SAGE was founded in 1965 by Sara Miller McCune to support the dissemination of usable knowledge by publishing innovative and high-quality research and teaching content. Today, we publish over 900 journals, including those of more than 400 learned societies, more than 800 new books per year, and a growing range of library products including archives, data, case studies, reports, and video. SAGE remains majority-owned by our founder, and after Sara's lifetime will become owned by a charitable trust that secures our continued independence.

Los Angeles | London | New Delhi | Singapore | Washington DC | Melbourne

ADVANCE PRAISE

How should one place the past in the context of the present? In contemporary India, the sheer asking of this question makes it disappear and reappear in the form of an interminable, infructuous debate between revivalists seeking to restore an imagined past to its pristine glory and liberal modernists who would rather junk the past in its entirety and build the future on the premises of the European Renaissance. The timely contribution of Rajvir Sharma's book to this conundrum consists in postulating a third way in the form of 'critical traditionalism'. Sharma draws his inspiration from India's indigenous political knowledge and its relevance to contemporary politics. His analysis of Kautilyan thought and post-Kautilyan praxis shows how to conflate strategically selected elements of indigenous political thought with concepts drawn from general political theory to create a coherent, authentic and legitimate whole. His comprehensive discussion of the core elements of Kautilya's *Arthashastra*, the world's oldest comprehensive treatise on the science of statecraft, gains further traction with his incisive analysis of its mutations, as evidenced in the elaborate structure of politics and the 'rule of righteousness' under Ashoka.

Sharma's erudite text, with its superb juxtaposition of vernacular concepts and general political theory, is a challenge and inspiration to students of Indian and comparative politics to fill in the gap of our knowledge of the evolution of the Indian state during the long interval between Ashoka and Nehru.

— **Subrata Mitra, Emeritus Professor of Political Science, South Asia Institute, Heidelberg University, Germany**

Kautilya, a classical Indian statesman, also known as Chanakya, wrote his masterwork—*Arthashastra*—on economics and political science about 2,500 years ago. His contribution is still often ignored in presenting the intellectual history of social sciences. In the literature introducing Kautilya's social philosophy, Professor Rajvir Sharma's study on Kautilya's political philosophy is a welcome contribution. Sharma concentrates on four aspects in Kautilya's *Arthashastra*: theory of state, legal theory, interstate relations and women in society.

Professor Sharma knows Kautilya's thinking well and presents it in the context of pre-Kautilyan Indian social philosophy as well as Kautilya's impact on post-Kautilyan political philosophy, especially in the great King Ashoka's thinking. However, Sharma's ambitions go beyond that. In fact, an interesting aspect in his study is how he compares Kautilya's theorizing to some ancient Greek and later European classics. In doing this, Sharma demonstrates how the Indian classic was much ahead of European classics in his theorizing.

The other interesting aspect in Sharma's study is briefly discussing, in Kautilyan context, some modern political phenomena and events in international politics. In doing this, Sharma demonstrates the universal character of Kautilya's theorizing in the *Arthashastra*. While Professor Balbir Singh Sihag's study on Kautilya's economic theory presents Kautilya as a founder of economics, Professor Rajvir Sharma's study presents Kautilya as a founder of political science, although Sharma does not say that directly.

— **Jyrki Käkönen, Professor Emeritus,**
School of Management, Tampere University, Finland

POLITICAL PHILOSOPHY OF KAUTILYA

POLITICAL PHILOSOPHY OF KAUTILYA

The *Arthashastra* and After

RAJVIR SHARMA

Los Angeles | London | New Delhi
Singapore | Washington DC | Melbourne

First published in 2022 by

SAGE Publications India Pvt Ltd
B1/I-1 Mohan Cooperative Industrial Area
Mathura Road, New Delhi 110 044, India
www.sagepub.in

SAGE Publications Inc
2455 Teller Road
Thousand Oaks, California 91320, USA

Indian Institute of Advanced Study,
Rashtrapati Niwas, Shimla 171005, India

SAGE Publications Ltd
1 Oliver's Yard, 55 City Road
London EC1Y 1SP, United Kingdom

SAGE Publications Asia-Pacific Pte Ltd
18 Cross Street #10-10/11/12
China Square Central
Singapore 048423

Published by Vivek Mehra for SAGE Publications India Pvt Ltd. Typeset in 10.5/13 pt Berkeley by AG Infographics, Delhi.

Library of Congress Cataloging-in-Publication

Names: Sharma, Rajvir (Professor of social sciences), author.
Title: Political philosophy of Kautilya: the Arthashastra and after / Rajvir Sharma.
Description: New Delhi, India: SAGE Publications India Pvt Ltd; Thousand Oaks, California: SAGE Publishing Inc, 2022. | Includes bibliographical references and index.
Identifiers: LCCN 2021061833 | ISBN 9789354791000 (hardback) | ISBN 9789354791086 (epub) | ISBN 9789354791161 (ebook)
Subjects: LCSH: Kauṭalya. Arthaśāstra. | Political science–India–Early works to 1800. | State, The–Philosophy–Early works to 1800. | International relations–Philosophy–Early works to 1800. | Political science–Philosophy–History. | India–Politics and government–To 997.
Classification: LCC JA84.I4 S47 2022 | DDC 320.01–dc23/eng/20220218
LC record available at https://lccn.loc.gov/2021061833

ISBN: 978-93-5479-100-0 (HB)

SAGE Team: Amrita Dutta, Shipra Pant and Rajinder Kaur

Dedicated to my parents

Late Yad Ram and Late Smt Anardevi

Thank you for choosing a SAGE product!
If you have any comment, observation or feedback,
I would like to personally hear from you.

Please write to me at **contactceo@sagepub.in**

Vivek Mehra, Managing Director and CEO, SAGE India.

Bulk Sales

SAGE India offers special discounts
for purchase of books in bulk.
We also make available special imprints
and excerpts from our books on demand.

For orders and enquiries, write to us at

Marketing Department
SAGE Publications India Pvt Ltd
B1/I-1, Mohan Cooperative Industrial Area
Mathura Road, Post Bag 7
New Delhi 110044, India

E-mail us at **marketing@sagepub.in**

Subscribe to our mailing list
Write to **marketing@sagepub.in**

This book is also available as an e-book.

CONTENTS

Acknowledgements   ix
Introduction   xiii

Chapter 1   State and Governance in Pre-Kautilyan Indian
            Political Thought   1

Chapter 2   The Theory of State in the *Arthashastra*   36

Chapter 3   Legal Theory of Kautilya: A Modernist Philosophy?   97

Chapter 4   Mandala/Rajamandala Theory and the Theory of
            Interstate Relations   141

Chapter 5   Women in the *Arthashastra*   185

Chapter 6   Post-Kautilyan Political Science   210

Conclusion   252
Bibliography   270
About the Author   283
Index   284

ACKNOWLEDGEMENTS

It has been a matter of great fortune for me to be awarded fellowship to work on *Political Philosophy of Kautilya: The Arthashastra and After* for a period of two years at the most prestigious institution of India, the Indian Institute of Advanced Study (IIAS), Shimla. So I first express my sincere thanks to the director, IIAS, Professor Makarand R. Paranjpe, who not only provided me an opportunity to carry out a focused research on the subject, by selecting me as a fellow but was also continuously a source of inspiration and guidance that helped me gain confidence and analytical prowess to undertake this ambitious study. I am grateful to Professor Kapil Kapur, chairman of the IIAS, who went through my draft research proposal and encouraged me to go ahead with this project as the studies on Kautilya and his legacy by political scientists are very few and far between.

In the process of my undertaking, I have been the beneficiary of the knowledge and wisdom of many Indian and foreign scholars, which helped me decide my approach to the study and widened my intellectual endeavour to understand and interpret Kautilya in a comparative perspective. My greatest gratitude is due to Professor Subrata K. Mitra, retired professor of political science, Heidelberg University; Dr Marko Juutinen, a researcher, university teacher and author, Tampere University, and visiting fellow at Observer Research Foundation; Professor Jyrki Käkönen, retired professor of political science and international relations, Tampere University; and Professor Balbir Singh Sihag, professor of economics, University of Massachusetts, who spared their valuable time to go through some of the draft chapters of my research and gave insightful and relevant comments and suggestions, which proved invaluable in the completion of this work. I am, indeed, indebted to Professor Subrata K. Mitra, Professor Jyrki Käkönen and Professor Balbir Singh Sihag, additionally, as they provided access to their works on the subject of my research, which further enriched my understanding and analytical capabilities.

I am deeply indebted to some of the eminent Indian scholars, teachers and friends with whom I had long personal discussions as well as discussions through mail to receive their advice, numerous comments and appreciation and encouragement throughout this research journey. My special thanks are due to Professor M. P. Singh, former professor and head, Department of Political Science, University of Delhi, and National Fellow, colleague and neighbour at IIAS, Shimla. Professor Singh, like a true teacher and mentor, provided me free access to discuss any matter pertaining to my project and also went through some of the chapters, adding more clarity to the manuscript. I will fail in my duty if I do not thank Dr Deepshikha Shahi, University of Delhi, and Professor Tridib Chakraborti, retired professor of international relations, Jadavpur University, Kolkata, and former Indian Council for Cultural Relations Chair of Indian Studies, for reviewing a few chapters and giving good advice to bring in some additional content to the manuscript.

My thanks are also due to other fellows at IIAS, who, during my presentations in the seminars, made valuable observations, especially Professor Madhav Hada, Professor Balram Shukla and Professor D. R. Purohit. I owe special thanks to Dr Meenu Agarwal, the resident medical officer at the institute for her very caring and compassionate medical treatment with a human touch, whenever needed.

I am also thankful to all the members of the IIAS library—Dr Prem Chand, the librarian; Mr Deepak Sharma; and, most distinguishably, Ms Vanshika Guleria, who always helped me in getting the support research material, even arranging for the books not available in the IIAS library and extending all necessary support services. I shall fail in my expression of thanks if I do not add any and every superlative to describe the character and behaviour of each and every member of the administrative staff, more notably, Mr Ravinder Saini, Ms Ritika Sharma and Promila, Mrs Vijayalakshmi Bhardwaj, Mr Akhilesh Pathak, Mr Kulbhushan Sharma, Mr Hemraj Sharma, Mr Kesar Singh, Mr Devraj Sharma, Mr Khemraj (Johny) and all those who rendered direct or indirect help to me in the completion of this project. I also thank the drivers, especially Mr Padam, Halku Ram and Bhag Chand, who took me to any place wherever it was necessary for me to go as well as the security staff who were ever so sweet, kind, respectful and helpful.

I deeply and sincerely acknowledge the immense contribution of my wife Sushila Sharma in this endeavour by way of her unstinted support. Her sacrifice, patience, faith and confidence in me made me bring this manuscript to fruition. I have no words to thank my daughters—Nimisha, Niti and Suchi—who always stood by me, extended every moral support and took keen interest in writing this monograph.

INTRODUCTION

Political Philosophy of Kautilya: The Arthashastra and After offers a critical analysis of the whole range of political ideas and institutions in
the ancient political economy text of Kautilya—the *Arthashastra*. The
work has been described by many historians as the most significant
treatise on the science of wealth (acquisition of *artha*) and the science
of politics. Unarguably, the *Arthashastra* provides an amazing material
not only for those who are interested in theoretical political research
but also for those engaged in politics in practice and in making and
administering public policies and decisions. The *Arthashastra* acts as
a practical guide and assists the king to rule, guiding him in almost
every detail of administration. Kautilya's *Arthashastra* treats not only
the domain matters of political science but also the issues falling in the
territory of history, philosophy, economics, public administration, geog-
raphy, strategic studies and management, creating interest in the minds
of several scholars of these branches of knowledge as well. However,
the publication of the translation of the stupendous nature of his work,
the *Arthashastra*, in 1915, after the completion of its translation in
1909 by Rudrapatna Shamasastry, laid the foundations of study and
research pertaining to the Kauṭilyan contribution to political theory
and practice of governance and administration during the Mauryan
rule, circa 321–297 BCE, controversy over the age and authorship of
the book notwithstanding. The interest of the political scientists in
the *Arthashastra* can be attributed to the analysis therein of the vast
range of areas of political theory—the origin, nature and functions of
the state; the society–state relations; bureaucracy; interstate relations;

strategic culture; and defence and security in addition to the discussion about various political concepts that have become a focal point in the teaching and research in modern times such as justice, law and authority, and gender justice.

Regarding power, the study points out the three basic sources from where the king derives his power and authority: *prabhavashakti* (the power of the army and the treasury) apart from *mantrashakti* (advice from the *mantriparishad* and of the wise) and the *utsah shakti* (charisma and energy of the king). Elaborating the concept of power referred to in the book, Ananya Vajpeyi in her article, 'An Ancient Treatise and the Making of Modern India' (2016), comments that the *Arthashastra* refers to both the substance and the purpose of political power. If power is taken as an essence of kingdoms and as authority to enable the ruler to take decisions, then this book tells you in a rigorous and rational manner about the type of substance power, what it might do in the world and how to put it to best use—if you happen to be a king—to consolidate your own power, keep rivals in check and take care of your people.[1]

This book is an endeavour to comprehend the diverse aspects of power as enunciated by Kautilya with reference to the nature and role conditioning the political behaviour and policy decision-making by the king pertaining to prosperity and well-being of his people and the conduct of interstate relations; the aim and substance of power; and the dangers of vesting the king with excessive/absolute power apart from suggesting the ways and means to enhance and consolidate power of the state in the interest of peace, stability and security. The study proposes a fresh look at some dimensions of political theory, if not all, as developed by Kautilya with reference to both its antiquity and modern context since Indian tradition of political thought will, in my view, form an important part of the studies of non-European political theory and textbooks, here in India and abroad.

Ancient India remained, for the most part, a neglected area till about 1858[2] with limited and scattered studies on India's past.[3] The religion, culture, traditions and customs of India having political ramifications did not interest the West till 1858, the year of a revolt against the British in 1858,[4] who treated India, as stated by Max Muller, as a nation of philosophers and Indian intellect as lacking in political or material speculation, and that the Indians never knew the feeling of nationality.[5]

'The empires of the East were perceived mainly as the tax-collecting institutions exercising coercive power of the most violent kind on their people. Their laws were seen as no more than the particular and occasional commands.' In the opinion of several Western scholars such as Senart, Max Muller, Jannet Dunning, Willoughby and Bloomfield, the Indians never had an idea of the state, were not able to evolve any political constitution, even in conception,[6] and that the *Aryans* in India could never develop political science as an independent branch of knowledge and free it from its theological and metaphysical environment as the European *Aryans* did because their supreme faith in the divine creation never impelled them to enquire into the rationale of their institutions.[7] This research is a significant enquiry into the validity of the theory that ancient Indian literature does not offer anything or much for theory building or to understand and apply the principles of governance and foreign policymaking and application in the modern times, reflecting upon political speculations of pre-Kautilyan, Kautilyan and post-Kautilyan (Ashokan) age on state, law and justice, gender justice and international relations.

It can be observed that scholars like D. R. Bhandarkar questioned the validity of the Western thesis, particularly after the discovery of the *Arthashastra*, asserting that it was no longer correct to say that the Hindu mind did not conduce to the development of political theories, and that the Indians never set up politics as an independent branch of knowledge.[8] Further, the monograph seeks to put to rest some of the queries agitating the minds of the reader of the *Arthashastra* and the Ashokan edicts: whether there are elements of strategic thinking and strategic culture in the political philosophy of the author of the book, the *Arthashastra*. Did Kautilya subscribe to the *Dharmashastra* tradition or *Lokayata* school? Was Kautilya amoral and Ashoka moral? Were he and Ashoka administrative thinkers interested only in the outcome of a policy/decision? Did their political approaches do justice to the modern concerns of law, justice and rights of every section of the society of their times? Does Kautilya's principle of *yogakshema* and Ashoka's *dhamma* construe to mean that the well-being of the subjects must receive top priority as the end of the state even if it was a monarchical system of government?

In the process, the study draws parallel, where required, from Western political thought, concerning the state and its nature, or relating to the dimensions of justice, foreign policy and international relations, politics and ethics matrix, gender relations and the writings of the thinkers like Kautilya. I have argued, here, that the ideas concerning political science and political theory were developed much earlier than they developed in the Western world, and, therefore, the endogenous sociopolitical and cultural sources need to be explored, if not over, then certainly equal to Western sources to explicate the local influences on theory building with regard to the conduct and management of internal and external affairs of the state.

SCOPE OF THE STUDY

As stated earlier, Kautilya's thoughts cover a long range of subjects—economics, public administration, accounting, revenue, management and society. It is very difficult to have a comprehensive and meaningful all-encompassing research. However, this study confines itself to a comprehensive and meaningful analysis of the aspects of political and administrative significance.

Several questions have been raised and addressed within this broader framework of the project such as the following in addition to the ones stated earlier:

1. Whether political science of Kautilya's *Arthashastra* draws in any manner from the pre-Kautilyan political science.
2. Whether the ideas developed by Kautilya and Ashoka pertaining to politics and administration had a limited application confined to their times or are of enduring value beyond history.
3. Can a political theory be developed by applying historical and empirical data in relation to Kautilya and Ashoka?

4. How far the techniques and strategies of war, peace and foreign policy prescribed by Kautilya and Ashoka can be treated as valid instruments in the present times?
5. Can Kautilya and Ashoka be called realist, neo-realist or idealist and what is the similarity(ies) or difference(s) between the approaches of the two ancient thinkers and of the West.
6. 6 How far is it needed to reassert Kautilyan principles of judicial fairness as tools of ensuring legitimacy and political stability in the state internally and externally in a conflict-ridden environment conceived by the two great thinkers?
7. Did the Kautilyan political philosophy influence the political thought and practice of Ashoka and, if so, to what extent?
8. Did the women in the text receive fair, equitable and egalitarian recognition and treatment and to what extent they enjoyed freedom and human rights in the times of both Kautilya and Ashoka?

It is argued that the ancient Indian society and the political thinkers had a clear understanding of political science and contributed to the evolution of the science of politics. Reference sources comprising the texts from *Rigveda* to *smritis* and, more importantly, the *Arthashastra* and the edicts have been used to establish that (a) the Indian political science and political thought were ahead of the Western political science and political thought in terms of their germination for the purpose of developing several political concepts and theory. (b) Women received a fair deal in the Kautilyan political ideology and enjoyed an egalitarian, respectful status in the text under study. Similarly, Ashoka appointed a special officer to give attention of the state to the matters pertaining to women. (c) Kautilya and Ashoka were both realists and idealists. (d) Kautilyan theory of administration did influence the nature and character of the Ashokan state in more than one area of governance. (e) Kautilya's theory of international relations holds relevance in the modern arena of changing international politics in the context of multilateralism, and the role and importance of finding peaceful solutions to the problems facing the world and securing an international community interested in practising and spreading humaneness, reverence to life, cooperation, and love and compassion for the sake of prosperous, safe and stable, happy and developed peaceful international and local order, a theory propounded by Ashoka, is no less. (This paragraph may be taken to be the epilogue).

METHODOLOGY AND SOURCES OF THE STUDY

The work discusses the rise of state, kingship and political institutions in a situational setting of Vedic and post-Vedic times. Kautilyan political ideas and philosophy travelling to the period of Ashoka form the main body of this work and it is unique in that sense. No other study has compared Kautilya's work on a continuum from his times and latter period in an integrated manner by using historical analytical technique of investigation apart from the content analysis method to go through some of the translated primary sources like those by distinguished scholars such as Shamasastry,[9] L. N. Rangarajan,[10] R. P. Kangle[11] and Patrick Olivelle along with a study of secondary sources such as articles and books written and published by a number of foreign and Indian scholars apart from glossary of words/commentary, such as P. N. Vidyalankar,[12] Visakhdatta,[13] M. V. Krishna Rao,[14] R. K. Mukherjee,[15] N. C. Bandyopadhyaya,[16] Sten Konow,[17] Dikshitar,[18] U. N. Ghoshal,[19] K. P. Jayaswal,[20] R. S. Sharma,[21] J. C. Heesterman,[22] V. P. Verma,[23] P. V. Kane,[24] A. L. Basham,[25] H. N. Sinha[26] and V. S. Agarwal.[27] I have also consulted literature emanating from modern authors on the *Arthashastra*, such as Balbir Sihag, Subrata K. Mitra and Liebig, P. K. Gautam, Subramanium, Radhakrishnan Pillai, Arvind Gupta, Jawaharlal Nehru, Jhumpa Mukherjee, D. M. Brown, Sureshwar Jha, D. R. Bhandarkar, S. K. Sharma and Ravindra Shenoy. The source material has also been drawn from various *smritis*, *Jataka tales* and *epics*—the Mahabharata (Bhagavad Gita and the *Shanti Parva*), the Ramayana and oral and other textual references. The study of Ashoka is primarily based on the study of his edicts and several books and commentaries written by historians such as Romila Thapar, A. L. Basham, Upinder Singh, Patrick Olivelle, Nayanjot Lahiri, Ven S. Dhammika, Lucia Cosmano, Marilena Pisani, Alexander Cunningham,[28] Radha Kumud Mookerji[29] and R. S. Sharma,[30] and of all the inscriptions in Ashoka Library in Bibliotheca.[31]

Issues Not Covered

The present study has skipped the discussion and debate regarding:

1. The age and authorship of the *Arthashastra*
2. Kautilya's economic theory and thought
3. His thoughts on revenue and financial administration
4. His contribution to the science of management
5. The debate regarding the date of birth and times of King Ashoka

The sole consideration behind doing so has been the fact that any such endeavour could have led to a research lacking in focus, manageability and organization. It could have also been described as overambitious. Each of the aforementioned issues, in fact, is a matter of independent comprehensive enquiry. Further, none of the aforementioned matter has had a direct relevance to the investigation I had chosen to undertake.

SCHEME OF CHAPTERIZATION

Coming back to the discussion within the text, Chapter 1 discusses pre-Kautilyan ideas about the state and governance. It is a study of the origin of the science of politics and the nature of Indian political thought, especially relating to the origin and nature of the state, law and justice in the Vedic and post-Vedic period, referring to the works such as the *Brihadaranyaka Upanishad*, *Brahma Sutra*, *Yoga Vasistha*, the Ramayana, the Mahabharata, Vedas, *Arthashastra* and *Nitishastra*. The *Dharma Sutras* make the earliest texts on law and polity. Political ideas contained in the *smritis* such as *Manusmriti*, *Yajnavalkya Smriti*, *Naradasmriti*, *Brihaspati Smriti* and *Katyayana Smriti* and of several pre-Kautilyan political thinkers such as Manu, Brihaspati, Ushanas, Vishalaksha, Bhardwaj, Vatvyadhi, Kaunapadanta, Pishuna, Bahudaniputra, Pishunaputra and Ambhi find a relevant and analytical treatment. A perusal of the *Shanti Parva*, the Mahabharata, the Ramayana, *Manusmriti*, *Buddhacharita*, *Mudra Rakshasa* and *Dashakumarcharita* establishes the fact that a number of political thinkers in the pre-Kautilyan period had written on the subject of political science in the form of *gatha* and verse.

Chapter 2 discusses, in detail, the Kautilyan political ideas about the origin of the state with reference to the divine theory, social contract theory and the evolutionary theory of the origin of state and brings out that Kautilya did not pay exclusive attention to any of the theories, but he seems to be in agreement with the ideas expressed in this regard in the *Digha Nikaya* and *Shanti Parva*. He agrees perhaps that the state came into being to protect people and property against the conditions of *Matsyanyaya* and the people agreed to pay taxes and obey the state/king in return.

After having explained his views about the origin of the state, the next important aspect from the viewpoint of political theory that attracts the attention of the researcher is the matter relating to the meaning, definition and nature of the state as envisaged in the *Arthashastra*. He defines the state as constitutive of seven elements/ *prakritis—swami/swamin, amatya, janapada* or *rashtra, durga, kosa, bala/army/danda* and *mitra* (ally)—forming part of Kautilya's *saptanga* theory. It may sound strange that he treats the ally or *mitra* as an integral element of the state. But if one goes through the present international scene and the alliances, like the North Atlantic Treaty Organization or the European Union, one can easily understand the importance of an ally in the maintenance and protection of the sovereignty of the state, an essential constituent of the state as per the modern definition of the state. In what manner these elements are tied organically to each other and how the weakness/calamity/decline/ degeneration of higher elements is more detrimental to the state as integral elements are matters discussed in the context of the state being seen as an organic entity.

The nature of the state has been analysed with reference to the following questions: Was Kautilyan state a welfare state? Was it an unlimited monarchy? Was it a centralized bureaucratic state? What follows from the study of the *Arthashastra* is that the state was to follow the principles of a welfare state, a concept coined much later by the modern political scientists. Kautilya, time and again, stressed that the happiness of the subjects should be central to the policies and actions of the king. What constitutes the basic feature of the state and administration, during the Kautilyan times with regard to the centralization/decentralization of power, is not yet fully settled as R. S. Sharma thinks that after going through the governmental structure and functioning, one cannot but conclude that it was a highly centralized system, whereas the Indologist J. C. Heesterman opines the opposite to say that it was a decentralized system of administration going by a study of the text alone. I have gone into this debate to not only cogently arrange the arguments on both sides but to also find the true nature of state and administration by textual interpretation as well as historical evidence, at my end, and argue that the truth lay somewhere in between the two contrarian views insofar as the structure of government and administration was centralized, whereas the functioning of administration was decentralized; governance was centralized but administration was decentralized. Kautilya seems to be convinced that effective governance could be ensured through a system of centralized bureaucratic state. The second question is answered when Kautilya tells us that the state was not an absolutist monarchy; rather, a monarchy working under a system of checks and balances provided by the customs and dharma, the *mantrins* and *mahamatyas* and several associations. All matters of urgent public importance were taken by the king to the *mantrins/mantriparishad* for deliberation and advice, but their advice or recommendations were not binding on the king, even though it might not have been without risk to do so.

The state of Kautilya, it can be safely noted, performed manifold functions, including that of a police state; of welfare state whose sole concern was to pursue the happiness of the subjects besides discharging the role of a regulatory state. The king enjoyed the legislative, executive and judicial powers, apart from running an efficient financial administration.

The king's concerns to expand, defend and consolidate the geographical boundaries of his empire as *vijigisu* are discussed with reference to his philosophy of *mandala*, *shadgunya* and four *upayas*. The *rajamandala* theory is put to scrutiny with examples drawn from the modern times, especially with reference to the *ari–mitra–ari–udasina* model of international and neighbourly relations of the king and the kingdom alongside the six ways for the conduct of foreign policy (*sandhi*, *vigraha*, *asana*, *dvaidhibhava*, *samsarya* and *yana*) that were guided, in the eyes of Kautilya, by the thirst of the king/state for power and wealth. *Sandhi* or peace treaty; *vigraha* or hostilities, including the types such as conventional, secret or proxy war; *asana*, that is, staying quiet; *yana*, that is, preparing for war; *samsarya* or seeking protection from a stronger king; and *dvaidhibhava* or making peace with a neighbouring king in order to pursue, with his help, the policy of hostility towards another. His thoughts on diplomacy and foreign policy suggest that war was not the first instrument of meeting the interests and goals of the state. This theme forms part of Chapter 3.

The theme of Chapter 4 is Kautilya's conception of law and justice, which has been seen as the most advanced and modernist in its nature and scope. In fact, I have argued that his codification of law, the essential principles of justice and its administration are in no way behind the present theories, looking especially in the background of his time and culture of governance. What is important and distinct here is that he devotes himself to the question of sentencing policy and prescribes a uniform sentencing policy in relation to the type of an offence/crime, leaving no scope for the discretion or whims and fancies of the judges while pronouncing judgment(s), which is missing, at times, in the modern system of jurisprudence. Another important feature of his theory of justice is the independence that he grants to his judicial officers known as *rajukas*, a theory that is central to the constitutional governance of the modern period.

A separate chapter, Chapter 5, on the status of women in the *Arthashastra* has been included in the study to know the extent to which Kautilya was conscious to addressing the issues of gender justice and empowerment. The ancient Hindu thinkers are often criticized for treating women as subordinates to men and that they support patriarchy, thus suppressing the idea of gender equality. In the process, the *Manusmriti* and the *Arthashastra* are often quoted. However, I argue that the criticism is not wholly valid. After going through the commentaries and translations made by many historians, it is established that the views of Kautilya on women's rights and justice were even a step ahead of the modern social and political intellectuals. The rights and status of women in the Kautilyan scheme of government and administration, focusing on the issues of personal laws, including the rights to remarry and widow marriage, inheritance laws, rights of the widowed women, rights of the prostitutes as professionals and spies and after their retirement, etc., are quite radical and are clearly drawn in the *Arthashastra*.

Chapter 6 analyses the post-Kautilyan political theory with reference to the political thoughts of King Ashoka and discusses his theory of *dhamma* and *dhamma vijaya*. It has been argued that Ashoka, though carried out political ideas and ideology of Kautilya, in many ways, carved out for himself a new foreign policy and strategy to gain and maintain authority inside and outside his empire. He invented a new theory, known as the law of piety, love and compassion—the *dhamma*. The study explains that Ashoka followed the Buddhist philosophy, not Buddhism. There is a clear difference between *dhamma* of Buddha and *dhamma* of Ashoka. Ashoka's *dhamma* was a social–political and strategic concept to create a new set of relationship between society and the state and the interstate interactions. His idea of *dhamma* and *dhamma vijaya* has been analysed in a comprehensive manner with reference to his major, minor and separate edicts along with the analysis of his inscription on rock and pillar edicts. He prescribed and followed the principles of non-violence in all matters of governance and policy pertaining to domestic and international relations.

In the end, it can be stated that the whole monograph relates critically to the contributions of the pre-Kautilyan, Kautilyan and post-Kautilyan political thought to the evolution and development of political science in India, having much to impact the latter political thought and theory, including the Western political thought and theory.

NOTES

1. See https://www.publicbooks.org/an-ancient-treatise-and-the-making-of-modern-india/
2. Sharma, *Aspects of Political Ideas*.
3. Muller, *A History of Ancient Sanskrit Literature*.
4. Sharma, *Aspects of Political Ideas*, 1.
5. Quoted in Sharma, *Aspects of Political Ideas*, 1.
6. Senart, *Caste in India*, 212.

7. Sharma, *Aspects of Political Ideas*, 8.
8. Sharma, *Aspects of Political Ideas*, 8.
9. Shamasastry, *Kautilya Arthashastra*.
10. Rangarajan, *Kautilya*.
11. Kangle, *The Kautilya Arthashastra*, Pts I, II and III.
12. Vidyalankar, *Kautilya's Arthashastra* (Hindi translation).
13. Vishakhadatta, *Mudrarakshasa*.
14. Rao, *Studies in Kautilya*.
15. Mukherjee, *Chandragupta Maurya*.
16. Bandyopadhyaya, *Development of Hindu Polity*.
17. Konow, *Kautalya Studies*.
18. Dikshitar, *Hindu Administrative Institutions*; Dikshitar, *Mauryan Polity*.
19. Ghoshal, *A History of Hindu Political Theories*; Ghoshal, *A History of Hindu Political Ideas*.
20. Jayaswal, *Hindu Polity*.
21. Sharma, *Aspects of Political Ideas*.
22. Heesterman, *Inner Conflict of Tradition*.
23. Verma, *Studies in Hindu Political Thought*.
24. Kane, *History of Dharmsastra*, Vols I and III.
25. Basham, *The Wonder That Was India*.
26. Sinha, *Sovereignty in Ancient Indian Polity*.
27. Aggarwal, *Astadhyayi of Panini*.
28. Cunningham, *Inscriptions of Asoka*.
29. Mookerji, *Ashoka*.
30. Sharma, *India's Ancient Past*.
31. https://www2.hf.uio.no/polyglotta/index.php?page=library&bid=14

State and Governance in Pre-Kautilyan Indian Political Thought

Pre-Kautilyan ideas about state and governance relate to the study of the origin of the science of politics and the nature of Indian political thought in the Vedic and post-Vedic periods up to the *Arthashastra*. The science of politics was known in those days as *Dandaniti, Kshatra Vidya, Rajshastra, Rajniti, Nitishastra and Nitisara*. This science carried an imprint of the ideas of several pre-Kautilyan political thinkers such as Vishalaksha, Bhardwaj, Vatavyadhi, Kaunapadanta, Manu, Brihaspati, Ushanas and Gaurisiras.[1]

A very important development in the 6th century BC was the emergence of the *Lokayat* philosophy, which did not accept the authority of the Vedas and underlined the supremacy of reason. This philosophy, later on, formed part of the *Arthashastra* or science of politics.[2] Here, a reference to *Brihadaranyaka Upanishad, Brahmasutra, Yoga Vashistha*, the Ramayana, the Mahabharata, Vedas, *Arthashastras* and *Nitishastras* is worth mentioning as some of these texts exclusively deal with state and government, both in theory and practice. The *Dharmasutras* are the earliest texts on law and polity. According to A. K. Majumdar, the *Dharma Sutras*, which share some common topics with the *Grihyasutras*, mainly deal with rules of conduct as well as the government and law, both civil and criminal.[3]

Further, it has been said that the contribution of several other *smritis* such as *Manusmriti, Yajnavalkyasmriti, Naradasmriti, Brihaspatismriti* and *Katyayansmriti* to the evolution of the concepts of law and government is significant. Kautilya himself admitted that his work was based on a number of treatises on the science of politics and named some of the pre-Mauryan political thinkers on the subject, such as Manu, Brihaspati, Ushanas, Vishalaksha, Bhardwaj, Vatavyadhi and Kaunapadanta. The political ideas of Pishuna, Bahudaniputra, Pishunaputra and Ambhi also find a mention in his text. A perusal of the *Shanti Parva* of the Mahabharata, the Ramayana, *Manusmriti*, *Buddha Charita*, *Mudra Rakshasa* and *Daskumaracharita* establishes the fact that a number of political thinkers in the pre-Kautilyan period had written on the subject of political science in the form of *gatha* and verse. The *Vamsa Brahmana* of the *Samaveda* and *Vamsa* of the *Sankhyayana Aranyaka* and *Shatapatha Brahmana* also provide a long list of teachers, although their main contribution is more to the idea of sacrifice and theology than to the subject of political science.

This study critically questions the arguments that the *Dharmashastras* and the *Arthashastra* were nothing but mere didactic poetry in which *dharma* and *artha* were taught as subjects in the curricula of the study meant for the education of a prince[4] or that 'the subtle and profound spirit of India, which finds its fullest expression in the absolute idealism of the *Vedanta* of *Samkara* and the sceptical nihilism of *Nagarjuna*, is alien to the conception of the political man and that India offers nothing that can be regarded as a serious theory of politics'.[5] Or the Aryans could never free their politics from the theological and metaphysical environment.[6] A message of these opinions is 'that politics in ancient India had no independent status, that it was always tied to the apron-strings of religion and metaphysics and that the ancient Hindus, unlike the Greeks, were perfectly innocent of politics as a distinct branch of knowledge'.[7]

Some contemporary Western scholars have, however, expressed contrarian views on the earlier thesis that Hindus in India had no clear idea of the material social–political life and were interested in matters like *Moksha* and that they were dogmatic and unscientific in approach. However, it must be admitted that despite the dominance of religion, ancient India did produce a sizable body of political literature.

Moreover, there is always a scope for divergence in conceptualizing and narrating political thought and theory from culture to culture as, in the words of Beni Prasad, 'Political thinking is intimately related to social and political milieu in which it originates. Every thought, moreover, bears the stamp of the ethos of the people who give birth to it'.[8]

It may be reminded that political ideas and concepts in ancient India are older than the *Arthashastra* school of Kautilya, and Indian political theory, despite having religious overtones, was not theological or religious in nature, as it merely underlines the vital fact that political authority has to operate within a world of relationships which by their essential nature have a moral foundation.[9]

The students of ancient India, such as A. S. Altekar, R. S. Sharma, B. A. Saletore, K. P. Jayaswal, R. C. Majumdar, Shamasastry, N. N. Law, B. K. Sarkar, U. N. Ghosal, N. C. Bandyopadhyaya, V. R. R. Dikshitar and Ashok S. Chousalkar, have enquired into the questions of the origin and nature of the state, law and justice and of *Dandaniti* in the sense of sovereignty. A common thread in their scholarly writings is the argument that the ancient Hindus were not oblivious of the complexities of politics and political science and that politics was conceived as an independent science. It might be true to say that, at times, there seems to be no effort on their part to completely separate religion from politics in the early period of sociopolitical evolution, but as time progressed, the 'religious' ones were kept out of 'political' matters. That ancient Hindus were politically conscious can be noted in several incidental references in the *Prakrit* texts of the Jains, such as the *Uttaradhyayana Sutra* about the system of administration and government. The *Jain Puranas* and *Prakrit* texts on ancient Indian polity, which have been ignored for long by contemporary works on ancient Indian political science, bring us their ideas on gender justice and rights, which form an integral part of my study in Chapter 5.

Professor Ghoshal throws sufficient light on the importance and content of the works produced in the 5th century BC,[10] and the methods of observation, analysis and deduction used to theorize the political life. Ghoshal holds that the credit for separating politics from theology and raising it to the dignity of an independent science, and he belongs to the early *Arthashastra* thinkers. These thinkers brought a rich store of new material on the science of government.[11]

Furthermore, the thoughts of Ushanas, Brihaspati, Bhardwaj and Vishalaksha on the *Rajshastras* inform us that Brihaspati's *Rajshastra* embraced all aspects that could not be covered in the *Rajdharma*. Wilhelm and A. D. Pant also studied in detail the political ideas and theories of the pre-Kautilyan age. A. D. Pant discussed the material and intellectual milieu of the period that gave birth to the *Arthashastra* tradition and pointed out that the *Brahmana Parivrajakas* were interested in studying social and political problems as well as philosophical questions.[12]

The study of the pre-Kautilyan perspectives on state and governance is significant as it will enable us to understand not only the background of the *Arthashastra* and the areas of convergence and divergence between the political thoughts of the two periods, but it will also explain the processes of the evolution of political theory and thought in India. The material has been drawn mainly from *Manusmriti*, *Yajnavalkyasmriti*, the Mahabharata, the Ramayana, *Brihaspatismriti* and *Digha Nikaya* after briefly surveying the Vedic literature.

The nature of ancient Hindu politics and political tradition can be best understood by referring to the different schools of thought and their understanding of the term science/*vidya*. It may be pointed out in the beginning that there is no unanimity on the number of sciences among the sociopolitical thinkers of the pre-Kautilyan age. For example, Manu mentions three sciences, namely *Trayi*, *Vartta* and *Dandaniti*, while Brihaspati excludes *Trayi* from the list of sciences and contends that *Vartta* and *Dandaniti* were the only sciences. Ushanas, on the other hand, argues that the science of politics is the real science from which all other sciences originate.

With the exception of Shukrachary's conception of *Arthashastra*, which includes the sciences of economics and politics, all the other classifications treat politics as independent of *Trayi* and *Anvikshiki*, i.e., independent of theology and metaphysics … it is remarkable that the doctrines of *Nastikas* (*Sceptics*), *Arthashastra and Kamshastra* are much distinct branches of learning as *samkhya*, *Vedanta* and the various Vedas.[13]

It is not wrong to argue that *Nastividya*, an independent branch of learning, recognizes the predominance of reason as against the theological and metaphysical and denies the existence of the Vedas, which ascribes the origin of all things to nature and not to God.

One also notes that the ancient political thinkers gave different names to political science, namely *Rajdharma* (*Manusmriti* and other *smritis*), *Rajyashastra* (Mahabharata, XII.i), *Dandaniti* (*Manusmriti*, VII.19; *Arthashastra*, I.i), *Nitishastra* and *Arthashastra*. The science of politics or the science of state and government was also termed as *Kshatra Vidya*[14] *as well as Dhanur Vidya*[15] or military science.[16] However, the *smritis* and epics written in different time periods (200 BC to 200 AD), including *Manusmriti*, *Vishnu Purana* and *Yajanavalkya*, dealt with social (*Varnashrama*), philosophical (*triverga*) and religious matters along with the discussion of the matters that are considered political in nature, such as the duties of the king, functions of the administrative officials and rules governing the dispensation of civil and criminal justice and the conduct of foreign policy.

The outlook of the writers of that time was semi-religious and semi-moral. Often, we find that social and political theory is co-presented in the same works dealing with other areas of human thought. Indian political thought seems to be inspired by both the 'real' and the 'ideal' or 'normative'. In India, the state was never conceived as merely a coercive institution responsible for preventing or imposing certain sanctions on the activities of the people/society; its functions also included the promotion of a virtuous society and a moral order.

> The King was to be a virtuous ruler, devoted heart and soul to the welfare of the people; if he was not such, then the gods will punish him. The subjects had no secular remedies feasible in normal times; gods were expected to destroy a bad king.[17]

It was stated that a king could be killed like a mad dog if he failed to perform his duties as recommended, but it is not clarified who could do it and how. A. S. Altekar writes, 'Abstruse thinking and daring speculation which is characteristic of Hindu thought in other departments like philosophy and poetics are strangely enough conspicuous by their absence in the works on the science of polity'.[18]

ORIGIN OF THE STATE AND ITS THEORIES

The origin of the state and its nature and functions have been central in the writings of the authors of all ages, though it has received a larger space in the writings of modern thinkers when we refer to theory building and clarity in that regard. How and when people organize themselves into a political organization from a social community is a matter of speculation in the realm of which different narratives are provided by different teachers of political science and political theory formation. Some of the theories about the origin of the state are examined below.

Theory of Divine Origin

This theory proposes that the state came into existence when God ordained a person to take responsibility for bringing chaos to an end and for protecting the people against anarchy, thus claiming the rise of the state to be an act of divinity and the king to be the God's nominee on earth. It is mentioned in the *Shanti Parva* that, after the disappearance of society that lived happily without any coercive authority and the emergence of the jungle rule, men went to God with a request of getting them rid of the environment of the *Matsyanyaya*. *Brahmadeva* created a king who could be entrusted with the responsibility of not only framing a code of law but also enforcing it. 'He composed a comprehensive code, created an asexual son named *Virajas*, appointed him king and men agreed to obey his orders.'[19]

According to another story in the *Shanti Parva*,[20] it is said that people, tired of the chaos and disorder, came to an agreement/contract to subject person/persons found guilty of acts like misappropriation or adultery to social expulsion. This arrangement/universal social agreement, however, did not work, perhaps because of the absence of a law-enforcing authority/king. So they approached God, Brahma/Prajapati, for appointing a king who could command the popular respect and protect them as well. God then appointed Manu as the king.[21]

Though Manu initially refused to accept the responsibilities of a king, he agreed to perform the functions of the state/government when he was assured by the people of not only their loyalty and obedience to the laws but also their willingness to pay 10 per cent of the merchandise and one-sixth of the agricultural produce as taxes in return for their protection and development—moral and economic. Nonetheless, we can conclude from both the stories that the state came into existence on account of the prayers of the people to God and the consequent creation of the king by the Creator. In that sense, the state was a divine institution, even though it also implies a contract in which people agreed to obey the orders of the king and pay taxes in return for the kingly protection.[22]

One also notices that the Europeans, especially in the Middle Ages, subscribed to the theory of the divine origin of state and the divine rights of the king to rule. The difference between the Indian theory and the Western theory is that the Western theory gave unrestrained power to the king without any rights to the subjects to oppose or criticize the king as he was the God, while the Indian thinkers did not assign any divine rights to the king, even though they accepted the divine origin of the state. To quote Bandyopadhyaya,

> ...Monarchy never became as irresponsible as in Europe after the Reformation. The king was venerated; his office was highly extolled; his functions were compared to those of the rulers of the universal forces—the Devas, yet the Indian people never accepted the king as the counterpart or the vicegerent of the omnipotent deity. Nor did India ever see any Caesar cult as we find in the history of decayed Rome after the world conquest and no prince dared to pretend to be invested with 'the right divine of princes to govern wrong'.[23]

Referring to *Digha Nikaya*,[24] Altekar points towards the oblique acceptance of the divine-cum-social contract origin of the state. He writes:

> Buddhists did not believe in god and so the Brahmadeva as the creator of the first king and code does naturally not figure in it. But we are told that in the dim and the distant past, there was a golden age, when men who had ethereal and refulgent bodies, lived in virtue and happiness. Somehow there was a fall from this ideal state; there arose anarchy and chaos, and people wondered how to put an end to it. Eventually, there arose on the scene a person named *Mahajan Sammata* (one acceptable to the great community), who was born asexually.

He was a man of virtue, wisdom and ability who agreed to the public request to become their king.[25]

Even in *Adi Purana*, we find that the first *Thirthankara*, Rishabhanatha, introduced kings, officers, castes and professions.[26]*Taittiriya Brahmana* attaches divine sanction, as in its absence, no political institution could really claim complete allegiance and obligation on the part of the subjects. According to the story, Indra was given the powers to protect and rule by the creator, Prajapati. Beni Prasad elaborates and says:

> Religion figured prominently in the installation of every new king on earth. The act of consecration or coronation was the most momentous one. It drew the consecrated close to the gods. Indeed it made him one of them. It lifted him above punishment. Thus is defined the character and birth of the king in *Aitareya Brahmana*[27] and *Satapatha Brahmana*.[28]

Further, *Manusmriti* and other similar books stated that the science of the state and politics, namely *Rajyashastra* and *Rajdharma*, is based on *Dandaniti*, which is the ultimate foundation for the state. 'It is *danda* (physical force or physical punishment) which rules over all the subjects, it is *danda* which protects them; when all else is sleeping, *danda* keeps awake; law is nothing but the *danda* itself.'[29] *Danda* seems to be an instrument for protection of the subjects. *Manusmriti* says, 'For, when these creatures, being without a king, through fear dispersed in all directions, the lord created a king for the protection of the whole creation'.[30] Vainya/Vena, the first king, not Manu, was called upon by the God and Rishis to take an oath to carry out his duties as per the science of government and not by his fancies.[31]

Dandah shasti prajah sarva danda evabhirakshati
Dandah supteshu jagarti dandam dharmam vidurbudha[32]

It is *danda* that ensures well-being and social stability in the state. Explaining the *Dandaniti* and its relevance, Ushanas says that all relationships are rooted in the *Dandaniti*; the *Dandaniti* enables the state to cause and pursue achievements and integrates social, economic and political relationships with one another.[33] In the eyes of Manu, the *Dandaniti* was the real king, the real leader and the real protector.[34]

The doctrine of royal divinity finds expression in the following verse of the law book of Manu:

When the world was without a king and dispersed in fear
in all directions
The Lord created the king for the protection of all
He made him of eternal particles of Indra and the Wind
Yama, the Sun and Fire Varun, the Moon and the Lord of Wealth
And because he has been formed of fragments of all those gods,
The King surpasses all other beings in splendour.
Even in infant king must not be despised, as though a mere mortal,
For he is a great god in human form.[35]

What follows from the above verse is that Manu implies that the king had a higher divine status and people were supposed to support and obey him as he was the product of the work of many Gods, which is quite contrary to other epics and Vedas in the sense that they assure the subjects of the right to revolt and even kill the king like a mad dog if he contravenes the conditions of kingship, that is, the duty to protect the kingdom and the life, property and *varna* and *dharma* of society. On the other hand, it would be hasty to draw this conclusion as Manu seems to be backing the idea of people's rights elsewhere in his book, *Manava Dharmashastra*.

Social Contract Theory

There are two important questions regarding the social contract theory: first, what was the process of the theory and between whom was the contract entered? And second, whether the social contract theory of the origin of state that evolved in ancient India could be termed as a counterpart to the Western social contract theory. It is pertinent to note the ideas on this theme in Chapter 67 of the *Shanti Parva* and in the Buddhist *Agganna Sutta* of *Digha Nikaya* and *Mahavastu*, which indicate that sovereignty in ancient India originated in a social contract.[36] Giving a description of the social contract in pre-Kautilyan India, D. R. Bhandarkar states, that the state of nature as described in the above theory was one of war, 'which came to end only when men agreed to give their liberty into the hands of a sovereign'; that this theory bears remarkably close resemblance to the one propounded by Hobbes; but while Hobbes expounded this notion of agreement by saying that absolute power was irrevocably transferred to the ruler, the social contract theory as advocated in the pre-Kautilyan political literature and also in *Arthashastra* maintained that the king was still the servant of the people.[37]

It follows from Bhandarkar that the Indian social contract theory, in this sense, was much superior and more advanced than the one expounded by Hobbes. The Indian social contract did not give unlimited powers to the king, or we can say it propounded a theory of limited monarchy. Is it really a true exposition of the social contract theory of the origin of the state? The answer has not been unanimous, as many historians of ancient Indian political science disagree with Bhandarkar on this count. They say that the social contract mentioned in the *Brihadaranyaka Upanishad*, *Shanti Parva*, *Digha Nikaya*, *Atharvaveda* and other works of the political thinkers of the post-Vedic period points out clearly that the king was not a part of the contract and that God ordained the king and the people agreed to pay taxes and obey his commands.

Further, there is no evidence in the old political literature which establishes, like the Western theory, that men themselves came together to abandon the state of nature and agreed to surrender their liberty and rights to a common authority. *Digha Nikaya*, on the contrary, establishes that, after the arrival of the age of the decline of pristine purity, people gradually concluded a number of agreements amongst themselves and established the institution of family and private property. Even in this condition, there emerged several activities such as theft and clashes of interests on account of race and unequal family status, which were inimical to a harmonious and happy social living. Therefore, people gathered to elect a chief endowed with capability and intelligence, known by different names as *Mahasammata* (one elected by the people), *Khattiya* (means the lord of the fields) and *Raja* (a person who charms people by means of *dharma*).

Digha Nikaya defines the qualifications of a king and also specifies the obligations of both the electors and the elected. The functions of the king included punishing the guilty, maintaining social order, preventing violation of laws, protecting the property of one against encroachment by the other and pleasing the people, while the people were under an obligation to pay one-sixth or one-tenth of their produce as tax to the head of the state.[38] It should be noted here that the king was oath-bound to devote himself to the well-being and safety and security of the people. It can be therefore inferred that the king by accepting the conditions of kingship indirectly became party to the contract. People reserved the right to not only remove but also kill a king who failed to perform his *Rajdharma*. In other words, people did not completely surrender their sovereignty to the ruler in so far as they retained the right to disown a ruler or revolt against a ruler if he failed to meet the desires and needs of the society.

History of the post-Vedic period also suggests that there were instances when the non-performing kings were removed and another was brought in place, like when King Prathu replaced Vena, the earlier king who became a tyrant and authoritarian, and people were unhappy with that situation.[39] I maintain that the origin of the state in ancient India is the result of both the divinity and social contract. Even in the Western social contract theory, the government/king was not a party and was under an obligation to execute the general will akin to the one found in the Indian version of the theory of social contract, whereby he was to execute the commitment to ensure the well-being and safety of the people. The only difference between the Western and Indian theories of social contract is that the king was above the law and the people in the Western theory, while in the Indian scheme of the contract, he was like a public servant.

The *Vana Parva* draws a very happy sketch of the state of nature when it records that it was a situation where every person lived a pure godly life; they hardly faced any miseries or deprivations, all their desires were met without any fear or pressure, and they lived a long life of even hundreds of years. The *Shanti Parva* also calls it a Golden Age with no king and no sovereignty. Righteousness informed people's behaviour in relation to each other in protecting one and all. But there came a sharp fall in these values when greed and avarice, unrestrained sexual indulgence, loss of difference between virtue and wrong/vice and an end to righteousness took over the earlier happy society.[40] One sees somewhat of a parallel with the theory of the state of nature in both Locke and Rousseau when compared with the ancient Indian description. David Slakter remarks in this context:

> Like Hobbes, Indian theorists consider the state of nature to be one where basic social concepts such as property are inapplicable. They share with Locke however a belief that people in a state of nature can still be bound by obligations beyond pursuit of brute self-interest. While the Indian theorists have in common with Rousseau a belief in the goodness of pre-social community the former believe such is due to humankind's prior perfection and proximity to the gods, rather than due to peoples' innate goodness.[41]

Taittiriya Brahmana attaches divine sanction, as in its absence, no political institution could really claim complete allegiance and obligation on the part of the subjects. According to the story, Indra was given the powers to protect and rule by Prajapati. Religion figured prominently in the placement of every new king on earth. The act of consecration or coronation was the most momentous one. It drew the consecrated close to the Gods. Indeed, it made him one of them. It lifted him above punishment. These are the definitions of the character and birth of the king in *Aitareya Brahmana* (VIII, 4, 12) and *Shatapatha Brahmana* (III, I, I, 8; V, 4, 4, 7).

John Spellman[42] addresses the theories of the origin of the state and asserts that the legends in Vedas found the divine and warrior king. *Rigveda* mentions in this regard:

> if one accord they made and formed for kingship *Indra*, the Hero who in all encounter overcometh; most eminent for power, destroyer in the conflict, fierce and exceedingly strong, stalwart and full of vigour; Bards joined in songs to *Indra* so that he might drink the Soma Juice, the Lord of light, that he whose laws stand fast might aid with power and with the help he gives.[43]

Samaveda echoes the same view when it says that heroes of one accord brought forth and formed the kingship (*Samaveda*, 4.2.4.1) That the king was conceived as a warrior becomes further clear from the following statement in the *Shatapatha Brahmana*:

> We are in an evil plight; the *Asura-Rakshasas* have come in between us. We shall fall prey to our enemies. Let us come to an agreement and yield to the excellence of one of us. They yielded to the excellence of *Indra*, wherefore it is said, *Indra* is all the deities, the gods have *Indra* for their chef.[44]

U. N. Ghoshal traces the origin of the state as provided in *Digha Nikaya* and *Mahavastu*.[45] It should also be noted here that the *Sutras* do not give any attention to the issue of the origin of the state, as it is assumed that it was difficult to imagine a society led by the observance of *swadharma* without a king. 'The social structure of *varnashrama* is eternal and the concept of *dharma* is prominent. The declaration of law is made by the *Brahmans*, and the king is a mere executive sovereign.'[46]

COMPARISON OF THE INDIAN THEORY WITH THE WESTERN THEORY OF SOCIAL CONTRACT

There have been attempts on the part of the Indian scholars to compare and contrast the Indian and Western theories of social contract of the origin of the state, but no unanimous conclusions were reached. Some portray Indian theories of social contract as not only close in approach to the Western theories but also as one ahead of that, while others like A. B. Saletore maintain that it is not clear in the Indian literature regarding whether people abandoned the chaotic and anarchical state of nature themselves of their own will or were forced to do so.[47] However, this argument seems unconvincing because one can easily imagine that the people might have been forced by the *arajaka* or anarchic conditions to come together on the necessity of a political authority.[48] It may be stated, however, that unlike the Western view of social contract wherein the people surrender their rights to a person or group of people and entrust the ruler with unhindered powers, the Indian theory does not divest the people of their rights, and the king/state was duty-bound to fulfil the responsibility of their protection, failing which they could revolt against him. It is also not difficult to find similarities between the two theories with reference to the state of nature. The Indian exposition of the pre-political state of society is close to that of Locke and Rousseau in the first instance, as it draws closer to the view that the state of nature was not unhappy and inharmonious and that people lived in a righteous manner and, in the later stage, close to the Hobbes's idea when it is said that there was a decline of the righteous and the virtue was overtaken by the vices of greed and caprice and the people entered into a state of war against each other.

However, the nature of the contract as given under the Western and Indian viewpoints is different, as mentioned earlier. Like in Locke's theory, the Indian philosophy of contract leaves the right to life and property in the possession of the people. It will not be out of place to point out that there are some Indian historians who do not subscribe to the contract theory of the origin of the state. A. S. Altekar, for example, comments:

> It is now generally recognised that the contract theory of the origin of gov-
> ernment is bad history and worse logic; it can no doubt explain the origin
> of a particular form of state among people who have already developed
> governmental institutions, but it cannot explain how the first agreement
> took place among the members of a community, which was still in the
> state of nature. Contract is possible only in a society where mutual rights
> and obligations are respected; and this is obviously impossible in a society
> where law of jungle prevails.[49]

This logic of Altekar is inattentive to the fact that a chaotic state of nature, inflicted by the law of the jungle, could only force people to come together to create a coercive authority to usher in a liveable state of affairs. Had there been no compelling chaotic conditions, there might not have been any need, of a state. Further, the contract was supposed to be strengthened by following the conditions of the contract by both sides—the king and the people. The twin conditions integral to the contract were as follows: the king shall protect the family, property and the *varna* system, uphold *dharma* and ensure the goals of the state—*dharma*, *artha* and *kama*. People, on their part, will remain loyal to the state and pay taxes. Thus,

> the contract theory of the origin of state should be regarded as a unique
> contribution of ancient Indian thinkers to political thought, for even the

Greek thinkers like Plato and Aristotle, who had established political science practically as an independent discipline, did not think in terms of contract between the king and the people. Plato points out in the *Republic* that when even three, four people come together for the satisfaction of their mutual needs that leads to the rise of the state. This, therefore, implies some idea of social contract.[50]

EVOLUTIONARY THEORY OF THE ORIGIN OF STATE

The evolutionary theory seems to be the most acceptable, rational and more relational idea as it provides an account of pre-political, political and pre-state society gradually transforming itself into a political organization/state passing through different phases rather than being a product of any one time. It traces the formation of the state in the context of changing social, economic and agrarian relations in society, thus interlinking the social and political evolution, that is, the transformation of society from one form to another, culminating in the establishment of the state. Some questions become relevant for enquiry, such as the nature of social organization in a pre- and post-political stage; the nature of the economy and economic relations; the place of family in social relationships and the role it played in the process of political/state formation; and the nature of society–state relations in regard to the questions of political obligation. The early ancient Indian system of social living indicates, as documented in several Buddhist, Jain, Puranic and Brahmanical traditions, that it was a society of wanderers and food gatherers. The means of livelihood were forest products like fruits and roots/*bhumiparpataka*.[51] This view has found support in the writings of scholars such as Childe[52] and Morgan.[53]

The shift of society occurred from a pastoral/tribal living system to a settled community with economic claims on land and property to a political community; religion, ethics and spirituality formed intervening variables of the socio-religious and eco-political growth. The evolutionary process of the origin of the state has been described in the *Atharvaveda* (Chapter VIII, Hymn 10) in the following manner:

The first stage of the organization of human life was one of *Vairajya*, where there was no king and no state, often said to have led to the state of anarchy, followed by the emergence of an agricultural, stable and settled society giving rise to a sense of ownership of material objects and also to the institution of family so as to meet the resulting needs of this agricultural social formation. There was a head of the family who held the authority to regulate the affairs of the family and later over a number of other tribes/ families. This Head could be equated with the institution of the kingship as came to be known in the later period. Thereafter, the life of the society became complex; the settled clans, as the story goes, began to fight between themselves over pasturelands, sources of water and animals like cows necessitating the appointment of strong leader to lead them in war. Accordingly a leader was chosen by the members of the clan who rendered to him obedience. He finally became the king. This view finds support in John Spellman who after citing several examples from different sources (*Rig Veda, Samaveda, Aitareya* and *Satpatha Brahmanas*) saw the ancient India king primarily as the military leader.[54]

It follows that a number of factors, including force, played a significant role in the evolutionary process of the origin of the state. Cincy M. Thomas[55] divides the stages of the evolution of the state into the following six categories:

1. Tribal military democracy. The age of *Rigveda* is primarily a period of tribal welfare and assemblies.
2. The age of the breakup of tribal polity under the constant stress of conflicts between the *Rajanya Kshatriya* and the *Vis* (described as an ordinary businessman).
3. Full-fledged state formation with the emergence of large territorial monarchies of Kosala and Magadh and tribal oligarchies in Northwestern India.
4. The Mauryan period that saw the establishment of a centralized bureaucratic state.
5. The stage is marked by the process of decentralized administration.
6. Period of decline of the centralized state and appearance of decentralized proto-feudal polity wherein land grants played a significant role in shaping political structure and administrative privileges.[56]

Historians, though, are divided on the issue of the existence of the institutions of private property, marriage and institution of family as well as about the existence of the institution of state in the primitive society.[57] The *Shanti Parva* mentions about the institution of family and marriage as follows: 'A householder's home, even if filled with sons, grandsons, daughters-in-law and servants, is regarded empty if destitute of the housewife. One's house is not one's home; only one's wife is one's home'.[58] It has been recorded in the *Puranas* that it was a classless society,[59] with no *varna* system before the society changed from a pastoral to an agrarian one and the concept of private property and family entered to determine social conduct.[60] This gave rise to the fight to grab more and more, by force, the fields of others and ushered therein a system of *Matsyanyaya*, which in turn necessitated the urge to establish a legal authority that could protect them against the robbery and theft of their materials—land, gold, etc., bringing into existence the office of the ruler, the *Mahakhattia*.[61] *Mahavastu* and *Tibetan Dulva* tell us that family, a result of building separate houses and boundaries around the property, also played a very significant role in the origin of the state.[62]

The *Puranas* deal with the contribution of the *varnas*—*Brahmanas*, *Kshatriyas*, *Vaishyas* and *Sudras*—to the origin of the state. According to the narratives, people were classified/divided into four *varnas*, which were meant to perform different functions. The *Brahmanas* were to be engaged in the acts of teaching, studying and praying and in priestly activities; the Kshatriyas were to perform the acts of warriors and fighters; the Vaishyas were to be involved in the acts of production and trade; and the Sudras were to assist in manual tasks. It has been stated in the *Vay Puran* that, because of the conflict between the *varnas*, Lord Brahma created *danda* (justice) and war as the profession of the Kshatriyas.[63] Thus, it is said of Manu, who, after being approached by the members of the *varnas*, produced Priyavrata and Uttanapada, the two kings vested with *danda*, the power to establish the rule of law and justice. Thus, the institution of the state came into being to protect the institutions of property, social classes and family.[64] The theory finds its echo later in the *Arthashastra* and historical interpretations given by R. S. Sharma[65] and F. Engels.[66] It was the necessity to seek protection for the people and for punishing the abductors of others' wives and robbers of others' wealth, and instilling confidence among all classes of people that Gods created the institution of the king.[67] Prathu, at the time of his consecration, thus declared, 'I shall establish the *swadharma*, *varna dharma* and *ashrama dharma* and enforce them with the rod of punishment'.[68]

But why people suddenly left the golden conditions of living, characterized by a virtuous, cooperative and helpful environment, for the one informed by greed, avarice, hatred, malice and selfishness? R. S. Sharma credits this situation to the introduction of family, property, caste and states, and to keep these tendencies under check that *danda/vyavahara*, the power instrument of the state, arose. It was unimaginable that private property, family and *varna* could exist without the protection of *danda/vyavahara*. This is clearly described in *Manusmriti* and *Katyayana*. Out of 18 crimes mentioned to be looked into by the king in *Manusmriti*,[69] 10 are related to property and 2 to family. A similar picture emerges in *Katyayana* wherein it is said that out of 10 offences requiring the attention of the king, five are connected to property and one to family. Even the duty of the king to uphold *dharma*, finding place in the *Dharmashastras* and having connection with property laws, marriage relations and caste is rooted in the protection of these three institutions.

It is only when the king upholds *dharma* that everyone can claim their wealth and wife as their own. It is through the promulgation of *dharma* by the king that the *varna* system and morality can find protection.[70]

Therefore, it seems that in concrete terms, the king's maintenance of *dharma* signified nothing but the defence of the social order based on the institutions of family, property and caste. The deal set forth for the realization of the king also reflects the purpose of the kingly office. The dominant ideal that moved the kings in ancient India was the attainment of *dharma, artha and kama.* If the term *artha* is taken in the sense of enjoyment of property, the term *kama* in the sense of enjoyment of family life and the term *dharma* in the sense of maintenance of the legal system, it would be clear that the conceptions of property, family and caste dominated in the *triverga* ideal also.[71]

What follows from the preceding account of the theories of the origin of the state in the pre-Kautilyan literature is that the ancient political thinkers of Vedic and post-Vedic periods made a defining contribution to the development of political science and political theory, throwing light on the origin, concept and definition of the state, and that all the three theories have their distinctive ideas and philosophy. For instance, the divine theory of the origin of the state is distinct as far as it talks of the creation of the king by the Gods; yet it does not surrender people's right to life and property and pre-supposes political obligations being observed by both the godly representative as well as the people. The king, therefore, would administer justice and uphold social order, and the subjects would obey him and pay taxes to the state. The social contract is also unique in the sense that it does not grant the king absolute powers, as Hobbes does, and combines the features of the theories of Locke and Rousseau. The evolutionary theory lays emphasis on the gradual development of the state linked with social and economic changes in society at different times. It may be pointed out that the European scholars have laid undue and one-sided emphasis on the religious aspects of the ancient Indian social-political thought. It cannot be denied that various schools of thought of political and social philosophy clearly established that there was a distinction between the religious and the political while seeing through the ethical foundation of the state as a guarantee of a stable society and an effective state. Moreover, the Hindu thinkers were of the firm view that the state is a necessary institution for the orderly progress of society and that the existence of a country would be difficult, if not impossible, without a government.

DANDA AND DANDANITI: INGREDIENTS OF SOVEREIGNTY AND LEGITIMACY

Danda and *Dandaniti* occupy a central place in the theory of the state. The political philosophy tradition in the pre-Kautilyan texts such as *Manusmriti*, the Mahabharata, the Ramayana and Buddhist and Jain texts establish that *Dandaniti* was an important practical science as it concerned with the conduct of the kings and the *Rajniti*. *Danda* is defined as the force or coercive power of the state and *Dandaniti* as the science of government. There can be no conception of a state in the absence of a coercive power. In fact, *Dandaniti* can be defined as the science of governance—the way *danda* should be used to enforce the rule of law and enable the subjects to pursue and enjoy the *triverga*—*dharma*, *artha* and *kama*, whereas *danda* can be taken as the science of government. *Dandaniti* refers to the process of achieving and administering happiness for the people and provides a source, for that purpose, for the use of *danda*. Manu envisaged that it was the untiringly infliction of punishment on the wrong/evil doers that could save the weak from being roasted by the stronger, characterizing *Matsyanyaya*.[72] *Danda* is the authority or power itself, representing the sovereignty of the state. Manu says,

> The ultimate sanction behind the state is force. If it is not used, the alternative is the law of the jungle (*Matsyanyaya*). It is *danda* (physical force or physical punishment) which rules over all the subjects, it is *danda* which protects them; when all else are sleeping, *danda* keeps awake; law is nothing but *danda* itself.[73]

Danda is the real king, the real leader and the real protector.[74]

The Yudhishthira–Bhism discourse, narrated in the *Shanti Parva*, reveals that *Dandaniti* is all-encompassing and straddles *Varnashrama dharma* as well as *Rajdharma*. The Golden Age (*Kritayuga/Satyuga*) dawns when the king enforces the norms and values of *Dandaniti* in full measures. However, if he enforces the *Dandaniti* to three-fourths of the extent, the community descends to the Silver Age, the *Treta*. If the shortfall is one-half of the *Dandaniti*, the community further descends to the Bronze Age, the *Dwapara*. If the *Dandaniti* is completely abandoned, the community sinks to the depths of the Iron Age, the *Kaliyuga*, where oppression and tyranny are the order of the day.[75]

Dandaniti is not concerned merely with imposing sanctions or engaging in a prohibitive action involving punishment; it is also a means of instilling in the members of society a natural desire to obey law rather than the fear of punishment, as well as ensuring religious, philosophical and economic well-being of every individual by ascertaining proper distribution of the gains between the individuals and the state, on the one hand, and between the individuals themselves, on the other. All relationships—social, political and economic—are the subject matter of *Dandaniti*, to borrow from Ushanas. Describing *Dandaniti* as the science of politics or political science, Kautilya asserts that *danda* is a means to maintain *Anvikshiki, Trayi* and *Vartta* and that the method of proper use of *danda* is called *Dandaniti*.[76] Though the two terms are used quite often interchangeably, one can infer a fine distinction between the two in so far as *Dandaniti* deals with the actual process of governance and the goals it aims to pursue. Thus, the goal of *Dandaniti* is *yogakshema*, which consists of *yoga* and *kshema*, denoting thereby the acquisition of the *artha* and peaceful enjoyment of the same. The concept came to be used for *Rajdharma, Nitishastra* and *Rajniti* and *Niti* in the works of many thinkers such as Kamandaka, Somadeva Suri, Shukra, Chandesvara, Bhartrihari and Malhar Ramrao later in the non-Kautilyan texts.

The theory of *Dandaniti* as brought out in the pre-Kautilyan political literature shows that its emphasis is on the responsibilities of the state to use *danda* to fulfil the aspirations of the people—social, economic and political—by ensuring all-round development of society, including moral and spiritual, and to protect the weak against the encroachments on them by the powerful by awarding *danda* (punishment) on the wrong doers or the violators of law so as to prevent the rule of the jungle or *Matsyanyaya*. *Dandaniti* was not a code of profitless and relentless precepts. It reflected the actual conditions in which man lived.[77] It enabled people to realize the goals of life—*dharma, artha, kama* and later *Moksha* also—as prescribed by the *Dharmashastras*, and it aimed at the maintenance and promotion of righteous conduct in the social and political arenas.

DHARMA AND DHARMASHASTRA IN ANCIENT INDIAN SCIENCE OF POLITICS

Danda and *Dandaniti* are supposed to be under the control of *dharma*, which played a significant role in the origin as well as the functioning of the state.[78] In *Taittiriya* and *Aitereya Brahmana*, it is stated that the concept of *dharma* is based on truth. *Shatapatha Brahmana* says that Varuna made the sacrificer *dharmapati* or the upholder of *dharma*.[79] According to the *Aitereya Brahmana*, the king, after *Aindrabhisheka*, was declared *dharmasyagopta* or the protector of *dharma*.[80] The legitimacy of the authority of the king was dependent on the extent to which the king followed the law of *dharma* and that self-government (swaraj) was dependent on self-control (control of senses) If the king forgot *dharma* to establish his self-importance, he would cause great harm to the state and the people.[81] However, the concept of *dharma* has been subject, like many other concepts, to many interpretations and definitions. To have an overview of some of them would be necessary to reach a correct understanding of the term. Let me begin with the definitions provided by some Indologists: Heinrich Zimmer defines *dharma* as 'the fixed order of heaven and earth' taking *dharma* to mean akin to *rita*, which 'means eternal order',[82] a view shared by Rudolf von Jhering in his book, *The Evolution of the Aryans*, translated by A. Drucker, London, 1897. In the opinion of Saletore, these views do not explain either the context or the significance of *dharma* in the ancient Indian political philosophy.[83] Later, some scholars from the West and India countered this definition of *dharma* as incorrect and erroneous. Macdonell, as an example, says that *dharma* or *dharman* is a law or custom having for its purpose both civil and criminal law and morality.[84] The term *dharma* has also been defined to mean 'house' or its inmates[85] and also as 'Ordinance' or law and as religion and morality. A. B. Keith equates the term *dharma* with custom, law and righteous conduct.[86] Attempts to find the correct meaning of the word have yielded no conclusive results, mainly because there is no equivalent term to the word *dharma* in English language.[87] That Indian historians have failed to arrive at an exact meaning of the term is evident. Rangaswami Aiyangar, who interprets *dharma* as virtue or precepts at one place and as canonical law at another place, tries to define it with reference to its forms: *saddharma* (ordinary equity and morality) and *asadharana dharma* (dharma of a special character comprising *varna dharma*, *ashrama dharma*, *Varnashrama dharma*, *guna dharma* and *naimittika dharma*); he further classifies *dharma* into *acara dharma* (valid usage), *vyavahara dharma* and *prayascitta dharma* (rules of penance). Though this classification, for the sake of convenience of understanding the contents of *dharma*, emanates, without denial, from the ancient texts and from *Vijnaneswara*, it does not come to any concrete definition of the term as one.

Dharma, as we know from different narratives, was used to define and regulate intra-society relations as well as relations between society and the state. The *Purush Sukta* tells us that Indian people were classified into four *varnas*—*Brahmanas, Kshatriyas, Vaishyas* and *Sudras*. Out of these, the first two were regarded as the ruling class and the last two were part of the common citizen or common mass, though there is evidence which puts only the Kshatriyas in the ruling class superior to the other three, as all of them were to obey the king. This view seems to be untenable, as the *Brahmanas*/priests/*purohits* performed sacrifices and the coronation of the king, and it is also specified in several Vedic books that the king was to keep the *Brahmanas* happy to secure his authority and supremacy.

Upanishadic records further tell us about the conception of *dharma* as political power. The legend has it that Brahma created four classes in order to perform his worldly duties. But when he saw that they failed to perform their duties well even after the creation of these four sections of society, he created *dharma*[88] to control or check the Kshatriyas also. So *dharma* became the king of kings and the law of laws, as *dharma* was truth and *dharma* and truth were integral to each other. In other words, the law of the jungle could be banished and replaced with the rule of law and justice on the basis of *dharma*. *Dharma* was, however, dependent on *danda and Dandaniti*. It was imperative in *dharma* that *danda* should be judiciously exercised. Legitimization of the political authority was also ingrained in the popular belief that the *Raja* was upholding the cause of *dharma*.

> The authority of the king should be obeyed because it was based on righteousness, it was said. One, who is respected by his own people, becomes an object of esteem with enemies also, while one who is disregarded by his own people is set at naught by his enemies.[89]

The idea that a king can do no wrong, like in the Western theory of the divine origin of the state, was never a part of the Indian theory of divinity and kingship, according to which a king could be entitled to divinity only till he observed virtuous and righteous behaviour towards the people. The people treated him as *Rashtrabhrita* and obeyed him for the purpose of getting protection for *dharma*, life and property. According to Coomarswami,

> In ancient India, the spiritual authority legitimised the temporal authority in order to establish people's faith in the efficacy of the government. Spiritual

authority had a power to control temporal power but it could not replace latter because the moment it tried to usurp power for itself, it had acted against the principles of *dharma* and as a result, it would lose its authority. Temporal power had to act according to principles of *dharma*; otherwise it would also lose its sanction to govern.[90]

Incorporation of the principles of the *Dharmashastra* into government and governance while concluding a social contract with Kapavya further shows the mutual commitment between the king and the people to observe *dharma* in the discharge of their duties. According to the Mahabharata story, Kapavya conceded to the request of his tribesmen to accept kingship, subject to the conditions[91] that they would not kill women, children, ascetics and those people who did not want to fight war; would protect cows and *Brahmanas*; would not disrupt marriages or other ceremonies organized by the people; and shall not destroy standing crops and fruit-bearing trees. *Danda* is created not to kill the people but to protect them, and they should punish those who gathered wealth by plundering their own country. Bhism tells that these *Dasyus* agreed and followed the principles of the *Dharmashastra*.[92]

The foregoing discussion suggests that the prescriptive, normative and practical elements of the ancient Indian political philosophy pronounced in the Vedic and post-Vedic literature, including that of Buddhists, Jains and the Mahabharata, have immensely influenced the structure, organization and functions of political authority and the institution of kingship. Politics was based on ethics, and the king was not a seat of an arbitrary authority. He was to use his authority for the sake of the common good instead of serving his own self-interests. This view is echoed in the Mahabharata: 'The subjects being united would kill that sinful and cruel king who does not protect, misappropriates money, destroys things and is not charitable.'[93] They should shun such a king like a leaky boat. In conclusion, it may be stated that *dharma* was understood in the sense of duty, law, morality, virtue, justice and righteous conduct in relation to others and the self; it was a check over the irresponsible and arbitrary use of power by the king; it was a basis of faith of the people in the king as far as he followed the righteous path and protected those following the righteous rules of behaviour; and *dharma* strengthened the legitimization process in the kingdom.

THE CONCEPTION OF SOVEREIGNTY IN
THE ANCIENT INDIAN POLITICAL THOUGHT

Sovereignty forms a definitional construct of the term state. There was no ambiguity in the minds of the Indian political thinkers of the Vedic and post-Vedic periods that sovereignty determines the status of the sovereign and the kingdom and that the political problems are of immense value in the political thought and political life of the people and the state. It will be interesting to know here whether there was any centralized power in the Vedic period, like the one mentioned in the *Arthashastra*; whether they clearly differentiated the state and the government, denoting the residence of sovereignty in the former and the instrumentality of the sovereign in the latter; and whether there was a clear separation between the state and the religion? Though it is difficult to give a definitive answer to these questions in view of the lack of unanimity among the ancient political and social traditions, it can be maintained that the ancient texts, especially the *Shatapatha Brahmana*, *Manusmriti*, the Mahabharata and the Buddhist and Jain literature, provide us with enough evidence that the ancient Indians were quite aware of the science of politics and that the political ideas and ideals developed in that age carried the significance they deserved from the viewpoint of political theory, the issue of sovereignty being no exception. One can vaguely say that the king represented the government and that kingship could mean the state. Manu, who defined a state as an entity consisting of seven elements, considers Swami as a part of the larger concept of the state. One may, therefore, settle to accept that the ancient Indian political science paid attention to the analysis of the relevant political issues and political institutions with futuristic connotations and differentiated the state from the government, as implied in Manu's theory of state.

There are two dimensions to the term sovereignty—religious and political. 'Shatapatha Brahmana discusses sovereignty with a religious perspective'.[94] From a political science perspective, sovereignty presupposes the existence of a government that exercises or may exercise sovereign power[95] and implies independence of action in the internal and external affairs of a state. Sovereignty refers to a condition wherein people extend habitual obedience to the laws and decisions of the government failing which the government can force compliance with the law/s of the state. Two pertinent questions arise here: one, whether and how far the Indian theory of sovereignty meets the definitional elements of the concept; and two, whether sovereignty as conceived by the Indian political thinkers of ancient times was monistic and close to Austin's idea of sovereignty or was it closer to the pluralist model. Going through the accounts of those times, it can be asserted that sovereignty in India was neither totally monistic nor completely pluralist. The study discovers that it was a mix of both the theories. It was monistic in the sense that the king enjoyed indivisible authority because only then he could provide protection to people, family, property and caste. This idea is supported by the fact that *raja* was known as *samrat* or *adhiraj* or *maharajadhiraj*, indicating the level and type of political power vested in the king and the dominant position he was placed in.[96] The sacrifices such as *Rajsuya* and especially *Ashvamedha*, signified an 'assertion of power and a display of political authority such as only a monarch of undisputed authority could have ventured upon without courting humiliation'.[97] However, it is difficult to contend that the performance of horse sacrifice, *Ashvamedha*, did not necessarily make the king an absolute power.[98] The three theories/schools of the origin of the state do not grant, in explicit terms, absolutist status to the king, standing above the law, nor was he allowed to change the conditions of the social contract. He would receive unquestioned support and obedience from his subjects only till he protected them, their property and *dharma* and upheld *varnas*. It shows that there was no concept of an unbridled sovereign, and hence, the monistic theory of sovereignty was not visible in its purest form either in the Vedic or post-Vedic times. The concept of sovereignty has been further visualized from the standpoint of substantive sovereignty, real sovereignty and legal sovereignty. The first one resides in the state, which has the ultimate sovereignty, and the second one lies with the government. Saletore elaborates:

> In terms of sovereign power, the state is the ultimate sovereign underneath which lies the agreement of the general will of the bulk of the people; while government is only the legislative sovereign, which, during the term assigned to it by the ultimate sovereign, makes laws of universal validity within its own competence, and possesses the right to exercise force in the maintenance of such laws and to maintain its own authority.[99]

The discussion on the theory of sovereignty may be closed here by stating that, although there seems a divergence of opinions about the nature of sovereignty, in the sense of whether it was monistic or pluralist, it is generally observed that it was technically close to the Austinian philosophy, but was more of a pluralist type in practice. As far as the monarchy as an institution was a limited one in terms of freedom, 'general will' is found to dominate in the case the monarch did not live up to the canons of agreement. There were checks on the exercise of power by the king in the form of other institutions such as the *Amatya*, the *sabha* and *samiti* of the republican period and public opinion, sometimes going to the extent of revolt by the people. Therefore, Macdonell wrote that 'the king's power was by no means absolute, being limited by the will of the people expressed in the tribal assembly—*samiti*'.[100] Even so, it cannot be denied that the sovereign could exercise unhindered authority in order to discharge multiple functions—social, political, financial and defence.

SOME POLITICAL INSTITUTIONS IN THE ANCIENT INDIAN POLITICAL SYSTEM

A discussion of any system of political governance would be incomplete without referring to the existing important political institutions, their origins and their role in the functioning of the state. A brief account of some ancient political organizations as referred to by the Vedic and post-Vedic texts, namely, the *sabha, samiti, vidhatha, parishad, janapada* and *the mahajanpadas*, is in place. R. U. S. Prasad traced the development of the system of governance from early to late Vedic times, paying careful attention to correlate the development of power structures with early tribal movements and dynamics.[101] It is worth noting that references to monarchy and the republics in the pre-Kautilyan period continue in the Kautilyan period and after. The system of elected kings, for example, finds mention in the Vedic and post-Vedic works such as *Telapatta, Panchgaru Jataka*, the Mahabharata and the Ramayana, which tell us that only a person with good qualities and possessing piety and capability, physical and intellectual, was chosen by the people as their king. Referring to *Telapatta Jataka*, R. C. Majumdar says, 'the youngest son of Brahmadutta, the king of

Banaras, goes to Takshila in Gandhar and is elected king there due to his innate qualities and control over himself.[102] In *Panchgaru Jataka*, there is a reference to people offering the throne to *Bodhisatva* and celebrating his election by decorating the town and the royal palace as the palace of Indra.[103] The Ramayana provides another instance of the democratic way of choosing the king. According to the story, the king Dashratha decided to coronate Rama, his eldest son, as the crown prince, but not before giving an opportunity to the chiefs of the cities and villages of his kingdom to think and give their opinion on the matter. The assembly was given the authority to even suggest new measures, if his own proved them of little worth.[104] According to the Mahabharata, Pratipa wanted to appoint Devapai, his elder son, to be his heir, but could not do so because the popular will was against this on the ground that his skin disease made him unfit for the position of king. Thereafter, his brother was made the king.[105] We may conclude that there was a system of elected monarchies besides the existence of a system of limited monarchy.

THE SABHA, SAMITI, PARISHAD, VIDATHA, JANAPADA AND MAHAJANAPADAS

The institutions of the *sabha*, *samiti* and *vidatha* are described in the *Atharvaveda*, which refers to the *sabha* and *samiti* as the two daughters of Prajapati. *Sabha* appears in the *Rigveda* but without clarity about its exact meaning. The *Rigveda* defines *sabha* as a hall used for gambling, recreation or dance or to discuss the matters related to cattle and other aspects of social life.[106] For Professor Alfred Ludwig, *sabha* was the assembly of the *Brahmanas* and the rich/*Maghvavans* who are referred to as *sabheya* or persons worthy of assembly.[107] It means the *sabha* was not open to all people. There is reference to *sabha-saha* as 'eminent (persons) in the assembly', *sabha-sthanu* as 'pillar of the assembly hall', *sabheya rayihsabhavan* as wealth fitting for the assembly, *sabhapati* and *sabha-pala* as the guardian of the assembly hall, *sabhasad* as sitter in the assembly and *sabhacara* as assessors or judges of the *sabha*. The nomenclature of various offices suggests that the *sabha* was not merely a meeting place or a place for gambling, but it was an institution that came to play an important role in the governance process, especially in the period of the *Brahmanas* and *samhitas*. Bloomfield opines that *sabha* was not used as an assembly at all, a view refuted in the *Vedic Index* (II, p. 427). *Sabha* has been described as the assembly of the high dignitaries, not to be equated with the village council as viewed by Heinrich Zimmer. Jayaswal terms *sabha* as a popular body of the elders and a body of men selected under the authority of the *samiti*, and its function was that of the judiciary, acting like our modern-day criminal courts. With regard to its functions, N. C. Bandyopadhyaya seems to be in agreement with Jayaswal when he says that the 'sabha held a conspicuous place in the political institutions of the country, which we may designate as the political council', adding further that it was a 'central aristocratic gathering associated with the king. It was an advisory body to the king; and it acted as a judicial assembly'.[108] Ghoshal views this institution as a deliberative body, a parallel institution to the *samiti*.[109] Altekar attaches three meanings to the *sabha*—as village assembly, meeting for social and political purposes; *sabha* being the same as *samiti*; and the *vidatha* and *sabha* as a cabinet and equates its status with the king himself. Overall, one tends to agree that the *sabha* was an assembly of people that performed both the social and political roles.

Samiti

Samiti is another institution often mentioned in the early Vedic accounts of the state and government without any unanimity among the scholars about the definition, structure and functions of the *samiti*. Professor Altekar, like Hillebrandt, believes that *samiti* and *sabha* are not different from each other. *Atharvaveda* describes them as the twin daughters of Prajapati and therefore not having similar organizations. For Ludwig, *samiti* included all the people, primarily the *visah*,[110] implying that *sabha* was a smaller body than *samiti* stated to exercise restraint on the powers of the king. It is argued that the king could discharge his functions effectively only if the general/popular will was honoured through the tribal assembly,[111] a view contested by Saletore, because if the *samiti* was a tribal assembly, then who composed the *sabha*?[112] There seems to be an agreement between Zimmer, Jayaswal and Ghoshal on the subject of the composition and functions of the *samiti*, who said that the *samiti* consisted of the *visah* and sometimes even elected the king. Zimmer sees the Indian *samiti* as comparable to the ancient German assembly known as *Tacitus*. However, neither Ghoshal nor Zimmer were able to remove the confusion regarding the candidacy of the king. That is, whether the *samiti* elected the king from among all the members of the *samiti* (*visah*), and what happens when one comes across the revelation that the institution of the king was hereditary. Jayaswal terms *samiti* as the sovereign constitutional body that is used to discuss matters of the state.

The authors of the *Vedic Index*, Keith and Macdonell, take it 'reasonable to assume that the business of the assembly was general deliberation on policy of all kinds, legislation, and judicial work. But of all these occupations there is, perhaps, as a result of the nature of the text, little or no evidence directly available'.[113] Some historians assert that the *samiti* had the power to control the distribution of public funds too.[114]

Vidatha

Vidatha is the third significant political organization that means 'order', a body issuing an assembly deciding religious and war matters[115] besides being seen as ordinance, 'dispose', 'ordain' and 'sacrifice'.[116] *Vidatha* is also described as one concerned with religious matters. Macdonell, Keith and Bloomfield see *vidatha* as a house and as a sacrifice. Here, too, nothing conclusive about its meaning and functions comes out. A plethora of vague views on these institutions beginning from the *Rigveda* and even epics exist, but clouds of confusion regarding their respective organization, functions and their mutual relationships persist, as pointed out by J. W. Elder. 'Despite occasional references to *sabhas, samitis and rajans* in the Vedas, none of the Vedas provided an unambiguous description of how *sabhas, samitis* and *rajans* related to each other. This did not prevent subsequent scholars from suggesting that *sabhas* and *samitis* engaged in democratic (possibly even unanimous) decision-making, served as councils to rulers, elected and removed rulers, collected taxes and declared war. Nor did it prevent them from suggesting parallels between the Vedic *sabhas* and *samitis*, anthropological descriptions of clan and tribal gatherings,

Homeric agoras, Roman Senates, Teutan councils of chiefs and Anglo-Saxon Witenagemots.[117]

Janapada

The *janapada* finds different meanings in the ancient texts, including people from the city and the village, and subjects from all the four *varnas*, guilds, and so on, as well as land in the *Brahmana* works. The importance of people has been brought out in the *Maitrayani Samhita*, *Taittiriya Brahmana* and *Atharvaveda*. In the Ramayana, the term is used in the sense of *paurajanapada*, which consists of people from the *paura*, the cities and the *janapada*, the countryside. Both the types of people acted together as assembly on certain occasions. It is also seen as Realm, *Rashtra or desa*.[118] Paura, in *Divyavadana*, has been referred to as a corporate body or a commercial organization that looked after the municipal affairs of the capital and constitutional matters. *Paura* administration of the municipalities is recognized later under the Mauryan rule, with reference to the city of *Pataliputra*.[119]

It follows that the scholars could not reach a commonly agreed view of the meaning, organization and functions of *sabha, samiti, parishad, janapada* or *paurajanapada*, but they existed in the republican and monarchical regimes; were entrusted with the social, religious and political functions; and often acted as checks over the arbitrary and authoritarian behaviour of the king. *Rashtra/Desa-signified* areas falling under the jurisdiction of the kingdom are referred to as *janapada* and *paurajanapada*.

CONCLUSION

It has been attempted here to explain the Vedic to post-Vedic theory of polity in India and to explore how the political problems of the state and the antecedent issues like law, justice, sovereignty and legitimacy were addressed in the political thought of those times, which bears a resemblance to modern political science.

Primarily, the ancient Indian political science, though rooted in the *Dharmashastras*, pointing to a close relationship between ethics and politics, was secular in nature and substance. There are different theories of the origin of the state with a common view that the state arose out of the emergence of chaotic social conditions, making it incumbent on the establishment of political authority to establish the rule of law and restore social order apart from pursuing the common well-being of the society and preventing *Matsyanyaya*. In addition, *Dandaniti* or the science of governance, legitimacy and sovereignty formed the core of the ancient Indian political theory, with a connotation quite similar to that found in the modern political thought and theory. The question of the classification of governments, as was done by Aristotle, is dealt with in the ancient political texts, wherein we find governments being divided into monarchies, limited and elective monarchies and republics. Equality, fairness and impartiality/neutrality are the foundational elements of the concept of law, and justice and order are based on the Indian political thought. It was obligatory for the enforcers of justice to make a judicious use of force or coercion against the criminals or violators of the law. It can be observed that the king was also subject to the commands of the law according to *Dharmashastras*. The basis of law and justice was *Dandaniti*. Even in modern times, justice is defined as a system where there is no fear of *Matsyanyaya*. Protection of the poor and provision of *yogakshema* was the end of justice in ancient India, as it continues to be so even now, irrespective of the system of government or the form of state.

NOTES

1. See Mahabharata, 12.58-1-3.
2. For further information, see *Sarva Darshan Sangrah*, *Vishnu Purana*, the *Naishadhiya Charitam* and Panini's *Ashtadhyayi*.
3. Majumadar, *Concise History of Ancient India*, Vol. II, 2.
4. Winternitz, 'Kautilya Arthashastra', 23.
5. Law, *Aspects of Ancient Indian Polity*, V.
6. Sen, *Hindu Political Thought*, V.
7. Sen, *Hindu Political Thought*, 1.
8. Pant, *Theory of Government in Ancient India*, p. ix; Mortimer Wheeler, *The Indus Civilization: Supplementary Volume to the Cambridge History of India* (New Delhi: Cambridge University Press, 1960), 3.
9. Pant, *Theory of Government in Ancient India*, xv.
10. Ghoshal, *A History of Indian Political Ideas*.

11. Chousalkar, *Authority and Forms of Political Protests in Indian Tradition*, 9.
12. Chousalkar, *Revisiting the Political Thought*, 10.
13. Chousalkar, *Revisiting the Political Thought*, 2.
14. Olivelle, *Chandogya Upanishad*, VII. 1.2, 1.4, 2.1, 7.1.
15. Keith, *Classical Sanskrit Literature*; *Kshatravidya*; Hopkins, *India Old and New*, 104.
16. Agrawal, *India as Known to Panini*, 304.
17. Prasad, *Theory of Government in Ancient India*, 3.
18. Prasad, *Theory of Government in Ancient India*, 17.
19. Altekar, *State and Government in Ancient India*, 27.
20. *Shanti Parva*, Chapter 58, 12.
21. *Shanti Parva*, cited in Altekar, *State and Government in Ancient India*, 28.
22. *Tambrivanpraja ma bhih karttri naino gamishyati, dhanyasya dasham bhagam dasyamah koshvardhanam* (*Shanti Parva*, Chapter 67, 23).
23. Bandyopadhyaya, *Development of Hindu Polity*, Part I, 5.
24. Walshe, *Digha Nikaya*, Vol. III, 84–86.
25. Altekar, *State and Government in Ancient India*, 29.
26. *Adi Purana* III, 30 ff; Altekar, *State and Government in Ancient India*, 29.
27. Prasad, *Theory of Government in Ancient India*, p. 17.
28. Prasad, *Theory of Government in Ancient India*, 17.
29. *Manusmriti*, VII.
30. Buhler, *Manusmriti*, Vol. VII.3, 216.
31. Mahabharata, *Shanti Parva*, Chapter 59, 106–108.
32. *Manusmriti*, VIII, 14, cited in Altekar, *The Position of Women in Hindu Civilization*, 1.
33. See Mahabharata, XII. 62.28–29.
34. *Sa Raja purushodandah san eta shasita cha sah* (*Manusmriti*, VII.17).
35. *Manusmriti*, VII, 3–5, 8.
36. Saletore, *Ancient Indian Political*, 142.
37. Saletore, *Ancient Indian Political*, 142–143.
38. *Baudhayan* fixes it at one sixth of the produce.
39. See Altekar, *The Position of Women in Hindu Civilization*; Chausalkar, *Revisiting the Political Thought of Ancient India*.
40. *Vana Parva*, CLXXXIII.
41. Slakter, *Sovereignty and Dharma*, 7–8.
42. Spellman, *Political Theory of Ancient India*, 1.
43. *Rigveda*, 8.86.10–11.
44. *Shatpatha Brahmana*, 3.4.2.2.
45. Ghoshal, *A History of Indian Political Ideas*, 62.
46. *Vasistha*, I, 39–41, S B E Vol., 14.
47. Saletore, *Ancient Indian Political*, 146.
48. One can recall in this connection the records in Buddhist, Jain and other Hindu literature.
49. Altekar, *State and Government in Ancient India*, 31.
50. Sharma, *Aspects of Political Ideas*, 61.
51. *Vayu Purana*, I, VIII.84; *Padma Carita*, III.55.

52. Childe, *Man Makes Himself*, Chapter 4, 54–73.

53. Morgan, *Ancient Society*, 20.

54. Spellman, *Political Theory of Ancient India*, 21–22.

55. Thomas, *Concept of State and Nation*.

56. This classification or periodization of the development of the institution of state seems to be based on the description of the process of evolution provided by Sharma, *Aspects of Political Ideas*.

57. *Na vairajyamnarajasinnadandonacadandikah* (*Santi Parva*, 59.14); Sharma, *Aspects of Political Ideas*, 49–50.

58. *Santi Parva*, 144, 5–6; *Mahabharata*, 1.4.9–12.

59. *Vayu Puran*, VIII.60; *Mahavastu*, I, 340–346; *Sacred Books of the Buddhists* (SBB), IV, 62–67; Rockhill, *The Life of the Buddha*, 2–6.

60. *Tasmin vanalate antarhitetam salim akanam atusam surabhitandulaphalam aharamaharanta ciram dirghamadhvanam tisthenshu* (*Mahavastu*, I, 343).

61. Rockhill, *The Life of Buddha*, 6–7.

62. *Mahavastu*, I, 343; Rockhill, 4.

63. *Brahma tamartham buddhva yathatathyena vai prabhuh, kshtriyanambalam dandam yuddhamajivamadisat*, I, VIII.161.

64. This can be ascertained from the recurrent themes in the *Shanti Parva*; the *Ayodhyakand* of the *Ramayana* and the *Vishnudharmottara Purana*.

65. Sharma, *Aspects of Political Ideas and Institutions*, 35.

66. Engels, *The Origin of Family*, 244.

67. *Santi Parva*, Chapter 67, 14–15; 17–18; 19.23–24.

68. *Samrangana Sutradhara*, VIII, from Sharma, *Aspects of Political Ideas*, 38.

69. *Manusmriti*, VIII, 4–7.

70. *Arthashastra*, Book III, I.

71. Sharma, *Aspects of Political Ideas*, 45–46.

72. *Manusmriti*, VII, 39.

73. *Dandah shasti prajah sarva danda evabhirakshati. Dandah supteshu jagarti dandam dharmamvidurbudhah* (*Manusmriti*, VIII, 14).

74. *Sa raja purushodandah san eta shasita c sah* (*Manusmriti*, VII, 17 cited in Altekar, *State and Government in Ancient India*, 2).

75. Verma (1959) as quoted in Singh, 'Two Contrasting Major Theories', 7–11.

76. Chousalkar, *Revisiting the Political Thought*, 44–45.

77. Saletore, *Ancient Indian Political*, 28.

78. Refer to the literature in *Shatpatha Brahamana, Taitreyi* and *Aitereya Brahmana*.

79. Chousalkar, *Authority and Forms*, 22.

80. Ghoshal, *A History of Indian Political Ideas*, 23.

81. Coomarswamy, *The Spiritual Authority*, 11.

82. Griffith, *The Hymns of the Rigveda*; *Rig Veda* 1896–1897, I. 123. 9; IV.7.7; VII. 36.5.

83. Saletore, *Ancient Indian Political*, 11.

84. Macdonell and Keith, *Vedic Index*, I, 390–398.

85. *Rigveda*, I, 144, *Atharvaveda*, IV, 25, 7.

86. Keith, *Classical Sanskrit Literature*, 92, 450, 451, 455, 457; refer to Saletore, *Ancient Indian Political*, 585.
87. Keilhorn, *Epigraphia Indica*, IX, n. (7), 113; Kane, *op. cit.*, I, 1.
88. Chousalkar, *Authority and Forms*; *Brhadaranyaka Upnishad*, 14.11–14.
89. Mahabharata, 12.69.34; refer to Chousalkar, *Authority and Forms*, 37.
90. Chousalkar, *Authority and Forms*, 39.
91. Chousalkar, *Authority and Forms*, 36.
92. Mahabharata, 12–133.
93. Banerjee, *Indian Society in the Mahabharata*, 157.
94. *Shatpatha Brahmana*, XII. 9.4.1; S.B.E., XIV.
95. Saletore, *Ancient Indian Political*, 58.
96. For details, see *Shatpatha Brahmana*.
97. Saletore, *Ancient Indian Political*, 62.
98. *Taittiriya Brahmana* and *Apastamba Dharmasutra* too do not subscribe to this theory propounded by *Shatpatha Brahmana*.
99. Saletore, *Ancient Indian Political*, 63.
100. Macdonell, *A History of Sanskrit Literature*, 158, quoted in Saletore, *Ancient Indian Political*, 96.
101. Prasad, *Rig-Vedic and Post-Rig-Vedic Polity*.
102. Majumdar, *Corporate Life in Ancient India*, 105.
103. Cowell, *The Jataka*, 289.
104. Majumdar, *Corporate Life in Ancient India*, 108.
105. Misra, *Ancient Indian Dynasties*, 83–4.
106. See Macdonell and Keith, *Vedic Index* I and II.
107. Ludwig, (Rpt), 1948, 51, cited in Saletore, *Ancient Indian Political*, 390.
108. Bandopadhyaya, *Development of Hindu*, Part I, 113.
109. Cited in Saletore, *Ancient Indian Political*, 395.
110. Ludwig, *Rig Veda*, 3; Saletore, *Ancient Indian Political*, 397.
111. Macdonell, *A History of Sanskrit Literature*, 158.
112. Saletore, *Ancient Indian Political*, 397.
113. Saletore, *Ancient Indian Political*, 398–399.
114. See Ghoshal, *Beginnings of Indian Historiography*, 149; *Shatpatha Brahmana*, VII. 1.4, 299.
115. Roth, citation from Macdonell and Keith, *Vedic Index*, II, 296.
116. Oldenberg, *Sacred Books of the East*, XLVI, 26ff.
117. https://www.encyclopedia.com/international/encyclopedias-almanacs-transcripts-and-maps/sabhas-and-samitis
118. Jayaswal, *Hindu Polity*, 320.
119. Saletore, *Ancient Indian Political*, 381–390.

The Theory of State in the *Arthashastra*

I

This chapter has four sections. In Section I, an enquiry into the extent of linkages of the pre-Kautilyan political science to the development of political theory and thought revealed in the *Arthashastra* of Kautilya, the most eminent political thinker of ancient India, is in place so as to enable the reader to comprehend and analyse the political legacy inherited by him in terms of political concepts and institutions and also to understand his original contribution to the theory and practice of politics. It is often said that the pre-Kautilyan political literature helped Kautilya to organize his political thought and theory systematically and logically and influenced his political vision as well.

It may be stated at the outset that the greatest contribution of Kautilya, and a unique one, was that he developed a unified and integrated view of the state. In the words of Naresha Duraiswamy, 'The *Arthashastra* provided a political philosophy to unify previously small political units, weld divergent groups into a broader cohesive identity and integrate diverse linguistic groups. The emphasis on the common weal was intended to cement a diverse and heterogeneous population. The end goal was social cohesion'.[1] In fact, the *Arthashastra* provides an opportunity to the student of politics to know the archetypal political thought that exposes him to the idea of Hindu political theory similar to the one presented by Plato in his *Republic* in the case of ancient Greece. Kautilya was the first ancient political thinker who adopted a scientific approach in his writings on the science of politics and economics. The work has a mention of the *Purva paksha*, the *Uttara paksha* and *ekanta* or the conclusion that is reached after adopting all the steps involved in the process. Krishna Rao holds that Kautilya discussed facts in relation to place, procedure, doubt, implication, contrariety, *viparyaya, vakyasesha, anumata, vyakhyana, nirvahana* and *anagatavekshana* apart from the references to the previous portions and to alternatives, *vikalpa*.[2] But this discussion focuses on knowing: (a) Whether the *Arthashastra* was based on the analysis of political tradition and thoughts expounded in the Vedic and post-Vedic literature on political science or a product of his own original thoughts. (b) Was the *shastra* a work in continuity of historical explanation of political problems or were there variants in the method and thoughts pertaining to the analysis of the political institutions, concepts and problems of his time? (c) Did he devote himself to political theory building and seek to answer the questions regarding the origin and nature of the state and the theory of the functions of the state, and if so, were his political ideas in consonance with the ideas propounded in that context by the thinkers preceding him, that is, the thoughts contained in the Vedas and texts such as the Ramayana, *Shanti Parva, Digha Nikaya, Jatakas, Jainas, Dharma Sutras* and *Dharmashastras*? In other words, is there a legacy of pre-Kautilyan political science in relation to the political science and theory of Kautilya?

VEDIC AND POST-VEDIC LEGACY OF THE *ARTHASHASTRA*

The aforementioned questions relating to the Vedic and post-Vedic legacy of the *Arthashastra* are analysed in the following pages.

1. Origin of the state

A general view of the theory of the state in terms of its origin is that Kautilya did not give much attention to how the state came into existence and that he did not develop a theory of the state in that regard. There is no mention in any of the 15 books or any of the 150 chapters thereof, such as the stories in the *Brahmanas*, the Ramayana, the Mahabharata or *Digha Nikaya*, either of a state of nature or *arajaka* state in explicit terms and the creation of a divine king to help the people get rid of that situation or of any social contract between the social groups and then again between the people and the *Mahasammata*, nor is there a discussion of the evolutionary emergence of the state. But why did Kautilya escape the question of the origin of the state? It could be, as scholars like Ajit Kumar Sen think, because 'Kautilya took state as a natural Institution in the sense that it exists from the very dawn of *Varnashrama* or Hindu society. Since the state is ingrained in the human nature, it needs no explanation as to its origin historically'.[3] The second explanation could be that Kautilya did not disagree with the theory that the state or the king was the creation of Brahma, the creator, or that he took the existence of the state for granted in the sense that the social order was maintained because of the presence of the king/state, and it was because of the power of the king to punish and wield the rod that the subjects not only observed *swadharma*, but they also obeyed the orders of the sovereign. It is the rod wielded by the king that ensured the pursuit of philosophy, the three Vedas and economics; its administration constitutes the science of politics, involving the acquisition of things not possessed, the preservation of things possessed, the augmentation of things preserved and the bestowal of things augmented to a worthy recipient. On it is dependent the orderly maintenance of worldly life.[4] Thus, the existence of the wielder of the rod is already recognized by him. The argument in the *Arthashastra* seems to be that the king enjoys his position and power not because of any divine claim but because of the qualities and qualifications he possesses. In spite of these arguments, it would be wrong to suggest that Kautilya did not express himself on the matter of the origin of the state at all. There is enough evidence to show that he did not overtly support, if not reject, the theory of the divine origin of the state. Further, Kautilyan speculation about the contractual basis of the state comes across in his work.[5] R. S. Sharma opines,

> [T]he earliest *brahmanical* exposition of the contract theory of the origin of state in clear terms occurs in the *Arthashastra* of Kautilya. Just as in *Dighanikaya* this theory is propounded incidentally in connection with the refutation of the *brahamana's* claim to social supremacy, similarly in the *Arthashastra* it is expounded casually in the course of a talk amongst the spies about the nature of royal power.[6]

It is no one's argument that Kautilya made any deliberate attempt to discuss the contract theory in as much detail as he did about the conception of state by pointing out the seven elements that constitute the state. Yet as stated by R. S. Sharma,

> into the terms of contract it introduces certain new elements which are absent in the *Dighanikaya*. It states that overtaken by the state of anarchy the people elected Manu Vaivasvata as their king and undertook to pay 1/6 of their grain, and 1/10 of their articles of merchandise in addition to a portion of their gold. In return for these taxes the king guaranteed social welfare to the people by undertaking to suppress acts of mischief, afflicting the guilty with taxes and coercion.... This account of the origin of the state closes with the moral that the king should not be disregarded.[7]

In the contract theory of Kautilya, the king enjoys more powers than the subjects. The restrictions on royal authority do not come so evidently and so openly as the number of obligations that the subjects are put under in order to buttress and strengthen the authority of the king.

> It is argued that the king, who assures security and well-being to his subjects by eliminating wrongful acts through coercion and taxes should never be disregarded. Hence, Kautily's contract theory is purported to buttress royal power as that of Hobbes, rather than to limit it as that of locke.[8]

Kautilya's ideas about the social contract theory can be derived from his understanding of the political anthropology of the individual and the community. Speaking of the human nature or *sanskriti*, Kautilya argues that the *artha* is the logical and practical condition of *dharma* and *kama*. Kautilya makes two assumptions: first, the man, by nature, is selfish and suffers from the *vyasanas* such as greed, lust and desire to dominate others, and second, these dispositions give birth to conflicts between communities and within individuals. The continuing conflicts ultimately create conditions of anarchy or *Matsyanyaya*. In the opinion of Liebig, Kautilya argues that in this anthropologically derived basic situation of anarchy and arbitrariness, men feared for their lives and property and felt the need for a ruler with supreme executive power—that is, armed with the rod of force and punishment—against those who would illegally use force (in the form of murder, assault or robbery) within their territory, and thus, he indicates that the people should be grateful for having the king and should not complain about paying taxes to him.[9] It can be concluded on the basis of the understanding derived from the above discussion that Kautilya referred to the question of the origin of the state only incidentally or casually instead of giving it some serious attention. With regard to the nature of government, Ilhan Niaz comments that 'Kautilya does not debate the merits or demerits of different forms of government. For Kautilya, that issue has already been settled in favour of absolutist monarchical states that operate through salaried professional bureaucracies and military forces'.[10]

However, he was the first Indian political thinker to provide a concrete meaning and definition of the state as revealed in his *saptanga* theory. It is interesting to note here two things: One is that Kautilya, for the first time in the history of ancient India, defined a state which resembles, rather expands, the modern definition of the state, and two, he also developed a theory of the functions of the state going beyond the defence of the *Dharmashastra* and the people and their property to include the responsibility to defend and expand the frontiers of the empire.

2. **Dharmashastra** and the **Arthashastra**

In the pre-Kautilyan age, we have found that the *Dharmashastra* tradition played an important role in guiding and, to some extent, controlling the sociopolitical order of the Vedic and post-Vedic times, and *dharma* was an important basis of the law. The *Brihadaranyaka Upanishad* describes *dharma* as the king of kings and that the weak could rule over the powerful only with the help of *dharma*. *Dharma* was created in view of the failure of the four *varnas* to meet the growing needs of society.[11] *Dharma* came to be identified with the law and was the ruling principle of the state.[12] For Kautilya, both the *Arthashastra* and *Dharmashastra* belonged to *Itihasa Veda*, considered the fifth Veda and were mentioned along with the *Atharvaveda*, of which the *Arthashastra* was considered as *Upa Veda*. It may be noted that the *Atharvaveda* was considered the Veda of the *Kshatriyas*.[13] The *Atharvaveda* and the *Itihasa Veda* dealt with the science of politics, known as *Kshatra Vidya*, and their purpose was to ensure the well-being of the people. The king did not enjoy the legislative authority without restraint. His executive authority was also meant to uphold *dharma* among others. *Danda* and *dandaniti* were responsible for maintaining social order, based on the *Varnashrama dharma*, and for preventing *Matsyanyaya*. *Dandaniti* was to be in the service of mankind, dispensing justice without discrimination, favour or prejudice. It was interpreted

> as a means to maintain *Anvikshiki, Trayi, Varta* and the method of proper use of *Danda* is called *Dandaniti*. It helps man acquire the thing not acquired, preserve the thing acquired and bring about its increase, distribute the increased wealth among the needy. It encourages proper well-being of the people.[14]

The discussion may be closed on the note that though Kautilya describes four sources of laws, namely the sacred (*dharma*) law, *vyavahara* (evidence/practice), *charitra* (culture/custom) and *rajasasana* (state law or edicts of the king),

> whenever there is conflict between the customary law and the sacred law or between *vyavahara* or law based on evidence, the sacred law will prevail. But whenever sacred law is in conflict with rational law (king's law), then reason shall be held authoritative; for there the original text (on which the sacred law has been based) is not available.[15]

Thus, the *Arthashastra* can be taken as a departure from the past in the sense that it establishes the superiority of the state over the *Dharmashastra* without denying the relevance and importance, which the *Dharmashastras* command in the life of a society as codes of righteous conduct. Kautilya gave a new interpretation to the concept of sacred law and was of the view that *anviksiki*, defined by him as the philosophy of *Sankhya, Yoga and Lokayata*, occupied in the chronology of the four sciences—*trayi* (the triple Vedas), *varta* (agriculture and trade or wealth), *artha* and *dandaniti* (the science of government) a place of precedence. When seen in the light of these sciences, the science of *anviksiki* is most beneficial to the world; it keeps the mind steady and firm in weal and woe alike, and bestows excellence in foresight, speech and action. The science of *anviksiki* has always been held to be a light to all kinds of knowledge, an easy means to accomplish all kinds of acts and a receptacle of all kinds of virtues.[16]

Kautilya seems to have taken a significantly divergent view from his predecessors on the relationship between the sacred law and the state law, while upholding the superiority of the Vedas in relation to history and customs. He takes a rational and logical approach to politics by differentiating between the *Dharmashastra* law and the *dharma nyaya*: 'The king who administers justice in accordance with sacred law (*dharma*), evidence (*vyavahara*), *samstha* (precedents, History), and *nyaya* (King's law, Equity) which is the fourth, will be able to conquer the whole world bounded by the four quarters'.[17] Kautilya argues in favour of the subordination of the sacred law to the state law in the case where the first is at variance with the second.

3. Political institutions

The pre-Kautilyan, Vedic/*Rigvedic* political literature refers to several political institutions existing at that time. *Janapada and paurajanapada, sabha, samiti, vidhatha and parishad*—social and political organizations under different states—were seen playing a significant role. They could be termed as the symbols of decentralization of power or as examples of pluralist sovereignty. It would be pertinent to point out that the institutions such as *sabha, samiti and vidhatha* lost their significance earlier than later, and that these organizations could not be explained and analysed by the scholars writing political and social history of early ancient India in a unanimous manner as they were termed differently by different historians, beginning with Ludwig, the writers of the *Vedic Index*, Bloomfield, Heinrich Zimmer, Alfred Hillebrandt, K. P. Jayaswal and N. C. Bandyopadhyaya and ending with A. S. Altekar and U. N. Ghoshal. Some described them as village assemblies/councils, while others termed them parallel to the king, and yet others saw them as advisors to the king as well as the judicial assemblies. Some considered all of them as one and the same, while others differentiated between them.[18] With reference to the *Arthashastra* discussion on politics and political science, it is found that any reference to *sabha, samiti or vidhatha* is missing there. There is only one concept that has been mentioned in this great book, and that is *janapada*. Here too, it is noticed that early ancient Indian political literature observes a lack of agreement regarding the meaning, organization, nature, scope and functions of *janapada* and *paurajanapada*.[19] Some describe them as mere people/assemblies of people from the countryside and the town areas, whereas others define them as a realm or territory. Some describe them as institutions having political responsibilities, whereas others do not agree with this interpretation. The *Arthashastra* does refer to the concept of *janapada* in his work, but as one of the constituent elements of the state. The reason for the neglect of the *sabha, samiti and vidhatha* could lie in the fact that they had already disappeared before the *Arthashastra* was written. So far as *janapada* was concerned, Kautilya agreed to treat them as people and territory. This term will get a detailed treatment later in the discussion of the *saptanga* theory of state developed by Kautilya.

4. Forms of the state

Identification and classification of the forms of the state and government have been part of the intellectual exercise among the authors of political treatises both in ancient and in modern times. Many political thinkers have tried to analyse the distinctive fundamental features of states and governments and grouped them or categorized them accordingly. So far, political science teachers, from Aristotle to modern ones, have classified the states and/or governments on the basis of (a) the location and nature of sovereign power—monarchy, aristocracy, oligarchy and democracy; (b) separation of powers—parliamentary, presidential and parliamentary–presidential; and (c) division of powers on a territorial basis, comprising more than one set of government—unitary and federal.

The ancient political theorists, as their works show, have also referred to the existence of several forms of state/government. The *Aitareya Brahmana* mentions 10 forms of governments such as *Swarajya*,[20] *Rajya* and *Vairajya*.[21] These forms of the state were in existence in the North as well as in the South.[22] Kautilya tells us that '*Vairajya* was a form of government and that too a bad one because no one feels in a *Vairajya* government the feeling of mine (with regard to the state); the aim of a political organism is rejected; anyone can sell away (the country), no one feels responsible; or one becoming indifferent leaves the state'.[23] M. Haug says that *Vairajya* in the *Aitareya Brahmana*[24] assigns two meanings to the term: (a) without a king and

(b) a very distinguished king. In this passage, we must take it in the first meaning, for here are the *janapada*, that is, people in opposition to the king mentioned as *abhishikta*, that is, anointed, while, in all other passages of this chapter, we find instead of them, the *rajnah* or kings[25] and *Bhaujya*, which are differentiated on the basis of the nature of power vested in the ruler.[26] R. S. Sharma maintains that some of these forms of government may have been obtained among the non-Aryan tribal people not yet brought under Vedic influence. Though most terms used for these forms cannot be precisely defined for the Vedic period, *ekaraja* may mean a ruler whose authority was undisputed in his domain.[27] The evidence collected from the Vedas, the *Brahmanas*, the epics and the *Arthashastras* suggests that the most popular form of the government was a monarchy, which could take the form of hereditary, elective or a limited monarchy. Quoting from the *Taittiriya Samhita* and early Yajus collection, Sharma says the king is announced in 'this tribe (vis)'and 'in this kingdom (rashtra)', which shows that the tribe and the geographical region occupied by it were becoming coeval.[28] Then, there is evidence of republics and corporations of warriors described by Panini as *Ayudhajivins*, besides there being self-governing clans—Malavas, Ambasthas, Cathaeans and Ossetians. Buddhist literature mentions other clans such as the Licchavis, the Vajjians, the Sakyas, and the Mauryans. Discussion in many books and essays also leads the reader to the conclusion that the rule of these clans was seen as a system of oligarchies, where there was a council of the notables presided over by the king to rule the kingdom. However, with the passage of time, these oligarchies or republics almost disappeared by the 5th or 6th century AD. History tells us that there were confederations as well in ancient India.[29] A. S. Altekar tell us about Kuru-pancalas of the later Vedic period who formed a composite state ruled by a common king. Licchavis formed alliances with Mallas and Videhas, and the Licchavis Federal Council consisted of 18 members, nine of whom were elected by each of the confederating state, but 'normally, however, states in ancient India were unitary in character'.[30] Kautilya also devotes his energies to the topic of the forms of the state in Book XI, Chapter 1, where he discusses, among others, oligarchy, aristocracy, republics and monarchy as forms of the state. He talks of sovereign clans who are described by Rangaswami Aiyangar as free aristocracies. He was also cognizant of the fact that the small kingdoms, whether republics or republican monarchies or oligarchies in the form of *ganas* and *sanghas*, with variations in terms of their organization, nature and role and that various sources in Buddhist literature also do not help the reader much in that regard. One is not clear as to whether the rule of the Buddhist religious *sanghas* was equally applicable to the political *sanghas* as well or whether the model of political *sanghas* was not the same as that of the religious *sanghas*.

Coming back to Kautilya, the forms of government were put into two *shrenis*/corporations: the corporations of warriors of (the *Kshatriyasreni*) Kambhoja, Surashtra and others who lived by performing agriculture, trade and wielding weapons; and the corporations of Licchavis, Vrijika, Mallaka Mudraka, Kukura, Kuru, Panchala and others who lived by the title of Raja. Kautilya recommends that the conqueror

> should secure and enjoy the services of such corporations as are invincible to the enemy and are favourably disposed towards him. But those who are opposed to him, he should put down by showing the seeds of dissension among them and by secretly punishing them.[31]

This is an indication of the policy of the state towards the republics intended to be a part of the empire. Kautilya places this policy quite clearly when he says:

> Acquisition (conquest) of a *Samgha* is more desirable than an alliance of goodwill or military aid. Those which are united (in a league) should be treated with the policy of subsidy and peace, for they are invincible. Those which are not united should be conquered by army and disunion…. Thus should the monarch (*Ekraja*) behave towards the *samghas*.[32]

It may be inferred from this policy of selective subjugation of the republics by the empire that the stronger republics remained free, while the weaker republics that were not united were first divided through the use of spies and women and then dismembered through the use of force. The republics were characterized by mutual rivalries and jealousy. Further, the nature of the republic states was dissimilar.

For example, the republics of Kambhojas, the Bhojas and Pitinikas were non-monarchical and were self-governing communities under the Mauryan Empire. Kautilya also tells us in the *Arthashastra* about another form of state known as *Dvairajya*[33] where two rulers exercised a joint claim over sovereignty. Kautilya is not favourably inclined towards such a state, as such a state would always suffer from disharmony and factionalism. However, Kautilya probably was convinced that a monarchy was one of the best forms of state as it could bring all states operating independently under one political umbrella to obtain the objectives of general good of the people and pursue the policy of *yogakshema*. 'The king shall be the only monarch of all the corporations, and the corporations also, under the protection of such a single monarch, should guard themselves against all kinds of treachery'.[34] A monarchy was the best form of government because, in it, there was neither the strife of sections nor the dominance of class interests. The king was, thus, the chief necessity for a state.[35]

Following the aforementioned discussion, it can be surmised that Kautilya had gone through a major part of the *Arthashastras* preceding him, but he did not carry forward the political theory and thought developed in the times of the Vedas and the epics preceding him as it is. Rather, his work was a departure from his past in many ways. For instance, the theory of the origin of the state was to him of lesser importance than the state itself, which he very precisely defined. Second, he does not seem to be much interested in discussing the political institutions like *sabha, samiti, parishad and vidhatha*, except the institution of *janapada*, which impacts the rise and growth of political theory. Third, the classification of the states finds him favouring the monarchical form of the state, which is considered by him as a better system as it will be more stable, prosperous and peaceful as compared to other forms of the state of the times preceding him. Put in this perspective, it can be asserted that the *Arthashastra* is the first book, and Kautilya is the first political thinker of ancient India who ventured into the field of political inquiry free from the ecclesiastical pressures and who could be vested with the credit of developing and documenting a science of politics and political theory comparable to the political science and theory of his contemporary and the later period Western political thinkers, including Plato, Aristotle and Machiavelli, as far as the theory of state goes or as far as the art and science of government is concerned.

NATURE OF KAUTILYAN STATE

Any analysis of the Kautilyan theory of state would be incomplete without referring to the views of the author of the *Arthashastra* on the nature of the state. Several questions arise here: Was the state a form of absolute monarchy wherein the word of the king was the law? Was it a monarchy punctuated by a system of checks and balances, that is, a limited monarchy? Was it a benevolent monarchy or could it be described as a welfare state? Was it a centralized bureaucratic state or a pluralist decentralized system of government? Was Kautilya's state a federation or unitary in its structure and operation? Historians are not unanimous, and even the *Arthashastra* is not completely free from vagueness on these questions.

In Kautilya's monarchical system, the king appears to have wide-ranging powers to govern the country, as evidenced from the long list of functions and duties of the king, indicating a complete grasp and control over the administration, and yet the king is described by Kautilya as a public servant, an agent of the people. He was to seek the company of the elderly and the learned, as they were regarded as the guardians of the social and moral order in the society. In general, it can be easily agreed, therefore, that Kautilya does not support the idea of an absolutist state; rather, he is in favour of a limited monarchy. Note, for example, his insistence on the ruler to observe the principle of participatory decision-making, involving consultation with the *mantrins and mantriparishad* in that process. One is reminded of his famous statement—one wheel alone does not turn[36] and therefore cannot pull the cart. *Arthashastra* Book I, Chapter 15, says that even in the matters of urgency, the council should be summoned and the decision of its best men be adopted. Even so, Kautilya nowhere makes it obligatory for the king to abide by such advice in such explicit details. The abiding nature of consultations is implicit, not explicit. For example, Kautilya advises the king to set the preceptors or ministers as the bounds of proper conduct (for himself), who should restrain him from occasions of harm, or when he is erring in private, should prick him with the goad in the form of the indication of time for the performance of his regular duties by (means of) the shadow of the gnomon or the *nalika* (water clock).[37] He insists that all kinds of administrative measures are to be preceded by deliberations in a well-formed council.[38] *Dharma* and customs and local usages formed another set of checks on the exercise of authority by the king. Though the king was given a vast range of powers, he exercised them within the bounds of law and justice; he was not above the law, even if he was one of the sources of law. One comes across several rules and procedures in the *Arthashastra*, which govern the conduct of business of the state by the wielder of authority in the state. The king is to follow a predetermined work schedule to discharge his activities concerning the people and the state with hardly any scope for deviation. He was under obligation to hear the grievances and problems of the people daily in a public place, establishing that it was a responsive and responsible state instead of being an autocratic one. It was the responsibility of the state to provide conducive conditions for harmonious and happy living in the society and enable people to obtain the four goals of life—*dharma, artha, kama* and *moksha*. The king and officials were bound by the principles of ethical conduct that paved the way to bliss and prosperity, as a society based on contracts alone is less productive and more anxiety-prone than the one based on conscience and compassion. Moreover, a predominantly ethical social environment is in need of defensive measures to protect against opportunism[39] one may underline here that 'an ounce of ethics was better than a ton of laws'. Ethics and foresightedness could improve governance and bring sustainable prosperity for the whole of humanity. The Kautilyan view of the state is in line with the modern dictum which states that the state came into existence for the sake of life and continued to exist for the sake of good life.

A Welfare State

Another question to understand the nature of the state is whether the Kautilyan state was a sort of welfare state.[40] To be true, Kautilya does not devote any chapter in the books to a separate discussion of the subject of welfare; it can be inferred from various passages that the state qualifies itself to be called a welfare state if it means that the state owns special responsibility to help the helpless and take care of the hapless. In other words, a welfare state helps those who cannot help themselves. It was not enough for the king to follow the path of righteousness, but to follow the path guided by *yogakshema*. He shall follow the path that guarantees his people spiritual and material well-being: *praja sukhe sukham rajnah, prajanamcahitehitam; Natmapriyamhitamrajnah, prajanamtupriyamhitam* (in the happiness of the subjects/people lies the happiness of the king and in their welfare, his welfare. What pleases him is not good, what pleases the subjects is good) and, further, *Natyadhikarah Karyasthe, rajanahpriya hiteratah*[41] (peoples' welfare is an end in itself for the king/state, and political power is the means to that end, and the good and the virtuous ruler should constantly endeavour to attain that end).

Aiding and assisting the people in carrying out their work was an essential component of the welfare role of the state. Rao comments:

> it was remarkable that the state's ideal of public and social duty towards the subjects was very high. The state aid comprised of state's initiative in starting private industries, experimental in character, making the provision of expert scientific advice and commercial intelligence. Direct financial assistance was given by means of loans or subsidies to stimulate production, and grants of land, and supply of materials, and water on favourable terms....[42]

The state's welfare schemes included direct assistance to weaving, agriculture and dairy products, and even tax remissions were granted by the state to certain people in order to promote the production of certain goods or to encourage individuals to carry out their business or trade without much hindrance. To care for the proper nourishment and material progress of the citizens was one of the most important duties of the king in the scheme of Kautilya. Similarly, labour welfare attracted attention, much like in modern times, in the *Arthashastra* also. The *Arthashastra* prescribes punishment to those who conspired to lower the quality of the artisans or to hinder their income or obstruct their sale or purchase or heavy fines on those who failed to pay wages according to contract.[43] Aradhana Parmar is right in her remarks that never before Kautilya was this function raised to such a level as when he compares it to the performance of a great religious sacrifice. In another context in the *Arthashastra*, Kautilya lays further stress on the supreme importance of this function when he writes that strength is power, but happiness is the end.[44]

The care of the weaker/vulnerable sections equally formed part of the duties of the government. Kautilya writes, 'the king shall provide to the orphans (*bala*), the aged, the infirm, the afflicted and the help-less with maintenance. He shall also provide subsistence to helpless women when they are carrying and also to the children they give birth to'.[45] Also 'when a capable person other than an apostate (*patita*) or mother neglects to maintain his or her child, wife, mother, father, minor brothers, sisters or widowed girls (*kanya vidhavas cha*) he or she shall be punished with fine of twelve *panas*'. This social obliga-tion of the capable member(s) of the family forms an integral part of our social (legal) conduct even in present-day India. According to the Maintenance and Welfare of Parents and Senior Citizens Act, 2007, passed by the Indian Parliament, it is a legal responsibility of the capable member/son/daughter to look after the parents or a senior citizen; behaving otherwise is a punishable offence. Kautilya makes it legally punishable if someone embraces asceticism without providing for the maintenance of his wife and sons, while making it the duty of the superintendent of weaving (Book II, Chapter XXIII) to employ widows, crippled women, girls, mendicant or ascetic women (*pravrajita*), women compelled to work in default of paying fines (*dandapratikarini*), old women servants of the king, and prostitutes (*devadasis*) who have ceased to attend temples on service to cut wool, fibre, cotton, panicle, Tula, hemp and flex.[46] Similarly, 'those women who do not stir out of their homes (*anishkasinyah*), or whose husbands are gone abroad, and those who are cripple or girls may when obliged to work for subsistence be provided with work (spinning out threads) in due courtesy through the medium of maid-servants (of the weaving establishment)'.[47] Thus, the state was obligated to meet the survival needs of women in certain circumstances, as mentioned earlier.

The state was supposed to protect even a prostitute who has lost her beauty by appointing her as nurse (*matrika*). Prostitutes, female slaves and old women incapable of rendering any service in the form of enjoyment (*bhagnabhogā*) shall be appointed to work in the storehouse or kitchen of the king.[48] Furthermore, prostitutes were protected against abduction or confinement by a man against their will or disfiguring them by causing injury or hurt. Doing so was a punishable offence.

The legitimacy of the government, in addition, rested on its capability to protect the people against calamities such as fire, famines, floods, diseases and epidemics. Kautilya gives more attention to floods than to fire, as fire may destroy only a village or half a village, but floods carry away hundreds of villages; so is true of diseases, which may afflict only one region, and remedies can be found for it, whereas famine afflicts the whole country and leads to an absence of livelihood for living beings. In all, Kautilya refers to eight calamities of a divine origin.[49] However, it is difficult to agree with this view of Kautilya because even a disease like COVID-19 might take into its coverage an extensive area of more than one region and even the whole kingdom if not effectively contained. Again, it was the responsibility of the king to not only protect villages from the molestations of courtiers (*vallabha*), workmen (*karmikas*), robbers and boundary guards but also keep them safe from being destroyed by herds of cattle. This was so because the helpless villagers, who were always dependent on their fields, needed protection against disruption and harassment. Farmers were also helped by the state by way of the provision of pastureland in the village. The children's protection finds a special mention in Book III, Chapter 12.20, wherein it is provided that a slave less than eight years of age shall not be compelled against his will to serve in a foreign land. The property of a minor was held in a trust to be looked after by the elders of the village.[50]

The state protected the interests of the employees against the excesses of the employer 'by regulating the relations between the two through enforcement of the contracts; by fixing the rates and manner of payment of wages and making non-payment or part-payment of wages for full work punishable'. An employer who engaged a labourer to do a piece of work had to pay that labourer for the full work even if he did not take a whole day's work from him.[51] A labourer was also subject to punishment, however, if he neglected his work, committed theft or destroyed the material.[52]

In sum, it can be stated that the essence of the duties of the king underlie not only in the performance of *rakshana and palana* of the subjects, but it was equally, if not more, concerned with the discharge of the function of *yogakshema* (welfare), which goes beyond the basic functions of the state. Welfare can be rightly taken to mean prosperity, well-being and happiness of the people, which embraces the whole range of activities—economic, social, moral and legal. 'In fact, the Kautilyan state', observes Parmar pertinently, 'partakes practically in full the nature of a welfare state today and even goes beyond the modern concept of the welfare state by associating it with the idea of human happiness'.[53] The discussion on the topic can be closed with a significant assertion of V. R. Ramachandra Dikshitar that the king was a constitutionalist who promoted the welfare of his people at all times, in all places and at all costs.[54] 'Solicitude for the welfare here and hereafter of all his subjects, high and low, is manifest throughout, and it extended even to people beyond his boundaries in an all-embracing humanity'.[55]

A CENTRALIZED BUREAUCRATIC UNITARY STATE?

Like other questions, there is no uniformity on the issue of whether the state had a centralized bureaucratic structure with delegation of powers to the subordinate administrative units and whether it was a federal or unitary system. Some scholars, like N. C. Bandyopadhyaya, opine that the state was a perfect example of centralized polity and administration as

> the king was the sole repository of all powers and political functions. He was the supreme executive head, the head of the armed forces and also the fountain head of justice (*Dharama-pravartaka*). The officers of the government took directions from him and communicated directly with him. For his own information, he had spies employed throughout the country, not only to watch over the opinions of the people but to examine the conduct of all officers of the realm.[56]

Historians such as Professors R. S. Sharma and Romila Thapar also seem to buttress this view; while scholars like J. C. Heesterman, on the contrary, believe that the state in Kautilya was a decentralized structure and had several peripheral political institutions, meaning a pluralist power structure with several co-sharers in sovereignty. Kautilya himself refers to many social/political units in the form of *srenis*, *puga*, *kula*, *gana* and *sangha*, which were said to be autonomous. It may be averred, however, that it was only in some limited spheres, and the king was there to regulate them through laws, rules and regulations. For example, the guilds were free to lay down rules for their collective good. The customs and laws of the caste/society, not at variance with the societal customs as a whole, were not interfered with by the state. It is interesting to note that deference to the customary laws and practices did not in any manner compromise or make ambiguous the status of the king as a secular ruler, even though Radha Kumud Mukherjee goes so far as to state that the local guilds and associations enjoyed independent political status and had the power to enact their own laws, rules and regulations with commonality of interests, thus indicating the decentralized and non-unitary character of the state.[57] However, some writers on ancient politics and the political system do not entertain this view that sovereignty resided in different centres instead of one place or person—the king. It might be pointed out that Kautilya suggests nowhere, explicitly or implicitly, that, while recognizing the existence of a number of social groups and guilds, there were any institutions enjoying parallel or coordinated powers with the state, or that the state was one of the many associations or 'an association of associations'. Furthermore, as pointed out by Krishna Rao, the groups never distrusted nor regretted state interference and never attempted to delimit the sphere of the state; on the other hand, the groups desired that the authority of the state should be exercised over the whole of the social and economic life of the community.[58]

In fact, it would be more appropriate to term the Kautilyan state as a system of centralized governance with decentralized administration, for it was easy to govern an empire of the size that it was from the centre but difficult to administer from the centre. So it established a system of delegated powers to the administrative units established up to the level of the village, the township, the district and the province. Maintenance of law and order, collection of revenues from all sources, and maintenance of social and moral order in the respective spheres of their responsibility were treated as the domain of local obligation of the local officials with a system of supervision and control by the officers at higher levels. That the village affairs were under the control of the state is evident from the fact that there were a number of departments headed by a superintendent to regulate the activities of the guild, including the fixation of the rate of profits over the fixed price of the local and foreign produce and punishment to violators with fines. There is a reference in Kautilya's *Arthashastra* to a large number of officers working at the local level, such as *sthanikas*, *nagrikas*, *gopas* and *anikastha*, who supervised over the machinery engaged in administering the rural and urban areas. A land survey for the purpose of determining and ascertaining the taxpaying capacity of the village was also carried out by the central-level officers of the state. From the aforementioned discussion, one can drive home the point that the Kautilyan state was neither federal nor a decentralized system of government in character but a unitary monarchical political system with a decentralized structure of administration.

II

CONCEPTION OF THE STATE IN THE *ARTHASHASTRA*: SAPTANGA THEORY

It is commonly agreed among the readers of Kautilya's *Arthashastra* that the most notable contribution of Kautilya to political theory is the theory of state. He provided a clear definition of the state, as an entity comprising seven elements/*angas* (parts)—the *swami*, the *amatya* (the minister), the *janapada/rashtra* (the country/people), the *durga* (the fort), the *kosa* (the treasury/economy), the *danda/bala* (the army) and the *mitra* (the friend/an ally).[59] He believes that the state is an organism or an organist institution based on the seven *prakritis*. Indicating the defining feature of the state, Kautilya said that no territory deserves the name of kingdom (state) unless it is full of people and controlled by an agglomeration of power with absolute authority over the territory.[60] It is apt to refer to the meaning assigned to the term *prakriti* by several scholars such as Kangle who translated it as the constituent elements of the state; Rangarajan defined *prakritis* as the seven elements of any state, Modelski described them as elements of the state, and Liebig called them state factors. It is appropriate to mention here that even the Greek political thinkers such as Plato and Aristotle did not attempt to define the state and discuss its constituents the way Kautilya did. Though one may treat Plato's philosopher king, his warriors and his husbandmen as comparable to some extent with the *swami*, the *danda* and *janapada* of Kautilya, respectively, and for Aristotle, the households and citizens constitute the state, but none of these conceptualizations can be treated as complete and expansive as is the definition provided by Kautilya: 'On the contrary Kautilya surpasses the Greek Philosophers in this field'.[61] As for the ancient Indian political thinkers, it would be wrong to say that political thinkers before Kautilya did not address the political problems of their times, but they did not really deal with the concept of the state as such. Their focus was on ethical aspects of the polity and society, encompassing the issues of finding out the ways and means of ensuring righteous political and social conduct of the king and the subjects. There was hardly any difference between the state and government; rather, they were used as synonyms. The questions relating to the king and kingship found adequate treatment in the Vedic and post-Vedic political literature reflective of the theory and thought related to the origin and functions of the state. The concepts of power, sovereignty and political obligation also entered into the body of political discussions taking place in the law books, epics such as the Mahabharata and the Ramayana, and in *Panchtantra*, *Buddhist Digha Nikaya* and *Jataka* and *Jaina* literature. But all this is found more as scattered ideology than a well thought-out comprehensive analysis of the state, its machinery, its functions and role in both the domestic and external domains. It is here that Kautilya's contribution becomes distinct. He separated the concept of the state from the concept of the government that exercised the sovereign power of the state and was responsible for the management and conduct of the affairs of the state. Many texts refer to the institution of the king[62] and the *amatyas*, yet they can be better understood as components of the government than of the state as is taken to mean in modern times. This could be because the state really did not assume the status of an established entity as it did after the establishment of the states of Kosala and Magadha, necessitating proper conceptualization.

Accordingly, it can be asserted that Kautilya, for the first time, perceived a state as a corporate body consisting of seven elements stated earlier, despite the concept of *astangika rajya* described in the *Shanti Parva*, critical edition, as the eighth element is not mentioned anywhere. He established the state as an independent unit. His theory of a state goes beyond the confines of the internal administration and organization; he also places the state in the context of international relations and policy.

SAPTANGA THEORY EXPLAINED

Saptanga theory of Kautilya can be understood in terms of his theory of conflict, driven by the greed and lust and struggle for domination over the others, seen in the context of establishing supremacy of power. Kautilya's concept of power finds expression in his *saptanga* theory, which tells us about the seven *prakritis* that represent the state power. This new understanding of state power is one of Kautilya's outstanding theoretical achievements.[63] Kautilya discusses these seven *prakritis* in a sequential form as indicated earlier already. Before discussing them in detail, it is pertinent to note that the hierarchy of the seven *prakritis* spoke of the weight he assigned to them. According to Liebig, the ranking of the seven *prakritis* is an expression of a logical and substantive hierarchy and generative principle. The state factor, *swamin*, is the 'generative condition' of the state factor *amatya*—without a ruler or a government advising him. 'Ruler and the government constitute the institutional framework of the state territory and the people living and working therein (*janapada*)—the undertakings of the fort, the treasury, the army, the waterworks and the occupations for livelihood have their source in the country. And bravery, firmness, cleverness and large numbers are found among the country people'.[64]

We will discuss them in the following sequence.

Swami/Swamin

Out of the seven constituents (*prakritis*) of the state, the most important is the *swami*. It should be borne in mind that the concept of *swami* or *swamin* is not new as almost all the previous texts and sacred laws talk about it with regard to the analysis of politics and political science of the Vedic and post-Vedic period of ancient India. King and kingship occupied a large space in the political theorizing of the early ancient India as well. But the term came to be given a more comprehensive and inclusive coverage in the *Arthashastra* than in the earlier ones or in the works following Kautilya's *Arthashastra*. His definition of state came to be accepted as a standard definition.[65]

> The treatment of the seven elements in this text is thorough and systematic, and we have no parallel to this in other texts... the subsequent texts have something different to say on the mutual relations of these elements, otherwise they do not add anything of substance to the Kautilyan definition.[66]

The term *swami* refers, as in the other sources of ancient history, to the head of the government, irrespective of whether they were in the form of monarchies or non-monarchies or republics or democracies. The term *swami* occurs for the first time in the Saka inscriptions.[67] *Swami* is also used for the institution of the head of the state, literally meaning the master or the owner. R. S. Sharma adds, 'The intention is to stress the sense of possession exercised by the head, who occupies a very exalted position in the scheme of Kautilya'.[68] Scholarly opinions differ on the question of whether the institution of the kingship was hereditary; it is safe to assert that it were the qualities of the *swami/* king than his birth that determined his claim to the throne. Kautilya gives a long list of the qualifications of the person claiming his right to be a king[69] that include, among others, being born in a family of high status; possession of valour; should be godly; capable of seeing through the medium of aged persons; should be virtuous and truthful; should have large aims and should be highly energetic and enthusiastic; he should not be addicted to procrastination, and he should be of resolute mind with a taste for discipline; should possess the qualities of quickness and probity; and should be the owner of sharp intellect, strong memory and keen mind besides being energetic, powerful and trained in all kinds of arts. Moreover, he should possess dignity and be capable of taking remedial measures against dangers and should be ready to avail himself of opportunities when afforded with respect to place, time and manly efforts in addition to being clever enough to discern when to cause cessation of treaty or war with an enemy or to wait and keep treaties, obligations and pledges or to take advantage of his enemy's weak points. A king was not supposed to browbeat and cast haughty and stern looks. In fact, Kautilya dreamt of a sagely king, and he says that he 'should be free from passion, anger, greed, obstinacy, fickleness, haste and back-biting habits and should be observing customs as taught by aged persons etc.'[70] It is relevant to point out here that the king occupies an unassailable position in the scheme of governance of the country. And yet, he enjoys no divinity or divine status to claim any divine attributes. In the words of B. A. Saletore, there is nothing in the *Arthashastra* to suggest that Kautilya ever considered the king as a God on earth. On the other hand, all the regulations, which he has mentioned in connection with the education and duty of the king point to a member of the Hindu society, who was only one amongst the many who could hope to become a king.[71] In a similar vein, Aseem Prakash argues:

> since Vedic belief system encourages pantheism, it was not possible for the king to claim to be the vicar of the millions of gods and goddesses, many of which are in conflict with each other. This also implies that the king could not gain legitimacy by claiming to be the protector of religion—he could only make a claim to be a protector of the moral order—to enable the individual to follow his dharma.[72]

The second thing worth remembering in relation to the position of the king, despite being accepted as omniscient power in the context of the knowledge of the Vedas, is that he was neither above the law nor had any absolute authority. Rather, he worked under several restraints, including public opinion, the customs and *dharma*. He was considered as the servant of the people.

However, it cannot be denied that the king was someone more than the first among equals. Safety of the king and his kingdom has always been a matter of utmost importance in all the discourses of the *Arthashastra*. This is evident from the Kautilyan discussion of calamities of the elements of the state. Kautilya draws an order of precedence of the seven elements and tells in Book VIII, Chapter 1 that 'my teacher says that of the calamities, namely the king in distress, the minister in distress, the people in distress, distress due to the bad fortification, financial distress, the army in distress and an ally in distress—that which is first mentioned is more serious than the one coming later in the order of enumeration'. Though Bhardwaj disagrees with this view and opines that ministerial distress is more serious as it is the minister who takes the remedial measures against calamities and is engaged in the protection of the kingdom and much more responsibilities fall on the minister, such as deliberations in the council, the attainment of results as anticipated while deliberating in the council, the accomplishment of works, the business of revenue collection and its expenditure, recruiting the army, driving out the enemy and wild tribes, and the protection of the heir. Like a bird deprived of its feathers, the king loses his active capacity and the king's life itself comes into danger if the minister is in distress. But Kautilya rejects Bhardwaj on the ground that it is the king who attends to the business of appointing ministers, priests and other servants, including the superintendents of several departments, the application of remedies to reduce the troubles of his people and his kingdom, and the adoption of progressive measures; when his ministers fall into trouble, he employs others; he is ever ready to bestow rewards on the worthy and inflict punishment on the wicked; when the king is well off, by his welfare and prosperity, he pleases the people; of what kind the king's character is, of the same kind will be the character of his people; (*yatha raja, tatha praja*) for their progress or downfall, the people depend upon the king; and the king is the aggregate of the people. He does not agree with Visalaksha in whose estimate the troubles of the people are more serious than the troubles of the ministers as it is they from whom are secured the finance, army, raw products, free labour and collection of necessities. Kautilya argues against it and says that all activities, including successful accomplishment of the works of people, security of the people and property from internal and external enemies and collection of revenue and bestowal of favour proceed from the minister. Thus, he goes on to defend the descending order of the seven elements and concludes that when a part of one of the elements of sovereignty is under threat, the extent, affection and strength of the serviceable part can be the means of accomplishing a work.[73]

Functions of the King

The functions of the king have been a part of the scheme of political thinking and analysis from the period of the *Brahmanas* to the period of the Mahabharata, the Ramayana, Buddha and the later periods. In the *Brahmanas*, the main functions of the king centred around the protection of the people, the property and *dharma*, which did not see any major change even up to the post-Vedic times. Another function of the king, as our earlier discussion of the rule of the kingship suggests, was to ensure the application and upholding of the *Varnashrama* system. In the Mauryan times also, the king was supposed to maintain social order, collect revenue and protect his subjects. But some more functions termed as *palana*, *rakshana* and *yogakshema* and the conduct of international relations were added to his responsibility. In brief, the functions of the king, in Saletore's view,[74] can be classified into executive, legislative, judicial, administrative, ecclesiastical, revenue, military and cultural and patronage functions.

The same list of functions can also be found in the *Manusmriti*, substantiating my argument that the nature of functions performed by the king according to Kautilya was an example of continuity and change, that is, besides the functions enumerated by the law giver Manu, Kautilya added a few more as per his political ideas on the state and its international environment after the invasion of Alexander and the weakened position of the then existing kingdoms.

With regard to the executive functions of the king, it has been found that the protection of the individual, the family, the society and the property and of the *Varnashrama dharma* and facilitation of the pursuit of the four goals of social life—*artha, dharma, kama* and *moksha*—were the most significant executive functions of the ruler. Ensuring *yogakshema*, the well-being of all the people, and making provisions for social security for the old, the orphans, the infirm, the afflicted and the helpless were also the executive functions of equal value. Creation of state-run orphanages, widow homes and assistance centres for the infirm and their maintenance was a part of his executive domain. Saletore[75] says that these functions were a part of the executive functions provided in the *Manusmriti*, which Kautilya's king continued. We will discuss these functions elsewhere when we discuss the analysis of the theory of functions of the state. Here, it would be more pertinent to deliberate on the pursuit of those functions of the king that strengthen his calibre, character, popularity and loyalty and his capability and capacity to protect the kingdom and the self and to enjoy legitimacy of his government. These functions are documented in Kautilya's *Arthashastra* in Books I and II.[76] Further, the king, according to Kautilya, is to lead a much disciplined political and personal life. He should divide his day and night into fixed hours for fixed duties and shall ever be wakeful for both the day and night.[77] Kautilya further says that in view of maintaining efficient discipline, he (the king) shall ever and invariably keep company with aged professors of sciences in whom alone discipline has its firm roots.[78] He describes discipline as artificial and natural. He lays emphasis on the qualities of a learner as well as of a leader in a king, which include the mental faculties such as obedience, hearing, grasping, retentive memory, discrimination, inference and deliberation for the purposes of learning sciences—*anviksiki* (philosophy of *Sankhya*, *Yoga* and *Lokayata*), the *trayi* (triple Vedas), *varta* (agriculture, cattle breeding and trade) and *dandaniti* (science of government)—from which all that concerns righteousness and wealth is learnt.

Another question that is often asked about the Kautilya's king is whether he was an autocrat, a dictator or a tyrant, one of the terms used generally in the Greek political thought. Before an answer to this question can be attempted, it is necessary to know the activities and practices of a tyrant as provided by Aristotle. He seems to be of the view that a tyrant engages himself in the construction of such buildings as to occupy the people and keep them poor; in multiplying the taxes besides making war in order that his subject may have something to do and be always in want of a leader. The tyrant is also distrustful of his friends and sows dissensions among the people and weeds out all opposition, including the men of high spirit.[79] Are these qualities common to Kautilya's king? There are records in the *Arthashastra* to show that Kautilya's king shares some of these traits of the Aristotle tyrant, particularly relating to the system of espionage used to sow dissensions among the enemy and pried into the revenue collection and is termed as a faithful reproduction of the Greek model.[80]

Spies were also the mechanism used by the king to keep a watch over the officials, including the ministers of the state and the people as well. Pointing this out, Saletore says,

> With such a huge octopus-like network of spies, the kautlyan autocrat could feel the pulse of the people better than his counterpart in Greece or Macedonia. Judged from the manner in which he held the people within his iron grip, it seems that there was no difference between him and the tyrant described in Aristotle.[81]

Still, in my view, it would be an injustice to treat the Kautilyan king and the tyrant of Aristotle on the same level because the intentions and activities of the two might not have been driven by similar considerations. For instance, the evidence suggested in the *Arthashastra* about the wars launched by the king was to seek the stability and prosperity of his kingdom instead of merely for the sake of diverting the opinion and attention of his people. Similarly, sowing dissensions was meant only in relation to the enemy, which was justified as winning or weakening the enemy, and not for his subjects to fight with each other. *Dandaniti* again was dictated by the canons of judicious application instead of the dictates of arbitrariness.

Kautilya also does not support the idea of imposing heavy taxes in order to enrich the treasury at the cost of harming the subjects. Rather, it was the prosperity of the people and the king that formed part of the economic policies of the state. 'In the happiness of the subjects lies the happiness of the king'.[82] That the interests of the people were kept high in the mind of the king becomes further clear when one notes the insistence on the learning of four sciences of which the science of *Varta* was given an important place by Kautilya. He very explicitly maintains that the state shall avoid such large profits as will harm the people as an 'impoverished people are ever apprehensive of oppression and destruction (by over taxation etc.) and are desirous of getting rid of their impoverishment, or of waging war, or of migrating elsewhere'.[83] Even in the case of financial emergency, Kautilya approves mobilization of resources through several unusual means, yet there also he prohibits the raising of demands more than once because that might be tantamount to extortion. What makes the king different from the tyrant of Aristotle is the fact that Kautilya very specifically asks the king to abjure six vices/enemies, which, if not done away with, shall cause harm to the kingdom and the people. These are stated in the *Arthashastra* as follows:

> Restraint of the organs of the state, on which success in discipline depends, can be enforced by abandoning lust, anger, greed, vanity (*mana*), haughtiness (*mada*) and over joy (*harsa*)... Strict observance of the precepts of sciences also means the same; for the sole aim of all the sciences is nothing but restraints of the organs of senses.[84]

Kautilya gives a number of examples in the *Arthashastra* text of such kings who perished because they did not observe the principle of keeping the organs of senses under control.[85] These examples include that of Bhoja known also by the name Dandakaya, the Vaideha, Janmejaya, Talajangha, Aila, Ajabindu, the Sauvira, Ravana, Duryodhana, Dambhodbhava, Arjuna of Heheya and Vatapi kings who fell prey to the aggregate of six enemies and perished together with their kingdom.[86] Therefore, he prefers a wise king over a wicked one as the latter will certainly destroy the most prosperous and loyal elements of his kingdom, while the former can make even the poor and miserable elements of his sovereignty happy and prosperous.[87] In conclusion, it can be said that Kautilya's perception of a king is of one who is easily approachable and the one who should be truthful, pious, true to his promise, liberal, full of energy, resolute, desirous of learning and endowed with great fortune[88]; a good king should also be the owner of certain personal excellences to successfully manage the affairs of the government and the kingdom.[89] And for this to happen, the king, as it comes out from the foregoing discussion, should be the owner of high character and the excellences following the policy of *yogakshema* and keep the happiness of his subjects above everything else, including his own happiness and interests; he should be easily approachable to his subjects, should be honest in his thought and action besides being able to reject what is false and misleading and should be able to differentiate between the righteous and the unrighteous.

These prescriptions for the head of the government and of the state contained in the legendary work—the Arthashastra—are admittedly relevant even in the modern times, particularly when the entire global community is yearning for the achievement of the goal of good governance with a renewed focus on putting into practice an important attribute of the state for the good of the whole people.

Amatya

The second constituent of the state in order of preference is *amatya*, which, in fact, constitutes the agency of the sovereign power of the state and is mentioned in the texts on political science in the ancient period. There is absence of agreement on the nature and organization of ministers or *amatyas*. There are scholars who differentiate between the *mantrins* and *mantriparishad* in which the latter is taken as a bigger body, while the former is described as a smaller organ. Some perceive *amatya* as a regular cadre of the civil service out of which were recruited other officers of the state to the different departments of the government such as the chief priest, ministers, collectors, treasurers, officers to be employed in the department of criminal and civil administration, officers in charge of the harem, envoys and the superintendents of various government departments.[90] Furthermore, for Kautilya, the number of the ministers was not to exceed three or four, while the size of *amatyas* was dependent on the capacity to employ. This means that the number of *amatyas* was not fixed and was subject to variation. In pre-Mauryan times, *amatyas* were also appointed as village headmen, supervisors of sales transactions, judges, guides in worldly and spiritual matters and surveyors, etc.[91] Tracing the position of *amatyas* in the Arthashastra, R. S. Sharma finds it compatible with their position in the Jatakas. He assigns them agricultural operations, fortifications, welfare of the territory, prevention of adversities, punishing the criminals, collections of royal duties, etc.[92] The ministers, on the other hand, are those who advise or counsel the king. In post-Mauryan times, also, *amatyas*, termed as *sachiva* also sometimes, were treated as a general cadre of officers as it appears from the inscriptions of Rudradaman[93]; they find a lower place to the *mantrins* in the discussion of Kautilya's *Arthashastra*. It may be further observed that the selection of the *mantrins* was based on rigorous tests on merit, were paid a defined salary, had been given a definite domain of functions and were governed by public service conduct rules. Kautilya was convinced that the government of the kingdom could not be carried single-handedly by the king in the most effective and efficient manner without the assistance of the ministers. According to him, sovereignty (*rajatva*) is possible only with assistance. A single wheel can never move. Hence, he shall employ ministers and hear their opinion.[94] Like the king, Kautilya also mentions the qualifications of the ministers who, in his opinion, should be native; born of high family; influential; well trained in arts; possess foresight; should be wise; should have a strong memory; should be bold, eloquent, skilful and intelligent; should possess enthusiasm, dignity and endurance; should be pure in character, affable and firm in loyal devotion; should be endowed with excellent conduct, strength, health and bravery; free from procrastination and fickle mindedness; and should be affectionate and free from such qualities as excitement, hatred and enmity.[95] On the basis of the list of qualifications of the ministers, it is observed that Kautilyan *mantrins* and *mantriparishad* was an elitist organization in character and was distinguishable with regard to merits. Second, there seems to be congruence, to quite an extent, between the qualities of the king and that of his ministers. This similarity seems to be necessitated by the requirements of governmental objectives as well as the need for creating geometrical thinking at the level of the king and of the ministers on national issues. Even in the modern period, one sees the practice of police verification and intelligence reports and clearance from vigilance commission before placing the civil servants in the higher positions under the state. This is done in order to ensure that only the people of high character and commitment enter into the administration. Even now, in the council of ministers, such ministers are held in high esteem by the public and the bureaucracy, who is endowed with the qualifications assigned to the ministers by Kautilya. In the words of Saletore,

It speaks volumes for the Mauryan Prime Minister that he could with such acumen lay down the hardest qualifications which any progressive modern government could have prescribed for recruiting the highest officials of the state; and that he could, at the same time, make ample provision for finding out whether the prospective ministers really possessed them.[96]

Besides, it may be pointed out that foreigners were debarred from being appointed to the chief offices for which only the natives of the soil were entitled.[97]

The size of the council of ministers (*mantriparishad*) has also attracted the attention of Kautilya. But before reaching at any reasonable conclusion, he cites several authors/political thinkers preceding him. For instance, he tells us that Manu thought it fit to have a council of 12; Brihaspati, 16; and Ushanas, 20. However, Kautilya did not think it proper to impose any numerical limitation on the composition of the council. Rather, he left it to the exigencies of the needs of the kingdom. It shows that Kautilya was alive to the fact that the king should have the freedom to organize and reorganize the council as per the emerging needs of policy and governance. We observe in the modern regimes that the ministries are merged, created and re-created as new demands appear on the political and administrative scene in the country.

The most significant matters of the state, such as the declaration of war and concluding peace, matters of defence, finance, agriculture, pensions, etc., were taken to the council. The members were free to place their point of view in the presence of the king who presided over the meeting. The king, though was free to accept or reject the opinion of the council, generally went by the view arrived at in the council either unanimously or by majority.[98]

Second important aspect of the working of the council was the principle of secrecy about the proceedings. In the modern times, also, the council of ministers functions under the oath of secrecy. Secret agents were appointed for the purpose of detecting any breach of faith. Any violation of the secrecy of the council was subject to severe punishment. It was open for the king to consult the council as a collective or the members could be asked to give their counsel individually. He could call three or four members together for discussion and advice or could take the matter to the whole council. Though one does not find any direct evidence of collective responsibility of the council of ministers, they were in subordination to the *mahamatya* who could be seen as equal to the *wakil* of the Mughal period; he was the representative of the king and the vicegerent of the empire.

Janapada

Janapada constitutes the third element of the Kautilyan state. Further, one notes that the term or unit referred by Kautilya is not new as it appears in the ancient political literature written before him. *Janapada, paurajanapada* and *paurajanapadajana* find a mention in the *Manusmriti*, Ramayana's *Ayodhyakand* and before them in the *Satpatha, Maitrayaniya* and *Tattiriya Brahmana* as well. Then, we come across several political institutions that are said to reflect the expression of the general will or the peoples' will. These terms used in the pre-Kautilyan times included *janapada, paurajanapada, sabha, samiti, parishad* and *vidhatha*, representing the importance of people and the territory in the formation of a state.[99] It is impossible to imagine a state without people. The Western political scientists also in their definition of the state include people as one of the constituents of the state. Kautilya gave a very clear connotation of the term in the *Arthashastra*, who uses it in the sense of a realm or countryside. This concept is clearer when one reads the chapter on the organization of villages (*janapada nivesha*) in the *Arthashastra*. The conclusion one draws from the passages of *Arthashastra* is that *janapada* indicates both the people and the territory. Professor Aiyangar does not agree with the use of *janapada* as territory when he remarks:

> Conditions of later times should have somewhat reduced, in practice, the importance of one of the essentials according to the old definition of the state. In the epochs of wide popular and tribal movements represented in the Vedic and epic periods, it was of course not to be expected that the territorial aspect of the state should be grasped, or stressed, even if understood. Even in the days of Kautilya, powers are referred to by the name of peoples and not by geographical limits.... It is, however, clear that in the epochs that followed the disruption of the Mauryan Empire, when invasions and immigrations from outside followed one another in an

unending procession, frequent unsettlement of the population and of the political boundaries became inevitable, and the state had to be thought of independently of a fixed territory.[100]

This argument of Aiyangar, however, does not seem to be convincing because the mere change in the boundaries of a state does not render territory irrelevant as part of the definition of state. Saletore is right in saying that 'It is not denied that in a vast country like India there were periodical movements of tribes. But this is not equal to saying that people had no concept of territory as being one of the elements of the state.'[101] Similarly, it is difficult to agree with Dr Kane who says, 'it should be noted that neither Kautilya nor Kamandaka defines *Rajya*'. Territory as a concept has been quite old as is evident from the fact that the term appears as territory in the name of *rashtra* even in the *Rigveda* as well as in the *Atharvaveda* and later *samhitas*. How can a state be conceived without a people having a claim over certain land or territory, which they could call *rashtra*? Saletore rightly asserts: 'If the ancient Indian had not possessed the concept of territory, as some imagine, it is impossible to explain the terms *rajya*, *samrat*, *sarvbhauma*, etc.'.[102] Kautilya exposes the concept and importance of territory in the definition and running of a state in the following statement on the definition of *janapada sampada* (good country):

> Possessed of capital cities both in the centre and extremities of the kingdom, productive of subsistence not only to its own people, but also to the outsiders on occasions of calamities, repulsive to enemies, powerful enough to put down neighbouring kings, free frommiry, rocky, uneven and desert tracts, as well as from conspirators, tigers, wild beasts, and large tracts of wilderness, beautiful to look at, containing fertile lands, mines, timber and elephant forests, and pasture grounds, artistic, containing hidden passages, full of cattle, not depending on rain for water, possessed of land and waterways, rich in various kinds of commercial articles, capable of bearing the burden of a vast army and heavy taxation, inhabited by agriculturists of good and active character, full of intelligent masers and servants, and with a population noted for its loyalty and good character—these are the qualities of a good country.[103]

One can further gather the Kautilyan idea of territory from his following averment: *desahprithvitasyamHimavat-samudrantam-udicin-myojan-sahasra-parimanam-atiryak-cakravarti-ksetram*.[104] (country means the earth; in it the thousand *yojanas* of the northern portion of the country that stretches between the Himalayas and the ocean form the dominion of no insignificant emperor; in it there are such varieties of land, as forests, villages, mountains, level plains and uneven grounds).[105]

Durga/Fort

Continuity of the elements of the state from the Vedic period till the *Arthashastra* and later periods can be seen when it is noted that *durga* or fortifications are treated by Kautilya as another important constituent of the state. The term has been used in many senses like a fort or a stronghold or as *pur* or a rampart or *prithvi* and *upasad* or siege, fortification, etc. In the opinion of Macdonell, the forts were probably the places of refuge against attack, ramparts of hardened earth. That fort/*durga* occupied the fourth place in importance among the elements of the sovereignty becomes clear from two sources in the *Arthashastra*: Book VI, Chapter 1 that contains the list of elements of state and Book VIII, Chapter 1 that discusses the aggregate of the calamities of the elements of sovereignty. Kautilya focuses on the types of forts—*audhaka* or water fortification, *vanadurga* or forest fortification and *parvata* (hill) fortification or a fort on land; the fortification on all the four quarters of the boundaries of the kingdom, defensive fortifications against an enemy during war constructed on the ground naturally fit for the purpose. Next, Kautilya talks about the ways and means of their construction, their use and relevance in the political sphere and securing the lives of the subjects of the state. To quote Kautilya,[106] of these, water and mountain fortifications are the best suited to defend populous centres; desert and forest fortifications are habitations in wilderness (*atavisthanam*). He further asserts, 'or having no refuge in times of dangers, the king may have his fortified capital (*Sthaniya*) as the seat of his treasury (*samudayasthanam*) in the centre of his kingdom; in a locality naturally best fitted for the purpose, such as the bank of the confluence of rivers, a deep pool of perennial water, or of a lake or tank, a fort, circular, rectangular or square in form, surrounded by an artificial canal of water, and connected with both land and water paths (may be constructed)'.

The *durga*, he advises, should have a passage for chariots and that should be made of trunks of palm trees or of thick slabs of stones. He presents a blueprint of his theory of fortifications fitted with an architectural map in which a rampart, apart from other things, must have provision for an unassailable part, a passage for the flight (*pradhavitikam*) and a door for exit (*nishkuradwaram*). Kautilya assigns great significance to the fort in the scheme of defence and security of the state, which is a necessary factor in achieving and maintaining sovereignty of the state. This is the reason why Kautilya places great importance on the construction of canals and storehouses that can hold weapons, such as spades, axes, varieties of staves, hammers, discus, machines, etc. (which could destroy hundreds of people at once) together with spears, tridents, bamboo sticks with pointed edges made of iron, camel necks, explosives (*agnisamyogas*).[107]

Kosa

Kosa or treasury is the fifth most important element of the state. Further, it is evident that Kautilya believed in the efficacy of finances and financial administration to be a necessary condition for the stability, security and prosperity of the state, as well as for the increase in the *prabhavashakti* of the king and the kingdom. No state, when one looks at the modern power dynamics in international politics and relations, is in a position to safeguard its independence in the face of its depleting finances. Any financially dependent state cannot be better than a mere case of suzerainty and not of sovereignty in the absence of sound financial position of its own. He was also convinced that a strong army/*bala* was also dependent on the strength of the *kosa*. In the case of weakening economy and resources, as the common sense reveals, the state will not be in a position to defend its boundaries as the necessary war tools and technology cannot be obtained or produced either from inside or from outside without adequate money. Second, a weak treasury, which is indicative of bankrupt treasury, may also lead to a military revolt if the armed forces are not paid and maintained adequately. Talking of the excellences of a treasury, Kautilya says: 'Acquired lawfully by the ancestors or by oneself, consisting mostly of gold and silver, containing various kinds of big jewels and cash, one that would withstand a calamity even of a long duration in which there is no income'.[108]

The king should not neglect the depletion of the treasury and replenish it by means mentioned in the *Arthashastra* Book 5.2.3—he should demand a third or a fourth part of the grains from a region, whether big or small in size, that is not dependent on rains and yields abundant crops; from a middling or inferior one, according to yield; he should not demand from a region that is useful for building a fort or embankment or trade routes or new settlements or mining or material forests or elephant forests, or from a region small in size, which is at the frontier. Besides raising demands on the farmers, the king should raise demands through a tax of 50 *panas* from the dealers in gold, silver, diamonds, gems, pearls, corals, horses, elephants, etc., whereas the dealers in yarn, cloth, copper, steel, bronze, perfumes, medicines and wines should pay a tax of 40 *panas*, which may continue in the descending order to 30, 20, 10 and 5 *panas*, respectively, in the case of traders engaged in different trades.[109] The prostitutes and actors should pay half their wages. Kautilya suggests that every section should be duty-bound to contribute to the replenishment of the treasury whether it is a farmer, a trader, a cattle breeder, dealers, workmen or a professional or administrators, or even the treasures of the temples in the fort or through the donations from the rich according to their wealth and benefits conferred on them, or on their own will. The donors should be bestowed upon with position, umbrella, turban or decorations in consideration for money. These measures are taken only in the case of financial emergency.[110] Kautilya also suggests that the king should not levy taxes more than once, and that he should take from the garden as they ripen and he should avoid unripe fruits that may cause an uprising, for fear of his own destruction. According to K. N. Jha and L. K. Jha,

> Chanakya paid supreme importance to the maintenance of a rich treasury, which favourably affected entire activities of the administration. It was pointed out that the augmentation of the treasury depends mainly on the abundance of the harvest (*Sasya-sapat*), opulence of the industrial production (*PracharaSamridhi*), prosperity of trade and commerce (*Panabatulya*) as well as a good fiscal management.[111]

A rich treasury, suggests Kautilya, had to serve some important goals as the nation's wealth was treasured and meant to be utilized to defend the realm, to secure peace at home or maintain law and order, to dispense justice and to support and develop the economy, and to ensure efficient operation of the state machinery.

One is confronted with a question here. Why did Kautilya grade the treasury after the fort at number five? Kaunapadanta was right in saying that when calamity befalls on the treasury and the army, the calamity on the army is more serious, but Kautilya was against this view. He said that the army, indeed, is rooted in the treasury; in the absence of treasury, the army attacks the enemy or kills the king. As for the preference to the fort over the treasury, he says, 'dependent on the fort are the treasury, the army, the silent war, restraint of one's own party, use of armed forces.... In the absence of a fort, the treasury will fall into the hands of enemies'. In other words, Kautilya was of the opinion that the treasury could be strengthened and re-strengthened if the other constituents preceding it are strong and healthy.[112]

Bala/Army/Danda

Bala or the army is given the sixth place in the hierarchy of the elements of sovereignty in the *Arthashastra*. He envisaged the best army as one coming down directly from father and grandfather (of the king) ever strong, obedient, happy in keeping their sons and wives well contented, not averse to making a long sojourn, always invincible, endowed with the power of endurance, trained in fighting different kinds of battles, skilful in handling various forms of weapons, ready to share in the weal or woe of the king and, consequently, not getting into trouble with him, and purely composed of soldiers of *Kshatriya* caste. Furthermore, Kautilya was interested in carrying out a systematic study of the institutions and conditions amenable for the effective and efficient governance of the kingdom and not governance based on chance. Sovereignty was to be secured against any form of attacks either from inside or from outside and for that, *bala* or the army in its strongest form was necessary. *Danda*, in Kautilya's view was the symbol of power. The emphasis on the army as one of the constituents of the sovereignty also spoke of the foresight and a realist political thought as he rejected the dependence of the king on fate and fortune or stars. He was a realist and rationalist to provide for the mechanisms for safeguarding the king, his people and his kingdom. Thus, *bala*/danda/coercive authority capable of inflicting punishment represented the power or the authority of the state, enabling it to exercise sovereign functions. *Danda* was also identified with different connotations such as punishment, law, power, justice, *bala* or army and force. The idea of an army and its various kinds can be traced to the Vedic period and to the works of Manu, Panini, the Mahabharata and the Ramayana[113] apart from the theory of the army developed by Kautilya.[114] Kautilya took cognizance of six types of armies—*maula* (hereditary troops), *bhritya/bhritak* (hired), *sreni* (army of the corporations), *mitra*, (army or troops of the ally or allied forces), *amitra* (army consisting of the deserters or belonging to the enemy) and *atavibalanamsammuddanakalah* (the wild tribes)—and advised the king about the uses of different types of army as per their demand and occasion. Further, Kautilya suggests that the types of aforementioned armies enjoy their importance in a descending order. It cannot be ignored that in the present times too, the status and prestige—the *prabhavashakti* and *utsahashakti*—of a nation flow from the military resources of a country, among others. The history of the United States, China and the erstwhile USSR are examples to that effect. It holds equally true that a country equipped with such arms, ammunition, warheads and the most modern technology is more powerful than countries that do not have such advanced military arsenal. Defence preparedness of a country and the fear it can create in the minds of the rivals reflect the status of power of that country. In other words, the power relations between the countries are quite often dictated by their military and economic strength. Kautilya suggests three types of strengths—intellectual strength (the power of dialogue and deliberation), a prosperous treasury and a strong army—as the strength of a sovereign country.[115] Army is also used sometimes in the matters of internal security. So the army is the factor in peace, progress, stability and paramountcy of power of the state. What we are observing today in relation to the role and importance of the army as an element of state power, Kautilya could perceive it thousands of years ago. Possession of power makes a country superior in comparison to others, and that is the reason why countries are interested in enhancing their capabilities, both military and economic.

Mitra/Ally

One of the distinguishing features of the Kautilyan conception of state is the inclusion of the *mitra* or an ally as a constitutive element of the state. This is not found anywhere in the political discourses on state theory beginning from the ancient to the modern definitions of the state. Malay Mishra aptly remarks that 'a unique insight is obtained from Kautilya incorporating *mitra* or ally as an integral element of a state.... Consideration of an ally as a source of state power is exclusive to Kautilya's theory'.[116] There is a reason behind the inclusion of a friend and an ally as the determinant of state sovereignty. Interestingly, making allies is so pragmatic and relevant in modern-day international environment that it can be vividly observed in initiatives by even the most powerful nations of the world today who are vying to build allies in regions that are distant from their territory. Example of the United States reaching out to make new allies in the Asia-Pacific region and a similar exercise by other nations in the Gulf region aptly exemplify the importance of allies in contributing to the initiator's national power. This insight on the ally makes Kautilya's *Arthashastra* a timeless masterpiece on polity.[117] In fact, even now, the independent entity of a state does not become a reality unless it is given formal recognition by the existing countries. Naturally, it cannot happen if countries are hostile. Only a friendly political ally would stand by the state to enable it to acquire the status of a sovereign power. Again, it is the ally who will stand by the side of the friend in case there is some threat from the enemy to her sovereignty. Thus, suggests Kautilya, 'Coming down directly from father and grandfather, longstanding, open to conviction, never falling foul, and capable of making preparations for war quickly and on a large scale, is the best friend'.

The preceding discussion on the *saptanga* theory of state suggests that the seven elements of state with their attached excellencesconstitute the limb-like elements of sovereignty; The elements are, though arranged in the descending order from the viewpoint of importance, in fact interdependent like the organs of a body, which all function to perform their separate roles as assigned to them, and yet the malfunctioning of one may render other organs ineffective and non-functional unless corrected and repaired quickly. The king is the chief coordinator of the government and also the source of policy, law and good governance; the king is the promoter of dharma, a *vijigisu* and learned in Vedas. *Saptanga* theory has a bearing on almost all aspects of the science of politics–political philosophy and theory and thought, law, administration, economics, diplomacy and foreign policy, defence and military affairs, and governance and focus on the seven power factors—*prakritis*[118]—agriculture, trade, commerce, business and industry together form the basis of a strong *kosa* meant to be pressed into the service of the state and the society. It may be noted here that, despite the hierarchy of the elements, Kautilya was not rigid enough to follow that order irrespective of the conditions requiring a different treatment. This is obvious from his following statement: 'Lastly, a calamity which threatens to destroy all other elements shall be considered as the most serious, irrespective of what position the element occupies in the list of priorities.'[119] Kautilya finally reduces the number of elements of the state to two only, the king and the kingdom[120] as they are treated by Kautilya as the soul and the heart of the state.

A mixed model of sovereignty, which was neither monistic in the Austinian sense nor an entirely pluralist system characterized the nature of the state. The king was generally led by the advice of the *mantrins* or even the *purohit* (not a part of the elements of the sovereignty).

Kautilya not only expounded the importance of each element, *prakriti* but also prescribed that the king should be vigilant against the *vyasanas* that might ruin the *prakriti*. The calamities or *vyasanas* should be anticipated by the ruler, and if they take over the *prakriti*, the king should take action to protect them according to their priority in the scheme of elements of the state. This is in the interest of the king and his kingdom to obviate the calamities by taking proactive measures as they could prove the nemesis of the *prakritis* and cause decay of the state.

The state draws its power from three sources: *utsah shakti* (power of energy, drive and direction, equivalent to leadership of the king), *prabhavashakti* (power to generate influence, cause effects in favour of the state. This is possible through the power of the economy and the army of a state) and *mantrashakti* (power to influence, attract and induce co-opting; good council and diplomacy).[121] Kautilya's *saptanga* theory

> means that state power is no longer an abstract, relational magnitude, but an aggregate of material and immaterial variables. That implies that state power can be operationalised by breaking it down into its seven components. Thus state power can, if not precisely measured, at least be adequately evaluated and estimated. That includes assessing the positive or negative developmental trends of each of the seven prakriti.[122]

Economic, human and physical resources alone are not enough to determine the quality and character of state power but the skilful king and the advisors also matter equally in the process. According to Kautilya, all the *prakritis* together in an aggregate form determine state power. Hence, neither one nor two state factors should be given exclusive importance in assessing state power as each one of them is dependent on the other. This interdependence or interaction is very lucidly explained by Liebig who observes that the power potential of a state and its strong military power factor appear to be linked particularly to a quantitatively large armed forces. But the same state with a weak economic power and financial resources may face non-payment of salaries, low-grade equipment and insufficient supplies, thereby reducing the army's combat power. Conversely, territorially and demographically, small states with modest armed forces might become powerful states in a relatively short period of time if the state factors like the *swamin* and *amatya* are of excellent quality, promoting and expanding the country's economy (*janapada*) and the cities' economy (*durga*), thus increasing tax revenue (*kosa*), allowing the armed forces to be upgraded (*danda*) and conducting a wise foreign policy (*amatya*)[123] Kautilya's concept of *prakriti* is analogous to the contemporary concept of national power.[124]

For Kautilya, a strong treasury was not an end in itself, but a means to an end. He suggests that laying up too much treasure in the king's treasury may not be desirable as it would deprive the subjects; similarly, it would not be wise on the part of the king to save and accumulate money at the cost of the defence and security of the country.

In sum, the *saptanga* theory of Kautilya revolves around his theory of power, legitimacy and sovereignty. In doing so, he appears to be quite close or ahead of his times as well as of others like Machiavelli, Weber and Morgenthau. His classification of the sources of power; his analysis of the *prakriti* in terms of the conduct of foreign policy and politics; and his insight into the matters of defence, national unity and development make him a political thinker relevant not only to his times but also to the present-day political science. He developed a theory of a centralized bureaucratic state, an extraordinarily powerful state dominating both the Brahmanas and the powerful economic classes[125] though there are scholars like J. C. Heesterman who disagree with this view and argue that Kautilyan state represented a pluralist decentralized polity and power.[126]

III

FUNCTIONS OF THE STATE

This section relates to the Kautilya's theory of functions of the state analysed in the context of political theoretical discourse, which gave birth to several theories of the functions of the state, the liberal and Marxist theories being the most discussed ones. There are divisions further among them as neoliberal and neo-Marxist view of the role of the state later in the present times. How did Kautilya visualize the role and position of the state/king vis-à-vis the regulation, ownership and administration of the economy and the role of the various sections of the society? To put the issue differently, did Kautilya visualize a comprehensive domineering role to the state where it was the exclusive owner of the means of production and distribution or was it merely concerned with performing the promotional and regulatory role where in it only facilitated other persons and organizations to undertake production roles within the confines of the rules and regulations? A close study of the *Arthashastra* suggests that the Kautilyan theory of functions of the state resembles liberal view of the state functions and includes broadly the following.

1. Basic functions

These can be generally understood as law and order or police functions or the functions that are recognized in the Vedas, epics and the *Arthashastra* as protection functions. Even in the modern times, it remains a fundamental obligation of the state to provide freedom from fear of death or injury to the individual citizen as well as the social groups comprising the society. Kautilya, like the narrative of the duties of the king in the Vedas, epics and *smritis*, suggests that no state shall survive in the absence of a stable, peaceful and prosperous society and the absence of anarchical conditions known as *Matsyanyaya*. It is the foundation of the sovereignty that the state is effective in ensuring the citizens an environment in which they could fully enjoy their property and live a happy family life. Regulating the conduct of the people in relation to each other in accord with the requirement of law and rules constitutes the primary duty of the state and the government. Maintenance of the *varnas* and *dharma* forms another important function of the state that finds an elaborate treatment in the *Arthashastra* (Book I.3, 5.17). Kautilya emphasizes the importance of observing the specified duty by each *varna* as its observance leads to heaven and to endless bliss and the transgression of the rules by them would end into their extermination through the mixture of *varnas*. Therefore, the king is to dutifully enforce adherence on the part of a member of each *varna* to perform his/her assigned role in the system. 'For, people, among whom the moral laws of the *Aryas* are established, among whom the (rules of the) *varnas* and the states of life are stabilized and who are guarded by the three *Vedas*, prosper, do not perish'.[127] The king was supposed to establish that people remain on to the path of *dharma* with the help of *danda*, as it was inevitable for the protection of the whole population as well as for the preservation and development of philosophy, the three Vedas, agriculture, trade and commerce.[128] Administration of *danda* is the science of politics; on it depends the orderly maintenance of life. The tasks of *rakshana* and *palana* form the important ingredients of the state responsibility towards its subjects. It is the functional obligation of the state to enable the individual to pursue his *dharma;* thereby it is the protector of the moral order.[129] We come across a similar list of functions of the state or the three duties of the sovereign by Adam Smith. According to him, the first duty is to protect the society from the violence and the invasion of other independent societies; the second duty is to protect, as far as possible, every member of the society from the injustice and oppression of every other member of the society or the duty of establishing an exact administration of justice; and, third, the duty of erecting and maintaining certain public works and certain public institutions, which can never be for the interest of any individual or small number of individuals because the profit could never repay the expense to any individual or small number of individuals, though it may frequently do much more than repay it to a great society. Thus, the provision of basic infrastructure fell into the category of basic functions of the state.[130]

2. Financial role of the state

Kautilya visualized an active role of the state in the management of finances and financial administration. He was convinced that the sovereignty, security and legitimacy of the state were loosely related to the strength of the treasury, which, in turn, was dependent on the management of the sources of revenue and the proper use thereof. Levying and collecting taxes by the state was necessary to meet its obligations to the people with respect to their welfare and well-being along with the maintenance of social order and a big standing army. The financial role of the government was critical to the running of the affairs of the state. In terms of finances, the government discharged direct and indirect roles. The state was in the direct mode of performing certain financial functions like owning and running the minefields and acted as a fiscal regulator and adjudicator of the functions and disputes involving the private actors in the areas of business, trade and commerce. It should be noted here that Kautilya was closer to the neoliberal view of the state that enjoins upon the state a duty to uphold individual freedom and pursue social welfare by promoting the coexistence of the public and private sectors. Promotion of an active trade and commerce with the development of agriculture was an important functional duty of the state. The neoliberal theory has been conceptualized not as a laissez-faire state, but as a state that takes a leading role in shaping the economy and the society without hurting the private initiatives and without letting the private sector violate the rule of law and the regulations determined by the administration at the same time. Furthermore, this theory pays attention to the welfare of the subjects, in general, and of the poor and the helpless such as the aged, the infirm, the widows, the prostitutes, etc., in particular. Kautilya took a liberal welfare approach to the role of the state. He advocated the idea of *yogakshema* in the conduct of the affairs of the state. Thus, it can be inferred from the *Arthashastra* that the state played an important role not only as the owner of some of the means of production and distribution but the economic administrative functions of the state could also be identified with its role as a regulator, facilitator, promoter and follower of welfare principles of governance. As a player in the field of economic administration, the state was concerned with carrying out a land census at intervals so as to assess the taxpaying capacity of the agricultural households. Besides, the traders were taxed; there was a tax collected for using roads and waterways in addition to the passport being taxed. Tax was levied on the service industry, the prostitutes, the dancers, pilgrims and the citizens (*pranaya kriya*) for the acts of benevolence, and this formed the part of the revenue of the state. An effective and efficient administration of taxes and revenue matters was, Kautilya suggested, central to strengthening the resources of the country.[131] In a nutshell, financial powers of the state included the power to—

a. impose taxes and collect revenue;
b. maintain a treasury full of gold, jewellery and gems, etc., and to see that it was never depleted;
c. look into the accounts of receipt and expenditure;
d. appoint the officers to carry out the responsibility of financial administration;
e. regulate trade, commerce and industry;
f. regulate the market prices of the commodities;
g. develop agriculture, business, industry and tax system;
h. fix percentage of profits, for example, it was not to exceed 10 per cent in foreign trade;
i. control private enterprise;

j. efficiently run the state-owned enterprises like the ones relating to natural resources and treasure troves;

k. possess crown land and uncultivated wasteland; and

l. own and run transport and cotton industry falling within the domain of the state.

3. Political functions: Executive, legislative and judicial

In the modern state, we generally observe that the tasks of law-making, law execution and law adjudication are vested in three different organs of the government, that is, legislature, executive and the judiciary, following the principle of separation of powers. But the ancient Indian records show that with the decline and disappearance of the *samitis* and assemblies, these three functions came under the direct control of the king and the state officials appointed and empowered by him. The king was the source of law, executive authority and justice. However, it is true that the king while using his powers, legislative, executive or judicial, shall keep in mind the importance of customs, *dharma* and the secularity of the relationship between the citizen and the state. It can further be stated that any legal powers enjoyed by the officials was in the nature of delegated one and not separate from the ruler as constitutionally defined, even though the executive powers were shared by them with the king. What constituted the executive wing of the government was not really clear in the *Arthashastra*, but from the discussion therein, it followed that the king was the head of the executive administration and the *amatyas*, the *mantrins*, the *purohit*, the *yuvaraja* and the *senapati* were the integral constituents of the executive. It may, however, be noted that the role and place of the *purohit* in the *Arthashastra* appears to be quite significant in relation to the king as Kautilya in his Book I.9.9-10 asks the king to select a person as the *purohit* who not only possesses good character but is also well versed in the Vedas and its auxiliary science, divine signs and *dandaniti* and capable of counteracting divine and human calamities, and that he should follow him as a pupil to his teacher and as a son to his father. He further adds (Book I.9.11) that the *Kshatriya* power is rendered prosperous by the *Brahmana* (*Purohit*) and fortified by the *mantra* (counsel by the *mantrins*) rendered to the king. Does this arrangement in the treatise suggest that Kautilya's concept of sovereignty was pre-modern as it was in Europe before the Westphalia treaty? The answer is no because the *purohit* was not above the king. The *purohit* was treated as a civil servant and occupied a position equivalent to the *mantrins, senapati*, the prince and dowager queen. He could be punished and dismissed by the king like any other servant of the state. It does not seem to be similar to the one described in the Rig Veda or the *ratnin* of the *Shatapatha Brahmana* or as mentioned in the *Baudhayana* (I.18.7.8) and *Vasistha* (XIX.3.6). There appears some decline in his status.[132] Kautilya divides the entire administration into 32 departments each under the charge of an *amatya* (*superintendent/ adhyaksha*) concerning a defined list of functions. According to A. K. Majumdar, 'Kautily's scheme of arranging departments and allocation of duties may be said to be his permanent contribution to ancient Indian administration'.[133] At the same time, it can be inferred from the administrative narrative provided in the treatise that the inter- and intra-departmental relationships have not been treated clearly enough; one does not know whether the heads of departments were tied in any hierarchical arrangement or each one of them was directly account-able to the ruler. For example, it is not clear whether the *amatyas* were under the supervision of the *mahamatya* or the *mahamatya* was or was not the head of the *mantrins* or the *mantriparishad*. Was the *mantriparishad* only a deliberative body on certain national issues or merely a larger body to render advice to the king when called into session? Similarly, were the *mantrins* given the charge of coordinating and controlling the department/group of departments or did they form a core advisory committee to the king only is again left unanswered in the *Arthashastra*. A closer reading of the text shows, however, that the king was the chief coordinator, supervisor, controller and com-mander of the whole executive. In the *Arthashastra*, Kautilya suggests that a person appointed by an order to a particular department shall communicate to him (i.e., the king) the real nature of that work and the income and expenditure (both) in detail and in the aggregate.[134]

Expanding further the scope of the executive powers of the state, Sir William Petty maintains in his book 'Treatise of Taxes and Contributions' that the military and defence functions, providing religious and other education, administration of justice, care of the impoverished, the incapacitated and the unemployed, and the construction and maintenance of roads, bridges, navigable rivers, ports, etc., which are conducive to the general welfare of the community as a whole are integral to the list of duties of the state.[135] In the field of legislation, the state was concerned with the promulgation of laws and maintenance of the common law as reflected in customs and usages of the country. The rules and regulations or the orders of the king were primarily meant to enable him and his officers to discharge their political and administrative obligations. Writing about the legislative powers of the king in Kautilya's *Arthashastra*, M. V. Krishna Rao asserts, 'it is manifest in Kautilya's legal theory that the king could legislate and exercise authority to direct and regulate the life and conduct of guilds, corporations and other associations'. Kautilya says:

> whenever there is disagreement between history and sacred law or between evidence and sacred law, then, the matter shall be settled in accordance with the sacred law, but whenever sacred law (*sastra*) is in conflict with rational law (*dharmanyaya*) then reason shall be held authoritative, for there the original text on which the sacred law has been based is not available.[136]

It is the edicts of the king, therefore, that provide a definite, unambiguous and authoritative explanation to the customs and the prevailing norms and ideas, including that of various guilds—agriculture, crafts and trades.

About the judicial functions, the *Arthashastra* maintains that the king was the fountainhead of justice. It was the foremost duty of the king to protect *dharma* as he was the *dharmaparavartaka* and had to protect his subjects with justice, for its observance would lead him to heaven. *Swadharma svargaya, Prajadhamena Rakshitah*.[137] In the words of A. S. Altekar, 'the king was the supreme judicial functionary in ancient India from the post *Vedic* period; but in actual practice considerable powers were delegated to the local popular courts. The kings and the government officers usually declined to entertain suit at first instance'.[138] It was the duty of the king to appoint three judges who were to sit in each court having the qualifications of an *amatya*. According to some accounts, 'village councils and town corporations enjoyed complete freedom in their local affairs; the courts, whether royal or popular, usually administered the traditional law as embodied in the *jatidharma* (local caste customs), *srenidharma* (guild rules) and *janapada dharma* (local customs)'.

4. Administrative functions

Kautilya pays utmost attention to the administration and administrative officials. Beginning from the organization and principles of public administration to the problems of personnel administration, Kautilya touches upon each and every aspect of administrative machinery of the state that might impact the quality, character and performance of an organization, which may have implications on the service and welfare of the citizens and the defence and security of the kingdom. This was the reason why Kautilya laid emphasis on organizational loyalty, organizational commitment, integrity, capacity and capability[139] of the candidates who were to be appointed to various offices of the state. Kautilya maintains that ministers should be appointed to ordinary offices in consultation with the councillors and the chaplain and the integrity, piety, uprightness and freedom from greed and lust, loyalty and courage, etc., of each one of them should be tested through secret tests (Book I.10.6.1). He identifies necessary qualifications for the candidate(s) keeping in mind the nature of work to be carried out. For example, only those commanding high moral character and loyalty should be selected to the palatial administration; those who proved loyal by the test of piety should be appointed to offices in the judiciary and for the suppression of criminals; those who proved upright by the test of material gain should be appointed to offices of the administrator and in the stores of director of stores; those who proved pure by the test of lust should be appointed to guardianship of (places of) recreation inside the (palace) as well as outside; those who proved loyal by the test of fear should be given duties near the person of the king; those who proved honest by all tests should be made his councillors (Book I.10.2-16). It is beyond comprehension as to why Kautilya says that those found dishonest by every test should be employed in mines, in forests for material produce, in elephant forests and in factories (Book I.10.15). Another point to be noted is that the methods of tests prescribed by Kautilya are in the nature of a utopia, beyond the possibility of practicability. Take the test against lust. 'A wandering nun, who has won the confidence (of the different ministers) and is treated with honour in the palace, should secretly suggest to each minister individually': 'the chief queen is in love with you and has made arrangement for a meeting with you; besides, you will obtain much wealth'. If he repulses the proposal, he is pure (Book I.10.7). True—only a minister not in his senses would ever fall prey to such a proposal. The virtues requisite of an employee under the state, finding mention in the *Arthashastra*, are found even in modern-day India and elsewhere and form part of the recruitment tests, both written and oral, or what can be termed as technical and psychological, personality tests.

Detection of corruption and punishing the corrupt were the most significant functions of the king as it continues to be so in the present modern times. Kautilya recognized that man is fallible and those who were involved in dealing with the financial matters were more vulnerable to corruption. Therefore, he favoured the system of vigilance and spying over the officials of the kingdom. Moreover, he was of the view that it was difficult for the person not to be corrupt when opportunity existed and also that detection of corruption was not an easy task. He first suggests that just as it is not possible not to taste honey or poison placed on the surface of the tongue, it is not possible for one dealing with the money of the king not to taste the money in however small a quantity. In the same tone, he asserts, 'just as fish moving inside water cannot be known when drinking water, even so officer appointed for carrying out works cannot be known when appropriating money' or 'it is possible to know even the path of the birds flying in the sky, but not the ways of officers moving with their intentions concealed'.[140] The *Arthashastra* talks of 40 ways of embezzlement. The underlying message, therefore, is that the king (the anti-corruption agencies and the institutions in the modern administrative system) should have to be extra cautious and extra vigilant over the employee behaviour everywhere but more so in case of those associated with the management of treasury, and collection and expenditure of state revenues.

Another significant element of administrative functions of the king was to develop the employee by imparting training to them. Book II of the *Arthashastra* is specifically devoted to the topic of training.

5. Functions relating to the conduct of foreign affairs and national security

It can be observed in the whole text of Kautilya's *Arthashastra* that foreign policy and international politics attracted deeper attention of Kautilya than any other question. Even the question of protection of the king's subjects is seen not only in the context of protection of the person, family and the property from the internal disruptive forces, but it includes, more importantly, protection from external aggression. He devotes a full-fledged Book VI on how to conduct and manage foreign relations, how to deal with the questions of war and peace expressed through his theory of *mandala*, *Shadgunya* and four *upayas*. In fact, it seems that nothing engaged the efforts and energies of the king and his council of ministers greater than deciding the policy of the state on security and safety of the state. Further, it would not be an exaggeration to say that nothing in the *Arthashastra* has received so much attention of the scholars from India and abroad involved in the study of government and politics in ancient times as the theory of international relations that is considered as the most significant contribution of Kautilya to the political theory and thought.

An overview of the functions of the state, as discussed earlier, suggests that Kautilyan view foresees the modern liberal welfare theory of the state. The state of Kautilya was neither a socialist state nor even a police state. Kautilya envisioned a state that played an active role in the economic as well as political spheres for he believed that there was a close linkage between politics and economics. At the same time, the protection of private property and promotion of commerce, trade, business and industry under private ownership was a part of the responsibility of the king.

IV

DANDANITI AND THE CONCEPTS OF SOVEREIGNTY AND LEGITIMACY

The ideas of sovereignty, wedded to the territory and power, and of legitimacy, acquired more salience with the emergence of a territorially settled population and emergence of a universally accepted supreme political authority to provide efficacious and effective governance, enabling the people to peacefully enjoy happiness and the material progress. Two versions of sovereignty were taking shape in the minds of the ancient Indian political thinkers—one ideological and the other pragmatic. The pragmatic dimension of sovereignty related to the attention slowly turning towards the issue of external sovereignty as well as originating from territorial expansionism, subjugating other rulers and the population outside its jurisdiction as separate political entities. Performance of *Ashvamedha* sacrifice was indicative of this development, where to be *chakravartin samraat* became another basis of support of the natives as well as of the conquered population to the king. Kautilya made these ideas more explicit by combining the idea of the practical and the ideological, that is, the *Dharmashastra* theory of sovereignty and the legalist theory of sovereignty. The major elements of Kautilya's theory of sovereignty can be discerned in his theory of *dandaniti*.

We noted in the *saptanga* theory of state that *danda* and *dandaniti* is an important constituent of the state. In fact, the whole concept of *dandaniti* in the *Arthashastra* is based on the conception of power, an integral part of the existence of the sovereign state. The function of protection, maintenance of law and order, and observance of the principle of *yogakshema* necessitated endowing the king with the authority of *danda* without which it was impossible to enforce public compliance to the decrees, rules and regulations or orders issued by the sovereign. Therefore, the basis of the coercive power of the state lay in its obligation towards the citizens to provide them protection from internal and external threats to them as a society and as an individual, while the citizen was duty-bound to follow the edicts of the state, in return, faithfully. Any breach of contract by either the citizen or the state would contribute to the return of anarchy in which both were to perish. A. S. Altekar explains:

> state is the necessary institution if the individual is to live according to his *dharma*; it is the coercive authority of the state which produces the automatic mental habit of following once own *dharma*. State in ancient India claimed absolute allegiance and there was no other rival civic corporate body in this respect.[141]

In another sense, *dandaniti* can be described as a synonym of the modern concepts of sovereignty and legitimacy emerging out of the perception of power and its use. It is envisaged in the text that *dandaniti*/sovereignty is concerned with the establishment of the authority of the state to carry out the will of the people and of the state over the subjects with their consent and/or with the award of punishment to the people resisting the laws of the state. Coercive power of the state is also a prerequisite for upholding the *varna* system in which every person is supposed to perform the functions defined or assigned for his *varna*. Any deviation from that is to attract punishment/*danda*. In Book I, Chapter 4, Kautilya mentions that 'the people (*Loka*) consisting of four castes and four orders of religious life, when governed by the king with his sceptre, will keep to their respective duties and occupations'. In the opinion of U. N. Ghoshal,[142] *dandaniti* represents the science of politics and is concerned especially with the application of the coercive authority of the ruler.[143] Thus, it may be understood as 'lawful infliction of punishment' and also as the 'principle of government'. Even before Kautilya, in the *Manusmriti* and the Mahabharat, the importance and relevance of *danda* has been recognized as the means to enforce the political obligations of the king and to uphold the state authority, which is applied to all without favour or prejudice.[144] *Danda* and *dandaniti* together form the essence of the government. S. N. Dhar reinforces the same view by quoting one of the verses, which means *danda* alone rules all subjects, *danda* alone protects them, *danda* is awake when others are asleep and the wise declare *danda* to be identical with *dharma*.[145] In another context, one gets an impression that the basis of the legitimacy of power or the legitimization of power was the divinity of the king. In the previous chapter, while discussing the theories of origin of state, it was found that the *Shatapatha Brahmana* talks of divine authority as the king was ordained by the *prajapati* to put the environment of anarchy to an end. That the king enjoyed divine power was the argument in the *Rigveda* and the *Atharvaveda* in which the king was seen as semi-god or Parikshit was described as god among men, respectively. 'The growing sway of religious ideas and notions produced an atmosphere in the *Brahmana* period which was more favourable to the notion of divinity of the king'.[146] There was an attempt here to develop a concept of a universal and indivisible sovereignty. The king was seen as the sole lord of the mankind, the one and the only one lord.[147]

One can observe the same political philosophy of legitimacy of power in the latter political literature produced in the post-Vedic period. This theory of sovereignty and legitimate political power can be traced in the Mahabharata, *Matsya Purana*, *Sukraniti* and *Naradasmriti*. Furthermore, the people obeyed the king as he was the creature of god; it was their duty not to despise him and to always respect him and his orders. However, the divine basis of the royal power did not remain as a permanent feature of Indian political theory and did not receive acceptance beyond certain localities. The king never became irresponsible to the people or accountable to the god alone, as in Europe. He remained a human personage, a servant of his people, whose immense duties outweighed the privileges and prerogatives of his office.[148]

Another narrative regarding sovereignty and legitimacy of the state, finding place in the ancient Indian political thought including that of Kautilya, is that the king received an unflinching support of the people because he was perceived by them as the upholder of the moral and social order, the *dharma* and *varna* system, and he was considered the career of the prosperity—the social, moral, cultural and economic well-being of the subjects. Thus, holding people and himself to the path of righteousness formed a significant basis of power of the king and ensured a passive obedience from the public to the state. It is interesting to note that *dandaniti* in the *Arthashastra*, as coercive authority, was inherent in the state, first, in order to secure unhindered application of law to maintain law and order; to free people from fear of being attacked from the rivals or from being robbed of their belongings; and second, the *danda* should be applied by the sovereign power in a just and righteous manner. *Danda* should neither be overused nor underutilized. If it was unjustly used, it would make the king a tyrant in the eyes of the subjects; the subjects in that situation may challenge the sovereign by staging a revolt; if it was utilized less than what was required, people would despise the king, undermining his authority; or when the authority was not used when required, there was a possibility of the failure of the king to prevent the return of the conditions of *Matsyanyaya* again. A king should neither be severe with the rod, nor lenient with the rod because the former would generate disharmony and the latter would give rise to contempt. The underlying idea behind this advice of Kautilya seems to be close to the opinion of a contemporary philosopher Guglielmo Ferrero opposing the imposition of power by brute force. He should be just with the rod as it will dispel the misfortunes overtaking the people.

In fact, the state has to work as a trust and as public servant to obtain public obedience to his laws, rules and regulations. In other words, Kautilya suggests that, at various places, political trust of the people provides an unshakable loyalty to and faith in the intentions and actions of the state. The king is the 'aggregate of people' is how it is expressed in Kautilya's *Arthashastra*. It may be emphasized that sovereignty would be under severe stress in the absence of legitimacy attached to it. It would survive the challenges, on the other hand, if the people perceived that the power being used by the authority was for the sake of achieving and sustaining common good, and that the king had a legitimate right to rule/govern. As David Hume declares: 'it is an opinion that government is founded, and this maxim extends to the most despotic and most military governments as well as to the most free and most popular'.[149] Alternatively, legitimacy, in fact, means consent of the people to be commanded and administered by the ruler, which should be available with the state till it respects the articles of the contract reached between them and the state. In the words of Li Ma:

> as soon as these rules are no longer respected, or if the ideology is questioned, the contract is broken, the power is no longer legitimate, and the members of the society have no reason to obey spontaneously. It is then necessary to use force in order to obtain obedience.[150]

Kautilya also does not rule out the use of force if necessary to bring about and support an ideal social order based on the principle of honestly discharging the assigned *varna* related functions without deviation from the principle of righteousness by any individual or a group. If we look into the sources of legitimacy, we observe that Kautilya's thoughts were a forerunner to that of Max Weber who argued that the people obeyed the ruler either on account of tradition/ custom or charisma or on the basis of a legal rational authority. In the later relationship between the state and the citizen, it was the law and the institutions that assigned legitimacy to the power, whereas, in the second case, it was the exceptional leadership qualities and capabilities of the heroic person that determined legitimacy. In the case of the customary power, the wielder of authority enjoys it because it is recognized to be the mechanism traditionally since long. Kautilya defined power as strength, a theory of power emanating and sustained by *jnanabalam* (the power of knowledge), *koshdabalam* (power of treasury) and *vikrambalam* or the power of might *or* the power of valour, the energy.[151] Kautilya says the position of the king will depend on the availability of these three powers.[152]

Tabhirbhyuchchitojyayaanbhavati, apchitoheenah, tulyashaktihsamah |35|
Tasmachchaktimsidhimcaghatetatmanyaveshayitum,
sadharanovadravyaprakritishvananantaryenshauchvashenva |36|
Dushyamitrabhyamvaapkrashtumyatet |37|

(Thriving with these, the king becomes superior; reduced
in these, inferior; with equal powers, equal. |35|
Therefore he should endeavour to endow himself with
power and success, or, if similar, [to endow with power and
success] the material constituents in accordance with their
immediate proximity or integrity. |36|
Or, he should endeavour to detract [these] from
treasonable persons and enemies. |37|)[153]

A few words regarding the nature of sovereignty would not be out of place before putting a full stop to the discussion on this topic. As regards many other debates on the *Arthashastra*, the nature of sovereignty in the theory of Kautilya is also not above a controversy. There are three interpretations: one says that sovereignty envisaged by the author of the text really meant the supremacy of the king exercising absolute powers without any hindrances; that the state was glorified in which the king was the apostle of all legal and moral powers as well as the foundation and embodiment of all sovereign authority, as all other footprints vanish in the footprints of the elephant, so all *dharma* disappears in the *rajdharma*. And that *danda*, which protected the people, was the womb of civilization. The king was the *udyatadanda* and in whom all the *prakritis* or elements of government were concentrated. However, the second opinion disagrees and maintains that the sovereignty was pluralist in nature as there were many peripheral institutions enjoying decision-making powers at the local level. They refer to the existence of various guilds, *srenis*, *ganas* and *sanghas* almost parallel to the central authority. So there were other centres of power. Kautilya has not given any indication by which it suggests that these institutions were either independent or autonomous. The third view asserts the middle way and says that Kautilya visualized a pluralist monistic sovereignty. This opinion was also not tenable as the king was supposed to exercise his powers in both virtuous and coercive manner so as to enjoy the confidence of the people. All the checks either in the form of *dharma*, the prosperity of the subjects or peace were there merely to prevent the use of power by the sovereign in an autocratic manner. Public interest, thus, was the basis of the unlimited power of the king. Sovereignty was indivisible in every sense of the term.

NOTES

1. Duraiswamy, *Commentary*.
2. Rao, *Studies in Kautilya*, 2.
3. Sen, *Hindu Political Thought*, 148.
4. *Arthashastra*, Book I, Chapter 4, Sections 3–4.
5. *Arthashastra*, Book I, Chapter 13, 5–10.
6. Sharma, *Aspects of Political Ideas*, 68.
7. Sharma, *Aspects of Political Ideas*, 69.
8. Sharma, *Aspects of Political Ideas*, 69.
9. Liebig, 'Kautilya's Arthashastra'.
10. Niaz, 'Kautilya's Arthashastra'.
11. Muller, *Brihadaranyaka Upanishad*, 1–4, 11–15.
12. Chausalkar, *Revisiting the Political Thought*, 41.
13. Bloomfield, *Hymns of the Athrva-Veda*, 37.
14. Chausalkar, *Revisiting the Political Thought*, 44–45.
15. *Arthashastra*, Book III, 1.
16. *Arthashastra*, Book 1, Chapter 2.7; cf. Saletore, *Ancient Indian Political*, 185.
17. Saletore, *Ancient Indian Political*, 186.

18. For details, see Sharma, *Aspects of Political Ideas*; Saletore, *Ancient Indian Political*.
19. In a personal interaction, Professor M. P. Singh remarked that the emergent centralized state in *Arthashastra* swallowed them and aggregated them into *janapada/rashtra* as a constituent element.
20. A system of self-rule in which the ruler was called *svarat* or *svarajya* literally means becoming the 'leader of equals'.
21. This form of the state was in existence in the North as well as in the South.
22. *Aitareya Brahmana*, VIII, 14.
23. *Arthashastra*, Book VIII.2, 323; Jayaswal, *The Hindu Polity*, 83–84.
24. *Aitareya Brahmana of the Rigveda*, Vol. II, 518.
25. Jayaswal, *Hindu Polity*, 82.
26. Sharma, *Aspects of Political Ideas*, 360.
27. Sharma, *Aspects of Political Ideas*, 360.
28. Sharma, *Aspects of Political Ideas*, 359.
29. Sudas is said to have defeated a confederacy of 12 kings in the *Rigveda*.
30. Altekar, *State and Government*, 22; for further details, see Saletore, *Ancient Indian Political*, 91–130.
31. *Arthashastra*, Book XI, Chapter 1; Shamasastry, *Kautilya's Arthashastra*, 455.
32. Jayaswal, *Hindu Polity*, 119.
33. *Arthashastra*, Book VIII, 2.
34. Shamasastry, *Kautily's Arthashastra*, 459.
35. Bandyopadhyaya, *Development of Hindu Polity*, 57.
36. *Arthashastra*, Book I, Chapter 7.9.
37. *Arthashastra*, Book I, Chapter 7.8.
38. *Arthashastra*, Book I, Chapter 15; Book VIII, Chapter 1.
39. Sihag, 'Kautilya and Modern Economics'.
40. 'Welfare state' has become a conceptually and theoretically developed term contextually located in the post-Second World War world—a capitalist and democratic polity. Kautilyan state does not exactly fit into this construction, though it had many features of a welfare state.
41. *Arthashastra*, Book I, Chapter 15.
42. Rao, *Studies in Kautilya*, 120.
43. Rao, *Studies in Kautilya*, 124.
44. Parmar, *Techniques of Statecraft*, 37.
45. *Arthashastra*, Book II, Chapter I, 47–48, Shamasastri, *Kautily's Arthashastra*, 53.
46. Shamasastri, *Kautilya's Arthashastra*, 140.
47. Shamasastri, *Kautilya's Arthashastra*, 141.
48. Shamasastri, *Kautilya's Arthashastra*, 154; *Arthashastra*, Book II, Chapter 27, 124.
49. *Arthashastra*, Book VIII.4; Kangle, *The Kautilya Arthashastra*, Pt II, 397.
50. *Arthashastra*, Book II, Chapter 1, 27.

51. *Arthashastra*, Book III, 14.9; Parmar, *Techniques of Statecraft*, 39.
52. *Arthashastra*, Book III, Chapter 14, 26–27.
53. Parmar, *Techniques of Statecraft*, 45.
54. Dikshitar, *Mauryan Polity*, 100.
55. Rice, *Mysore and Coorg from Inscriptions*, 14; Dikshitar, *Mauryan Polity*, 61.
56. Bandyopadhyaya, *Development of Hindu Polity*, Pt II, 22.
57. Mookerjee, *Local Self Government*, 124.
58. Rao, *Studies in Kautilya*, 42.
59. *Arthashastra*, Book VI, Chapter 1.
60. Kaur, 'Kautilya', 59–68.
61. Sharma, *Aspects of Political Ideas*, 21.
62. *Raja, rajan* and the system of sacrifices and coronation of the kings through the practice of *rajasuya and ashwamedha*.
63. Liebig, 'Kautilya's Arthashastra'.
64. Liebig, 'Kautilya's Arthashastra'; *Kautilya's Arthashastra*, Book VIII, Chapter 1, 29–30.
65. Sharma, *Aspects of Political Ideas*, 15.
66. Sharma, *Aspects of Political Ideas*, 15.
67. Sharma, *Aspects of Political Ideas*, 15.
68. Sharma, *Aspects of Political Ideas*, 15.
69. *Arthashastra*, Book VI, Chapter 1.
70. Shamasastry, *Kautilya's Arthashastra*, 287.
71. Saletore, *Ancient Indian Political*, 299.
72. Prakash, 'State and Statecraft'.
73. *Arthashastra*, Book VIII, 322–325.
74. *Arthashastra*, 310–313.
75. *Arthashastra*, 310.
76. Shamasastry, *Kautilya's Arthashastra*, 9–13; Chapters 5–7, 10–12.
77. Refer to *Arthashastra*, Book I, Chapter XIX; Shamasastry, *Kautilya's Arthashastra*, 36–39.
78. Shamasastry, *Kautilya's Arthashastra*, 39–60, 9.
79. Saletore, *Ancient Indian Political*, 315.
80. Saletore, *Ancient Indian Political*, 315.
81. Saletore, *Ancient Indian Political*, 316.
82. *Arthashastra*, Book I, Chapter 19.34.
83. *Arthashastra*, Book VII, Chapter V, 277, 306.
84. Saletore, *Ancient Indian Political*, 318.
85. *Arthashastra*, Book I, Chapter 6.
86. Shamasastry, *Kautilya's Arthashastra*, 11.
87. *Arthashastra*, Book VI, Chapter 1.
88. Kangle, *Kautilya Arthashastra*, Pt II, 314.
89. See the long list of these excellences in Kangle, *Kautilya Arthashastra*, Pt II, 314–315.

90. Sharma, *Aspects of Political Ideas*, 16.
91. Refer to Fick, *Social Organizations*, 144–149.
92. Sharma, *Aspects of Political Ideas*, 17; *Janapadasyakarmasiddhayahsvatahpara tas'cayogakshemasddhanamvyasanaprtikarahsunyanivesopacayaudanadakaran ugrahas'ceti*; *Kautilya Arthashastra*, Book VIII.i.
93. Sel.Inscr. 174.I. 17.
94. *Sahayasadhyamrajatvamcakram-ekamnavartatekurvitasacivan-tasmat-tesamcasrinuyan-mata*; *Kautilya Arthashastra*, Book I, Chapter VII.13, 12, text p. 13.
95. Saletore, *Ancient Indian Political*, 345.
96. Saletore, *Ancient Indian Political*, 345.
97. The Mahabharata: 'The person who achieves celebrity, who observes all restraints, who never feels jealous of others, who never does an evil act, who never through lust or fear, or covetousness or wrath, abandons righteousness, who is clever in the transaction of business, and who is possessed of wise and weighty speech, should be the foremost of ministers. *Arthashastra* maintains that Persons well–born, and possessed of good behaviour, who are liberal and never indulge in brag, who are brave and respectable, learned and full of resources, should be appointed subordinate ministers in charge of the different departments.'
98. Some scholars like Jayaswal went to the extent of saying that the position of the king was that of a constitutional head, though not supported by a majority of other historians including N. C. Bandyopadhyaya.
99. Refer to *Brahmana* literature, which uses the term *janapada* in the sense of both the people and the land or realm.
100. Saletore, *Ancient Indian Political*, 425.
101. Saletore, *Ancient Indian Political*, 425.
102. Saletore, *Ancient Indian Political*, 427.
103. *Arthashastra*, Book VI, Chapter I.258, text p. 258.
104. *Arthashastra*, Book IX, Chapter 1, 17–18.
105. Saletore, *Ancient Indian Political*, 428–429.
106. *Arthashastra*, Book II, Chapter 3, 50–51.
107. *Arthashastra*, Book II, Chapter 2, 52; Shamasastry, *Kautilya's Arthashastra*, 52.
108. *Arthashastra*, Book VI, i.10; Kangle, 1972, 316.
109. *Arthashastra*, Book V.2, 17–23.
110. For additional measures for replenishing the treasury, see *Kautilya's Arthashastra*, Book V.2, 37–70.
111. Jha and Jha, *Chanakya*.
112. For further details, see Kangle, 1972, 385–390.
113. The Ramayana, *Bal Kanda, Yuddha Kanda*.
114. See *Vedic Index I*; *Manusmriti*, VII, 96, 172; Panini, II.4.2, Vi.2; Aggarwal, *India as Known*.
115. Saletore, *Ancient Indian Political*, 291.

116. Mishra, *Kautilya's Arthashastra.*
117. Mishra, *Kautilya's Arthashastra.*
118. Liebig, 'Kautilya's Relevance', 99–116.
119. *Arthashastra*, Book VIII.1.63; Mishra, *Kautilya's Arthashastra*, 77–109.
120. Saletore, *Ancient Indian Political.*
121. Mishara, *Kautilya's Arthashastra.*
122. Liebig, 'Kautilya's Arthashastra'.
123. Liebig, 'Kautilya's Arthashastra'.
124. Modelski, 'Kautilya'.
125. Boesche, *Kautilya*, 54.
126. Refer to the debate between R. S. Sharma and J. C. Heesterman in Sharma, *Aspects of Political.*
127. Majumdar, *Concise History of Ancient India*, Vol. II, 52.
128. *Arthashastra*, Book I.4.3–16 and Book I.5.1–2.
129. Sarkar, *The Positive Background*, 174.
130. See Marder, 'Adam Smith'.
131. Rao, *Studies in Kautilya*, 209–210.
132. Majumdar, *Concise History of Ancient India*, 67.
133. Majumdar, *Concise History of Ancient India*, 73.
134. Kangle, *Kautilya Arthashastra*, Pt II, 90.
135. Shodhganga.inflibnet.a.in/bitstream/10603/138406/8/08_chapter%201.pdf (accessed on 19 May 2020).
136. Rao, *Studies in Kautilya*, 45.
137. Rao, *Studies in Kautilya*, 69.
138. Altekar, *State and Government*, 61.
139. *Arthashastra*, Book II, Chapter 9, 1.
140. *Arthashastra*, Book II, Chapter 9, 81–84; Kangle, *Kautilya Arthashastra*, Pt II, 91.
141. Altekar, *State and Government*, 73.
142. Ghoshal, *A History of Indian Political Ideas.*
143. Dhar, *Kautilya and the Arthashastra*, 79.
144. See *Manusmriti*, VII, 14–13; I, 340–341; *Matsyapurana*, 225.9.18.
145. Dhar, *Kautilya and the Arthashastra*, 81.
146. Altekar, *State and Government*, 89; *Satpatha Brahmana*, XII, 4.4.3.
147. Bandyopadhyaya, *Development of Hindu Polity*, Pt I, 98.
148. Bandyopadhyaya, *Development of Hindu Polity*, 99.
149. Ma, 'A Comparison of the Legitimacy', 52.
150. Ma, 'A Comparison of the Legitimacy', 49–59.
151. Kangle, *Kautilya Arthashastra*, Pt II, 319.
152. *Arthashastra*, Book VI, 35–37.
153. Kangle, *Kautilya Arthashastra*, Pt II, 319.

Legal Theory of Kautilya

A Modernist Philosophy?

Administration of law and maintenance of order has been the most important function of the state since its inception. A system of law and justice is the foundational necessity of the legal theory and action. Kautilya was quite conscious that the social, economic, cultural and political stability was intricately linked to the trust and faith of the people in the objectivity of law, in both form and application, which again was dependent on the existence of fair, independent and impartial judicial administration. It was only through the rule of law that society could be prevented from being pushed into the darkness of lawless, normless and selfish intra-society behaviours.

Kautilya treats the subject of law and justice comprehensively in Books III and IV to include the formal law as well as the procedures and processes of justice and suggested (Book III) that clear procedures of civil and criminal codes, use of evidence and provision of transparent and honest judiciary could save the state from being surrounded by several calamities (hindrances and challenges). Rule of law could guarantee a righteous conduct of the social, political, economic and cultural being.

For Kautilya, *danda* and the *dandadhara* are the two vital instruments of establishing and sustaining a just and good system of governance; the state may fall or perish and society pushed back to the age of *Matsyanyaya* if there is no coercive authority and there is no rule of law.[1] In order to invoke and maintain the trust and faith of the people in the rule of law and fairness of justice, it is imperative to make apt use of *danda* or power of punishment, which in turn is determined by the system of merit-based bureaucracy and the impartial, objective and honest judiciary. An effective and efficient administration of law and justice strengthens the state to perform its political obligations of *rakshana*, *palana* and *yogakshema* of its subjects. The legitimacy of power and sovereignty are intimately linked with the fair and impartial implementation of law and just adjudication and settlement of disputes between the subjects themselves and between the state and the people.

It is pertinent here that Kautilya's legal theory is examined with reference to the conception of law, the sources of law, the ambit of law, the principles and nature of law and the instruments of the application of law, besides its consonance or discordance with the modern theory of law in the following pages.

CONCEPTION OF LAW IN THE *ARTHASHASTRA*

In general terms, law is defined as a system of governance or regulation of the conduct of society and the state with respect to their rights and duties. Law is that bundle of rules and regulations, one may say, which determines the boundaries of action or non-action on the part of an individual, a group or the state; a form of sanctions relating to the freedom or restriction on the ways of behaviour—social, political or economic—of the people. Law in the *Arthashastra* is the set of rules meant to serve the common good. Thus, law is the expression of sovereignty that enables the king (the government) to issue orders and secure obedience of the people. Law is the command of the sovereign, in the vocabulary of Austin. Furthermore, according to Kautilya, the king was the supreme executive authority, and the checks applicable on the use of that authority was more procedural in nature than having any implication on the nature of law and the authority attached to it. Kautilya's king could issue orders to the officials and institutions of the state even by superseding the *dharma nyaya* or the customs in case they were contrary to the royal edicts or to the interest of the nation. The sovereign's commands (*sasana/rajsasana*), which is justice and is thus identical with the truth, represent universal human conscience. The commands of the king are documented in *sasana patra* by *lekhaka* who clearly and in unequivocal language promulgates the king's law.[2] Moreover, for Kautilya, law was both a restraint on the acts that deviated from the right track or that which inflicted harm to others and a facilitator to differentiate 'good' from 'bad'. Law is thus a moral imposition/compulsion as well as a coercive force to mould the actions and the relations of the society against anarchy and despotism. 'Law is the spiritual efficacy and power'. Kautilya, like Aristotle, in the name of *dharma*, appeals to the sense of honour and duty, human dignity, moral responsibility and enlightened patriotism. Neither tyranny nor *arajaka*, but ordered liberty, satisfied Kautilya, and this implied a delicate adjustment and a combination of principles that are apparently opposite but harmonize conflicting claims; this is because the Hindus, like the Greeks, possessed a sense of flexibility and a faculty of compromise.[3] That law, therefore, is the expression of both the spirit and reason, and mind is the essence of the argument of the *Arthashastra*. His support to *Lokayata* philosophy of politics consistently made him favour a system of law that was free from irrationalism. Furthermore, law included not only the one enacted by the king, but it also included the sacred law and the customary law. The ambit of law was comprehensive as it covered the aims and objectives of society and the state, the whole cultural environment of the time period, and legal and social organizations/institutions.

> Social ends determined the content of law, and the relativity of law to ends extended from content even to form and source. The sources of law were pre-eminently determined /contemplated by the society to which the law applied and varied with a change in social ends and ideas.[4]

Therefore, we can say that a law could be seen in the body of the text in the context of its purpose or goals, which is, in the ultimate analysis, to serve the social aspirations—material and spiritual. Kautilya's treatment of the concept of law seems to include a legal system ordained to adjusting relations and controlling conduct of individuals, corporations and guilds, merchants, etc., and the legal precepts and procedures prevalent in a political society that really form the basis of administration and delivery of justice in an impartial manner.

IMPORTANCE OF RULE OF LAW IN THE *ARTHASHASTRA*

The concept of rule of law is an important element of constitutionalism and the existence of the conditions against *Matsyanyaya*. For Kautilya, rule of law implied that the government should be run on the basis of the principle of accountability and non-arbitrariness in giving award or inflicting punishment or performing other administrative functions under the state. It is evident from Books III and IV that law is based on justice, morality, order and fairness and not based on the whims and fancies of the king and his officers. For Kautilya, rule of law was the expression of equality before law, even though the *varnas* were not treated equally, a modern concept in legal discourse. That law shall not discriminate between the son of the king and his enemy when it comes to awarding punishment is established in his Book III.1.42, which says: 'For, it is punishment alone that guards this world and the other, when it is evenly meted out by the king to his son and his enemy, according to the offence'.[5] It is interesting to note that the Kautilyan concept of *danda* and *dandaniti* are wedded to the concept of rule of law, that is, the king was invested with the authority to use force to achieve the ends of law and society, though he was not to be an autocrat while administering *danda* or implementing *dandaniti*. Kautilya has time and again emphasized upon *danda* being used neither in excess nor less than required if the interests of the state, the king and society are to be properly preserved. Further, a robust system of rule of law pre-supposes the existence of an honest and impartial judiciary and a high calibre of judges. The classical text not only prescribes the qualifications for the judges but also provides for their punishment in case they have deviated from the righteous path of dispensing justice to the people.[6]

The *Arthashastra* refers to the rule of law as an unqualified obser-vance of one's duties (functions) without transgressing the functional territory of the other, and the social order was not disrupted because any act contrary to this law would destroy the state and society and disturb the process of adjustment of relations decided upon by the existing laws—*dharma*, custom or *vyavahara*. Kautilya talks about the administration of law to yield a lawful public behaviour and that the law should be administered in accordance with the procedure established by law, a dimension of constitutionalism, which is the bedrock of modern jurisprudence. He further holds that only the valid laws/transactions should be taken into account while arriving at any conclusive judgement in a given case. In other words, the validity of law formed the actionable limitations of the king, his officials and the courts. 'Law is the king of the kings' forms part of the politico-legal thought according to Kautilya's *Arthashastra*. That nothing is above the law is what guarantees the impossibility of the return of the dark rule of anarchy, and it is under the rule of law that even a weak individual can be hopeful of standing against the powerful. He argues in various parts of the text that law should be upheld in the righteous manner when he gives a narrative of the duties and functions of the different heads (*adhyakshas*) of the departments in Book II. To take one example, he tells us that the superintendent of jails would be punished if a person was put in jail without informing him of the reasons thereof. This procedure is very much in consonance with the modern theory of detention and punishment. Another example relates to the use of third degree, like torture, against the accused in the process of investigation of a crime. It was recommended in the text that no prisoner was to be meted out an unjust and excessive torture.[7] Though this idea is out of tune with the modern legalism and constitutionalism, it still is a part of a collection of evidence or confession in practice, and the civilized world is still struggling to find ways and means to eliminate it from practice.

SOURCES OF LAW IN THE *ARTHASHASTRA*

The *Arthashastra* recognizes clearly three sources of law, that is, *dharma*, custom and the royal edict or order. Thus, dispensation of justice was based on *dharma*, evidence that is based on witnesses; custom, customs accepted by people and continuing from a long time; and the edicts of the king, meaning law as promulgated. Let us discuss these sources of law in the following pages, seeking alongside their continuance as part of the modern legal theory.

Dharma

Dharma Sutras, and later the *Dharmashastra*, known to be the manuals of human conduct are our earliest sources for the Hindu Law, the most important being those, opines Basham, attributed to Gautama, Baudhayana, Vasistha and Apastamba.[8] It should be noted at the outset, however, that *dharma* has no equivalent in English. The term religion, if used as a synonym, would be a misnomer because in Indian philosophy, the term *dharma* connotes the sacred law or the righteous conduct or a man's duty to be performed as determined. It would, therefore, be wrong to derive that the ancient Indian state was a theological state or that the law was not secular because it was based on *dharma*. In fact, *dharma*, in my view, is the moral, just and legal determinant of conduct, taken together as it appears in the text. The *Dharmashastra* law is, in fact, indicative of those spiritual and intellectual rules that control and govern the righteous and unrighteous conduct of the people at both the personal and the collective/group level. A. B. Keith equates *dharma* to custom, law and righteous conduct,[9] leading one to conclude that the dictates of *dharma* became law since they became part of the customs forming part of the duty and morality of the people, eventually forming the basis of law. Every individual is bound by his *swadharma*, and the king is tied with his *rajadharma*. While the first imposes obligation either determined by society or by the state/king, *rajadharma*, implies the state's obligation to uphold *dharma*, the *Varnashrama* system, the customs and, above all, the welfare and material progress of the subjects of the state. Seen in the legal perspective, the concept of law may be explained as

> a code of conduct supported by a general conscience of the people. It is not subjective in the sense that the conscience of the individual imposes neither it nor external in the sense that the law enforces it. *Dharma* does not force man into virtue, but trains them for it. It is not a fixed code of mechanical rules, but a living spirit which grows and moves in response to the development of society.[10]

In fact, *dharma* can be defined as a combined form of Veda, tradition and customs and the thoughts of the *rishis* meant for governing behaviour. *Dharma* is one of the foundations of justice. Pandit Deendayal Upadhyaya echoes this idea of *dharma* in his theory of 'Integral Humanism'. He maintains, 'that constitution which sustains the nation is in tune with dharma. *Dharma* sustains the nation; hence we have always given primary importance to *dharma* which is considered sovereign. All other entities, institutions or authorities derive their power from *dharma* and are subordinate to it'. In the Kautilyan scheme of law and justice, *dharma* was assigned a higher place of priority as a source of law. Does it mean that the state according to Kautilya could not violate the sacred law or what is called *dharma* law? Or could the king interpret the meaning and content of *dharma* and make law, which is in conflict with the *dharma* law? As a response, it is interesting to note that the *Arthashastra*[11] itself maintains that the king should follow the *Dharmashastra* law over the customary law if they are in conflict with each other and should uphold the law of reason in case the *Dharmashastra* law and *raj nyaya* are contrary to one another. It follows that the king could modify the ambit of *dharma* even though it has been the refrain of certain commentaries that despite the great deal of influence wielded by the king and despite the fact he was the upholder of *dharma* in society, the king had no power to decide what constitutes *dharma* because his role was confined to ensuring that all the people lived their lives according to *dharma*. In a way, he was merely an executive like the one in the present times. R. P. Kangle argues that 'rajasasana is the highest authority on the basis of which a case is to be decided does not amount to saying that the king is regarded in this text as the law maker'.[12] It is, no doubt, stated that when all types of *dharma* perish, it is the king who sets the *dharma* going (that is why he is known as *dharmaparavartaka*) (Book III.1.38); if the *shastra* that is, *dharma is* in conflict with *nyaya* (*rajasasana*) the latter is to be regarded as authoritative, since there the written word (*path*) goes under (Book III.1.43–45). It clearly establishes the supremacy of the *rajasasana* over every other law for the purposes of jurisprudence. Explaining *dharma* as the source of law, Kangle states that the first of these, *dharma*, appears to refer to the law as administered by the *dharmasthas*, which is expounded in the remaining 19 chapters of Book III. It is supposed to be based on *satya*, apparently in the sense of eternal truth, because it has been handed down from times immemorial.[13] R. K. Chaudhary points out that 'Kautilya accepts *dharma* as coincident to the dictates of a moral sense or the observation of an established usage; and he insists that the exigencies of *rashtra* demand *dharma* as being understood as a deliberate order issued by and authority with that of punishment'.[14] Contrary to the *Dharmashastra*, the royal ordinances override the others, if need be.[15] It may be observed that though *dharma* as enunciated by the ancient political thinker in Kautilya has almost lost its relevance, its incarnation in the form of religion still holds good as an influencing element of law. For instance, the state has not been able to enact a uniform civil code in India despite the demand from the social reformers and the proponents of social justice as well as the suggestions of the judiciary several times to that effect. Cases of marriage, property rights of Muslim women and divorce are still governed by the dictates of Quran and Sunnah.

Custom

Custom or tradition has formed a vital source of law in almost every age of history. It may be recalled that *dharma* and customs were the two pillars of regulating the social action and behaviour when there was no state and no king to control and regulate social, economic and cultural relations in the society. We are told that before the emergence of the institution of a state, people were living happily by observing their respective *dharma*/duty to oneself and towards each other. Robert Langat's remarks seem plausible inasmuch as he sees custom as a purely social phenomena and finds the place of customs, known to have formed a special law regulating the various social groups, castes, corporations or guilds, families or the different regions of India, in the scheme of things as unambiguous.[16] It is undeniable that custom acquires the force of law when people repeatedly observe a particular norm or practice as the basis of the conduct of common affairs and individual behaviour over a period of time as a matter of fact. The *Manusmriti* maintains that the whole of the Vedas is the source of the sacred law (*dharma*), followed by the tradition and the virtuous conduct of those who know the Vedas, f the customs of the holy men and finally self-satisfaction. And then, 'the sacred tradition (the *smriti*), the customs of the virtuous men, and one's own pleasure, they declare to be visibly the fourfold means of defining the sacred law (*dharma*)'.[17] Macdonell treats *dharma* in the sense of custom or law, covering both the civil and criminal law and morality.[18] It is interesting to note that customs as a source of law have been well recognized by Kautilya who makes it crystal clear that custom should be given priority in deciding matters pertaining to inheritance among the mixed castes. He says: 'Desasya jatya sanghasya dharma gramasya vapi yah ucitah-tasya tenaiva dayadharmam prakalpayet', meaning that it should be decided in accordance with the customs prevalent in the country, caste, guild or the village of the inheritors.[19] In Book II, Chapter 7, he makes it obligatory for the state officials to record and maintain registers of the usages of regions, villages, castes, families and organizations. Even in the event of conquered territories, he makes it the duty of the king to 'initiate the observance of all those customs which, though unrighteous and practised by others, are not observed in his own country, and give no room for the practice of whatever is unrighteous though observed by others'.[20] *Dharma* of ancient India was not consciously made by the law-givers or by a legislature; it was generally enforced by social approval or the dread of hell and not by the force of the state. It was not static; it was, however, changed by the arbitrary will of neither a king nor the noisy method of legislation but by the slow and prolonged process of change in social customs and practices.[21]

Kautilya establishes the connection between law as a product of legislation (*rajasasana*) and law as a product of society germinating either from the moral foundations of society or the traditions and conventions/customs as prevailing at a given point of time and locale. Kautilya stressed the coexistence of both the laws—civil and customary—which was emphasized by a number of European and South Asian countries as well. Since the customary laws may vary, it can be agreed—from community to community and one geographical area to the other—that the individual members are habitual of claiming certain prerogatives on account of their membership of the specific community. For example, some personal laws are enjoyed by the Muslims or the Christians by reason of their belonging to a particular religious group. Even the decisions of the caste *panchayats* (Khap Panchayats) in the state of Haryana in Indian fall in the aforementioned category, even though not recognized by law on several occasions, but still customs hold good as they are the rights or laws propounded and practised by the community to be followed individually by each member generally. In fact, the importance of custom as the source of law has never escaped the eyes of the lawmakers, policymakers and law adjudicators, which emphasizes on making our legal system more inclusive and decentralized, not only structurally and organizationally but also operationally in both the horizontal and vertical spheres. Kautilya was conscious of the reality that certain localities/regions and societies, like the tribals, have their long established laws, rules and regulations governing them since the time immemorial, and unless they come in conflict with national interests and the interests of the king, they should be not only allowed to prevail, but it should also be the duty of the king to uphold them. Not doing so may cause upheaval in society, leading to political and social instability. It has been argued that common law tradition was popular in Britain, and from there, it was exported to her colonies. However, it is open to question as Kautilya included the customary law in his list of laws centuries before Britain transmitted the concept and efficacy of conventions as the source of law; in fact the colonial power realized the importance of the pre-existing social customs and allowed the social segments to be governed by them for the large part of their rule and interfered with some of them only when the demand for doing so emerged from society itself, for example, the sati system was abolished under pressure from the Hindu social reformers.

It is appropriate to point out that many customs have the force of law even after India became independent. Separate provisions have been made under schedule five and six of the constitution of India, for instance, in relation to some parts of the states of the north-east, and the tribal communities observe different community-determined rules in relation to marriage, inheritance and gender relations alongside the rules of judicature.[22] The Parsi personal laws are based not on their religion, but are governed by the Hindu customary laws in India even after the enactment of marriage, inheritance and divorce laws by the then colonial government in India like the Parsi Marriage and Divorce Act of 1936 and the Indian Succession Act of 1925. The aforementioned discussion suggests that India and many other countries, despite having a constitutional democratic system of government, are still struggling to introduce a uniform legal system across their communities and societies. A system of legal pluralism, to borrow from legal Anthropology, based on religious and customary boundaries still prevails.

Royal Edicts

Another source of law mentioned in the text is the orders or edicts issued by the king. It would, however, be relevant to note here the debate regarding the law-making power of the king. Whether he was entrusted with the authority to make fresh laws or only to execute the rules of behaviour recognized under the sacred law and/or the customs is the issue on which it is difficult to pass a judgement as the opinion among the scholars appears to be divided. For example, R. P. Kangle is of the view that, 'supremacy of the *rajasasana* in deciding cases of disputes in the court notwithstanding, the king cannot make fresh laws in supersession of those already prevalent in society...'. In any case, it is hardly possible to agree with K. A. Nilakanta Sastri that the supremacy of the royal decree (*rajasasana*) maintained in this text is exceptional among Indian writers and 'marks an attempt to evolve a new norm in civil law, in the establishment of which the royal authority will be actively exerted'.[23] He adds that

> the word *rajasasna*, which is used in the context of *vivadartha*, that is, matter in dispute, can only refer to a judgement by the king in that case, and not to a new law promulgated by the king. There is in fact no evidence that the king has the power of legislation according to this text.[24]

Kangle's argument, however, is weak when confronted with the assertion of Kautilya in Book III.1.38 that 'when all laws are perishing, the king here is the promulgator of laws, by virtue of his guarding the right conduct of the world consisting of the four *Varnas* and four *asramas*'. He further emphasizes in Book III.1.39: 'A matter in dispute has four feet, law, transaction, custom and the royal edict; (among them) the later one supersedes the earlier one',[25] indicating the supremacy of the king-made law over any other law.

Reference is found in Book II.10.71[26] about the power of the king to issue orders or commands and the procedure of forming royal writs (commands or orders of the king, *sasanas*) The *lekhakas* with ministerial qualifications, acquainted with all kinds of customs, smart in composition, good in legible writing and sharp in readings were supposed to convert the king's order to writing. He describes writs as of great importance to kings inasmuch as treaties, ultimately leading to war. Further, a writ, in order to be clear and unambiguous, should have necessary qualities such as arrangement of the subject matter (*arthakrama*), relevancy (*sambandha*), completeness, sweetness, dignity and lucidity, which imply the mentioning of facts in the order of their importance, no contradiction between the just and previously mentioned facts and subsequent facts till the completion of the letter, providing reasons, illustrations and examples to make the subject matter clear and impressive, and avoiding redundant words along with the use of appropriate and suitably strong words, description in exquisite style of a good purport with a pleasing effect, the use of words other than colloquial and the use of well-known words, respectively.[27] Whether the edicts could be treated as law or as executive orders/directions to officers to restore the treasure and so forth unlawfully retained by them, is, however, anybody's guess. Besides, such orders were concerned with the bestowal of rewards or punishments upon the king's servants and others, with the gift of honour to someone, with the grant of remissions, with the attestation of the act of subordinate, with communications, with replies and, lastly, with offering of universal safe conduct to travellers.

The quasi legislative authority of the king is implicit in his power to make rules and regulations for the guidance of the *adhyakshas* (heads of the departments, Book II) as well as to the magistrates, *pradestas* (Book IV). It may, therefore, be agreed upon that the edicts of the king had the force of law in the political and legal theory of Kautilya, and king's law was accorded a place of judicial supremacy[28] in matters of adjudication. M. V. Krishna Rao points out:

> But, the Kantaka Shodhana courts appear as a phenomenon in the legal history of ancient India. The expression, 'removal of thorns' confirms the thesis that the *dandadhara* actuated by the sole desire of preserving the state's integrity becomes relentless in the suppression of any form of wickedness that militates against the welfare of the *Janapada*. The judges of the courts were of magisterial authority disposing of cases without the formalities of the civil procedure Code and without the assistance of the jurists.[29]

Kautilya invested the king with the power to pronounce what is and what is not law when it related to the individuals, groups and guilds.

The existing law might need modification or replacement in order to meet the new needs of society and to synchronize practical need and the economic condition. But the right of the king was very much limited as far as the direction or invention of law according to his own judgement was concerned.[30] Kautilya argues that a royal legislation could modify existing *vyavahara* and *achara* and jurisdiction so as to obtain integration of states and their solidarity against the threats from the internal and external enemies.[31]

Thus, it is clear that though the state was usually expected to enforce the customs and laws mentioned in the *Dharmashastra*, it began to be invested with some powers to make its own regulations from about the 3rd century BC. The power of issuing *rajasasana* or royal decree was, however, not as extensive as the modern power of legislation. Personal, civil and criminal laws were usually determined by custom and the *smriti* rules and were hardly affected appreciably by the royal power to issue ordinances. But in the realm of administration and taxation, kings could introduce several changes and reforms by the new powers conceded to them. They could create new offices and departments, promulgate (like Asoka) their new policies and tap fresh sources of taxation.[32]

Are the royal orders or the edicts of the executive still valid as the source of law? It is to be noted that much has changed from the monarchical days of Kautilya inasmuch as political institutions and structures and legal processes of the past have been replaced by the new forms and designs. The separation of powers and their investment in separate institutions have established distinct political roles and functions to be performed by the state apparatus. Now, the lawmaking, law execution and law adjudication are placed with separate agencies unlike in the ancient treatise on statecraft. Nevertheless, it would be difficult to deny that, in India, the executive orders have the force of law, even though they are not the source of law in the strict sense of the term, as the source undoubtedly continues to be the law passed by the legislature. In a way, one can say that the executive continues to command semi-legislative authority[33] like the one described by Kautilya under the title of royal edicts in the *Arthashastra*, Book III.

When we examine the scheme of lawmaking in India and elsewhere in the present times, we find that the executive performs certain legislative functions like issuing executive orders and framing rules and regulations under the system of delegated legislation or what is called subordinate legislation. However, the exercise of these powers by the executive is subject to the control of the legislature. In the age of Kautilya, this check was applied by *dharma*/sacred law as there was no separate political institution like parliament or legislative assembly to hold the king accountable in that regard. Even now, like in the *Arthashastra*, law and coercive power of the enforcement machinery are interlinked. It is difficult to imagine rule of law in the absence of the provisions for punishment to the violators of law. It is the well-accepted principle of the modern theory of law and justice that law should be administered without bias, prejudice and partiality, which was the core of the argument of Kautilya in his theory of law and administration of justice. Even the judges and the king were subject to punishment for miscarriage of justice, for example, punishing an innocent man.

It can easily be argued, after the foregoing discussion, that Kautilya made a significant contribution to the evolution, development and growth of law inasmuch as the concept, scope and importance of law, and its rule was conceived in the modern sense of the term. Kautilya's categorization of law into civil and criminal laws forebears the Indian system of civil and criminal justice administration of the present times. He undertook pains to codify law and lay down procedures of law, as done earlier by the continental European nations, which belonged to the Roman and Germanic system of law. In modern India, we have two overarching types of laws: one, common civil and criminal codes, which illustrate what are called statutory or codified laws—codified by a constitution and a set of statutory laws, and two, religion-based personal laws and tribal customary laws. Both of them seem to be the guiding force of the judicial philosophy of Kautilya.

In fact, Kautilya's legal philosophy presented a synthesis of the ideas and principles of law preceding him. His political thought on the legal system is influenced by the principles and maxims of law and jurisprudence enunciated by his predecessors, at least partially.[34]

He presented an advanced theory of law, which can be compared in many ways to the modern theorization of law. Law, in his opinion, should be the agent and facilitator of discipline in society and also in the individual and to secure the promotion of *yogakshema*, the welfare of society and the security and prosperity of the kingdom.

Law, instead of being the mechanism of autocracy, was to be a balancing link between authority and legitimacy, and hence, it was to be just in form and application on which was dependent the legitimacy of the government. The subjects were given the right to disobey a law contrary to the objectives of the state and life of the society. Since the king was entrusted with the task of upholding the *dharma* and maintaining social order, it was necessary for him, under the prescriptions of Kautilya, to use law for that purpose effectively without bringing in the element of cruelty beyond the needed proportion in the process of administration of law and justice. Further, the royal edicts could not change or modify the nature and scope of the king's duties as ordained under the law. Kautilya provides a detailed list of the duties of the king and his officials in Book I of his treatise. If he did not do so, he would be subject to public disapproval, entailing a loss of legitimacy and a danger to the political and social stability, thereby weakening himself and the country. The provision in the *Arthashastra*, it can be said, for the king to compensate for the loss to his subjects on account of robbery and theft implied that the royal orders or edicts could not write off this royal responsibility from the list of his legal obligations.

CODIFICATION OF LAW

Codification of law goes back to the times quite early in the history of antiquity. Before Kautilya enunciated his scheme of the codes of law, there were others who developed such codes. Hammurabi's code of about 1700 BC, said to be actually inspired by Sumerian and Acadian codes, which could be treated more as a compendium of previous cases meant to supplement customs than a true code.[35] There were also in existence some other codes such as Gregorian code, promulgated in 291; the Theodosian code published in AD 438 and the Justinian code promulgated in AD 534.

In India, Kautilya can be credited with providing a comprehensive compendium of laws and legal provisions, regulations and rules on several legal matters. His code of law consists of a complete corpus of law relating to civil, criminal and personal matters. It is a code presenting systematically general and specific rules or laws governing the specific areas of law in ancient India. However, it is not clear from the text whether the codifications were driven out of the sacred law, customs and royal edicts, that is, from the existing system of rules and were merely their re-statement and consolidation or were constructed from some new system. On the other hand, it can be argued that the legal provisions emerged from all the three sources of law.

The threefold classification of law in the text speaks not only of Kautilya's rational and systematic identification of the rules, regulations and the laws, it is also typical of his foresightedness and developed legal intellect reflecting much of what prevails in India today. The substantive codification attempted by him are almost akin to the classification of laws in the fields of civil, criminal and personal laws, even if they have been modified, updated and replaced in view of the emergence of new experiments, experiences and changing needs in contemporary India. The codes of law are purposive in nature as far as they provide a basis for the application of true justice in a given case.

Civil Code

It would be correct to state that Kautilya does not assign a separate chapter on codification of law as such. Whatever is being discussed is by way of interpretation and inference of various pages from the text. I have separated some of the rules, regulations and laws and grouped them as civil, criminal and personal laws in that order. In the civil code, Kautilya provides us with an array of laws, rules and regulations that cover the matters relating to transactions, sale and purchase of property and matters relating to business, trade, labour and industry; the field of inheritance; and division of property.

1. Transactions/agreements
Kautilya begins by identifying the valid and the void transactions so as to eliminate any possibility of deceit. Talking about the agreements

(vyavahara), Kautilya mentions that any agreement entered into seclusion, inside the houses, in the dead of night, in forests, in secret or with fraud shall not be valid, and the proposer and the accessory and the witnesses shall be punished (Book III.I.148). However, it can be observed that there are exceptions to this rule, such as agreements concluded within the hearing of others; those that are not otherwise condemnable; agreements relating to the division of inheritance, sealed or unsealed deposits, or marriage; or those which concern women who are either afflicted with disease or who do not stir out; as well as those entered into by persons who are not known to have a sound mind shall be considered as valid even though entered into inside houses. Similarly, the transactions concerning robbery, duel, marriage or the execution of the king's order and the agreements entered into by persons who usually do their business during the first part of the night will not be void even though executed at night[36]; the agreements entered into forests by those who live most part of their life in the forests as merchants, cowherds, hermits, hunters or spies; fraudulent agreements entered into by spies; and the agreements reached by the members of any association among themselves.[37] Furthermore, if any dependent or unauthorized persons, for example, father, mother, a son, a father having a son, an outcast brother, the youngest brother, a family of undivided interests, a wife having her husband or son, a slave, a hired labourer, any person who is too young or too old to carry on business, a convict (abhishasta), a cripple or an afflicted person or an authorized person if he was under provocation, anxiety or intoxication at the time of making the agreements or if he was a lunatic or a convicted person, it shall be void.

Contracting a debt by mortgaging one's property like a house or a field when the property is not seen at the time or a debt contracted in addition to one already contracted and other aspects of civil law are clearly provided in Chapter I of Book III of the classic.[38] In addition, the Arthashastra defines what constitutes property of a woman as means of subsistence and jewellery, wherein means of subsistence valued at above 2,000 were to be endowed in her name, while there was no limit to jewellery, the ways to enjoy that property by the woman and her husband, the father-in-law, etc. (Book III.2.152). In a sense, the questions regarding the slaves or dasas and the labourers, *karamkaras*, undertaking in partnership, sale of property without ownership, encroachment on other's property, adverse possession and revocation of a sale or a purchase among others also form part of the civil code[39].

2. Division of inheritance

Chapter 5 of Book III of the *Arthashastra* deals with the question of division of inheritance in which we are told that ancestral property could be divided only after the death of both the father and the mother, while grandsons will also have a prescribed share in the ancestral property. Self-acquired property of any of the descendent sons is indivisible, unless it was acquired with the help of parental property.

If a man has no male issue, his own brothers, or persons who have been living with him (*sah jivino va*) shall take possession of his property (*dravyam*), and in their absence, his daughters (born of marriages other than the first four) shall have his property. If one has sons, they shall have the property; if one has only daughters born of such marriage as is contracted in accordance with the customs of any of the first four kinds of marriage, they shall have the property; if there are neither sons nor such daughters, the dead man's father, if he is alive shall have it; if he too is not alive, the dead man's father's brothers and the sons of his brothers shall have it; if there are many brothers of his father, all of them shall divide it.[40]

Moreover, the father shall not discriminate between his sons with regard to the division of property among them, nor any of his sons shall be deprived of his share without any valid reasons. This is true even today in India, but only in the case of property inherited by the father.

3. Recovery of debts

Chapter 11 of Book III tells us in detail about the interests (at different rates in relation to an individual, a commercial or *vyavahariki*, forests, sea traders) per month per cent on the debt taken by a debtor and the fine to be imposed on those charging over and above the prescribed rate. A creditor claiming four times the amount lent by him shall pay a fine of four times the unjust amount. No debt could be recovered if not taken note of for 10 years, except in the case of a minor, the aged, the sick, person in a calamity, a person migrated from the country or disorder in the kingdom (Book III.11.13). The debt shall not increase if a person is confined in a long sacrificial session or by illness or in the preceptor's house, or in the case of a minor or an insolvent (Book III.11.10). The sons and grandsons shall be obligated to pay back the debt with interest or heirs inheriting the property of the deceased or co-debtors or sureties. The suretyship of a minor shall be void in law. If a person had taken debt from two persons, he could not be sued by them at the same time, except when he was about to leave the place (Book III.11.19). However, a wife cannot be forced to pay back the debt taken by her husband without her knowledge and consent. However, a husband shall be liable to repay the debt incurred by his wife if he has gone abroad without making any provision for her.[41]

4. Pledges/Mortgages, deposits

This law deals with the lost, used-up, sold, mortgaged or misappropriated pledges. A usufructuary/productive pledge/mortgage shall never be lost to the debtor, nor shall any interest on the debt be charged. Till very recently, I do not know of the present practice, if the debtor mortgaged his or her property, he was not charged any interest on the debt. The assumption was that the one giving loan on mortgage shall recover interest from the commodity mortgaged. On the other hand, interest on the debt shall accumulate in case of hypothecation of the pledge lost, but the pledgee shall be fined 12 *panas* if he does not re-convey the pledge when the debtor was ready for it. It is further maintained that an immovable property, pledged and enjoyable with or without labour shall not be caused to deteriorate in value while yielding interest on the money lent, and the profit on the expenses incurred in maintaining it. This law also includes many more details related to share of profits, forfeiture of debt, etc. The *Arthashastra* also lays down the rules governing the reclamation of the lost deposits, loss of value of the deposit(s) due to its use, loss or mortgage of the deposits, etc.

Criminal Procedure Code

Criminal law and criminal procedure code are complementary and supplementary to each other insofar as they define crime and establish the procedure to administer justice. Criminal law code consists of that body of rules and laws that prohibit the conduct or behaviour of a person that may harm public safety and welfare of society. Criminal law deals with crimes that may entail punishment like the ones related to felonies or misdemeanours. Felonies include crimes like murder and are further classified into different categories of cases with varying degrees of punishment. Criminal procedure code refers to the actual procedure adopted in the process of administration that brings clarity to the discussion in Book III and to some extent in Book IV, relating to a vast range of matters such as law of contract, acts of murder, fraud and cheating, adultery, plea-bargaining, common intention and common object, and power to order and recover costs of the case, etc. Criminal laws further include verbal or physical injury, defamation or slander, contumely or threat, defiling of body, intimidation and assault, violation of laws related to the cutting down of trees, flowers or fruits, or the bushes, or trees at the cremation grounds, holy places or trees serving as the marks of a boundary, laying down rules for the regulation of gambling, touching the brother's wife, causing hurt without blood, forcible seizure of articles, commodities of high or low value, forest produce, jewels, theft, robbery, damage to fields, etc.

It may be added that the regal ordinances defining punishment of those who transgressed the royal commands were the prerogative of the king, and the regal interventions could be seen in the social and religious affairs of the people, and most of the laws discussed by Kautilya form part of the modern Indian jurisprudence under criminal procedure code.

1. The law of treason

The text refers to the laws of treason, which is similar to the situation in Britain under the Plantagenet. Any person who causes harm to the kingdom; forcibly enters the king's harem; instigates wild tribes or enemies against the king; or creates disharmony in forts, other regions of the country or in the army was to be burnt alive from head to foot. However, if that man happens to be a *Brahmin*, he shall be drowned (and not burnt).[42]

2. Cases of adultery

The list of crimes includes adultery, witchcraft, forceful relationship with a harlot and unnatural intercourse. It may be observed that he provides different punishment for different castes for their involvement in the act of adultery. For example, a *Kshatriya* committing adultery with an unguarded *Brahmin* woman was subject to a fine of highest amercement; if it was done by a *Vaishya*, he shall be deprived of his whole property, while if the same act is committed by a *Sudra*, he was to be burnt alive. Similarly, a man committing adultery with the queen of the land shall be burnt alive in a vessel; a man shall be banished in case he commits adultery with a low-caste woman besides being branded on his forehead. A man who has an unnatural sexual relationship with a woman shall be punished with the first amercement as also a man having sexual intercourse with another man (Book IV.13.236).

3. Misconduct with women

Kautilya was conscious of the fact that a woman could be violated/dishonoured in many ways, and, therefore, he provisioned for punishing such violators who dishonoured women whether a slave or a woman from a respectable family. Kautilya writes: 'For guards misbehaving with a slave woman shall be meted out lowest fine; with one not a slave, the middle fine; with one in the exclusive keeping (of someone), the highest fine and with a woman from a respective family, the punishment shall be death'.[43] He further states that a person who forcibly violates a widow living by herself or a *chandala* touching an *Aryan* lady shall be fined with 100 *panas*.[44]

Witchcraft to a woman other than to an indifferent wife, a beloved or by a husband to a wife was punishable under law with a varying degrees of punishment. He emphasizes that

> When a man performs witchcraft to win the sister of his own father or mother, the wife of a maternal uncle or of a preceptor, his own daughter-in-law, daughter or sister, his limbs were to be cut off and also to be put to death, while any woman who yields herself to such an offender was to get the same punishment and so shall be the fate of a woman yielding to a slave, a hired labourer or a servant.

4. Rape

Kautilya was very harsh on the offenders committing rape. For example, anyone who violated a maiden of the same *varna* who had not attained puberty was to be imposed a fine of 400 *panas* or was to have his hand cut off; if the woman died, the penalty was death. The matter has been further covered in ss 2–7 of Section 87 of Chapter XII of Book IV. The act of forcible intercourse (rape) committed even against a prostitute was a punishable offence. If a man wants to enjoy with a prostitute by force, according to Kautilya, the fine shall be 12 *panas*; if a group of men want to enjoy forcibly with one prostitute, each one of them shall have to pay a fine of 24 *panas*.[45] In another part of the text, in the *Arthashastra*, it is stated that a person committing rape with a captive, slave or a hired woman in a lock-up shall be punished with the first amercement; a man who rapes the wife of a thief or the wife of any other man who is dead in an epidemic shall be punished with the middlemost amercement; and a man who rapes an Aryan woman during lock-up shall be punished with the highest amercement. Kautilya provisioned death penalty for an offender who committed rape on an Aryan woman in the same lock-up; an officer was to get death penalty if he arrested an Aryan woman in the night on the pretext of raping her.[46]

5. Act of murder

Book IV, Chapter 11.229 of the *Arthashastra* provisions different punishments for committing the murder of a person. For example, a murderer shall be given death penalty with torture if the person has been killed in a quarrel and instantaneous death if the person wounded in a fight dies within a period of seven nights; an offender shall be fined the highest amercement if the wounded person dies within a fortnight; and an offender shall be fined 500 *panas* along with an adequate compensation to the bereaved. Anyone causing violent death either to men or women shall be punished with hanging. Going further he says that any person who murders his father, mother, son, brother, teacher or an ascetic shall be punished with death by burning both his head and skin; when a man wantonly murders another, or steals a herd of cattle, the punishment shall be beheading.

6. Miscellaneous acts of crime

Any man engaged in meeting prostitutes often; inflicting unjust punishment to others; spreading false or contemptuous rumours; assaulting or obstructing travellers on their way; committing a house break; or stealing or causing injury to royal elephants, horses or carriages were to be awarded death by hanging.

Personal Laws

Personal laws formed the third category of laws governing the social and personal life of the people. Nevertheless we find a separate set of personal laws that regulate different aspects of their social living. For example, there are different personal laws observed by the Muslims, the Hindus and the Christians for marriage, divorce, desertion, maintenance, *stridhana* and remarriage apart from the laws of inheritance and succession and division of inheritance of property. Kautilya deals with all the dimensions and more of the personal laws in greater detail in Chapters 2–7 of Book III.

1. Law of marriage

Kautilya attached the greatest value to the institution of marriage, describing it as the beginning of all transactions (Book III.2.1), and then divided marriages into eight categories that included *Brahma* form of marriage, the *prajapatya*, the *arsa*, the *daiva*, the *gandharva*, *asura*, the *rakshasa* and the *paisaca*, but he focused more on the first four types. But I am not sure whether it would be correct to describe the last two forms as valid marriages since both of them involved an element of force or fraud.[47] How can the father and mother sanction a marriage, as provisioned by Kautilya, if it was performed under force or under fraud, is difficult to digest, except that such marriages could be accepted as merely imposed by circumstances.

2. Law of divorce

How can divorce be obtained by a woman or a man found an elaborate discussion in the *Arthashastra*. A woman hating her husband cannot dissolve her marriage with him against his will. Nor can a man dissolve his marriage with his wife against her will. But if both the man and the woman have mutual enmity, divorce could obtained (*parasparam dveshanmokshah*). Further, if a man apprehends danger from his wife and wants to seek divorce shall return to his wife what she received at the time of her marriage. Conversely, if a woman apprehends danger from her husband and desires divorce, she shall forfeit her claim to her property. However, marriages performed in accordance with the customs of the *Brahma*, *prajapatya*, *arsa* and *daiva* marriages were beyond dissolution, that is, in the case of these marriages, divorce was impermissible.[48]

3. Law of maintenance

Kautilya recognized the right to maintenance of a woman and emphasized that a woman who has a right to claim maintenance for an unlimited period of time shall be given as much food and clothing as is necessary for her or more than is necessary in proportion to the income of the maintainer and if the period is limited, then a certain amount of money, fixed in proportion to the income of the maintainer, was to be given to her; so also if she has not been given her *shulka*, property and compensation, due to her for allowing her husband to re-marry. At the same time, a woman shall not be able to sue her husband for her maintenance if she either goes under the protection of any one from the family of her father-in-law or begins to live independently.

4. Right of a widow to remarry

According to the *Arthashastra*, a widow had the right to live a pious life with a right over her endowment and jewellery along with the balance of *shulka*. In the case she decided to remarry, she was bound to return the endowment and jewellery with interest. In case she decided to marry a person not selected by her father-in-law, she would have to forfeit everything given to her by her father-in-law and her deceased husband. However, no woman could lay claim over the property of her deceased husband after she remarried.[49] Similarly, a woman who remarried could not possess her own property (*stridhana*) in the name of maintaining her sons from her former husband, except that she was to endow it in the names of the said sons.

A barren widow was entitled to enjoy her own property till her death to ward off calamities (Book III.2: 153).[50] The husband was eligible to remarry, even if the first wife was alive, if the first wife could not have a son or was barren for eight years after marriage and could remarry after waiting for 12 years if the first wife gave birth to only female children. However, if the husband went against these rules, he shall be bound to pay her not only her *shulka*, her *stridhana* and adequate monitory compensation but also a fine of 24 *panas* to the government.

A woman has a right to remarry any one whom she liked and who is capable of maintaining her and relieving her misery, even when her husband is alive but absent and not having maintenance, and is deserted by well-to-do kinsmen. Kautilya, further, emphasized the rights and obligations of a young wife when remarrying, for example, an absent husband who had gone abroad.[51] Book III also addressed the issue of conjugal rights that finds a place in the modern law books of family laws. It is interesting to observe that in independent India, many of the provisions governing various codes of law are similar to Kautilyan thought, whether it is in the area of spousal relationship, situation of marital discord, separation, divorce or succession and inheritance of property. For instance, Hindu Succession Act of 1956 clearly provides that a property acquired by a Hindu woman shall be absolutely her property—her *stridhana*. There is reference to *Meher* in the Muslim personal law. While the Hindu Succession (amendment) Act establishes parity between the son and a daughter in matters of inheritance of parental property, we find, in practice, that the daughters are still made to sign away their inheritance rights by the male members of the family; gender parity, under family law, is still missing.

In the end, it can be observed that Kautilya developed highly relevant theory of law and its classification into implicit codes, which predated the modern Indian legal thinking. R. P. Kangle very aptly summarizes Kautilya's contribution to the codification of law, and says[52]:

> This very brief review of the law found in Kautilya will, it is hoped, show how it has been treated by him in the most systematic manner. The treatment is also as full as possible. This is an aspect of Kautily's teaching which is generally ignored in most studies of this work. Compared with this text, the earliest works on *Dharamashastra*, namely, the *Dharamasutras*

of Apastamba and others, contain only scrappy rules on only some of the topics treated here. They mostly concern themselves with marriage and inheritance, and to some extent with debts and deposits. But they contain practically nothing corresponding to a large number of topics treated so fully in this text, which can legitimately form the subject matter of a dispute among subjects to be adjudicated in a court of law. The *Dharamasutras* works, therefore, can hardly be regarded as giving us a genuine code of law. Such a code we find only in the *Arthashastra*.

5. Sexual morality

The *Arthashastra* deals with the questions concerning sexual morality, an idea often seen out of sync with modern thinking based on freedom of body by some feminists; yet, it cannot be denied that the issue is important in terms of present-day relationship between a man and a woman in the contemporary period. Kautilya discusses the issue of sexual morality in Book IV.12.15-19 and maintains that for a bride to be not a virgin at the time of consummation, the fine shall be 54 *panas*; apart from that, she shall return the dowry and marriage expenses. If after maintaining that kind of condition, she fails, she shall pay double; for substituting other blood, the fine shall be 200; the man falsely accusing the bride of loss of virginity shall lose the dowry and expenses. He shall not have the right over her if she was unwilling. In the latter sense, was Kautilya talking against marital rape?

KAUTILYA'S THEORY OF JUSTICE: A FINE MIXTURE OF THE PAST AND THE PRESENT IDEAS

Kautilya underlines time and again that the righteous application of *danda* and *dandaniti* alone could obtain the well-being of the nation—the creation of wealth, the efficacy and efficiency of justice, suppression of rebellion and dissensions, the health of the treasury, etc. Establishment and effective implementation of law by the executive and the judicial organs alone could lead to a system that could award the honest and punish the corrupt in administration and bring to book a criminal. That it was the just rod that could guarantee a righteous conduct of every affair was the firm view of both the *Dharmashastra* and of the *Arthashastra*. 'The virtuous one despises', says Subramanian,[53] 'prosperity attained through ignominy. The bounds of good conduct should never be crossed; truth and charity are the roots of righteousness. Righteousness is the ornament of all'.

The state power—its acquisition, exercise and disruption—was dependent upon the king's capability to enforce internal discipline and peace to send the message across that the law was supreme.[54] According to Kautilya, the importance of the principles of justice and continuous vigilance over the administration and society could be neglected at the altar of disorder and instability, causing injury to the health of the kingdom and the people. Establishment and continuity of a free, fearless and lawful life was, therefore, closely attributed to the unfathomed respect for law and justice, the two symbols of a civil social order and the existence of state.

It is interesting to note that in the Vedic period, the victims of injustice hardly had any systematic arrangements to take recourse to, so as to get the wrong committed to him, such as theft, robbery and adultery undone. He had to fend for himself by means of sitting on a dharna in front of the gate of his wrongdoer till he was able to get justice, or if he was unable to carry out the sit-in, he could go to the elders.[55] It is only in the later Vedic literature that one finds mention of the office of someone in the name of *sabhapati* who might have exercised the power of a judge, implying also that the *sabha* could intervene to arbitrate between the contending parties to the possible extent.[56]

Kautilya, following the *Dharmashastra*, made enormous contribution to the development of the judiciary and the judicial process. According to Kautilya, justice formed the basic foundations of the state and society. It may be noted here that justice, according to Kautilya, was an outcome of all kinds of formal and customary laws, the legal procedures and codes of law, as well as the judicial institutions. We can observe the clarity of thought in Kautilya's mind from the discussion of the principles of jurisprudence that elaborately codifies penal code and the code of criminal procedure, and the machinery of judicial administration involving the king, the judges and the judicial officers dealing with cases of adjudication at the lower level.

Basic Features of Justice

We have, first, focused on finding out the guiding principles of justice simply because it is necessary to know whether, Kautilya, like the modern theorists of jurisprudence, was interested in dispensation of justice to the satisfaction of the people in general, and of the parties involved in a suit, because 'justice should not only be done, it should appear to be done'. A closer look into Books III and IV establishes that justice is to be governed by some set of principles identified or inferred as follows:

1. Principle of equity

The first and foremost guide to the administration/dispensation of justice is taken by the author (Kautilya) as the principle of equity that should form part of the approach to the disposal of cases, where subjects are assured of certainty and predictability of law and justice. R. P. Kangle makes it clear in his translation of verse 17–18 in Chapter 10 of Book IV in the *Arthashastra*[57]:

> taking in full consideration the person and the offence, the motive, seriousness or lightness (gravity of the offence), the consequences, the present (effects), and the place and time, the magistrate shall fix the highest, the lowest and the middle (amersement) in the matter of punishment, remaining neutral between the king and the subjects.

However, while everything else is in conformity with the principle of equity, the consideration of person as the basis of justice violates the basic concept of equity as the magistrate could discriminate between persons while deciding the quantum of punishment. It would be pertinent to point out in this context that the *Varnashrama* system, in which it was the duty of the king[58] to uphold, was perceived as discriminatory in itself inasmuch as the *Sudras* were assigned an inferior status as compared to the other three classes/castes. For example, the *Sudras)* were not even entitled to own property, and they were to be inflicted a harsher punishment in comparison to the *Brahmanas* even if they committed the same offence. However, this accusation is not sustained when we note that Kautilya does not differentiate between people on the basis of their caste or class in the cases pertaining to verbal or physical injury, gambling and betting, assault, damage to pastureland, fields and roads, etc. It may be recalled that Kautilya stood for equal protection of law, unlike Manu who believed in a discriminatorily biased arrangement against the loser in the matter of gambling, and emphasized that all gamblers, whether they won or lost, tended to cheat, and that none of them could be discriminated in matters of punishment as doing so would lead to loss of confidence in the courts of justice. If the loser was to be punished with a double fine, no one would approach the king for justice.[59] At the same time, it is to be noted that the king had some special privileges in civil and criminal matters, which was comparable to the president of India today. The following were some of the privileges[60]:

a. he could not be made a witness;
b. his property could not pass to others by prescription;
c. he had the escheat to property without heir;
d. he was entitled to all lost or stolen articles without claimants;
e. he was entitled to the service of the artisans for a specified period; and
f. he was entitled to treasure troves

It is really interesting to note that even a king shall not escape punishment if he violates justice like when he punishes an innocent person. Kautilya maintains that when the king punishes an innocent man, he shall throw into water dedicating to God Varuna a fine equal to 30 times the unjust imposition, and this amount shall later be distributed among the *Brahmanas*.[61]

2. Justice to be fast

Justice delayed is justice denied is the old dictum at the back of the discharge of judicial duty, which is regulated by the rules meant for the judges in this regard. Dealing with the issue of adjournment of the case, Kautilya eliminates the cause of delay when he makes it incumbent upon the plaintiff to rejoin/reply soon after the defendant has answered the questions at issue. Or, he shall be guilty of *parokta*, for the plaintiff knows the determining factors of the case. But the defendant does not do so. The defendant may be allowed three or seven nights to prepare his defence. If he is not ready with his defence within that time, he shall be punished with a fine ranging from 3 to 12 *panas*. If he is not ready with his defence even after three fortnights, he shall be fined for *parokta*, and the plaintiff shall recover the amount of the case from the defendant's property.[62] Further, it can be noted in this passage that Kautilya, by fixing the time limit for the submission of argument and counterargument by the plaintiff and the defendant had made it certain that none of the parties to the case were able to get the case adjourned beyond the fixed time; if they did so they shall be subject to fine. We know that, today, the cases get adjourned frequently on the very grounds which Kautilya sought to deny beyond a certain period of time.

In terms of the settlement of cases relating to causing of hurt or involvement in a quarrel, Kautilya says: 'Sentence of punishment shall be passed the very day that a defendant accused of assault fails to answer the charge made against him'.[63] The court could take up for its consideration, suo moto, if some special category of people was not in a position to approach the court. For example, it is provisioned, in Book III.20.22, that the judges themselves shall look into the affairs of God, *Brahmanas*, ascetics, women, minors, old persons and sick persons, who are helpless, when they do not approach the court, and they shall not dismiss their suits. Kautilya was in favour of expedient trial not only because that would enhance peoples' faith in the efficacy of justice but also because of the efficacy of investigation in the sense that the reliability of the evidence may be adversely affected with every passing day. This is evident from Kautilya's assertion (Book IV, Chapter 8) that interrogation after some days is unreliable, no one shall be arrested on suspicion of having committed theft or burglary if three nights had elapsed since the crime, unless he was caught with the tools of the crime.

3. **Impartiality, neutrality and objectivity in the delivery of justice**
It is fascinating to note the emphasis the *Arthashastra* lays on the importance of impartial and neutral judicial stance if only to win the trust of the people in the judicial integrity and honesty, as well as for the sake of a harmonious, just and rule-based social order. *Danda* is

the expression of law, which is said to have four pillars, that is, sacred law (*dharma*), evidence (*vyavahara*), *charitra* (history or custom) and edicts of kings (*rajasasana*).[64] It is power and power (*danda*) alone, which, only when exercised by the king with impartiality and in proportion to guilt, either over his son or his enemy, maintains both this world and the next, argues Kautilya.[65] Furthermore, the king who administers justice in accordance with sacred law (*dharma*), evidence (*vyavahara*), history (*samstha*) and edicts of kings (*nyaya*), which is the fourth, will be able to conquer the whole world bounded by the four quarters.[66] Inherent in these passages, one can infer, is the element of neutrality and objectivity in the discharge of judicial functions. In order to further eliminate the element of bias from the judicial conduct, Kautilya clarifies:

> whenever, there is disagreement between history (custom/samstha) and sacred law or between evidence and sacred law, then matter shall be settled in accordance with sacred law. But whenever, sacred law (sastra) is in conflict with rational law (dharma nyaya/kings law), then reason shall be held authoritative; for there the original text (on which the sacred law has been based) is not available.

Even though one comes across the situation where hermits, if fined, could be allowed to perform penance, in the name of the king, oblation to god, etc., equivalent to as many nights as the number of *panas* of their fines, they were to undergo punishment in the case of defamation, abduction of women, theft and assault. It means that the form of fines in the case of hermits and heretics could be realized through penance only in some limited cases. The king was authorized, under the penalty of fines, to forbid the wilful or improper proceedings of ascetics—for vice, overwhelming righteousness—will in the long run destroy the ruler himself.[67] He (Kautilya) further emphasizes, 'In this way the judges should look into the affairs, without resorting to deceit, being impartial to all beings, worthy of trust and beloved of the people'.[68] In addition, judicial accountability has been established by laying down punishments for dereliction of duty by the judges. For example, if a judge questions a wrong person or ignores the reply to his question or gives instructions to remind or prompt the person being questioned by him, he was subject to the prescribed punishment.[69] in terms of the responsibility of the king for impartial and quick administration of justice, A. L. Basham remarks:

> ...Impartial administration of justice brought him the same spiritual reward as Vedic sacrifices; Kings failing in their duty suffered in hell. Even delay in justice was visited with dire penalties, for a legendary king called Nrga was reborn as a lizard, because he kept two litigants waiting in a dispute over a cow.... Moreover, the king was believed to incur the demerit of criminals not brought to book, and to suffer in the next life accordingly, while from the secular point of view the king who perverted justice or was negligent in its administration was in danger of losing his throne.[70]

Pointing out the built-in fairness and deterrence in the delivery of justice, as ascertained from the *Arthashastra*, Balbir S. Sihag says:

> Kautily's goal was to attain a crime free society but the removal of thorns was to be achieved only by resorting to legal means. He proposed a legal system, which has built in fairness and crime deterrence. If a crime was not solved, the king had to compensate the victim.... There was a built-in incentive to minimize the costly errors of omission and commission.... Kautilya pointed out that excessive punishment due to anger, greed or ignorance was counterproductive since people lost respect for the law. Kautilya believed that fairness was essential for political stability, which was a pre-requisite for prosperity.[71]

Kautilya believed that judicial fairness and law-based protection of the people would protect this world and the next. (Book III.I)

Justice as Welfare

A just social order presupposes an environment that guarantees security of life not only from violations by the criminals but also in terms of the ability to live life. It is in this context that Kautilya paid special attention to the issue of justice to the weak. At various places, he makes it incumbent upon the state to help the widows, the sick, the aged, the handicapped, etc. So justice in its extended form is also social justice. N. C. Bandyopadhyaya comments[72]:

> It (the kingly government) certainly did not believe in the dogma of equality and as such did not try to sweep away the institutions and traditions of the

past. Yet it followed the principles and maxims of the past too closely to recognise the right of the subject to live and the duty of the state in helping him to live.... The dominance of the ideas of the governmental paternalism is apparent not only from the duties which the Arthashastra writer inculcates but also from the main heads of expenditure. In regard to the former, the theorist repeatedly calls upon the ruler not only to render aid to the various arts and industries, to maintain the widow and the orphan but to treat subjects as if they were the king's children.

A closer view of the theory of justice shows that Kautilya underlines that justice should be in accord with the aims, objectives and social scheme of the state, and that the helpless must be assisted and maintained by the state.[73] Moreover, Kautilya argues that an order issued by anyone shall not be disobeyed if it is for the benefit of all, and if anyone does disobey, he shall be subject to punishment with a fine of 12 *panas*. If there is any united assault on such an ordering person, every assaulter shall be fined double the amount of the fine usually levied for such offences. An interesting thing to be noted is that he prescribes punishment first to the *Brahmin* assaulter, if there was any in that crowd of offenders.[74] This idea of justice of Kautilya also establishes that he was in favour of the rule of law and not of man. In the case of judges themselves taking up the cases of those who do not approach the court, he said:

> The judges shall take charge of the affairs of God, Brahmins, Ascetics, women, minors, old people, the sick and those that are helpless (e.g., orphans), even when they do not approach the court. No suit of theirs shall be dismissed for want of jurisdiction, passage of time or adverse possession.[75]

The Popular Courts

There existed some popular courts to dispense justice in certain disputes in the ancient political literature perhaps until the beginning of the British rule, which later disappeared with the establishment of the royal courts at every level. Earlier, in the ancient period, we find a mention of *puga* court, *shreni* court, etc. These popular courts find a place in the *Arthashastra* and it can be noted that a number of cases/disputes like the settlement of boundaries were decided by the village elders, while the cases related to temples, Brahmanas, ascetics, women, minors, old and invalid persons were also to be decided by the *dharmasthas* (Book III. 20). According to A. S. Altekar:

> It was the considered and long established policy of the governments in ancient India to encourage these popular courts and to enforce their decisions. Though these courts were essentially non-official and popular, they had the royal authority behind them ... The government has been advised to execute their decrees because the state had delegated these powers to them.[76]

ADMINISTRATION OF JUSTICE: ORGANIZATION AND PROCEDURE

Delivery of justice presupposes the machinery responsible for administering it through a process of justice, that is, justice is awarded through a laid-down procedure, leaving no space, to the extent possible, for discretion with or bias of the judges or the investigative organization. In other words, judicial process must follow the procedure established by law. Kautilya's *Arthashastra* simply does that. As the duty of a king, says Kautilya, consists in protecting his subjects with justice; its observance leads him to heaven. He who does not protect his people or upsets the social order wields his royal sceptre (*danda*) in vain.[77]

Organizationally speaking, there was a decentralized system of courts to decide cases beginning from the top to the bottom. At the apex was the *Kantaka-shodhana* court with the king at its head. This court dealt with the following[78]:

1. Regulation of the guilds and laying down their duties and profits in order to check their high-handedness.
2. Regulation of the market and the sale of merchandise, including the regulation of the price, prevention and stopping adulteration of articles of consumption, lowering of the wages of the artisans and producing stocks of goods without license. The *panyadhyaksha* and *samsthadhyaksha* played important roles in this regard.
3. Controlling famines, pestilence, floods and removal of the depredation of wild animals, snakes and pests.

4. Detection of the youth with criminal tendencies or apprehending housebreakers, adulterers, makers of counterfeit coins, having post-mortem examinations in cases of sudden death, application of torture to make suspects confess and thoroughly watch over the criminals.

5. Detection of dishonest officials, clerks and judges and regulation of jails and lock-ups.

6. Assessing and realizing fines in lieu of corporal punishments in offences punishable with death or mutilation.

7. Administration of new laws for punishing persons committing murder, treason, libels, breaking of dams, poisoning, or adultery committed by women.

8. Adjudicating various cases of violence to women, including rape, adultery, unnatural intercourse (*kanyaprakarma*).

9. Trying various other cases, for example, violation of a *Brahmin's* purity, house-breaking (burglary), delinquency on the part of officials, collision or injury to passers-by in streets, incest of the worst description, outrages on nuns, unnatural offences or violations of social order.

The aforementioned functions listed are indicative of the range of king's intervention in the large areas of the social, economic, religious and administrative affairs of the state and its people. It also suggests the close resemblance between the situation prevalent under the British Plantagenets and the laws of treason guarding the position and personal safety of the king. It can be also inferred that the king was the fountainhead of justice, *dharmapravartaka* (Book III, Chapter I). The lower courts' functions were discharged by the village, family and corporations[79] who retained their lower criminal jurisdiction. For example, issues relating to the sale and purchase of buildings and boundary disputes between any two villages were to be investigated by neighbours or elders of five or ten villages; disputes about fields were decided by the elders of the neighbourhood or of the village. If these elders could not come to a decision, the disputants could divide the disputed holding in an equal share. In the event of failure of both these measures, the disputed holding shall be taken into possession by the king. Furthermore, there were the higher courts known as *sangrahana*, *sthaniyas, dronamukhas* and *kharvatika. Sthaniya* was constituted in the centre of 800 villages, a *Dronamukha* in the centre of 400 villages and *kharvatika* in the centre of 200 villages. These courts were to be manned by three *dharmasthas* and three *amatyas*.[80]

Judicial Procedure

Judicial procedure forms an important dimension of dispensation of justice without favour or bias in order to eliminate arbitrariness from the realm of judicial administration. The constitution of independent India makes it mandatory for the law and justice machinery to follow the procedure established by law, while depriving a person of the protection of life and his personal liberty. Echoing something similar to Article 21 of the constitution of India, Kautilya tells us that when the superintendent of jails puts any person in the lock-up without declaring the grounds of provocation, he shall be fined 24 *panas*; when he subjects any person to unjust torture, he shall be fined 48 *panas*; when he transfers a prisoner to another place or deprives a prisoner of food and water, he shall be fined 96 *panas*; when he beat a prisoner to death, he shall be fined with 1,000 *panas*. The judicial process, according to the author (Kautilya) of the text, involves a number of steps, which include filing of the suit, investigation and recording of the statements of both the plaintiff and the respondent; calling for the evidence and the witnesses; judicial conduct; and the types of punishment and the decision based on sentencing policy, or judges' discretion or both. Altekar gives us a summary of the judicial procedure when he writes that, to begin with,

> the plaintiff was first to file the plaint stating precisely his case and claim. The plaintiff was not allowed to vary his pleas. The defendant was then summoned with notice and required to submit his written statement in reply. He could either deny or admit the claim or plead estoppels or *res judicata*. After considering the plaint and the written statement, the judge would call upon the parties to cite evidence which could be oral or documentary. However, more weight was assigned to the written documentary evidence. Possession was also possible to be adduced in proof of a claim.[81]

It is also indicated by Kautilya that the investigation apart from his residence, the caste, the *gotra*, the name and occupation of both the plaintiff and the defendant both of whom had to be fit to sue and defend, having been registered first, must include the statements of both the parties and shall be taken down in such order as is required by the case. These statements shall then be thoroughly scrutinized. Kautilya explains the procedure of investigation much more elaborately in Book III, Chapter 1.[82]

One may infer from the foregoing discussion that the process was almost patterned like the one in place today, implying that the process began with filing a first information report (FIR), followed by an enquiry, which involved preliminary investigation, and then an intensive one for collection of evidence. The investigation was not always carried out in a scientific and lawful manner by not only recording the statement of the accused but also of the witnesses cited by him, as the state machinery responsible for the investigation could also employ methods like third degree in order to fetch confession from the accused. But the investigating authority shall apply any of the four kinds of torture:

> As to persons who have committed grave offences, the form of torture will be nine kinds of blows with a cane; 12 beats, two thighs: two knots; 20 beats with a stick of a tree; 32 beats on each palm of the hands and on each sole of the feet; two bindings, the hands, the legs being joined so as to appear like a scorpion; two kinds of suspensions, face downwards; burning one of the joints of a finger after the accused has been made to drink rice gruel; heating his body for a day after he has been made to drink oil; causing him to lie on coarse green grass for a night in winter.[83]

It can be noted, at the same time, that Kautilya was against the use of torture as a means to collect evidence in the first instance, as he prescribes for forensic examination as well. He maintains that in case of a sudden death, the corpse shall be smeared over with oil and examined; a corpse tainted with mucus and urine, with organs inflated with wind may be regarded as having been killed by suffocation and suppression of breathing; any person with contracted arms and inflated neck may be regarded as having been killed by hanging; a dead person with stiffened rectum and eyes, with tongue bitten between the teeth and with belly swollen may be considered as having been killed by drowning. Any dead person, wetted with blood and with limbs wounded and broken, may be regarded as having been killed with sticks and ropes.[84]

The other dimensions of judicial procedure implicit in Kautilya's analysis are related to the sentencing policy, the concept of perjury, the concept of hostile witnesses, evidence and the forms of punishments. Undoubtedly, those issues were as important then as they are today for dealing with the 21st century problems concerning crime and punishment. Several insights of Kautilya into the comprehensive judicial system include the honesty of the enforcers of law without which administration of justice could hardly be effective, and that punishment should neither be higher nor lower but commensurate with the nature and character of crime, that is, there should be a linear relationship between the level of crime and the level of punishment in order to have effective reduction of crime. Evidence is crucial in the reasoning of Kautilya so as to ensure that no innocent was punished and no error is committed in identifying and punishing the guilty. The enforcers should attempt to get additional evidence if necessary.[85]

There were many forms of punishments: Kautilya prescribes that the quantum of punishment shall increase from the initial to be double or treble for offences committed the first, second and third time by an offender. But the king shall decide any punishment, in his discretion, if the offence is committed for the fourth time. In addition, punishment could be awarded in the form of fines, non-monetary impositions, banishment and mutilation. The social shaming, particularly if the offender was an officer of the state stealing property other than that of the king, was another form of punishment in place of fines, recommended by him. These shaming acts included smearing with cow dung in public, smearing with cow dung and ashes in public, parading with a belt of broken pots and shaving of the head or exile as the amount of theft increased in place of fines— 3 panas, 6 panas, 12 panas and 24 panas, respectively. Kautilya suggested:

> When thieves and robbers are arrested, the chancellor shall parade them before people of the city or the countryside (as the case may be) and proclaim that the criminals were caught under the instructions of the king, an expert in detecting thieves. The people shall be warned to keep under control any relative with criminal tendencies, because all thieves were bound to be caught (like the ones paraded before them). Likewise, the chancellor shall parade before the people forest bandits and criminal tribes caught with stolen goods as proof of the king's omniscience.[86]

CONCLUSION

I have argued in the foregoing pages that Kautilya predated his understanding of the judicial system by giving a detailed analysis of the various aspects of administration of law and justice. Some of the notable features of his advanced and comprehensive judicial system can be recapitulated as under:

1. He gave a clear definition of law and its sources that are the part of our justice system till date, whether it relates to sources, codification, structure and functions of courts with some modifications here and there as required by the circumstances and the needs of the present times.

2. We find a great deal of similarity between the criminal procedure of the past and the present, beginning from the filing of the FIR to the conclusion of the case.

3. Kautilya has referred to some of the modern legal concepts such as the forensic science, perjury, hostile witnesses and the punishment to them, without using them as per title, of course, today (Book III and IV).

4. He was of the firm view that the judges should not only be competent with comprehensive understanding of law, but they should be honest and accountable and impartial as justice could neither be effective nor deterrent in the absence of these judicial qualifications. According to the argument of the author, it follows that an impartial, fair and honest delivery of justice was also necessary to establish and sustain peoples' trust in the efficacy and objectivity of justice.

5. He preferred a determinate sentencing policy to discretion in the hands of the judges, except in the case of some special sections of the society such as the infirm, the helpless, the aged, the cripple, the sick, etc. He perhaps reasoned that determinate sentencing policy is desirable for two reasons: first, there shall be most minimum space for corruption in the delivery of justice, and, second, the plaintiffs and the defendants would know the meaning of their acts in advance. This may have helped in crime reduction much more realistically. Another reason could be not to leave law for different and varying interpretation even when

the case and its details were the same, leading to minimization of legal errors.

6. The judges were subject to punishment had they erred in awarding punishment or in punishing an innocent person.

7. The king was the fountainhead of justice and could be taken as the supreme court of appeal.

8. He gave priority to the monetary punishment to non-monetary one as some of the convicts were allowed in his scheme of justice to pay fines instead of suffering physical punishments. Even a convict was permitted to make good the fine by his labour in case he did not have enough resources to pay.

9. He was of the firm view that justice should not be delayed. Investigation also should be prompt and fast as there was a possibility of loss of credible evidence if immediate steps were not taken without loss of time, in the cases under dispute.

10. He argued in favour of rule of law both in the sense of equality before law and equal protection of law. It is implicit in arguments that no person should be deprived of his life and liberty, except through the procedure established by law. His discussion on the seizure of suspects, detection of the youth with criminal tendencies, etc., is proof to that effect.[87]

11. The Arthashastra, while recognizing the jurisprudential relevance and importance of customs and sacred law like it was given under the Roman law, asserted the supremacy of royal edicts as the ultimate source of law.

12. Kautilya can be credited with developing a comprehensive code of law like the one developed by Justinian code of law.

13. Furthermore, the Kautilyan concept of justice is rooted in the idea of good governance and seeking the happiness of the subject: 'in the happiness of the subjects lie the happiness of the king'.

In the end, it would not be out of place to assert that Kautilya's contribution to the theory of law and justice has been immense and is of lasting value. In the present times, we need to go deeper into his ideas as they can guide us while determining and exploring the new fields of legalism and justice. The concept of justice, as evolved by Kautilya, let us say, may not prove right on the scale of rational arguments always relevant to its present context, yet he remains a legal luminary in the sense that he did not leave any aspect of justice untouched, including ethical, economic, religious and political–practical and addressed them, to my mind, in a coherent and harmonious and systematic manner. He did not leave any issue, including codification of law and crime, conceivable in his times and of cardinal value for the future. If justice is the right thing to do, as Michael Sandal perceives, he outdid the eminent legal theorists by describing justice as an act of righteousness, and if justice consisted of doing one's duty, as envisaged by Plato, Kautilya surpassed him by making it incumbent on the king to uphold the *Varnashrama dharma*, wherein everyone was obliged to perform one's duty according to his defined role in the system, that is, as per the division of work. Yes, one can argue that it was difficult to define the righteous in the absence of identifiable standard measures of the right with certainty. But it is not so in the case of Kautilya as he derived his concept of the righteous from the precepts of the *Dharmashastra* and *Dharma Sutras*. Further, justice has been visualized by Kautilya, as done by Buddha, as a system of fair reward and proper punishment, signalling the idea of righteousness. It is interesting to note that Kautilyan idea of justice seeks to determine relationships of law and society in the context of uncertainty, conflict and chaos, on the one hand, and stability and progress of society and the state, on the other. He connects his concept of justice and law with the normative concepts–virtue, heaven, sin, evil and the other world in the same way as one sees them in the works of Manu. At the same time, it is prudent to mention that Kautilya was really a modernist legal philosopher and theorist who needs to be brought out of the area of neglect and indifference where the practitioners of law and academic researchers abandoned him.

NOTES

1. Rangarajan, *Kautilya*, 119.
2. Rao, *Studies in Kautilya*, 81.
3. Rao, *Studies in Kautilya*, 109.
4. Rao, *Studies in Kautilya*, 111.
5. Kangle, *Kautilya Arthashastra*, Pt II, 195.
6. '[I]f the judge threatens, upbraids, drives away or browbeats a litigant, he shall impose the lowest fine for violence on him, double that in case of verbal injury. If he does not

question one who ought to be questioned, questions one who ought not to be questioned or after questioning dismisses (the statement), or instructs, reminds or prompts him, he shall impose the middle fine for violence on him. If he does nor ask for the evidence which ought to be submitted, asks for evidence that ought not to be submitted, proceeds with the case without evidence, dismisses it under a pretext, carries away one tired with delay, throws out of context a statement which is In proper order, gives to witnesses help in their statements or takes up one again a case which is completed and in which judgement is pronounced, he shall impose the highest fine for violence on him. In case the offence is repeated, double the fine and removal from office shall be the punishment' (*Arthashastra*, Book IV.9.13–16; Kangle, *Kautilya Arthashastra*, Pt II, 279).

7. Jois, *Seeds of Modern Public Law*, 102.
8. *Dharmashastras* were the verse form of the prose *sutras* and were the instructions in the sacred law. See Basham, *The Wonder That Was India*, 113.
9. Saletore, *Ancient Indian Political Thought*, 12.
10. Radhakrishanana, *The Heart of Hindustan*.
11. *Arthashastra*, Book III.1.43–45.
12. Kangle, *Kautilya Arthashastra*, Pt III, 223.
13. Kangle, *Kautilya Arthashastra*, 222.
14. Chaudhary, *Kautilya Arthashastra*, 33, cited in Singh, 'Kautilya's Conception', 47.
15. Basham, *The Wonder That Was India*, 114.
16. Lingat, *The Classical Law of India*, 177, 195.
17. Saletore, *Ancient Indian Political Thought*, 22.
18. Macdonell, *A History of Sanskrit*.
19. *Arthashastra*, Book III.7.165: Shamasastry, *Kautilya's Arthashastra*, 188.
20. *Arthashastra*, Book XIII, Chapter 5.
21. Altekar, *State and Government*, 261.
22. Ghosh, *The Politics of Personal Law*, 144–150.
23. Nilakanta Sastri, *Age of the Nandas and Mauryas*, 175.
24. Kangle, *Kautilya Arthashastra*, 223.
25. Kangle, *Kautilya Arthashastra*, Pt II, 195.
26. See Shamasastry, *Kautilya's Arthashastra*, 71.
27. Shamasastry, *Kautilya's Arthashastra*, 71–72.
28. Shamasastry, *Kautilya's Arthashastra*, 115.
29. Rao, *Studies in Kautilya*, 82, 91.
30. Chaudhary, *Kautilya Arthashastra*, 32, quoted in Singh, 'Kautily's Conception', 47.
31. Rao, *Studies in Kautilya*, 82.
32. Altekar, *State and Government*, 158.
33. A reference can be made, in this context, to the ordinance making power of the president of India and that of the governor of a state. These ordinances have the force of law for a limited period, that is, till they are replaced by a parliamentary law or allowed to expire if not approved as law by the concerned legislature.
34. Bandyopadhaya, *Development of Hindu*, Pt II, 76.
35. Bergel, 'Principal Features'.

36. Shamashastry, *Kautilya's Arthashastra*, 167–168.
37. Shamashastry, *Kautilya's Arthashastra*, 168.
38. Kangle, *Kautilya Arthashastra*, Pt II, 191.
39. Kangle, *Kautilya Arthashastra*, Pt III, 225–229.
40. Shamashastry, *Kautilya's Arthashastra*, 182.
41. *Kautilya's Arthashastra*, Book III.11.23–24.
42. *Arthashastra*, Book IV.11.229.
43. *Arthashastra*, Book II.36.41.
44. *Arthashastra*, Book III.20.16; Kangle, *Kautilya Arthashastra*, Pt II, 252.
45. For further details on the matters of violence against women, illicit relations, etc., see Kangle, *Kautilya Arthashastra*, Pt II, 285–287; *Arthashastra*, Book IV, Chapter 12.
46. *Arthashastra*, Book IV.9.226; Shamashastry, *Kautilya's Arthashastra*, 253.
47. For detailed description of the forms of marriage refer to *Arthashastra*, Book III.2–9. The last two forms, *Rakshasa* and *Paisaca*, have been defined by Kautilya as a forcible seizure of a maiden and seizure of a sleeping or intoxicated maiden respectively.
48. Shamashastry, *Kautilya's Arthashastra*, 176f.
49. Shamashastry, *Kautilya's Arthashastra*, 173.
50. Shamashastry, *Kautilya's Arthashastra*, 174.
51. Shamashastry, *Kautilya's Arthashastra*, 180–181.
52. Kangle, *The Kautilya Arthashastra*, Pt III, 230.
53. *Kautilya's Sutra*, 39, 47, 62.
54. *Arthashastra*, Book I.4 and 5.
55. Altekar, *State and Government*, 245.
56. Altekar, *State and Government*, 246.
57. Kangle, *Kautilya Arthashastra*, Pt II, 283.
58. When all laws are perishing, the king here is the promulgator of laws, by virtue of his guarding the right conduct of the world consisting of the four *varnas* and the four *ashramas* (*Arthashastra*, Book III.1.38) as the king is seen as *dharmapravartaka*.
59. Kangle, *Kautilya Arthashastra*, Pt II, 250; *Arthashastra*, Book III, Chapter 20, Section 74.5.
60. Bandyopadhyaya, *Hindu Polity*, Pt 2, 47.
61. *Arthashastra*, Book IV.13.236–237; Shamasastry, *Kautilya's Arthashastra*, 264–265.
62. *Arthashastra*, Book III.1.149, Shamasastry, *Kautilya's Arthashastra*, 170.
63. *Arthashastra*, Book III.19.196; see Shamasastry, *Kautilya's Arthashastra*, 221; III.19.22; in Kangle, *Kautilya Arthashastra*, Pt II, 249.
64. Shamasastry, *Kautilya's Arthashastra*, 170.
65. *Arthashastra*, Book III.I.150.
66. *Arthashastra*, Book III.i.150, Shamasastry, *Kautilya's Arthashastra*, 171.
67. *Arthashastra*, Book III.16.191; see Shamashastry, *Kautilya's Arthashastra*, 216.
68. *Arthashastra*, Book III.20.24; Kangle, *Kautilya Arthashastra*, Pt II, 253.
69. Kangle, *Kautilya Arthashastra*, Pt III, 221.
70. Basham, *The Wonder That Was India*, 115.
71. Sihag, 'Kautliya on Administration'.
72. Bandyopadhyaya, *Hindu Polity*, Pt 2, 41.

73. The king shall provide the orphans, the aged, the infirm, the afflicted and the helpless with maintenance apart from providing subsistence to pregnant women and to children they give birth to. When a capable person other than an apostate (patita) or mother neglects to maintain his or her child, wife, mother, father, minor brothers, sisters or widowed girls, he or she shall be punished with a fine of 12 *panas* (*Arthashastra*, Book II, Chapter 1, 48).

74. *Arthashastra*, Book III.10.173; Shamasastry, *Kautilya's Arthashastra*, 197.

75. *Arthashastra*, Book III, Chapter 2; cf. Sihag, *Kautliya*, 23.

76. Altekar, *State and Government*, 25.

77. Shamasastry, *Kautilya's Arthashastra*, 171.

78. Bandyopadhyaya, *Development of Hindu Polity*, pp. 34–35.

79. As regards the villages, it is mentioned that villages shall be formed consisting each of not less than a 100 families and of not more than 500 families of agricultural families of *Sudra* caste, with boundaries extending as far as a *krosa* (2,250 yards) or two, and capable of protecting each other. See Shamasastry, *Kautilya's Arthashastra*,. 45; *Arthashastra*, Book II, Chapter 1.

80. In the cities of *sangrahana*, *dronamukha* and *sthaniya* and at places where districts meet, three members acquainted with sacred law (*dharmasthas*) and three ministers of the king (*amatyas*) shall carry on the administration of justice (Book III.1).

81. Altekar, *State and Government*, 257.

82. Shamasastry, *Kautilya's Arthashastra*, 168–169. And for detection and seizure of criminals see Shamasastry, pp. 239–245.

83. Shamasastry, *Kautilya's Arthashastra*, 249.

84. Kautilya further furnishes a long list of crimes and suspects who needed to be examined (Book IV, Chapter 6).

85. Sihag, *Kautliya*, 2.

86. Sihag, *Kautliya*, 22.

87. See *Arthashastra*, Book IV, Chapters VI and VII.

Mandala/ Rajamandala Theory and the Theory of Interstate Relations

Kautilya is remembered the most by political scientists, foreign policy experts and students of strategic culture and defence and security experts for his contribution to the theory of interstate relations and conceiving the idea of *mandala* just as Sun Tzu is referred to and remembered in China. Kautilya was the first political scientist of ancient India who argued the importance of sovereignty, both internal and external, because it is sovereignty, which defines, among others, the state.[1] No *rashtra* can make a progress until it is free to pursue its policies independent of others.[2]

Shukracharya's idea of self-rule as the greatest source of happiness and the dependence on others as the ground of great misery also points in the same direction.[3] Elaborating the state of subjugation of a country by another, Kautilya said: 'Under it, the country is not treated as one's own land, it is impoverished, its wealth carried off, or it is treated as a "commercial" article'.[4] Sovereignty has been discussed by Kautilya in his *saptanga* theory of state. The *mandala* theory too is influenced by the concerns of external sovereignty without which the internal freedom to frame policies and take decisions would be unimaginable. This was the reason why Kautilya underlines the duty of the king to preserve the state and uphold its paramountcy, a prescription in the theory of political realism in the theory of international relations.

This chapter critically examines Kautilyan strategic thought and interstate relations, first, in relation to his concept of *mandala* with reference to its contents, constituents, validity and efficacy as a theory of peace and war; second, it proposes to analyse Kautilya's approach to diplomacy with reference to his *shadgunya* theory (six ways of diplomacy and foreign relations) and the strategy of four *upayas* and their importance in the conduct of interstate relations; third, it aims at knowing and ascertaining its applicability in the modern world of politics with reference to prevailing global politics and political relations (multi-polar and multilateral) with the help of some examples from Asia, South Asia and Southeast Asia specifically and from the Western world in general within the context of power politics, aiming at not only to preserve and enhance national interest but also to establish and promote balance of power in the field of international relations through the techniques of diplomacy and war; fourth, it shall reflect upon the admissibility of the view that *Mandala* theory was basically an expansionist philosophy consisting of a ceaseless effort to acquire and preserve earth and conquer other territories and how Kautilya strived to strike an equilibrium between expansion and consolidation; and finally, the research dwells upon realist–idealist debate in IR in relation to Kautilya.

The subject has received exhaustive treatment in the *Arthashastra*, Book VI as well as in other classics.[5] That the *Arthashastra* is,

> primarily a treatise on the governance of a state dealing comprehensively with internal administration and foreign relations and provides the ruler an education in the ways of attaining the overriding goal of expansion of his kingdom is stated quite often. It is not only wide ranging, it is detailed in its practical guidance, yet not so binding as to instil rigidity in the face of changing conditions.[6]

Many questions arise in the mind of the reader about *mandala* philosophy of Kautilya. For example, can it be interpreted as a dynamic philosophy of asserting and maintaining equilibrium in international politics or was it a theory to explain dominance, self-assertion and a struggle for existence/survival at the level of running power games in the international arena? Answers to these questions are sought in the following pages.

MANDALA/RAJAMANDALA: THEORETICAL/DOCTRINAL DIMENSION AND STRATEGIC EXPLANATION

In the first place, the *Mandala* doctrine is based on the principle of winning and expanding the territories of the kingdom.[7] Kautilya[8] asserts that 'peace and activity constitute the source of acquisition and security when activity is that which brings the accomplishment of works undertaken and peace refers to that which brings about security of enjoyment of the fruits of works'. Does this mean that Kautilya is a 'militarist' and 'imperialist'? No, this characterization of Kautilya is not tenable; first, because he does not propagate expansion beyond the Indian subcontinent; political unification or hegemonic control of the Indian subcontinent is the strategic aim. He might have voted for territorial expansion, but he underlined the preference for diplomacy and covert actions as a means to that end. Second, he treated military matters more from the theoretical and strategic perspective than as a battle-hardened military practitioner. Third, Kautilya's field was grand strategy, not military strategy and tactics—in that regard, he seems to be more like Machiavelli and different from Sun Tzu and Clausewitz. If there is equal advancement in peace and war, says Kautilya, he should resort to peace, for in war, there are losses, expenses, marches away from home and hindrances.[9]

Buttressing this view, Pt Nehru in his *Discovery of India* remarks that

> war was not an end in itself for Kautilya who advocated consistent power politics, in order to secure and expand the power of the state internally and externally, and in that he knew no scruples, yet he was wise enough to know that this very purpose would be defeated by means unsuited to the end.[10]

In fact, Kautilya did not prefer war as the first choice and being engaged in the act for the sake of expansion of territory in perpetuity.

It should be noted that the *Mandala* theory of *Kautilya* was the product of (a) the existence of several states competing for supremacy or survival or what can be termed as the state of anarchy and (b) the need for establishing political unification, to the extent possible, of territories. Elaborating the point, Sachin More says that the *Arthashastra*

propounded the theory of foreign policy called the Raja (king's)—
mandala (circle), more frequently called the circle of 12 states or the
mandala within the perspective of the concepts of the constituents
of a state, the state's aspirations of growth and the turbulent power
struggle between the states.[11]

Kautilya developed his ideas about *mandala* with reference to relative power, that is, the power, influence and capability of a state in
relation to other states, and emphasized upon cumulative power of
seven *prakritis*, which provides *utsah shakti* (power to provide drive,
energy and direction to the state and its elements and mainly relates
to the ruler or the king; in modern day, it can be equated to the leadership of a state); *prabhavashakti*, concerned with generating effects
and related with the military and economic power and strength; and
mantrashakti, the power of the counsel and intelligence and knowledge.[12] However, *mantrashakti* is considered as the most significant by
Kautilya as 'an arrow discharged by an archer may kill one person or
may not kill, but intellect operated by a wise man would kill even a
child in the womb'[13] even though he believed that the application of
all the three together in a varying manner produces the comprehensive national power. Equipped with the cumulative power generated
by the seven *prakritis*, the state is positioned by Kautilya in the midst
of its neighbouring states to make choices for foreign policies, which
should be rationally formed. This dynamic relationship between *shakti*
or power and progress when extended to neighbouring states with the
application of right foreign policy is called *mandala* or *rajamandala* or
theory of circle of states.[14]

Mandala, a Sanskrit word, literally means a circle according to
which[15] every state has circles of states around it, beginning with the
immediate neighbour in the front and the rear, neighbour of the neighbour, neighbour of the neighbour of the neighbour and the state at
the outer circle. Kautilya puts the neighbour in the probable category
of enemy and the next to the neighbour in the category of an ally or
a friend or enemy of the enemy. Explaining the circle of kings, he
writes: the king endowed with personal excellences and those of his
material constituents, the seat of good policy, is 'would be conqueror'
(*vijigisu*).[16] Encircling him on all sides, with territory immediately next

to his is the constituent called the enemy. In the same manner, one with territory separated by another territory is the constituent called the ally. Talking about the different types of enemies, he elaborates: 'A neighbouring prince possessed of the excellences of an enemy is the foe; one in calamity is vulnerable; one (reference) without support or with a weak support is fit to be exterminated; in the reverse case, fit to be harassed or weekend'. Arndt Michael explains that the theory of *mandala* is based on the geopolitical assumption that the *vijigisu* (the potential conqueror state) is located at the centre of the *rajamandala*; its immediate neighbour is most probably an *ari* (enemy); the state next to the immediate neighbour is the enemy of this neighbour and likely to be *vijigisu's mitra* (friend). Behind this friendly or *mitra* state is located another unfriendly state (*ari-mitra*) and next to that is a friendly state (*mitra-mitra*).[17]

The concept of *mandala*/circle is made quite clear in Chapter 2.18 of Book VI, which tells us that, 'beyond him (the king), the ally, the enemy's ally, the ally's ally, and the enemy's ally's ally are situated in front in accordance with the proximity of the territories; behind, the enemy in the rear, the rear enemy's ally and the near ally's ally (one behind the other)'. In this scheme of Kautilya, one with an immediate proximate territory is the natural enemy; one of equal birth is the enemy by birth and the one opposed or in opposition is the enemy made (for the time being), followed by one with his territory separated by one other territory shall be the natural ally. These natural allies are further classified as an ally by birth (one related through the mother or father) and an ally made for the time being (one who has sought shelter for wealth or life). The total number of kings, thus, comes to 12. Kangle explains this complex puzzle in the following way[18]:

> There are twelve kings: *vijigisu*, the would be conqueror; *ari*, the enemy, whose territory is contiguous to that of the *vijigisu*; *mitra*, the *vijigisu's* ally, with territory immediately beyond that of the *ari*; *ari-mitra*, the enemy's ally, with territory beyond that of the *mitra*; *mitramitra*, the ally of the *vijigisu's* ally, with territory beyond that of the *arimitra*; *arimitramitra*, the ally of the enemy's ally, beyond the *mitramitra*; *parsnigrah*, the enemy in the rear of the *vijigisu*; *Akranda*, the *vijigisu's* ally in the rear, with territory behind that of the *parsnigrah*; *parsnigrahasara*, the ally of the *parsnigraha*, behind the *akranda*; *akrandasara*, the ally of the *akranda*, behind the

parsnigrahasara; madhyama, the middle king adjoining those of the *vijigisu* and the *ari* and stronger than either of these and *udasina,* the king lying outside or the indifferent or neutral king, more powerful than the *vijigisu,* the *ari* and the *madhyama.*

Furthermore, he suggests that one with territory immediately proximate to those of the enemy and the conqueror, capable of helping them when they are united or disunited and of suppressing them when they are disunited, is the middle king (*madhyama*). Similarly, there are neutral kings who are outside the sphere of the enemy, the conqueror and the middle king; stronger than (their) constituents; and capable of helping the enemy, the conqueror and the middle king when they are united or disunited and of suppressing them when they are disunited.[19]

In other words, as Kangle presents:

there are four principal states, those of the *vijigisu,* the *ari,* the *Madhyama* and *udasina* (indifferent). Each of these has a *mitra,* (ally) and a *mitramitra,* (ally's ally) thus making a total of twelve kings. However one should not form an impression that a *mandala* necessarily needed the existence of twelve states, rather this narrative only tries to tell us the probability of relationships that might occur when the *vijigisu* tries to attempt his supremacy to be established over the neighbouring states. In this view, each of the four kings with his two allies constitutes a subsidiary mandala or circle, of which there are four in all (Book VI.II.24-27).[20]

A third view of the text states that there were 48 states, 12 of each of the 4—*vijigisu, ari, madhyama* and *udasina.*[21] One may also say that

Mandal/Rajamandala theory of inter-state relations is a presentation in a systematic manner of how the states in a condition of constant conflict of interests could behave and how to tackle them. Clarifying further the concept of *manadala,* Marko Juutinen, remarks that the central nodes in Kautilya's *manadala* system, the four circles of kings are four types of kings: conqueror, conqueror's enemy, middle power and neutral power. Of the four nodes, the most powerful state is the *Udasin* one, the so-called neutral king, who has the material capabilities to resist and even to subjugate each of the minor kings individually, but is situated their territories and regards the lesser states with indifference because, for Kautilya, enmity depends primarily on territorial proximity. The middle king, *Madhyama* state, is the second strongest state, but it also shares territory with minor powers. Conqueror and its enemy are the lesser states that also share the common border.[22]

In a way, Kautilya situates interstate relations in the context of conflict of interests within a framework of friend–foe circles with his concentric, geopolitical *rajamandala* scheme. The concrete circumstances and correlations of power may determine the way friends and enemies, the neutrals and bystanders are to be dealt with. The status of the actors is constantly in flux: friends become enemies and vice versa, while neutrals and outsiders become friends or foes and vice versa.[23] This view maybe supported with the example of new alignment of nations in the post-Taliban Afghanistan situation and from the scene emerging in the Southeast Asian region, where AUKUS (Australia, the UK and the United States), Quad 1 and Quad 2 are formed and a new friendship between China and Russia has developed to contain America.

It is interesting to see that Kautilya's ideas on *rajamandala* are an exercise in the science of warfare and peace with special reference to interstate relations. He anticipated the views of Machiavelli, where he advised his prince to never ignore the matters of warfare and suggested that the king should deal with military affairs personally.[24] At the same time, Kautilya seemed to be conscious of fair play in the conduct of war. For example, he advised the king not to attack those who had fallen down (*patita*); those turning their back in a fight; the *abhipannas* (surrendered persons); *muktakesa* (people with untied hair); *muktasastra* (those who have abandoned their weapons); *bhayavirupa* (persons whose appearance has changed through fear); and *ayudhyamana* (those not taking part in the fight).[25]

Coming back to the *Mandala* theory, it is seen as one assuming every neighbouring country an enemy and the enemy's enemy a friend and, wherein the *Matsyanyaya* and *Mandala* theory are seen the twin evils.[26] It is also viewed as essentially a doctrine of strife and struggle and a source of war when seen from the position of a *vijigisu*.[27] The aforementioned interpretation of Kautilyan perspectives on the theory of *mandala* is only a half-truth as it does not take a comprehensively correct view of what Kautilya really implies in the theory. R. P. Kangle points out, based on his interpretation of Book 7, Chapter 18, Sutra 29, 'That the neighbouring princes, *samantas*, may normally be supposed to be hostile. But it is possible that some may have a friendly feeling towards the *vijigisu*, while others may even be subservient to him. Neighbouring states, thus, fall in three categories—*aribhavin*, *mitrabhavin* and *bhrytyabhavin*—meaning hostile feelings/approach, friendly disposition and brotherly attitude, respectively towards the conqueror'.[28] George Tanhum finds in the *Mandala* theory a nation's contiguous neighbours as always enemies and their outer neighbours as friends in a series of circles.[29] However, it is necessary to state that Kautilya has nowhere indicated what Tanhum has said about his theory. It is in fact a narrow and perhaps wrong interpretation of the *Arthashastra*.[30] Yashwant Sinha, former External Affairs Minister, once said: 'Just as Kautilya talked of the circle of states, a useful conceptual framework for the consideration of India's foreign policy would be to view it as consisting of three concentric circles around a central axis—the first of our immediate region, the second of the larger world and the third of overarching global issues'.[31] Simply put, *mandala* is, indicative of complicated interstate inter-linkages contingent upon varying degrees of amity and animosity, where each state is a *mandala* by itself; the *mandala* then as a microcosm reflects the range of allies and adversaries of a state, whereas *mandala* as an international structure is the macrocosmic aggregation of these unit-level *mandalas*.[32]

The concept of *mandala* can be better grasped by extending its interpretation into seven elements of Kautilya's foreign policy perspectives as has been done by a number of scholars such as Benoy Sarkar,[33] Modelski,[34] Roger Boesche,[35] Zaman,[36] P. K. Gautam,[37] Subrat Mitra and Michael Liebig[38] whose studies of Kautilyan foreign policy framework bring the reader closer to the understanding of the local and transnational influences over the determination of approaches to the pursuit of power in order to bring about balance of power and seek welfare and happiness of the subjects of the country(ies). Marko Juutinen mentions, apart from the elements of the state, three ways of conquest or *vijaya*—*dharmavijaya* (righteous conquest), *lobhavijaya* (conquest for some greed) and *asuravijaya* (demonical)—and three ways of war (*prakashyuddha* or open fight at a time and place indicated;

kutayuddha or concealed warfare, involving use of tactics in the battlefield; and *tusnimyuddha* or silent fighting, implying the use of secret agents for enticing enemy officers or killing them.[39] This classification of conquest and war clearly explains the philosophy and ethics behind them. The *dharmavijaya* envisages a war for the right goal, irrespective of its consequences if the intention is right. A righteous conquest (*dharmavijaya*) aims at the welfare of both the *vijigisu* and the country conquered.[40] In a righteous conquest, the *vijigisu* is not interested in taking over the territory as such; a *dharmavijaya* is a just conqueror who is satisfied with mere obeisance.[41]

For example, the Mahabharata and Rama–Ravana *yuddhas* can be cited as the ones fought for *dharmavijaya*, not for greed or *asuravijaya* by Pandavas and Rama, respectively. For Kauravas, on the other hand, the Mahabharata war was fought for greed.[42] One can go further to treat the First and Second World Wars fought for the sake of *dharma/* ideal as the alliances were engaged in war for defending or establishing democracy and not for extending the territories, necessarily. Many scholars perceived it as war for a just cause, against injustice and tyranny.[43] In this sense, it can be added that power and legitimacy are contingent on righteousness, and that alone can produce stability. Ultimately, Kautilya is pleading for a collective mindset, based on *dharma*. Another tradition of thought on war is pointed out by Torkel Brekke in the form of consequentialist tradition followed by Kautilya, which asserts that acts are good or bad only with respect to their results.[44] Differentiating between the two traditions of warfare, Brekke argues that the *dharmic* or *deontolgical* tradition sees *dharma* as the fundamental part of human existence, whereas the other sees *artha* as the goal of all activity. One sees the war as an end, and the other sees war as a means.[45] So the philosophy and ethics of war are linked with the idea of fairness and use or no use of violence and coercion.

It is fascinating to note the similarity between the Kautilyan idea of wars and the categorization of the war in the modern IR theories. The modern warfare, for instance, takes due cognizance of the use of intellect or the *kuta*—a concept used by Kautilya in his *kutayuddha*. Further, in modern times too, the countries in hostile relationship do not resort to open/direct war (termed *prakashyuddha* by Kautilya) as a first resort but take recourse to many other manoeuvres like the *kutayuddha*, aiming at defeating the militarily powerful enemy. The modern theory of warfare uses several terms for *kutayuddha*, such as 'indirect approach', manoeuvre warfare, asymmetric warfare and guerrilla warfare.

Similarly, Kautilya's *tusnimyuddha*, which can be considered as his distinctive contribution to the ideology of warfare, is interpreted as 'silent war' and occupies a significant theoretical place in the modern political discourse. Roger Boesch points out in his book[46] the theoretical recognition of the concept of *tusnimyuddha* and says: 'Interestingly, *tusnimyuddha* is finding theoretical acknowledgement in the contemporary world due to the experiences of the real world in what saboteurs do, what intelligence operatives do and what is contained in wars like Pakistan's proxy war against India'.[47] The examples of cyberwars, misinformation and propaganda war and the use of deception and secret intelligence agencies (spies, etc.) can be easily counted as a part of *tusnim* or silent war. Gautam, therefore, rightly calls Kautilya as the father of 'information warfare'.[48] Kautilya's emphasis on evolving and using an effective system of intelligence as an element of *tusnimyuddha* leads Liebig to accept Kautilya's *Arthashastra* as the text of pioneering value on intelligence and further elaborates that the ideas underlying modern intelligence are very much present in the *Arthashastra* as Kautilya provides key methodologies and theoretical concepts for intelligence analysis, assessment, estimates and strategic planning. Kautilya's work and Sherman Kent's work bear 'structural homology', though the latter is regarded as the father of modern intelligence.[49]

The Kautilyan scheme of foreign relations visualizes that the first and the foremost responsibility of the ruler is to defend the boundaries of his state and expand his influence, power and territory. Therefore, the *vijigisu* must proceed with the issues of conduct of interstate relations with these clear aims in mind. This is at the core of Kautilya's philosophy of *mandala*. The conduct of foreign relations in the Kautilyan concept of power/*mandala* centres around the 'would-be conqueror' (*Vijigisu*) who uses sixfold policy (*shadgunya*) to assume the position of a universal ruler (*chakravartin*).[50] Kautilyan logic of war and interstate relations are elaborated crisply by P. K. Gautam in the form of an acronym or code UPSRVY with numbers 4-7-6-12-3-3 in which U refers to four *upayas* (4); P stands for seven *prakritis* (7); S for *shadgunya* or six measures of foreign policy (6); R for *rajamandala* (12); V for *vijaya* or conquest (3) and Y for *yuddha* or war (3).[51] Before dealing with the elements of the acronym provided by Gautam in further details, it is prudent to point out that Kautilya developed his theory of *mandala* within the intellectual background of the origin of the state and its attendant social contract theory. It has been discussed elsewhere that Kautilya subscribes to the political argument underlining that the state came into existence to establish order, peace and prosperity in the face of *Matsyanyaya*. As there was a need for some authority to achieve this goal of saving the weak from the excesses of the strong, so was the imperative in the arena of world politics to remove the environment of *Matsyanyaya*, wherein a powerful state was expected to bring order between the states engaged in hostility by establishing authoritative influence and in some cases, even annexation of territories as well. The application of the social contract theory in the interstate relations also calls for the formation of alliances based on the concentric circles to restrain or support the powerful king. As in a state, there was an established authority—the king—to safeguard the interests of society and follow the principle of ensuring happiness and welfare of the people of the kingdom, so was it necessary to establish the supremacy of the *vijigisu* among the other states through power and righteous policies to protect even the conquered population, besides one's own.

The role of the constituent elements of the state (seven *prakritis*) is difficult to ignore as their mutual interaction, or the lack of it, could secure or lose the chance to win any war. For example, Great Britain could secure victory and shatter the myth of invincibility of the German Luftwaffe because of the strong political leadership of Winston Churchill with a skilled council of ministers, unwavering support of the population, tapping into commercial civilian resources cultivated from decades of government policy supports, backed by an elaborate air defence infrastructure, prosecuted by valiant military operations and supplemented with extraordinary intelligence and spy networks.[52]

The example is indicative of Kautilyan emphasis that any king interested in promoting his state's interests vis-à-vis other states is to assess as to how closely are the constituents linked to the ideal and can be compared to the contemporary concept of national power. Liebig clarifies that 'state's seven factors are homologous with Morgenthau's concept of national power whose components are the geographical setting, population size, raw materials, agriculture, industrial potential and the armed forces of a state'.[53] However, the role of an international organization cannot be set aside as it alone can keep the potentially unstable quest for national power in check. In other words, *Mandala* theory is necessary but not sufficient to generate a global equilibrium.[54]

Does *mandala* visualize a fixed circle of states treating neighbours as always enemies and their enemy's friends? In other words, is the *vijigisu* in a perpetual state of enmity with his neighbours? The answer in the affirmative would suggest ignoring the strategic dimension of Kautilyan *mandala* scheme. This misconceived idea of *mandala* focuses more on the physical arrangement of the states in circles and overlooks completely the background content of Kautilya's theories: first, the intrinsic value of *yogakshema*; the emphasis on the organic structure of a state; interrelated *prakritis* with their strive for the defined excellences; the emphasis on economic prosperity; and all-pervading binding of Kautilyan ethics—the *dharma*. Second, it misses the Kautilyan methodology for preselected choice of foreign policies rationally derived on the basis of Kautilyan calculations. Third, it further misses the primacy of *mantrashakti* and, fourth, but most strikingly, the place of *mitra*—the ally—as an inherent element of the state.[55]

In recent times, the concept of *mandala* is assuming newer versions in the context of the emergence of new realities in the arena of world politics, particularly after the breakdown of the former Soviet Union–led block and the closure of the Cold War and the new *mandala* formations within the shifting poles of power from the unipolar to multi-polar ones. Is security and power struggle between the nations around the world moving around the Kautilyan model of *mandala*? Do the new realities fit into the strategic prescriptions of Kautilya? Several regional formations and the position of a state or states within them can be used as a means to address these questions.

The constituents of a regional *mandala* can be both *ari* and *mitra* at the same time. The BRICS (Brazil, Russia, India, China and South Africa) can be a case in point when China and India are members of that formation with differing economic and political goals and both being in race for attaining the status of superpower in the region. They are tied in the relationship of both conflict and cooperation—conflict locally and cooperation regionally. So Kautilya is proved right that the interstate relations are determined by national interests and the play of power games. Interestingly, it is noteworthy that maritime *mandalas* are taking shape in the light of the struggle for marine sovereignty between China and other nations, including her neighbours like Vietnam. Involvement and growing interests of America and India in that struggle again indicates that the circle of states is what is to be managed and established properly if the conqueror is to succeed in his campaign(s), referred as strategic transactions in Southeast Asia.[56] We come across three maritime *mandalas* of India: immediate *mandala* consisting of China and Pakistan; intermediate *mandala* made of East Africa, the Persian Gulf, Central Asia and Southeast Asia; and the outer *mandala* comprising Japan, Russia and the United States. This new interpretation or extension of *mandala* still is not free from debate; the reflection of Kautilyan thought, says Gautam, in strategic discourse cannot be ignored.[57] Situating Pakistan in the position of *vijigisu*, Sachin More explains how Pakistan's emphasis on the wrong *shadgunya* policy of *vigraha and dvaidhibhava* towards India along with the increase in military strength, resulted in predictable decline, as calculable by Kautilyan methodology. Despite the seeming achievement of its geostrategic goal decided by it for itself, while making a wrong choice of outward policy—of parity with India—what ensued has been the deterioration of the state's *prakritis* of Pakistan internally.[58]

THE CONCEPT OF SHADGUNYA

Kautilya's theory of *shadgunya*, the six measures of foreign policy and the defining reference of the theory of *mandala/rajamandala*, is of foundational value[59] when seen in the context of the prevailing situation(s) or in the light of the fluctuating nature of power equation: foes become allies, allies become foes; middle/neutral kings may disappear or diffuse to take new forms; and fluidity rules dynamism. To exploit this fluidity, Kautilya introduces *shadgunya*.[60] Kautilya maintains, he who sees the six measures of policy as interdependent in this manner[61] plays, as he pleases, with the rival kings tied by the chains of his intellect.[62] However, Kautilya believed that the circle of constituent elements is the basis of the six measures of foreign policy,[63] that is, *sandhi, vigraha, asana, yana, samsraya* and *dvaidhibhava*, which, respectively, mean making a treaty based on conditions, that is, the peace policy; the policy of war or hostility; the policy of keeping quiet; marching on an expedition; seeking protection or shelter with another king or in a fort; and following double policy of making peace with one king and *vigraha* or hostility with another simultaneously.[64] Gautam and Liebig find a close relationship between *Mandala* theory and *Shadgunya* theory evolved by Kautilya.[65] There is a bit of difference of opinion on the interpretation of *sandhi* among the students of the *Arthashastra*. For example, Mark McClish opines that *sandhi* is something beyond a mere peacemaking. It essentially signifies non-aggression pacts and strategic partnerships. According to Rangarajan, Kautilya's policy of *sandhi* or peace is an enabling period for the *vijigisu* to build his power before attempting to conquer the enemy and that it aims at the progress of the *vijigisu's* state through strengthening alliances, awaiting favourable opportunity to conquer the enemy, or using dual policy.[66] Referring to strategic partnerships, Kautilya writes in Book VII.4.19 about the alliances, incorporating alongside the power of morality. Out of various kinds of alliance-making, Kautilya gave preference to alliances based exclusively on word/honour.[67] Here, it may be commented that the element of morality in the process of alliance-building takes Kautilya to the mixed idealist plane from the position of a mere realist.

Kautilya, like a realist, recommends that a *vijigisu* should use *shadgunya* according to the existing situations, indicating pragmatic approach to international relations. For example, when one is weaker than the enemy, the principle of *sandhi* should be adopted, while in the reverse situation, one should follow the policy of *vigraha* or war; one should remain in the state of *asana*, in the case both are equal in power; but if one is very strong, *yana* should be the policy. Similarly, *samsraya* is the choice when one is very weak. In other words, when in decline, as compared to the enemy, he should make peace; when prospering, he should make war; when he thinks the enemy will not be able to harm him, or he cannot harm the enemy, he should stay quiet; when possessed of a preponderance of excellent qualities, he should march; when depleted in power, he should seek shelter; and when the job can be achieved with the help of an associate, he should resort to a dual policy.[68] As for the weaker king, Kautilya suggests that a weaker king should submit to the righteous conqueror, submit monetarily to the greedy conqueror and take counter-steps for survival against a demonical conqueror,[69] which Coetzee describes as a concept of 'strategic flexibility'[70] for the weaker king.

Kautilya is, thus, clear in his mind that the *vijigisu* should resort to one of these six policy choices based on his estimate of the consequential promotion of his own undertakings concerning forts, waterworks, trade routes, settling on wasteland, mines material, forests and elephant forests, or injuring these undertakings of the enemy. He should remain indifferent to the enemy's advancement if he perceives that he could advance quicker or greater or could lead to a greater advancement in the future; the reverse conduct will be that of the enemy; make peace in case the advancement takes the same time or bears an equal fruit (for both).[71] Similarly, the *vijigisu* should not follow the policies that might produce the reverse results such as ruin of his own undertakings.

In the same way, Kautilya advises that the king should remain indifferent to his stable condition in case he perceives that he will remain stable for a shorter period or in such a way that he shall make a greater advancement, the enemy will do so in the opposite way and should make peace in case the stable condition lasts for the same period or leads to equal consequences for both. Kautilya further observes that 'the *vijigisu* should secure advancement through peace if remaining at peace, shall ruin the enemy's undertakings by his own undertakings bearing abundant fruits...or he shall easily entice away the persons capable of carrying out the enemy's undertakings by offering a greater remuneration from his own undertakings, with facilities of favours and exemptions; or, the enemy, in alliance with an extremely strong king, will suffer the ruin of his own undertakings'.[72]

It follows that enhancement of power or service of the self-interest should be the guiding force behind keeping peace. For instance, if a king thinks, explains R. Shamasastry, 'that he can prolong his enemy's hostility with another king whose threats forced him to seek his protection or being allied with him his enemy can harass the country of another king who hates the king or by exploiting his own resources in alliance with any two (friendly) kings, he can augment his resources or if a circle of states is formed by his enemy as one of its members, he can divide them and unite with the others; or by threats of favour, he can catch hold of the enemy, and when he desires to be a member of his own circle of states, he can make him incur the displeasure of the other members and fall a victim to their own fury', then the king may increase his resources by keeping peace.[73]

When can a king keep open hostility with an enemy? Only if he has born soldiers and corporations of fighting men; owns natural defensive positions such as mountains, forests, rivers and forts with only one entrance; is in a position of repelling enemy's attack easily; and could harass the works of his enemy; or if he believes that, due to internal troubles and loss of energy, the enemy will suffer early the destruction of his works; or he could induce the enemy's subjects to immigrate to his country when his enemy was attacked by another king.[74] Kautilya further advises that the policy of keeping neutral as an option can be adopted by a king who thinks that neither his enemy nor he can cause destruction of each other's works or the king thinks that he can increase inflictions to the enemy without incurring any loss to his own works, in case the enemy comes to fight him like a dog with a boar (Book VII.1.266).[75] The policy of march could be undertaken by a king if he was convinced that by doing so it was possible to destroy the enemy's works (Book VII.1.266),[76] and that he had made proper arrangements to safeguard his own works.[77]

Besides, it will be prudent for a king to seek shelter/protection from a king of superior power and endeavour to pass from the stage of deterioration to that of stagnancy and from the latter to that of progress when he thinks that he is not in a position either to harass his enemy's works nor to defend his own against his enemy's attack.

In *dvaidhibhava* policy, it is prescribed in a condition where by making peace with one enables the king to work out his own resources, and by waging war with another, the king can destroy the works of his enemy.[78]

The focus in the adoption of sixfold foreign policy measures by the king in the circle of sovereign states is an endeavour to pass from the state of deterioration to that of stagnation, and from the latter to that of progress.[79] It is noteworthy that Kautilya gives a good deal of attention to the issue of the nature of alliances in Chapter II of Book VII. He prefers peace over war when the outcome of peace and war are equal in nature. For disadvantages, such as the loss of power and wealth, sojourning and sin, are ever attending upon war, he said. An analogy of ideas can be noted from the thoughts of Kautilya and Chinese strategist Sun Tzu who held that the best victories were the ones where aims were achieved without bloodshed.[80] The same holds true when one has to choose between neutrality and war. Similarly, Kautilya accords priority to the double policy (making peace with one and waging war with another) over the policy of alliance as, in his opinion, whoever adopts the double policy enriches himself, being ever attentive to his own works, whereas an allied king has to help his ally at his own expense.[81] As for entering into an alliance, the king must become an ally of a king stronger than one's neighbouring enemy, and if there is no such king, one should ingratiate oneself with one's neighbouring enemy, by either supplying money or army or by ceding a part of one's territory and by keeping oneself aloof, for there can be no greater evil to kings than alliance with a king of considerable power, unless one is actually attacked by one's enemy.[82]

It comes out from his theory of circles of states:

a powerless king should behave as a conquered king towards his immediate enemy but when he finds that time of his own ascendency is at hand, due to a fatal disease, internal troubles, increase of enemies, or a friend's calamities that are vexing his enemy, then under the pretence of performing some expiatory rites to avert the danger of his enemy, he may get out of the enemy's court; or if he is in his own territory, he should not go to see his suffering enemy; or if he is near to his enemy, he may murder the enemy when opportunity affords itself. Closer to the truth, he asserts that a king who is situated between two powerful kings shall seek protection from the stronger of the two; or from one of them on whom he can rely; or he may make peace with both of them on equal terms. He may then seek to put one against the other by telling separately that the other was a tyrant, causing utter ruin to himself. Once divided, he may put down each of them by way of overt or covert means.

Again, the king shall be able to defend himself against his immediate enemy under the protection of two immediate kings of considerable power. Or, having made alliance with a chief in a stronghold, he may adopt the double policy or, he may adapt himself to circumstances or he may make friendship with traitors, enemies, and wild chiefs who are conspiring against both the kings. Or, pretending to be close friend of one of them, he may strike at the other at the latter's weak point by employing enemies and wild tribes. Or, having made friendship with both, he may form a circle of states. Or, he may make alliance with the *Madhyama* or the neutral king; and with this help he may put down one of them or both. Or, when hurt by both, he may seek protection from a king of righteous character among the *madhyama* king and their friends or equals, or from any other king whose subjects are so disposed as to increase his happiness and peace, with whose help he may be able to recover his last position, with whom his ancestors were in close intimacy or blood relationship, and in whose kingdom he can find a number of powerful friends. Pointing out the best way to form alliance, it is averred that of the two powerful kings who are on amicable terms with each other, a king shall make alliance with the one who likes him and whom he also likes.[83]

Kautilya deals with the character of equal, inferior or superior kings as well as the forms of agreement made by an inferior king in Chapter 3 of Book VII and recommends that (a) the conqueror should employ the six measures of policy with due regard to his power and (b) the king shall make peace with the equal and superior kings while attacking the inferior king. This policy is in the interest of the king, as otherwise if he attacks a superior king, it will ruin him just in the same way as a foot soldier who opposes an elephant is bound to be crushed; or a war with an equal king would be destructive to both just as the collision of an unbaked mud vessel with a similar vessel is destructive to both, but a war with a weaker king is bound to be successful like a stone with an earthen vessel. However, it may become necessary in certain conditions for a weaker king also to wage war just as it might be necessary for a stronger king to either make peace or allay the fear of war, if when at war, he were to see, 'The enemy's subjects, greedy, impoverished or rebellious, do not come over, being frightened of war'.[84]

What one understands from the aforementioned discussion is Kautilya's rationalist thinking and very realist argument that power decides peace between any two kings for no piece of iron that is not made red-hot will combine with another piece of iron.[85] In Book XII, Kautilya suggests that when a superior king discards the proposal of an inferior king for peace, the latter should view himself as a conquered king, or play the part of an inferior king towards a superior. Peace should be made with an all-submissive inferior king without causing him troubles and anger because if provoked by any such behaviour, an inferior king, like wild fire, will attack his enemy and will also be favoured by (his) circle of states.

Political realism/pragmatism according to Kautilya suggests that the stronger king should stay quiet when he finds that resorting to peace or war is not going to either weaken the enemy or increase his strength. The stronger king should also make peace if he foresees that the calamities befalling him would be greater than the ones suffered by the enemy and that the enemy could overcome them easily and attack him. If the calamities of the enemy are irremediable, the weaker king should also attack him, just as the stronger king should seek shelter if his calamities are irremediable.[86]

The aforementioned prescriptions of Kautilya about the choices of *shadgunya* amplify that there is no perpetual status in the position of a state and interstate relations; therefore, the king should be able to read the political situation and should accordingly apply all the means, namely advancement, decline and stable condition as well as weakening and extermination.[87]

There is no need to overemphasize that foreign policy in Kautilyan raison d'être means the indirect optimization of one's own *prakritis* by exploiting for a time the state factors of an allied state to one's own benefit—either by providing protection against a third state of superior power or by helping to conquer a third state of inferior power. 'In the first case, one's own state factors are kept intact or can be improved behind the shield of *prakriti* made available by the allied state. In the latter case, the ally is helping in the conquest of a third state, which means the incorporation of that state's *prakriti* into one's own—that is, the optimization of the own state factors by enlarging them with those of the conquered state'.[88]

The aforementioned recommendations of the *Arthashastra* establish Kautilya as a grand strategist in the context of the power and capacity of a state being inseparable from the co-relational value of the political, economic, cultural and governance aspects as well as foreign policy, diplomacy, military power and intelligence factors. Was he an expansionist? Broadly, the answer is no because he seems to be aiming at political unification of the Indian subcontinent. Kautilyan foreign policy does not point towards imperial proclivities beyond the Indian geo-cultural space.[89] However, arguably, his theory is not incapable of extension to the modern geopolitics.

FOUR *UPAYAS* OR STRATAGEMS

Kautilya spends reasonable time on the use and utility of four *upayas* or stratagems to follow the *shadgunya* to be effective in a world order characterized by continuous conflicts of interests and an environment of power game quite similar to the views of Max Weber, regarding political struggle and power, particularly in the context of establishing dominance in relation to other states.[90] Four *upayas* or methods of political action include *sama, dana, bheda* and *danda*—wherein *sama* refers to conciliatory approach; *dana* refers to placating with rewards and gifts, *bheda* refers to sowing dissension, and *danda* refers to using force, including coercion and sanctions.[91] All the four are integral to foreign policy strategy[92] and could be used either singly or in combination; a total of 30 different combinations, depending on the seriousness of the situation.[93] He explains that it is easier to employ an *upaya* earlier in order than a later one. For example, placating with gifts is twice as hard as conciliation, sowing dissension three times as hard and use of force four times. Force also signifies waging wars, on which Kautilya brings greater theoretical uniqueness.[94]

Similarity between Kautilya and Morgenthau is apparent when both see international politics as a pursuit of power. Morgenthau defined power as man's control over the minds and actions of other men. It would be pertinent in this context to cite P. K. Gautam who remarks that, without any reference to Kautilya, the 20th century pioneer of power politics theory Morgenthau, in his book,[95] mentions that

> balance of power can be carried on either by diminishing the weight of the heavier scale or by increasing the weight of the lighter one by adopting the policy of Divide and Rule; Compensation; Armaments; and Alliances resembling quite closely the Kautilyan concepts of *bheda* (divide and rule), *dana* (compensation), *danda* (armaments) and *sama* (alliances).[96]

It is fascinating to note that both Kautilya and the modern foreign policy analysts and theorists underscore the importance of psychological tools (four *upayas* or methods) in the conduct of foreign affairs such as the conclusion of war, peace in line with the understanding of the power and nature of the enemy and his political behaviour. It can also be argued that Kautilya was certain about the result-oriented significance of these *upayas* and their importance and relevance as aid to *vijigisu's* thought process in choosing strategic policy options. Thus, as Modelski says, the *upayas* (stratagems) are the 'influencing techniques', which can be applied to both domestic and foreign policies'[97] and so is the opinion of Jayantanuja Bandyopadhyaya[98] that 'Morgenthau is nearer to Kautilya's concept of *Udasina* when he speaks of the "splendid isolation" of the balance who waits in the middle in watchful detachment'. It may not be wrong to assert that many contemporary examples establish the utility of the four *upayas* like the application of all four *upayas*—conciliation process (*sama*); monitory incentives (*dana*); dissensions (*bheda*); and economic sanctions/blockades (*danda*) by the world actors in dealing with North Korea. It is also evident in the latest case of Iran imbroglio, where the careful use of *sama, dana, bheda* and *danda* has seemingly led to an amicable solution, thus, to the fruition of policy methods in application'.[99] Again, the Chinese foreign policy can better suit the understanding and application of *upayas* with reference to its approach to the weaker as well as the stronger states in her vicinity and beyond.

It is interesting to find that the Kautilyan idea of the types of war can be seen in the modern IR theories. The modern warfare, for instance, takes due cognizance of the use of intellect or the *kuta*, a concept used by Kautilya in his *kutayuddha*. Furthermore, in modern times too, the countries in hostile relationship do not resort to open/direct war (termed *prakashyuddha* by Kautilya) as a first resort but take recourse to many other manoeuvres like *kutayuddha*, aiming at defeating the militarily powerful enemy. The modern theory of warfare uses several terms for *kutayuddha*, such as 'indirect approach', manoeuvre warfare, asymmetric warfare and guerrilla warfare.

Similarly, Kautilya's *tusnimyuddha* or 'silent war', his distinctive contribution to the theory of warfare, occupies a significant theoretical place in the modern political discourse and finds, as Roger Boesch remarks, theoretical acknowledgement in the contemporary world due to the experiences of the real world in what saboteurs do, what intelligence operatives do and what is contained in wars like Pakistan's proxy war against India'.[100] The examples of cyberwars, misinformation and propaganda war and the use of deception and secret intelligence (spies, etc.) can be easily counted as a part of *tusnim* or silent war, leading Gautam to call Kautilya as the father of 'information warfare'.[101] Thus, one may agree with the opinion that the ideas underlying modern intelligence are very much present in the *Arthashastra* as Kautilya provides key methodologies and theoretical concepts for intelligence analysis, assessment, estimates and strategic planning. Kautilya's work and Sherman Kent's work bear 'structural homology', though the latter is regarded as the father of modern intelligence.[102] The latent presence of these strategic thoughts of Kautilya can be discerned in the modern-day dictionary of 'conflict resolution', 'conflict termination' and 'stability operation' across countries.

Furthermore, the strategist Kautilya prescribes that the king who conquers should extend a fair and just treatment to the people of the conquered territory to win over their confidence and support. He says in Book XIII, Chapter 5:

> *After gaining new territory,* the king conqueror should cover the enemy's faults with his own virtues, his virtues with double virtues; carry out what is agreeable and beneficial to the subjects by doing his own duty as laid down; do as promised, apart from showing the same devotion in festivals in honour of the deities of the country, festive gatherings and sportive

amusements as do his subjects, for the contrary behaviour would make him unworthy of trust for his own and other people, and he should honour all hermitages, and make grants to men distinguished in learning, speech and piety, and render help to the distressed, the helpless and the diseased.[103]

What follows from the foregoing discussion is that his conceptualization of *mandala* is governed by the strategic function of *mandala*, postulating the possible strategic relations among the states besides his general statement that the natural enmity of a state is with its immediate neighbour. Even if it may not be proper to agree with Kautilya that all neighbours are enemies (in fact, he also does not say so very explicitly), it still calls for a systematic analysis of the reasons as to why Kautilya considered the neighbour as the probable enemy of the conqueror. Juutinen lists some of them as follows: (a) competition for the same resources like arable land, woods or metals; (b) dependence on the same source of water; (c) increases in population; and (d) migrations and the potential colonization resulting from it.[104] Juutinen seems to be convincing in his argument; yet, it is not necessary that these causes are the general rule for neighbourly conflicts. The conflicts between the states may not be rooted in neighbourhood rivalries alone, but in the emergence of conflicting strategic interests, shaped and determined by the often-changing economic and political scenes at the global level. While the basic unit in Kautilya's *mandala* is the state, the modern *mandala* also applies to international organizations and governance agencies in the global context of complex and interrelational webs of political authority. Along with states, these webs of authority can be situated as parts of a state-centric *mandala*, as elements of interdependent sovereignty 'affecting people and productive forces, treasury and allies'. But they can also be interpreted as actors in transnational *mandalas*, where, instead of states, the focus is on transnational agents or international organizations.[105] For example, the United States and China do not share boundaries with each other, yet remained enemies/rivals during the entire period of the Cold War and became friends after its end, mainly led by economic interests, to become unfriendly again after the breakout of COVID-19 in 2020.

Again, it is the strategic interests that have brought America closer to India and driven her away from Pakistan, her earlier strategic partner. In other words, enmity and friendship are dependent on the continuity or discontinuation of the circumstances and assessments of the interests being served by the present alliances. Kautilya also appears to be conscious of the fact that the circles of states and alliances do not have permanence. They are determined by power balancing needs.[106] This interpretation of *mandala* further leads us to another level, that is, the transnational level of *mandala* formations from the neighbourhood theory. So, while the concept of *mandala* revolves around the constitution or formation of circles of states and the relations between them, guided by their conflicting interests, it is not wrong to further expand the concept to include the circles beyond the immediate local boundaries of states or interactions beyond the proximate boundaries. Looking at the question of *mandala* from the angle of global governance and international agents, Daniel Elazar[107] writes:

> *mandala* can account not only for inter-state relations but also for global governance and international organisation. This is an important observation, because one of the major implications of the globalisation has been the transformation in the political sovereignty of states through various forms of shared authority and pooled sovereignty.

Referring to 'governance without government' Rosenau and Czempiel, as well as Jan Scholte, state that the concept encapsulates the resulting fragmentation of public authority and the emergence of new actors, including non-governmental and private actors, in addition to trans-governmental (between, for example, state departments) intergovernmental, intra-regional, trans-local (e.g., between two cities) and public–private hybrids.[108] These arguments lead us to two conclusions: first, that the concept of sovereignty is undergoing a change, especially the concept of external sovereignty wherein the interdependence—economic and strategic—among the nations has tended to interpret sovereignty differently from the traditional understanding in the present century and, second, there have emerged, sometimes, collaborative and, at other times competitors, new *mandalas*, groupings or alliances, along with their contradictory and opposite political and geographical concerns to challenge the pre-existing dominant power relations around the world. For example, SAARC, ASEAN, BRICS, EU and several other regional alliances are operating as separate actors and registering their presence in the power play internationally. Furthermore, the emphasis of the *Mandala* theory is invariably on the maximization of power because Kautilya thought that only a powerful state can guarantee the *yogakshema* of its people.

Thriving with three powers—*mantrashakti*, *prabhavashakti* and *utsah shakti*—the king becomes superior; reduced in them, inferior; with equal powers, equal. Therefore, he should endeavour to endow himself with power and success, or, if similar (to endow with power and success), the material constituents in accordance with their immediate proximity or integrity or he should endeavour to detract (these) from treasonable persons and enemies.[109] Pursuit of power is one of the factors that render Kautilya a realist because one of the basic premises in realism is that states seek to maximize their power and influence.[110] The policy of power maximization, according to Kautilya, is associated with the efficiency and excellence of the state factors or constituent elements of the state, that is, the king; the government; people; country; and the productive capabilities such as agriculture, fortified city, treasury, army and the allies. The first element refers to a king in possession of strong leadership qualities, including his ability to command an effective and decisive influence over his people. In fact, it would be correct to assert that the support and morale of the people is a pre-condition for a successful march and victory of the *vijigisu* in the sense that the productive capabilities of the people would not only sustain the internal demands of the citizens, but it would provide support to a strong army. Strong industrial base; outreach to and influence, if not control, over the global markets; position in the regional and global value chains; other competitive and productive elements like infrastructure; and a cohesive society are the facilitators of the process of power augmentation even in the contemporary world and play a vital role in the power-balancing activity.

A study of the Kautilyan foreign policy theorization suggests that the *mandala* is a strategic constellation of diverse interests around a governance issue or a constellation of state relations with regard to a matter of governance; then to conquer means to solve this issue. Juutinen claims that a key objective of foreign policy is righteous conquest in the context of multiple and overlapping circles consisting of transnational intertwined state factors, denoting successful leadership in optimization of welfare in the interconnected political entities through win-win solutions for common problems. 'The modern *vijigisu* has a mastery over the complex web of *mandalas*, knows how to keep them separate (e.g., does not mix political conflicts with economic cooperation)'.[111] There could be some element of truth in what Juutinen says with respect to the coexistence of a situation of political conflict and economic cooperation in the modern system of international relations followed by contemporary *vijigisu* even though there is evidence to the contrary in many cases. For example, in the modern operation of foreign policy, one finds that there is a break of relations between the states both politically and economically in a conflict situation (even when it is not a case of open war), conceding that the economic ties may not shatter completely and suddenly. Take the case of tensions between China and the United States in the post-COVID-19 period, and India and China over the territorial issues. The step taken by India to ban some social media companies of China, by saying they are engaged in spying and stealing strategic information besides cancelling the contracts of many Chinese companies and making it further obligatory for them to seek India's permission before investing on any venture in the country in the context of unilateral military action along the line of actual control (LAC), is proof of the preparations for any eventuality not only in terms of military and other infrastructure but also to weaken and reduce the economic capabilities of the enemy.

Kautilya's pragmatism is evidently reflected in his strategic thought encompassed in his idea of *mandala* with its validity in the contemporary times. The modern conqueror also generally seems to prefer subservience or allegiance by other states. So the intension is to extend the 'power circle'—the area of influence rather than annex the territories barring exceptions like China that still nourishes physical expansion of power with imperialist intensions. Further, it is said that just as Kautilya's *vijigisu* limited his expansion to *chakravartinkshetra*, today's rising *vijigisus* are also more inclined to keep themselves as regional *vijigisus* and dominate their regions. Kangle observes: if seen with a critical eye, Kautilya's *Arthashastra* concept was more of uniting the subcontinent than expanding, but it was regional in approach.[112]

The endeavour to geographically dominate in South China Sea by China; in South Asia by India; in East China Sea by both Japan and China; and in the Middle East by Iran, Turkey and Saudi Arabia are examples of regional *vijigisus*. Further, Kautilya was right when he pointed out the formation of new alliances, *mitra* or *mitra-mitra*, based on the application of *shadgunya* principles or measures. Some resort to *samsraya* (coalition/alliance) such as in the case of Five Power Defence Arrangements (FPDA), NATO, AUKUS and QUAD; few embrace *sandhi* like China–Japan and China–Russia; and few embrace *dvaidhibhava*—dual policy—like Pakistan seeking China's support to counter India. However, *dvaidhibhava* may not necessarily involve two action orientations involving friendship with one country and hostility with another; it can also be understood as a state with two intensions—overt and covert—one exhibiting friendship and covertly harbouring feelings of hostility against the same state.[113]

We can find the relevance and applicability of some principles of *shadgunya* in the Indian context as well. For example, it may be argued that India's 'Operation *Parakram*' in the aftermath of terror attack on the Indian Parliament in 2001, which involved large mobilization of the armed forces to the border, is conceivably based on the pattern of *yana* form of policy strategy. The *asana* of *shadgunya* can be equated to the policy of non-alignment, a policy of remaining stationary or uninvolved.

Looking back at the overall Kautilya perspective of international relations, one can say that Kautilya's theory is in fact a timeless masterpiece in the field of International relations. His unique contribution in the area is being increasingly recognized not only in India but also outside in the world, in both academic and political fields. The West is also coming to realize that it might have much to do with the foreign policy exposure emanating from the past and the present political literature of India, as well as countries like China, to come to terms with the understanding and explanation of current international politics and security challenges. The concept of comprehensive national power can be rooted in the Kautilyan philosophy of *prakritis*. It can be safely averred that the whole model of foreign policy, war and peace propounded by Kautilya has left a lasting imprint on the field of strategic thought and culture; on symbiotic links between foreign policy and interstate relations and between national goals/interests and power politics (the change of their nature, scope and range notwithstanding); on the approach to deal with questions of war and peace in the context of not only military power but also the collective power of the seven *prakritis*, specifically the monetary strength, that is, the health of the *kosa*; on the role and importance of knowledge and intelligence; and on the utility of Kautilya's thoughts in understanding, interpreting and explaining the present-day theory and practice of international relations. It would be true to say that Kautilya developed a vocabulary and a theory to define international relations that predated the Western theory of International Relations. Emanating from ancient Indian scholarly traditions, observes Deepshikha Shahi, the *Arthashastra* most certainly qualifies as a sample of systemic theorization with some adaptations in accordance with the realities of the contemporary modern and postmodern world before it can effectively break the myth of the Indian inability to formulate systemic theories.[114] His interpretation of power dynamics places him in line with original theorists with reference to his assertions that (a) the growing power of a country decides its place and role among the other competing or cooperating states, at the local, regional and global level; his stress on both strategic and tactical planning, which have short-term and long-term implications from the point of view of conducting relations with other states; and, finally, in his argument that the decision to wage war should be taken after a collective analysis of diverse inputs, including the assessment of the resources, capabilities and power of the enemy, which holds true in the modern context of world affairs.

WAS KAUTILYA A REALIST OR IDEALIST OR BOTH?

Whether Kautilya was a realist or an idealist has been a matter of debate, and consensus still eludes the reader. For some scholars like Pinak Ranjan Chakravarty, the *Arthashastra* was the first substantively written grand strategy in Indian history written in the 4th century BC, and Kautilya, often called the Sun Tzu of India, after the famous Chinese strategist, was a hard-nosed realist who did not consider war as an extension of diplomacy (as Clausewitz argued later), but he regarded every aspect of diplomacy as 'subtle war'. If victory is assured, then one should go to war, setting aside any agreement or treaty signed previously.[115]

Chakravarty's views find resonance in Jyrki Kakonen who thinks that, in the Western International relations intellectual history, Kautilya is presented as an ultra-realist, or he is mentioned as one of the classics in political realism and is often referred as Indian Machiavelli instead of presenting Machiavelli as a European or Italian Kautilya.[116] However, due attention has not been given to the fact, Kakonen says that he (Kautilya) presented a kind of a model for not only an idealist or just and ethical society, but he also presented the human system as it appeared to a realist observer. Based on his realist analysis, he advised his king or ruler how to construct a society/state that can provide the best security and welfare for ordinary citizens.[117] Morgenthau recognizes in his *Politics Among Nations* (1978) that his theory of realism is also derived from ancient Indian political philosophy and quotes from Weber's 'Hinduism study', which contains several references to Kautilya and the *Arthashastra*.[118] It cannot be said for sure, though, that Morgenthau had read the *Arthashastra*.

On the other hand, there are scholars who perceive that Kautilya was a neo-realist. For instance, Professor M. P. Singh, drawing a parallel between Kautilya and the neo-realist or structural realist Kenneth Waltz, observes,

> Just as Waltz postulated three levels of international politics, namely, the level where state behaviour is explained in terms of action and psychological motivations of individual functionaries of state; the level where international relations are shown to be a function of the domestic regime of state; and the level where international anarchy bereft of a sovereign power leads inter-state relations to be caused and conditioned by the structure of world politics, whether multi-polar, bi-polar or uni-polar, so do the notions of 'Saptang State' and 'Rajamandala' in *Arthashastra* show a sign of evolution in international relations.[119]

This semblance of opinion among many other scholars is visible when it is mentioned that the core ideas of the *Arthashastra* are a significant factor of influence in modern India's politico-strategic culture. Approvingly, Subrat Mitra opines, 'the reference to Kautilyan ideas is also explicit and discursive' in the sense of the 're-use of the past' in addressing current political and strategic problems.[120] It can be agreed to treat the *Arthashastra* as an important endogenous politico-cultural resource for understanding the politico-strategic culture of modern India in the multi-polar world system and consider the theoretical engagement with Kautilyan ideas and concepts and their induction into the political science discourse a desideratum in political science.

However, it is argued that in the case of Kautilya, as a realist or normative idealist, the principle of either–or is inapplicable, in the sense that he does not find any dichotomy between what is termed 'purposive rationality' and 'normative' philosophy' of ensuring happiness of the subjects. This idea of Kautilya can be easily discerned when he stresses that it is the cumulative strength of the seven *prakritis* that can ensure power, safety and security and the material well-being of the country. A weak state can neither succeed in protecting the sovereignty nor can add to the economic and political resources that guarantee the advancement of the nation. Therefore, he advises the ruler to ensure extension of power and control over others by any means, fair or foul, but, at the same time, he brings in the necessary moral aspect to the question of governing the conquered people with a sense of fairness, justice, equality and respect to their customs in order to not only win their trust and support but also to ensure internal order and balancing. Liebig observes in this connection:

> Without the optimisation of the *prakriti*—driven by purposive political rationality—the people would sink into poverty and *matsya-nyaya* would loom—the very opposite of the happiness of the people.... Growing state power by optimising the *prakriti*—notably with respect to economy—will also make the people materially saturated and politically content which guarantees of the stability and power of the state.[121]

Further, arguing against labelling the *Arthashastra* as a strand of realism, Liebig maintains that this opinion misses out on four points: it (the *Mandala* theory) focuses more on the physical arrangement of states in circles and overlooks the all-pervading binding of Kautilyan ethics—the *dharma*; it misses the Kautilyan methodology for pre-selected choice of foreign policies rationally derived on the basis of Kautilyan calculations; it misses on the primacy of *mantrashakti*; and it misses the importance of ally as a constituent element of the state.[122]

The people, in fact, provide support and respect to that ruler who is powerful enough to deal effectively with anarchy both internally and in relation to external powers. This seems to be the motivating factor behind his suggestion that a wise king should be careful against the existence or emergence of the causes contributing to the decline, greed and disaffection among the subjects because, the subjects, when impoverished, become greedy; when greedy, they become disaffected; and when disaffected, they either go over to the enemy or themselves kill the master.[123]

Meinecke observes that 'the well being of the state and the people enclosed in it are the value and goal (of *raison d'etat*), power, securing and expanding power are the means to that end'.[124] In the intellectual context, Kautilya prescribes that the basic principle of maximization of seven *prakritis* and power is above any other norm of ethical rule. It is to be recalled in this context that Plato in his *Politea* showed no difference with Kautilya in not differentiating between 'general ethics and the political ethics of the statecraft'. Plato did not object to the use of 'noble lies' in politics, not in line with his concept of truth. Platonic state was empowered to engage even in the act of eugenics, including infanticide.[125] However, there appears a fusion of political realism and normative ethic in the whole range of political ideas of Kautilya, concerning the foreign policy issues as well as the approach to the welfare and progress of the people.

To sum up, it is clear that Kautilya believed that the results determine whether the policy is good or bad. It may be reiterated that it was necessary for the king to understand the science of power because, as stated in Book VII.18.43-44, 'he who is well versed in the science of politics ... plays, as he pleases, with kings tied by the chain of his intellect'. Further, contrary to the common perception, he asserts, 'a king, though ruling over a small territory ... conversant with (the science of) politics, does conquer the entire earth, never loses'.[126] It is true that Kautilya recommends several crude and cruel means to establish supremacy and command in the internal and external areas of operation, such as torture and assassination, in the name of removal of thorns as appropriate methods in times of crisis. It was, however, to be used only when the safety and security of the kingdom and the people seemed to be in jeopardy or when threatened by an internal or external enemy. It is also true that Kautilya advises the *vijigisu* to not observe the promises made in a treaty if it did not serve the interests of the state or has become obsolete or bothersome since, in the eyes of Kautilya, 'international relations are lawless struggles among those who are strong and those who are weak'.[127]

For Kautilya, there was nothing unfair in the conduct of warfare, including propaganda, deception or disinformation, and religion[128] to keep the morale of his own troops high, planting false information or lies to spread fear or downgrade the confidence of the enemy or the use of beautiful women spies for the purpose of showing dissensions and rivalry among the opposite forces as well as assassinations.[129] Some scholars like Bruce Rich, therefore, think that, 'Kautilya's foreign policy was the ruthless *realpolitik*, intrigue and deception ... coldblooded realism and treachery with some remarkable enlightened policies'.[130] But Rich is really unfair in his judgement of Kautilya as he does not recognize the fact that Kautilyan recommendations for winning a war are in vogue and are used by all nations. 'Kautilya can be faulted only for his exposition of what is practised by the states everywhere'.[131] Like any other state, he also believed that power is the possession of strength.[132] So, Kautilya can be rightly described as 'the classic proponent of the political realism; of the foreign policy; of a craft of obtaining and increasing the power, without moralistic illusions ... his geo-strategic analysis is amazingly advanced in nature'.[133]. It cannot be ignored that he recommended fair treatment to those conquered. Kautilya proposed that a king who looks after his subjects, like a father does for his children, would be able to not only enhance welfare objectives but also add to the material well-being, political stability and advancement of the state with the support, confidence and trust of the people in the government. He argues that a king could successfully rule over the territory if he promotes social justice as, in the absence of provision for the helpless, needy or jobless or in case of imposing too high taxes and failure to protect against hunger and poverty or if he is unable to prevent wrongful arrests of the subjects, he is open to ruining himself either by a revolt of the frustrated and dissatisfied people within or by the attack of the enemy from outside as the enemy might find in this situation the most opportune time to weaken or defeat the king. This narrative speaks of Kautilya's realism or pragmatism and, therefore, could be termed as amoral or 'unmoral, not immoral'; he could be non-religious, but not irreligious in his thoughts.[134] Kautilya is on the side of a weak king when it comes to a choice between a strong king who unjustly behaved and a weak king who justly behaved, and he maintains that he should march against the strong king who had unjustly behaved.[135]

That Kautilya was not unfair, unjust or immoral in his treatment of matters concerning statecraft becomes abundantly clear from what he writes in Book VII.5.19-26:

> For, by discarding the good and favouring the wicked, and by starting unrighteous injuries not current before, by discontinuing customary practices that are righteous, by indulgence in impiety and suppression of piety, and by doing acts that ought not to be done and by ruining rightful acts, and by not giving what ought to be given and securing what ought not to be given to (him), and by not punishing those deserving to be punished and punishing those not deserving to be punished, by seizing those who ought not to be seized and not arresting those who ought to be seized, and by doing harmful things and destroying beneficial things ... by ruining human exertions, by spoiling the excellence of works done, by dishonouring those worthy of honour.... Through the negligence and indolence of the king and because of the destruction of well-being,—(through these causes) decline, greed and disaffection are produced among the subjects.

Further, we have examples from the modern practice of foreign policy and conflicts at the global and regional levels, which establish Kautilya as a source of action. The Chinese policy of aggression and expansion seems to be in line with Kautilyan and Sun Tzu's ideas on war and peace. Kautilya pleads for the operation of *kutayuddha* even during the peace time by constantly aiming at sowing dissensions and discord among the enemy's leadership. Further, Kautilya's emphasis that it is the money and military power of a country that determines its role and position in the international order makes him again a realist of the first kind and places him much ahead of the Western theorists and enables the foreign policy and defence analysts to look towards the non-Western models of war and peace insofar as the origin of today's existing theories are concerned and acknowledge the profound contribution of the oriental political thinkers, like Kautilya, have made. It is hard to deny that India's rising economic and military strengths have positioned her to be a major player in the 21st century international order, and that many factors are there to shift India from a passive regional power to a more assertive global one.[136]

It may be noted that Kautilya's *Mandala* theory was practical and dynamic to suit the situations of war and peace at all times. Kautilya's *mandala* system could be seen in operation vigorously applied immediately before, during and after the Second World War. Hitler's Germany in 1939 signed a pact with the Soviet Union to avoid an attack to Germany's eastern flank. And the (erstwhile) Soviet Union signed almost an identical treaty with Japan the same year to be safe on its own eastern borders. When Hitler became overambitious and posed threat to Great Britain, Winston Churchill, though ever suspicious of the Soviet Union, befriended the other authoritarian leader, J. Stalin, following the line enunciated by Kautilya's strategic thought. This happened because the national interest demanded that action instead of following the moral edicts of the policy[137] and 'Mandala theory held more power than the moral, religious, ideological and spiritual considerations'.[138] The goal to defeat the common enemies—Italy, Japan and Germany—was the most important. The relevance of *Mandala* theory in the modern times is further visible in America breaking the alliance in her open declaration that the United States would help any country under threat from the Soviet Union and brought Turkey and Greece, the immediate neighbours and enemies of the Soviets, under its net of friendship and broke the Soviet Union's hegemony. Extending the idea further, the example of General MacArthur is not far to prove Kautilya's strategy right by treating the fallen Japan with kindness, respect, dignity and generosity and extended massive financial and technological assistance to that country, besides extending her trade tremendously or when America established the Southeast Asia Treaty Organization in 1954 to contain the evil designs of the Soviet Union and China in relation to her Southeast Asian neighbours and Baghdad Pact was signed on 24 February 1955 to protect the Middle Eastern countries neighbouring the Soviet Union. 'So busy was the United States building friends around the Soviets that the then US Secretary of State, Dulles was accused of "Pactomania". The American *mandala* was complete'.[139]

Kautilyan political realism is further reflected in the Chinese foreign policy initiatives and its desire to expand its boundaries with about 14 of its neighbours with the effective use of money and military. China is making massive financial investments through various development/infrastructure projects like One Belt, One Road; China–Pakistan Economic Corridor; or the investment in Sri Lanka and the intended relational change between India and Bangladesh and India and Nepal in order to expand its power and influence in the South Asian region and, to a lesser extent, in the Southeast Asian region. Furthermore, in the case of India and Pakistan and other countries too, China seems to be following the *Mandala* theory of Kautilya. It is expanding the circle of states on the same lines, if I may say so. It cannot be easily set aside that China has made a massive transformation in terms of economy reflected in her big trade surpluses when compared to almost all the major economies of the globe, and the West has been facing diminishing returns. Viewed from this angle, China has thrown great political, security and economic challenges to India in relation to its relations with that country. Commenting on this, Chakravarty remarks,

> As China enters a phase of economic restructuring, it is attempting to integrate the Eurasian land mass ... the ancient silk routes are being revived with modern infrastructure.... The question arises as to how it will affect India? China's influence is on the rise through massive investment. There is always a strategic dimension to such projects.[140]

In order to counteract this significant rise of China, India has evolved a make-in-India policy to make some change in the arena of economic permutations and combinations so as to influence China's trade and business. In the same line, there have emerged some international trading blocs like US-led 12 countries (which include Japan, Australia, and Vietnam among others and exclude India and China) Trans-Pacific Partnership signed in October 2015 whose aim is to implement new rules for conducting international trade. That these initiatives are bound to impact the nature of international relations as well as the military capabilities of the targeted states cannot be denied. In the changing Asian and Southeast Asian political, economic and security strategic realities, one can note the formation of new alliances, which Kautilya viewed as the circle of states. For example, much closer ties are being developed between Japan, Australia, Vietnam and India as a mutually cooperative group, so much so that there are joint military or defence exercises to exhibit solidarity with each other, and it is quite possible that this closeness may give rise to new conflicts and formation of other circles. The relevance of *Mandala* theory can further be traced in the emerging approach to regional politics in South Asia and Southeast Asia when one relates Chinese foreign policy to countries such as Taiwan, Malaysia, Philippines, Indonesia and Vietnam apart from East Mongolia and Hong Kong. Many of these countries are in search of security protection/shelter, to borrow from the *Arthashastra*, with a powerful government like America, may be supported by Japan and Australia. India is also not discounting the over-imposing behaviour of China like a *chakravartin kshetra* and is reformulating its strategy using Kautilya's tactics, even if not mentioned into the body of the policy just as China might not mention Sun Tzu while practising imperialist or expansionist policy in relation to her neighbours. Thus, China and India, the co-equals in the race of positioning themselves in the regional or international sphere of political, economic and strategic supremacy, are now in almost a new regional cold war, attempting to contain each other in terms of power and influence. Both the countries seem to be led by their respective history of the local and world view of politics, having been interpreted as cultural- and value-based phenomena. The history of China and India gives a chance to ask how universal or exceptional is the European development into a Westphalia nation-state system as compared to Chinese and Indian development into civilizational empire.[141] There is an effort on the part of China to rebuild international relations on a hegemonic pattern with a view to, first, break the hegemonic intentions of the earlier polar leaders—America and Russia and, second, to replace them by its own with the help of enhanced economic and military resources. Henry R. Nay and M. Ollapally have examined afresh the world view of aspiring powers such as China, India, Iran, Japan and Russia to tell us about how in the emerging states, own traditions have been brought up in developing IR theories as well as in interpreting their own foreign policies.[142] This aspect of changing international order has also been indicated by several other scholars of the field of IR.[143]

Reiterating the foreign policy goals of China and that of the *vijigisu* of Kautilya, one finds clear congruence between the two. The core interests of China, in the opinion of Michael D. Swaine, are as follows: (a) the protection of the basic system (existing sociopolitical order of China) and national security of the People's Republic of China (PRC) state, (b) the preservation of China's national sovereignty and territorial integrity and (c) the continued stable development of China's economy and society.[144] These interrelated objectives—the preservation of domestic order and well-being in the face of different forms of social strife; the defence against persistent external threats to national sovereignty and territories; and the attainment and maintenance of geopolitical influence as a major, and perhaps primary, state[145]—correspond with the objectives of Kautilya's *vijigisu* whose aim in the pursuit of domestic and external policies is to protect the territory, ensure the well-being and *yogakshema* of its people and strengthen the economy and military. Further, like Kautilya, China considers military might as critical to the nation's march to achieving the status of a superpower, and that in case of a failure of diplomacy and other deterrence measures, the military must be able to defend its interests and territories.

It would be pertinent to indicate here another strategic thinking of China that is closer to the one enunciated by the classic treatise, that is, the role of the *prakritis* (the constituent elements of state) the *vyasana* or calamity and *bhumi sandhi*[146] (treaty for acquiring land) in the international relations in the geopolitical context. Gautam argues that China declared a unilateral ceasefire in 1962 and withdrew from the state of Arunachal Pradesh despite the country being in a winning position and so did India in the case of Pakistan in 1947–1948 when it decided not to recapture Pakistan-occupied Kashmir (POK) because of the inhospitable terrain and potentially hostile population.[147] Further, in the case of China, the influencing factor could be identified what Kautilya termed *vyasanas* like ungovernable nature of the hostile Indian population in Arunachal Pradesh. Major Abhishek Kumar[148] finds similarities between CCP's dominant position in China's internal political structure and Kautilya's highest prioritization of the state's leadership among the seven *prakritis*; Kautilya's support for the protection of the king's rule from internal strife and power struggles and the Chinese core interests of protecting the Chinese Communist Party (CCP's) rule over China; and also between China's policy focus on its economy before military aggrandizement and Kautilya's prioritization of the treasury over the army.

It can be averred that China, like many other contemporary *vijigisus*, has made many Kautilyan strategic ideas an integral part of her policies on war, peace, diplomacy and other interstate relational dimensions. As Kautilya stressed on the combined use of all elements of national power—political, economic, military and cultural—to achieve the goals of the state, China has been exhibiting the same strategic dynamic approach to policy framework in relation to other states. India is a late starter in this regard.

CONCLUSION

In sum, the depth and range of the strategic thought on the issues of war, peace and foreign policy framework were not only of the directional and empirical value in the times of Chandragupta Maurya, but the experience of the post-Mauryan empire, including the modern world, also shows that his theory of *mandala*, *shadgunya* and four stratagems (the four *upayas*) is transcendental of time and space. The nature of international politics and policy in the regions like South Asia and Southeast Asia is indicative of the far-sighted approach of Kautilya to foreign relations and his intellectual competence and ability to deal with his own times as well as to predict or visualize the future course and shape of the nature of struggles between nations around power, progress, balance of power and national interests and the core elements of new concepts like comprehensive national power and of relative power. That *Mandala* theory, whether named or not, is of critical operational value can be discerned with the help of the analysis of China's relations with her neighbours and other countries such as Taiwan, Japan, Australia, Vietnam, Malaysia, Indonesia, India and Pakistan, specifically with reference to the tensions between them on the issues of South China Sea, East China Sea and border disputes with India and several others over decades, more open in 2020, on the one side and the relations with America and Russia, which can be seen as *madhyama* and neutral powers. On the other hand, India is recalculating its neighbourhood and Act East Policy strategically and further exploring what is called sub-regional initiatives with Bangladesh, Bhutan and Nepal—a country trying to get closer to China in the recent past. In the context of Kautilya, India is pursuing the policy of *dana* reflected in the emergence of new connectivity links in the power sector, transmission lines, transportation by waterways and coastal shipping. India is also seeking to promote connectivity for trading corridor with Myanmar and Thailand.[149] These initiatives can be seen as measures to counteract China's rise in the east and the contestations in the seas. Kautilya's political realism as well as his idealist views regarding the treatment of the conquered country still holds valid in the contemporary world. His six foreign policy measures (*shadgunya*) on war and peace and the four *upayas* can be seen as the basis of rational formation of a nation's policy on war and peace as to when it should be pursued actively, when to remain quiet, when to conclude peace, etc.

Looking into Kautilya's contribution to the foreign policy in theory and practice, it is felt that the *Arthashastra* needs to be explored on a larger scale to see as to how he was different from his contemporary thinkers in the field and how and in what way his ideas were more or less influence-generating in his and later times, particularly in the present world. Further investigations into the utility of the *Arthashastra* as a tool of study and analysis of the global realities in the area of International Relations are imperative.

NOTES

1. Carl Schmitt argues in his *Political Theology* that 'no functioning legal order could be perceived if there was no sovereign authority'. He further tells us in *the Concept of the Political* that 'specific political distinction is that between friend and enemy.... Politics involves groups that face off as mutual enemies. Two groups will find themselves in a situation of mutual enmity if, and only if, there is a possibility of war and mutual killing between them.... The utmost degree of association is the willingness to fight and die for and together with other members of one's group. It may also be stated here that though Schmitt is an ardent supporter of sovereignty, he does not disapprove outright the international legality; rather, he searches for the situations wherein the sovereign political communities, with differing identities can coexist in a shared international legal order' (Stanford Encyclopaedia of Philosophy, the Metaphysics Research Lab, Stanford University, Carl Schmitt, 2010/2019).

2. Sarkar, 'Hindu Theory', 400–414.

3. *Shukra-Niti*, Chapter III, 646 (Sanskrit text translated by Binoy Sarkar). Also see Sarkar, 'Hindu Political Philosophy', 488–491.

4. *Arthashastra*, Book VIII, Chapter 2; Sarkar, 'Hindu Theory', 400.

5. *Shukra-Niti*, IV, I, lines 39–43; *Manusmriti* VII, 154, 157, 207, in Muller, *Sacred Books of the East*; Kamandaka, Chapter VIII, Sanskrit text in the *Bibliotheca Indica* series.

6. Vittal, 'Kautilya's Arthashastra'.

7. Sarkar, 'Hindu Theory', 402; Mahabharata, Book XII, Chapter 56; *Arthashastra*, Book VI, Chapter 11; *Kamandaka*, VIII, 1, 3.

8. *Arthashastra*, Book VI, Chapter 2, 1–3.

9. Liebig, 'Kautilya's Relevance', 103.

10. Nehru, *Discovery of India*, 122–127.

11. Quoted in Kumar, 'The Arthashastra', 32.

12. Mishra, 'Katilya's Arthashastra', 77–109.

13. *Arthashastra*, Book X:6.51; Rangarajan, *Kautilya*, 625; Mishra, 'Katilya's Arthashastra', 89.

14. Mishra, 89.

15. *Arthashastra*, Book VI, 13–23; Kangle, *The Kautilya Arthashastra*, Pt II, 318–319.

16. *Vijigisu* is said to be a Kautilyan vocabulary.

17. Michael, *India's Foreign Policy*.

18. Kangle, *Kautilya Arthashastra*, Part III, 249.

19. *Arthashastra*, Book 6.2.21-22; Kangle, *The Kautilya Arthashastra*, Part II, 318–319.

20. Kangle, *Kautilya Arthashastra*, Pt III, 248.

21. Ruben, 'Inter-state Relations', 139; Kangle terms this opinion as an outcome of a misunderstanding of the text. Kangle, *Kautilya Arthashastra*, Pt III, 249.

22. Kangle, *Kautilya Arthashastra*, 8–9.

23. Liebig, 'Kautilya's Relevance', 103.
24. *Arthashastra*, Book V, Chapter 3, 35–36.
25. Kangle, *Kautilya Arthashastra*, Pt III, 259–260; Gautam, *One Hundred Years*, 35.
26. Bhakri, *Indian Warfare*, 207.
27. Chakravarti, *The Art of War*, 181.
28. Kangle, *Kautilya Arthashastra*, Pt III, 250.
29. Sidhu, 'Of Oral Traditions', 174–190.
30. Sidhu, 'Of Oral Traditions', 174–190.
31. Quoted in preface-setting the scene, Scott, *Handbook of India's International Relations*, xix.
32. Set, 'Ancient Wisdom for the Modern World'.
33. Sarkar, 'Hindu Theory', 400–414.
34. Modelski, 'Kautilya', 549–560.
35. Boesch, *The First Great Political Realist*.
36. Zaman, 'Kautilya', 231–247.
37. Gautam, *One Hundred Years*.
38. Mitra and Liebig, *Kautilya's Arthashastra*.
39. Juutinen, 'Emerging Dynamics of Conflict', 8; see also, Gautam, *One Hundred Years*, 51–57.
40. Juutinen, 'Emerging Dynamics of Conflict', 17.
41. Chakravarty, *Indian Philosophy*, 197; Gautam, *Hundred Years of Kautilya's Arthashastra*.
42. Implied herein is the nature of man/king, acquisitive or altruistic and also that a war may aim at acquiring wealth and resources as dharma does not require everyone to be a world renouncer! (Comment by Subrata K. Mitra, Heidelberg University.)
43. Vance, 'The War That Justified Other Wars', a commentary on the book by Grimsrud (*The Good War*). He remarks, although it was the most destructive thing to life, liberty and property that the world has ever seen, the Second World War is viewed as a good war; although it took the lives of more than 50 million people, the Second World War is viewed as a moral war, a noble war, a just war. Also see Bess, *Choices Under Fire*; Burleigh, *Moral Combat*.
44. Brekke, 'Between Prudence and Heroism', 131; Gautam, *Hundred Years of Kautilya's*, 49.
45. Gautam, *Hundred Years of Kautilya's*, 50.
46. Boesch, *The First Great Political*.
47. Boesche, *The First Great Political*, 109.
48. Gautam, *One Hundred Years*, 36.
49. Liebig, 'The Kautilya-Arthashastra and Core Concepts'. Kautilya provides a detailed methodology and Machinery of intelligence collection, see Book i.I.12.1-25; Kangle, *The Kautilya Arthashastra*, Pt II, 23–27.
50. Ranbir Chakraborty, quoted in Gautam, *Hundred Years of Kautilya's*, 52.
51. See Gautam, 52–57.
52. Vittal, 'Kautilya's Arthashastra', 38.

53. Liebig, 'Kautilya's Arthashastra', 10; also see Modelski, 'Kautilya', 549–560.
54. A comment on my draft by Professor Subrata K. Mitra, Department of Political Science, Heidelberg University.
55. Mishra, 'Kautilya's Arthashastra', 92.
56. Sukhija, *Asian Maritime*, 280–284.
57. Gautam, *Hundred Years of Kautilya's*, 101.
58. More, 'Arthashastra'; Mishra, 'Katilya's Arthashastra', 102.
59. Modelski, 'Kautilya', 553.
60. Mishra, 'Kautilya's Arthashastra', 94.
61. See Book VII of the *Arthashastra*.
62. *Arthashastra*, Book VII.18.44; Kangle, *Kautilya Arthashastra*, Pt II, 384.
63. Book 7.1.1, Kangle, *Kautilya Arthashastra*, Pt II, 321.
64. *Arthashastra*, Book 7.1.6-11; Kangle, *Kautilya Arthashastra*, Pt III, 25.
65. See Gautam, *Hundred Years*, 52; Liebig, *Statecraft and Intelligence*, 49.
66. Rangarajan, *Kautilya*, 9548–9549, 9457–9462.
67. *Arthashastra*, Book VII.17.1-15; Kangle, *Kautilya Arthashastra*, Pt II, 375–376.
68. *Arthashastra*, Book VII.1.13-18.
69. Rangarajan, *Kautilya*, 11656–11696.
70. Coetzee, *Philosophers of War*; Kumar, 'The Arthashastra', 40.
71. *Arthashastra*, Book VII.1.20-27, Kangle, *Kautilya Arthashastra*, 322.
72. Kangle, Pt II, 323.
73. Shamasastry, *Kautilya's Arthashastra*, 294–295; *Arthashastra*, Book VII, Chapter 1.265; it may be added that the whole narrative in this context speaks of a realist Kautilya who is of the constant opinion that the *vijigisu* should take any step relating to the issues of war and peace only after weighing all pros and cons of the action and after assessing the situation.
74. Shamasastry, *Kautilya's Arthashastra*, 295.
75. Shamasastry, *Kautilya's Arthashastra*, 295.
76. Shamasastry, *Kautilya's Arthashastra*, 295.
77. One can take an example of Athens' strategy against Sparta and conclude that Athens resorted to a more realist policy as compared to Sparta that allowed Athens to grow in power, though initially it was the reason for Sparta to declare war. Further, Athens continued to be involved even after the Persians left, and the Spartans returned home. We are told that the Athenians opted for the path recommended by Thucydides, and, comparably, Kautilya, to build their security Walls, while keeping Sparta busy through deceptive and other strategic means. The same attempt is being made by China in strengthening the strategic defence points, while trying to engage India for resolving boundary disputes in a peaceful manner in the Ladakh region.
78. *Arthashastra*, Book VII, Chapter 1. The modern-day example of *dvaidhibhava* is China that seeks cooperation with Pakistan and hostile relationship with India; policy of friendship with Malaysia and aggression with Vietnam over the South China Sea; and policy of peace with North Korea and hostility with Japan.

79. Shamasastry, *Kautilya's Arthashastra*, 296.
80. Boesche, 'Kautilya's Arthashastra', 9–37.
81. Shamasastry, *Kautilya's Arthashastra*, 296.
82. *Arthashastra*, Book VII.2.267; cf. Shamasastry, *Kautilya's Arthashastra*, 296.
83. *Arthashastra*, Book VII.2.268; Shamasastry, *Kautilya's Arthashastra*, 297.
84. Kangle, *Kautilya Arthashastra*, Pt II, 327.
85. *Arthashastra*, Book VII.3.269; Shamasastry, *Kautilya's Arthashastra*, 298.
86. Kangle, *Kautilya Arthashastra*, 328.
87. *Arthashastra*, Book VI.2.4; cf. Liebig, 'Kautilya's Arthashastra'.
88. cf. Liebig, 'Kautilya's Arthashastra'.
89. Liebig, 'Kautilya's Arthashastra'.
90. Liebig, 'Kautilya's Arthashastra'; Max Weber, 1978, pp. 27, 38.
91. *Arthashastra*, Book II, Chapter 10.47; Rangarajan, 'Kautilya', 91.
92. *Arthashastra*, Book II, Chapter 10.47; Rangarajan, 91.
93. Dikshitar, *War in Ancient India*, 326, 335; *Arthashastra*, Book IX.7.73-77.
94. Mishra, 'Katilya's Arthashastra', 95.
95. Morgenthau, *Politics among Nations*.
96. Gautam, *Understanding Kautilya's*.
97. Modelski, 'Kautilya', 553.
98. Jayantanuja Bandyopadhyaya (1993).
99. Mishra, 'Katilya's Arthashastra', 99.
100. Boesche, *The First Great Political Realist*, 109.
101. Gautam, *One Hundred Years*, 6.
102. Liebig, 'The Kautilya's Arthashastra'; Kautilya provides a detailed methodology and Machinery of intelligence collection, see Book i.I.12.1-25; Kangle, *Kautilya Arthashastra*, Pt II, 23–27.
103. See also, Rangarajan, 'Kautilya', 491–493.
104. Juutinen, 'Emerging Dynamics of Conflict', 9.
105. Juutinen, 'Emerging Dynamics of Conflict', 18.
106. See Book VI and VII of Kautilya's *Arthashastra*.
107. Elazar, *Constitutionalising Globalisation*; cf. Zuutinen, ibid., p.10.
108. See Rosenau and Czempiel, *Governance without Government*; Scholte, 'Global Governance', 11.
109. *Arthashastra*, Book VI.2.35-37; cf. Kangle, *Kautilya Arthashastra*, 319.
110. Juutinen, 'Emerging Dynamics of Conflict', 11.
111. Juutinen, 'Emerging Dynamics of Conflict', 18.
112. Kangle, *The Kautilya Arthashastra*, Pt III, 64.
113. Mishra, 'Kautilya's Arthashastra', 100.
114. Shahi, 'Arthashastra', 69.
115. https://www.mea.gov.in/distinguished-lectures-detail.htm?410
116. Kokanen, 'International Relations'.
117. Kokanen, 'International Relations'.
118. Liebig, 'Kautilya's Arthashastra'.
119. Singh, *Indian Political Thought*.

120. cf. Liebig, 'Kautilya's Arthashastra'; Mitra (2011), Sidhu (1996) and Michael (2008).
121. Liebig, 'Kautilya's Arthashastra'.
122. See Mishra, 'Kautilya's Arthashastra', 92.
123. *Arthashastra*, Book VII.5.27-28.
124. Fredrich Meinecke, 1963/1924.
125. Alfred Hillebrandt, 1923, cf. Liebig, 'Kautilya's Arthashastra'.
126. *Arthashastra*, Book VI.1.18.
127. Boesche, *Kautilya*, 109.
128. *Arthashastra*, Book X.3.30; Book XIII.1.7-8; Liebig, 'Kautilya's Arthashastra', 13.
129. *Arthashastra*, Book X.6.48-50.
130. Rich, *To Uphold the World*.
131. Kangle, *Kautilya Arthashastra*, Pt III, 282.
132. *Arthashastra*, Book VI.2.30.
133. Karad, 'Perspectives of Kautilya's Foreign Policy', 331.
134. Sen, *Studies in Hindu Political Thought*, 17; Rao, *Studies in Kautilya*; Bandyopadhyaya, *Development of Hindu*.
135. *Arthashastra*, Book VII.5.16-17.
136. Pinaki Chakravorty, ibid.
137. Bhagat, 'Kautilya Re-visited and Re-visioned'.
138. Bhagat, 'Kautilya Re-visited and Re-visioned', 200.
139. Bhagat, 'Kautilya Re-visited and Re-visioned', 202.
140. Pinaki Chakravorty, ibid.
141. See Hui, *War and State Formation in Ancient China*; Shankman and Durrant, *The Siren and the Sage*; Vivekanandan, *Interrogating International Relations*.
142. cf. Kakonen, 2020 draft Article on International Relations in *Arthashastra*.
143. See Archer, 2014, *The end of American World Order*; Tharoor, *Pax-Indica*; Kumar, *Asia in Post-Western Age*; Mahbubani, *The New Asian Hemisphere*; Jacques, *When China Rules*.
144. Swaine, *America's Challenge*, 160–163.
145. Swaine, Tellis, and Greenwood, *Interpreting China's Grand*, x; cf. Kumar, 'The Arthashastra', 77–78.
146. Gautam, *Kautilya's Arthashastra*, 4–12.
147. Gautam, *Kautilya's Arthashastra*.
148. Kumar, 'The Arthashastra', 80.
149. Trilateral Highway Project with Myanmar and Thailand; Sittway project in Myanmar as Kaladan project.

Women in the *Arthashastra*

5

In previous chapters, we have discussed different dimensions of the political thought of Kautilya with a specific focus on the Kautilyan theory of state and governance; the theory of law, justice and its administration; and his thoughts on the theory of international relations and foreign policy with reference to his concept of *mandala, shadgunya* and the four *upayas*. In this chapter, I propose to examine his ideas on the treatment of women in the ancient Hindu polity and society with the reference to his work, the *Arthashastra*. One may genuinely ask a question: Why have I chosen this topic when I have not devoted much attention to the aspects of economics and social structure and organization during the times of the *Arthashastra*? There are two specific reasons for doing so: first, women constitute an important part of society and make a visible contribution to the cultural, economic and social development of a state and society; second, despite the increasing attention of the sociolegal studies of the status and position of women in contemporary India, the scholarship has given a scant attention to the historical analysis of the rights and place she enjoyed in the past to reach a point of comparison of the present with the past and to take note of the influences that law, culture and traditions carry on the evolution of the legal and social practices relating to the status of women.

This study further becomes salient as the status of women is not only an integral part of the research project but also there is a need to make an in-depth analysis of the different views in relation to their condition in the Indian context during ancient times. It has been said, for instance, that women lived a life of subordination and subservience to men and were treated as merely child (sons)-producing machines.[1]

It is here that one requires investigating the issue of rights and gender justice, followed by an enquiry into the role of women in Kautilya's work, and the change, if any, in terms of the nature of the regulatory mechanisms, whether legal, social and cultural, has informed the claims of women on the state and society with special reference to equality, education, health, marriage, divorce, maintenance and inheritance. Where did women figure in the religious–cultural framework of society and the law? Do the rights, duties and gender relations continue unchanged from those times or whether the ancient traditions are invalid and bypassed by the modernist tradition, and if it is so, to what extent? Did Kautilya treat women in a more egalitarian manner than what is projected about him? Was he in any manner different in this regard from Manu, Plato and Aristotle? An attempt has been made to answer all these questions.

The theme of the chapter has been discussed in the light of the material mainly drawn from the *Arthashastra*, as translated by L. N. Rangarajan, R. Shamasastry and R. P. Kangle who have also commented on the great book, followed by a number of secondary sources, including books and articles. For the sake of clarity and order, the discussion has been divided into a number of sections, out of which the first section relates to the matter of marriage. It is important to underline that the status of a woman is a combination of many things, including the opportunities and admission by society of a right to a woman to acquire knowledge, have a healthy body and mind and have adequate access to and ownership of property, but the most important of them all is the system of rules and laws governing her family and personal life, exhibited through the social institutions like marriage.

THE INSTITUTION OF MARRIAGE AND WOMEN IN KAUTILYA

For Kautilya, all transactions begin with marriage (*vyavahara*—dealing, in effect, with civil life),[2] and he begins with a sort of classification of marriages into eight types:

1. *Brahma* marriage is one where the daughter is presented for marriage by her father after adorning her with ornaments.

2. *Prajapatya* marriage is one where the performance of sacred duties is carried out jointly by both the parties (similar is the definition of this marriage in the *smritis* as well).
3. *Arsa* marriage is one in which the father receives a pair of cattle from the bridegroom and then gives his daughter.
4. *Daiva* marriage is one in which the father gifts his daughter to the officiating priest inside a sacrificial alter.
5. *Gandharva vivaha*/marriage is one where the lovers execute marriage by a secret association.
6. *Asura* marriage is the one committed after receiving a dowry.
7. *Rakshasa* marriage is one where someone forces a marriage by kidnapping a maiden.
8. *Paishacha vivaha*/marriage by way of seizure of a sleeping or intoxicated maiden.[3]

The law of marriage further provides that the first four types of marriage are lawful with the sanction of the father and the remaining with the sanction of both the father and mother, as these two receive the dowry of the daughter, or one of them in the absence of the other. The *Brahma* marriage, as elaborated in the classical text, implies that in the first four marriages, the consent of the mother is not mandatory and, further, that the first four *vivaha* are considered as pious and *dharma vivaha*. Another derivation from the reading is that the consent of the mother could be taken later; the *shulka* was also received at the time of consent. The second dowry is to be received by the woman.[4] It is plausible to assert, after reading the provision of *gandharva* marriage, that the young girls and boys enjoyed the right to a love marriage during the days of Kautilya, which remained a taboo until recent times in modern India, if not under law, under the social customary system and norms. So Kautilya could be seen as more progressive in the matters of freedom of women and in the matters of marital choice, though only in a limited sense. Kautilya, further, displays considerable modernity and originality in his approach to the understanding and explaining the place and role of women in society and the state. This is evident from his support to the system of inter-caste marriages. Kautilya also provisions for the division of shares of property among the sons of a man. In Book III, Chapter 6.17-22 he states:

among a Brahmin's sons from wives belonging to the four *varnas*, the son of the Brahmin wife shall receive four shares, the son of the *kshatriya* wife three, of *vaishya* wife two and the son of sudra wife shall receive one share and the Brahmin's son born of a wife belonging to the immediately next Varna is to have an equal share; that of a *kshtriya* or a *vaishya* is to have half a share or an equal share if endowed with manly qualities.... In the case of Brahmins, however, the son born of a *sudra* wife shall receive only one third of the property as his share.[5]

This narrative clearly establishes that Kautilya permitted inter-caste marriages, a radically modern proposition by all standards. He states in Book IV.12.10 that a maiden having menstruation for three years could approach a man of the same *varna*; after that, she can even approach a man of another *varna* without being accused of an offence. The only condition is that she goes without her ornaments for taking her father's property shall be liable for theft.

A person violating a maiden who has not attained the age of puberty from the same *varna* shall be awarded a punishment of the hand being chopped off or a fine of 400 *panas*, and if she dies, the offender will be awarded death sentence.

RIGHT TO REMARRY

Kautilya grants the right to remarry to both the husband and the wife or a widow or a divorcee in certain exceptional circumstances. For example, Kautilya states in Book III.2.38-39 that a husband could remarry a second wife with the object of getting a son after waiting for 8 years if the first wife does not bear offspring or does not bear a son or is barren; after waiting for 10 years if the first wife bears dead offspring; and after waiting for 12 years if the first wife bears only daughters. If a man marries in transgression of this rule, he shall have to hand over the dowry, the woman's property and half of that as compensations for supersession and pay a fine of a maximum of 24 *panas*.[6] Further, Kautilya states that a man could marry any number of women/wives by paying the dowry, the woman's property, and in the case of a wife without a dowry or woman's property of her own, a compensation for supersession equal in amount to that and a suitable maintenance, for wives are necessary for having sons.[7] Thus, one may assume that Kautilya was not opposed to the system of polygamy for the sake of procuring a son. By this narrative, Kautilya appears to be unjust as he provides no remedy against the transgression of the rule, but he, rather, seeks to approve it under the system of compensation and fines. At the same time, it must not be forgotten that Kautilya was writing in a certain sociocultural environment where these practices were being carried out under the sanctions of social laws, and in many parts of north India, the practice of remarrying for the sake of getting a son is still in vogue.[8]

However, it may not be a fair evaluation of Kautilya without noting that a woman has also been given the right to remarry under certain circumstances. For example, Kautilya states in Book III.4.24-27[9] that the wives of a *Sudra*, a *Vaishya*, a *Kshatriya* and a *Brahmin* who are away on a short journey shall wait for a period of one year, which can be successively increased by one year, if they have not given birth to children; for one more year, if they have given birth to children; for those who have been provided for are to wait for double the period; and one who is unprovided for shall be maintained by the trustees and kinsmen after four or eight years. They shall be released thereafter. It might mean that such women shall be free to lead the life of their own, including remarriage. Kautilya is very specific when he says in Book III.4.30: 'Or, when the affluence of the family has disappeared, she, being released by the trustees, may marry again as she desires, or when she is in distress, for the sake of livelihood'. Further, he states 'After the pious marriage, the maiden shall wait for her husband who has gone away without informing her for seven periods if no news is heard about him and for one year if news is heard; if he has gone away after informing her, she shall wait for five periods when no news is heard and for ten periods if news is heard; if he had paid only a part of the dowry, she shall wait for three periods if there is no news and seven periods if there is news about him. In case he has paid dowry in full, she shall wait for five periods if there is no news and for ten periods if there is news. Thereafter, she could remarry as she desires, with the permission of judges because Kautilya believed that the frustration of the period is destruction of sacred duty'.[10] In addition, a wife of a man, who became a *pravrajita* (ascetic), had the same rights to remarry if the man had gone on a long journey or had died.[11] The right to remarry was granted to a woman, including a widow, in the *Atharvaveda* and the *Dharma Sutras* as well.[12] On the other hand, the laws of Manu do not allow remarriage or even divorce as he considers that a woman is never freed from her husband by sale or rejection.[13]

It is delighting to note that Kautilya was the most progressive sociopolitical thinkers insofar as he argued in favour of widow remarriage for which many social reformers like Raja Ram Mohan Roy had to launch some sort of a movement during the British regime. If a woman loses her husband, she can choose either to lead a life of piety or could marry again. If, however, she was desirous of having a family, she shall receive at the time of remarriage what was given to her by her father-in-law and her late husband. But if she married against the wishes of her father-in-law, she shall forfeit what was given to her by her father-in-law and her late husband.[14] Naturally, a widow who wants to remarry shall forfeit her claim over the property given to her by the late husband; she also shall forfeit her woman's property if she decides to remarry even though she has sons. Why were a widowed woman's rights restricted in case she remarried? This was so to prevent the leakage of property from patriarchy.[15] In the case she remarries for the maintenance of her sons, she shall augment the woman's property for the sake of her sons.[16] In some cases, the wife enjoys more rights as compared to her husband. Book III.11.175 states that a wife who has not heard of the debt (*pratisravani*) shall not be caught hold of for the debt contracted by her husband, except in the case of herdsmen and joint cultivators (*gopalakardhasitikebhyah*), but a husband could be caught for the debt contracted by his wife. If it is admitted that a man fled the country without providing for the debt contracted by his wife, the highest amercement shall be meted out.[17]

Right of a Man to Remarry

As it was for women, the same laws applied to men in terms of the right of a man to remarry after waiting for eight years before marrying another if:

1. a woman gives birth to dead children;
2. has not given birth to a male child; or
3. is barren.

There seems to be an agreement between Vatsyayana, Manu and Kautilya on this count.[18] The husband shall wait for 10 years before remarrying if the wife bears only a dead child; he shall wait for 12 years if she gives birth to only female children. He could remarry if he was desirous of having sons. In view of the clear specification of the conditions in which a husband could marry another woman, one can say that the institution of marriage was sacred and not to be broken, or the first wife cannot be treated as a left out to live alone by herself. It has been mentioned by Kautilya that if any husband marries another woman in violation of the aforementioned rules or conditions, he shall have to pay the first wife not only the *shulka*, her property (*stridhana*) and an adequate monetary compensation (*adhivedanikamartham*), but he shall also have to pay a fine of 24 *panas* to the government.[19]

The husband, after having paid the *shulka*, the *stridhana* and the compensation even to a woman who did not receive any such things at the time of her marriage with him and after making adequate arrangements for their subsistence (*vrtti*), could marry any number of women, for the women were created for the sake of giving birth to sons.[20] It seems from this that though it might not have been a general practice, the system of polygamy was not inconceivable specifically for those who were very rich and were endowed with huge resources. The marriageable age for a girl was to be not lesser than 12 years, which was the age of her puberty/majority, and 16 years for a boy. At the same time, a woman and a man shall pay a fine of 15 *panas* and 30 *panas*, respectively, if they proved to be disobedient to lawful authority after attaining majority, [21]; the amount of fine was the same if they failed or knowingly did not carry out marital duties. A wife had the right to abstain from sexual relations with the husband if she was a barren, desirous of a pious life, already had sons, gave birth to dead offspring or one whose menstruation had stopped.[22] Kautilya suggests 'if unwilling, the man may not approach a (wife) who is leprous or insane'.

The aforementioned discussion on the prescriptions of conduct of marriage and marital laws suggests that Kautilya paid close attention to these matters with more clarity. His analysis goes deep into them and is indicative of his systematic understanding of the culture of the society of his times, which appears to be futuristic and universal in character. It is more comprehensive than what one gathers from the *smritis*. R. P. Kangle remarks that 'many of the sub-sections, which are fully treated here, are not even thought of in the *smritis*'. The provisions concerning the dissolution of marriage and the remarriage of women are, on the whole, foreign to the spirit of those texts. The *smritis* also miss the breath and length of coverage and outlook and the nature of the status a woman commands in the classical text of Kautilya.[23]

RIGHT TO DIVORCE

It is interesting to note that the genius of Kautilya could envisage a situation when it might become impossible for the wife to live with the husband or vice versa. Therefore, he provided for the right of a woman to divorce or to abandon a husband. For example, it is recommended in Book III.2 of the *Arthashastra* that a woman may abandon her husband who has become degraded or gone to a foreign country or has committed an offence against the king or is dangerous to her life or has become an outcast or even an impotent.[24] Furthermore, in Book III.3.13, Kautilya states that a woman is entitled to stay with a female mendicant, a kinsman or a guardian alone and the husband shall give his consent for that in case she is disliked by him. It means that husband and wife could live separately if there was disharmony between them. Kautilya, again, asserts in Book III.3.15-19 that a dissatisfied wife is not granted divorce from the husband who is unwilling; the same rule applied for a dissatisfied husband; a divorce shall be granted when there is mutual disaffection. If the husband seeks divorce because of the wife's offence, he shall give to her whatever he may have taken, but he shall not give her whatever may have been received if the wife seeks divorce from the husband on account of his offence. It should also be pointed out that divorce is not permissible in pious marriages.

A wife, again, could indulge haughtily in the sport of drink; could go on a pleasure trip with women or men, with the consent of the husband or if she paid the fixed fines, and this she could do even if she was prohibited from indulging in these activities. So, such women could be penalized with fines, but not in any other manner. Kautilya supports the right of a man to divorce his wife or reject brides (in Chapter 15 of Book III) before the marriage rituals are performed; a bride could also be rejected if she is proved to be guilty of indecorous conduct with another man. However, the *Arthashastra* also lays down that divorce can be effectuated without the will/consent of each other.[25] Manu is also of the view that the man has the right to divorce a woman if she does not bear children. Sudhir Ranjan Das mentions the following grounds for divorce of a woman identified by Manu and states:

> In the opinion of Manu, the wife is praised as equal to the husband in honour, only if she bears children, otherwise she may be divorced. But unpleasant speech on the part of a woman is a serious crime in the eyes of Manu and he allows the husband to divorce his wife in such a case ... a woman attempting to run away from the house of her husband can be divorced in the presence of the relatives and other persons.[26]

RIGHT TO MAINTENANCE

Kautilya's forbearance comes to the fore when he argues in favour of the right to maintenance to women both by the husband and by the state as well. It is stated that the king shall be obliged to maintain not only the orphans, the aged, the infirm, the afflicted and the helpless, but he shall also provide subsistence to helpless women when they are carrying and also to the children they give birth to.[27] Neglect by a capable person (male or female) to maintain one's child, wife, mother, father, minor brothers, sisters or widowed girls (*kanya vidhavashcha*) is a punishable offence with an imposition of a fine of 12 *panas* under the Kautilyan scheme of governance. Kautilyan law further makes it punishable if any person embraces asceticism without providing for the maintenance of his wife and sons with a punishment of first amercement and for any person who converts a woman to asceticism (*pravrajayatah*).[28] The wife is eligible to receive her due maintenance as long as she is devoted and obedient to her husband or to other lawful guardians. Every wife shall be given as much food and clothing as required and even more than that, but the wife who parts with her husband and lives independently or places herself under the protection of another person shall forfeit her claim to maintenance from her husband. A widow is to be provided by her own property and also by her sons, if she remains pure, but if she remarries, she shall be maintained by her second husband or her protector.[29]

PROTECTION OF THE DIGNITY AND HONOUR OF WOMEN OR THE PRESCRIPTIONS AGAINST THE SEXUAL CRIMES AND CRUELTY AGAINST WOMEN

Kautilya pays special attention to the issue of upholding the dignity and honour of women and provides for severe punishments for violating the modesty or chastity or for any crime or violence against women. For instance, Kautilya devotes an entire Chapter 12 in Book IV on the violation of the maidens and treats that act as a serious offence under the administration of law and justice in the *Arthashastra*. Kautilya's provision for cutting off of the hand or a fine of 400 *panas* for a person violating a maiden not reaching the stage of puberty and of the same *varna* and death sentence in case she dies is enough proof for his concern in this regard. Furthermore, he recommends, in Section 87.3, the cutting off of the middle and index fingers or imposing a fine of 200 *panas* on the person who violates a maiden who has attained puberty; in addition, he shall pay adequate compensation to her father; he shall not marry her against her will; if he has violated when she is already reserved by the dowry of another man, his hand shall be cut off or a fine of 400 *panas* shall be imposed upon him and he shall also have to make the payment of the dowry.

It can also be construed from Book IV.12.15 that maintaining the dignity and honour is as much a responsibility of women as that of men. Kangle writes:

> for a bride not a virgin at the time of consummation, the fine shall be fifty four panas and she shall return the dowry and marriage expenses. If after maintaining that condition she fails, she shall pay double; for substituting other blood, the fine shall be two hundred, also for the man falsely accusing

the bride of loss of virginity and he shall lose the dowry and the expenses and he shall not have right to her if she is unwilling. Similarly, Kautilya prescribes fines of different amount on persons found involved in the acts of abduction of a Maiden by force or abduction by a group.[30]

It can be noted that Kautilya makes it an offence (Book III.20.16) to forcibly violate a widow who lives independently or a *chandala* to touch an *Aryan* lady and the fine for violation is 100 *panas*. If anyone causes abortion of a female slave by medicines, he shall be imposed the lowest fine.[31] Similarly, touching the brother's wife with the hand or going to a prostitute in the exclusive keeping of another would fetch a fine of 48 *panas*.[32]

Kautilyan laws on adultery also show us that he was against the acts of adultery.[33] He suggests that a wife who misbehaves in the absence of her husband shall be kept under guard by the kinsman or his servant, and she shall wait for her husband to return; if her husband were to tolerate, both should be set free; in case he does not tolerate, she shall be punished with cutting off of her ears and nose, and the lover shall meet with a death sentence.[34] Adultery shall be taken as committed when there is mutual caressing of the hair, or from indications of bodily enjoyment or from the expert opinion or from the statement of the woman.[35] Further, Kautilya asserts that a man can enjoy the company of a stranger woman, as agreed upon, who has been rescued by him from being carried away by the enemy troops, or foresters or being carried away by a current or was abandoned in a forest or during a famine or was left under the impression of being dead. However, he shall have to return her back for a ransom in case the woman was superior to him in caste, is unwilling or has children.[36] Again, touching the brother's wife by hand or for one going to a prostitute in the exclusive keeping of another will attract a fine of 48 *panas*. Similarly, if anyone forcibly violates a widow who lives by herself or a *chandala* touching an Aryan lady, he shall attract a fine 100 *panas*. Indulgence by a man and a woman, in gestures with limbs or indecent conversation in secret (with sexual intercourse in view), a woman shall be fined 24 *panas* and the man with 48 *panas*.[37] The aforementioned passages clearly indicate that molestation or violation of a woman by a person was treated as a crime in the *Arthashastra* as it is treated as a crime in modern India.

CRUELTY AGAINST WOMEN

Kautilya touches upon another important aspect relating to a woman, which has a modern relevance, that is, the question of cruelty against women. That violence or cruelty, verbal or physical, against women in a modern democratic society is an offence legally punishable is a well-known position, but it was so in the *Arthashastra* is something that makes Kautilya a distinct thinker of the patriarchal times and in a monarchical system of government:

> The inculcation of modest behaviour (shall be done) without the use of expressions such as 'thou lost one', 'thou ruined one', 'thou cripple', 'thou fatherless one', or 'thou motherless one' or striking at the back three times with one of (the three, viz.,) a split bamboo cane, rope or hand (may be done)' seems unconvincing in view of his next prescription wherein he suggests imposition of fines half those for verbal and physical injury if there is transgression of the above rules.[38]

Roger Boesche points out the deep concern of Kautilya on the abuse of a woman by the husband:

> Kautilya was serious in his efforts to protect the wife against spousal abuse. For example, he urged the state to fine a husband for verbal abuse which was listed in the *dharmasutras* (G12.1-14) and have been provided above... Kautilya tried much harder than his contemporaries to protect women, and, as a parallel, he also was what Charlse Drekmeier has called 'a champion of the *Sudras*, espousing their rights as freedom citizens'.[39]

Kautilya states in Book III.3.10-11 that cruelty committed by a woman on her husband is also punishable.

> The same shall be the punishment for the wife whose offence against the husband is well known. On occasion of her enjoying herself outside the home out of jealousy, the penalty shall be as laid down. It follows that cruelty does not mean only a physical violence; it also includes mental or psychological hurt. Thus his insistence on equal treatment of women and men on account of cruelty is well taken as it is attracting the attention of the modern legalists as well as the proponents of gender justice in modern times.[40]

For the author of the classical text, having illicit relation with a woman is also a kind of foolishness and by inference a cruelty as it is ruinous and harmful. In Book VIII.3.56-61, he quotes Vatavyadhi in whose view indulgence between a woman and drink, indulgence in women is worst; and rejects his opinion by extending the argument that in the case of indulgence in women there is begetting an offspring and protection of oneself with wives at home, the opposite of this with outside women. Here, Kautilya appears to be distinguishing indulgence in women in the home from those outside the home. He further agrees with his teachers that a woman could go to the house of any one of the kinsmen of her husband, a trustee, the village headman, a guardian, a female mendicant or her own kinsman, if there are no males in it, on account of the husband's ill-treatment, besides permitting them to do so even if there are males in it because a chaste woman cannot commit deceit.[41] A woman, in addition, could visit her kinsman in case there is a death, illness, calamity or childbed without hindrance by the husband.[42]

Even in the matter of interrogating a woman, it is interesting thing to know that torture should either be half or only an interrogation for the purpose of investigation of a case against her should be carried and if she is pregnant or a woman within one month of delivery, she should not be put to torture under any circumstances whatsoever. Thus, he was milder towards women than men while applying torture for either fetching confession or evidences for the given offence.[43]

SEXUAL CRIMES

Kautilya can be further credited with addressing the problem of dignity, chastity, privacy and honour of a woman when it is observed that several *stangas* or *shlokas* were devoted to the question of having sexual intercourse with an unwilling woman or committing an act of rape. This is treated as an act of violence and, therefore, a punishable offence. For example, he refers in Book IV.12.30-35 to various such acts. He writes in Book IV.12.30:

> For one carnally approaching the sister of his mother or father, his maternal aunt, his preceptor's wife, his daughter-in-law, daughter or sister, he shall be punished with cutting off of his generating organ and testicles/*ling* and death (thereafter). So shall be the kind of punishment to a woman who

was willing, or has relations with a slave, or servant or a pledged man.[44] For a kshatriya fine shall be the highest if he has relations with a Brahmin woman, for a *Vaishya* the confiscation of his entire property and for a *sudra*, burning him in a fire of straw in the similar case. It can be noted here that *Arthashastra* does not approve, like in Mahabharata, of celebrating a rapist as a 'conquering hero.[45]

Similarly, in the Laws of Manu, rape of a *Brahmin* woman by a *Brahmin* man was punishable with a fine of 1,000 *panas*, but if a man raped a virgin, he was to be awarded with either a corporal or capital punishment.[46] The *Dharma Sutra* also prescribe a harsh deterrent against such heinous crimes in the form of cutting off of the penis and the testicles of the offender.[47] Kautilya prescribes different penalties for committing a rape of a minor girl or an unmarried woman and if the raped young woman dies and of an older and married woman—nurses, widows or prostitutes.[48]

We note that Kautilya was for protecting the dignity of even a prostitute and provided for punishing a rapist whether individual or a group. He says 'For enjoyment of a prostitute by force, the fine shall be 12 *panas*; for many men enjoying forcibly one prostitute, the fine shall be 24 *panas* for each one separately'. He was equally concerned with the protection of the slave women as well. In Book II.36.41, he says 'For guards misbehaving with a slave woman, with woman who is not a slave, with one in the exclusive keeping of someone, with a woman from a respectable family shall be imposed lowest fine, middle fine, the highest fine and death sentence respectively'.[49] However, he was careful about protecting the innocent, in general, and recommended 30 times the punishment to the king in case punishment is inflicted on those not deserving to be punished. The king was to place that fine in the water for Varuna, which was to be distributed among the *Brahmanas* after that. We are told in Book III.3.26 that touching the hair, the knot of the lower garment, teeth or nails, the lowest punishment for the violence (shall be imposed, double (that) for the man. It can be inferred that any such act, whether committed by a woman or a man, was a punishable offence, but it was harsher for men. In the same vein, a woman is prohibited to converse in a suspicious place, violation of which attracts a fine or whipping. The women could, in this case, be whipped by a *chandala* with five strokes with the lash in the region between the sides (i.e., on the back) in the centre of the village or she could avoid the strokes by paying a fine of 1 *pana* for each stroke.

RIGHT TO PROPERTY AND INHERITANCE

When the question of right to property of a woman is put to examination, it is observed that maintenance and ornaments constitute a woman's property, wherein maintenance is an endowment of a maximum of 2,000 *panas*; as to ornaments, there is no limit. However, Kautilya tells us about this right of women in different ways. For example, he mentions as to how a woman can claim or forfeit her right on property. He specifies clearly about when a woman is entitled to her right over property and when shall she be deprived of that right. Similarly, Kautilya seems to have one type of arrangement in this regard relating to a widow and another type in the case of other women. Let us first talk about the property rights of a widow. Kautilya argues that a widow is entitled to her property/late husband's property only if she decides to remain pious and pure/virtuous; in the sense, she remains unmarried after the death of her husband. Conversely, if she remarried, she would lose every claim on the property given to her by her husband or her father-in-law. Further, he lays down that a widowed wife, not marrying again, could only use the property of her late husband, but he could not lay claim over that property. In the event of her death before her husband, her property shall be divided among her sons and daughters. Kautilya further indicates that the daughters shall inherit the property in the case there is a property of a sonless man. The sons shall inherit the estate of a man with sons or the daughters born in pious marriages.[50] It is here that Kautilya talks about the right of a daughter in the property of her mother. Moreover, it may be underlined that, like the Mahabharata, the sisters have been denied the right to inherit; they will receive only a share of the bell-metal dishes used for meals and ornaments from the mother's personal belongings. It can also be taken as a denial to a daughter only if there are sons.[51] As for other women, Kautilya tells us that on account of disaffection towards the king and misconduct and by wilfully running away, a woman would lose her ownership over the woman's property, what she has brought from her kinsmen and dowry.[52] It may, however, mean that she can retain her claim over her *stridhana*. However, if she leaves home for the house of a kinsman on the occasion of death, illness, calamity or childbed, which is permitted, and conceals herself, she shall forfeit her woman's property (*stridhana*); the kinsmen who conceals her shall also forfeit the balance of the dowry.[53] It can be inferred from the aforementioned discussion that a woman did not have a claim over the property of her husband like land or any immovable property unlike the Vedic period when both the wife and the husband had joint ownership of property.[54] Why were women denied a share in the immovable property when she was not prohibited from inheriting her own property? Different explanations, though not convincing by any standard of modern thought, have been provided for this. For example, it is said in the *Dharma Sutra* that women do not have strength enough to inherit and manage property.[55]

TREATMENT OF THE PROSTITUTES IN THE *ARTHASHASTRA*

It may sound a little strange for the modern reader to read that Kautilya assigns a special discussion on the institution of prostitutes. But it is this aspect of his focus on the role and position of women in society and the state, which tells us about the distinctiveness of his thought and action. He not only did not ignore a woman generally seen in a low esteem, but he also raised her status in terms of treating prostitution as a profession and also by defining her role(s) of different natures and types, including that of being an agency for collecting intelligence meant to be used for internal governance[56] and for spying over the enemy king. She was also to act as an instrument of killing the rival ruler if the situation so demanded. In the words of Roger Boesche:

> Precisely because women are such a powerful addiction, the king could use them against an enemy. For example, if a king is trying to undermine a ruling oligarchy, he should make chiefs of the ruling council infatuated with women possessed of great beauty and youth. When passion is roused in them, they should start quarrels by creating beliefs (about their love) in one and by going to another.[57]

Kautilya recommended that 'the keepers of prostitutes should make the (enemy's) army chiefs infatuated with women with great beauty and youth and create quarrels among them when they are in the highest state of passion'.[58] Such a role gave her self-image, self-confidence and the ability to think critically and foster decision-making and action. Thus, he took a prostitute's function beyond her traditional stereotype of an entertainer or giving pleasure to those approaching her. By including prostitution in the list of a profession, he underlined her contribution to the generation of revenue resources for the state as well, as a percentage of their income was to be given to the state treasury as tax.[59] It is not that the *ganikas*/prostitutes were the invention of Kautilya or that they did not exist prior to him. In fact, there is evidence of this category of women even in the epics like the Ramayana. In the *Arthashastra*, there is a description of three types of *ganikas*/prostitutes: (a) one practising within a state-controlled establishment; (b) the *rupajiva* or a prostitute living and earning her livelihood and practising independently outside the sphere of a state-owned establishment or in establishments in which government intervention was minimal; and (c) the *pumsachali* or the concubine.[60]

It is worth noting that prostitutes were not only beautiful young women of exceptional type, but they were also imparted skills of their profession by a paid state employee who was responsible for imparting training in the field of art, dance, entertainment, singing, painting, lovemaking and music. In a way, it can be argued that the *ganikas* were not amateur artists, but they were well versed in their respective areas of expertise. The head and her deputy in charge of a brothel house were also given some lump sum assistance by the state to establish brothels and purchase jewellery, furniture, etc. Further, she was protected by the state against exploitation by making her rape a punishable offence, though the efficacy of this provision is a matter of conjecture. Moreover, Shirin points out that 'since the skilled prostitute earned revenue for the state, her ransom price for releasing her from service to the state was also high—24,000 *panas*—the second highest salary paid only to the top five officials of the state'.[61]

Though there is enough to suggest that a prostitute was skilful, intelligent and accomplished, the *Arthashastra* seems to ignore her due claims, as for example, consider the case of her son being denied a legal recognition in matters of inheriting his father's property, leaving the prostitute to herself to make arrangements for her children in that respect. However, it cannot be denied that she enjoyed legal protection against rape, which is described as an offence in the text.

FEMALES AS SLAVE IN THE *ARTHASHASTRA*

In this discussion on women, I have drawn the attention of the reader to the rights of a woman kept as bonded labour (pledged woman) or as a slave. We are told in the *Arthashastra* that such a woman had a right to protection against abortion as it was a punishable crime. If a slave woman gave birth to her master's child, she was entitled to freedom from bondage; at the same time, such a pregnant slave could not be sold or mortgaged without making proper arrangements for her welfare during the period of pregnancy. Further, the master was obligated under law not only to not rape a slave virgin or a bonded nurse but also to ensure that no one else could rape her. Moreover, a woman slave enjoyed protection against beating, violent treatment, violation of her virginity or giving bath to a naked man.

WELFARE AND SOCIAL SECURITY OF WOMEN

From the discussion on women in the *Arthashastra*, one may tend to conclude that Kautilya swings between treating women as independent, free and subordinate beings. However, it is fascinating to note that he makes it the responsibility of the state to

> provide means of livelihood to widows, crippled women, maidens, women who have left their homes and women paying off their fine by personal labour, mothers of courtesans, old female slaves of the king and to female slaves of the temples whose service of the gods has ceased by getting yarn spun out of wool, bark-fibres, cotton, silk-cotton, hemp and flax through them. (Book II.23.2)

The superintendent of yarns and textiles was responsible to fix wages, not arbitrarily or discriminately, but on the basis of the fineness, coarseness or medium quality of the yarn and on the basis of high or low in quantity, thus leaving hardly any space for bias in fixing wages. Besides, they should be given gifts and should be made to work by honouring them during festival times (Book II.23.3, 5). This kind of treatment to such women would undoubtedly make them not only self-reliant, independent and confident about their living, but it would also render them dignified life free from exploitation, frustration, depression and helplessness. In other words, Kautilya did not leave them at the mercy of others or to live on alms.

He also provides for those women who do not move out, like those living separately, widows, crippled women or maidens, and who wish to earn their living, should be given work by sending his own female slaves to them with (a view to) support (them): if they come to the yarn-house themselves, he should cause an interchange of goods and wages to be made early at dawn. Looking at the face of a woman or conversing with her on another matter than the matter concerning yarn, the lowest fine for violence shall be imposed, and the middle fine shall be awarded for delay in the payment of wages and for payment of wages for work not done.[62]

CONCLUSION

The foregoing discussion of the status of women in the classical text of Kautilya suggests an extraordinary thoroughness, practicality and realism; heedlessness of moral and religious standards and norms; and a distinct combination of the influences and features of the culture and tradition of his period inside and outside India. It is also possible to derivate from the *Arthashastra* study concerning women that the author touches upon several aspects relevant and important from the viewpoint of modern times as well. Therefore, it may not be wrong to argue that his ideas covering the issues of right to marry and remarry, divorce, rape, dignity and freedom; her protection against cruelty and violence; purity and sanctity of marriage and family; the right to property and the right of a daughter to inherit property; and the right to maintenance are not only reflective of the law and conventions of his age, but they are also indicative of the lasting value of certain cultural values and beliefs of contemporary India, social change informed by education, law and politics notwithstanding.

In some way, Kautilya predates modernity; rather, he is ahead of modernity, particularly when we go across the treatment and position of the prostitutes or the *ganikas*. He not only recognizes the economic and political as well as administrative use of those women, but he also provides them a respectable place in society by making prostitution a profession and ensuring and assuring a number of rights and claims like other women in a sense. I would also like to argue that Kautilya makes the reader feel that his ideas on women are in tune with the modernist perspectives, in several ways, of gender justice, a concept not popular, rather not known, in those days.

The investigation shows that Kautilya is a stand-alone ancient Indian political thinker who devoted one chapter to the discussion on women besides having referred to the gender issues in several other books, as stated in the body of the discussion, of the treatise. Again, it may be underlined that he made a unique contribution to the social welfare theory and justice when the socially, economically and physically handicapped and weak were to be helped by the state to lead a life of dignity and self-reliance, and here too, he laid special emphasis on women's welfare. Thus, he stands for human and humane treatment of this important section of society. Kautilya's women have been given a place that is given not because he considered them weak as compared to men, but on account of his insistence on maintaining and strengthening the system of *Varnashrama* and to that extent of upholding the principles of division of labour. This view of Kautilya appears to be in consonance with the idea of ideal state and society propounded by Plato in *Republic*, wherein he argues about the separate status of the guardian class from the other classes. Kautilya also talks about the four pious and pure marriages, which are to be governed by different norms than the remaining ones out of the eight categories into which marriages are divided by him.

However, as can be seen from the text of the chapter, Kautilya appears to be inconsistent in his thoughts about women. While, for instance, a woman enjoys almost equal freedom and rights in personal matters, in matters of inheritance and free movement out of her home, he sends a message that she was placed in a subjugate and inferior position in relation to man. Are women free from such conditions in India or in several other parts of the world? It is difficult to provide a straightforward answer to this question in the affirmative. In any patriarchal society—present or past—such practices and restrictions are still in vogue even after they have been rendered in law as irrelevant, outdated and illegal. Kola Olugbade, while answering to the criticism of Plato for being in-egalitarian in reference to women, also echoes the similar view and remarks: 'We should not ignore the fact that Plato was simply not egalitarian. Looking for a feminist in a culture that flourished several thousand years ago could be frustrating and unrealistic especially when the culture was resolved in its Hellenistic phase of patriarchy'.[63]

Customary law or practices still carry weight, and social sanctions prevail even today. It is still believed that such social norms are the guarantee of social balance and calm and cooperative social governance. Kautilya's ideas are a combination of feminism and conservatism, so to say. He talks about women slaves, but unlike Aristotle, grants them rights to beget freedom in certain conditions. It is conceded that the development of society, law and justice from ancient to the modern age have immensely changed the discourse on gender relations; yet, their range revolves around the issues and questions addressed by Kautilya in one or the other sense. He found many pathways of equality and justice and accorded desired adequacy to women issues at his end. His views on the rights and duties of a wife and other women indicate his commitments to social ideals, which were very high. Indeed, it was higher for the age in which he lived and strove for a higher tone in social and political life.[64] Furthermore, he did not find merit in the theory of communism of wives in order to ensure quality of mind and soul of the guardian class; rather, he insisted on maintaining the sanctity of marriage in accordance with the imagination of categories of marriages. However, Plato and Kautilya have one point in common that both supported polygamy,[65] but Kautilya is against indiscriminate sexual relations. Plato prescribes that a good man should have more wives than the rest, while Kautilya favours the idea of multiple marriages for getting a son, good or bad man notwithstanding.

To sum up, it can be safely asserted that Kautilya was not only deeply conscious of women issues, but he also understood them, and this is the reason why he is much above the shoulders of his contemporaries and even those following him. He may not be looked upon as someone revolutionary, but certainly not as a protagonist of denying any recognition in society. He strove for a better deal to women in her public and private life. It is true that Kautilya pleaded in favour of her role mainly as bearing and raising of children/sons, but this conception of the generative function of a female has not erased from the mind of man and society despite having made a huge progress mentally, culturally, materially and socially today. It is not easy to disagree with Sudhir Ranjan Das who stated:

> With regard to these aspects it can be said that Kautilya is careful enough to grant them their legitimate claims and rights allowing them to occupy an honourable position in the society. On the whole Kautilya's spirit about the woman is humane and enlightened. All these considerations will naturally lead us to the conclusion that women, in the age of Kautilya, occupied no inferior position in the Hindu Society.[66]

NOTES

1. See Kangle, *Kautilya Arthashastra*, Pt II, 200; Shamasastry, *Kautilya's Arthashastra*, 174.
2. *Arthashastra*, III.2.1; Kangle, *Kautilya Arthashastra*, Pt II, 196.
3. *Arthashastra*, Book III.2.2-9, Kangle, *Kautilya Arthashastra*, Pt II, 196–197.
4. Kangle, Pt II, 197. In the case of the first four marriages, it seems mother's consent was either not necessary or was obtained later; second, the marriage was pious or a *dharmavivaha*. In the case of the remaining three, it could be derived that the *shulka* was received at the time of consent, and by *dvaitiyam shulkam*, it may mean, *pratidana* or gifts given to the bride at the time of marriage. It is possible, remarks Kangle, that the second dowry may be that received when the woman happens to marry second time after the death of her husband.
5. Kangle, *Kautilya Arthashastra*, 213.
6. According to commentators, the list of permitted situations for remarriage also includes *aprajayamana*, which means who bears a child once and does not

conceive again. It may also mean who does not bear because of miscarriages or whose son died and a child was not born thereafter; see Kangle, *Kautilya Arthashastra*, Pt II, 199.

7. *Arthashastra*, Book III.2.41-42; Kangle, Pt II, 200.
8. I recall a story of a *Brahmin* farmer from my village who went in for seven daughters before finally succeeding to get a son. Though not very common, the living first wife still permits her husband to remarry if she has not been able to give a son or is barren. What I am trying to argue is that culture and society influence the thought process and legal status when it comes to women.
9. Kangle, *Kautilya Arthashastra*, Pt II, 207.
10. *Arthashastra*, Book III.4.31-36, Book III.4.37-41; Kangle, *Kautilya Arthashastra*, Pt II, 207, 208.
11. *Arthashastra*, Book III.4.37.
12. See Altekar, *The Position of Women in Hindu Civilization*; Boesche, 'Women in Kautilya's Arthashastra', 35. However, it may be pointed out that remarriage was condemned under Hindu laws and customs even for a wife ill-treated/maltreated or a widow. Altekar, 1995: 83, 150–159, further, it may be recalled that remarriage by a widowed woman or otherwise does, even in the recent times, not receive the natural social acceptance; rather, it is considered a stigma even now in most cases in modern India.
13. Laws of Manu (*Manusmriti*, 9.46, 202; 9.65, 205); Boesche, 'Women in Kautilya's Arthashastra', 35.
14. *Arthashastra*, Book III.2.19-23, 25.
15. Shirin, 'The Position of Women', 123–134.
16. Shirin, 'The Position of Women', 123–134; *Arthashastra*, Book 3.2.26, 28–30. Kangle, *The Kautilya Arthashastra*, Pt II, 198–199.
17. Shamasastry, *Kautilya's Arthashastra*, 199.
18. See Das, 'Position of Women', 542.
19. Shamasastry, *Kautilya's Arthashastra*, 174.
20. Shamasastry, *Kautilya's Arthashastra*, 174.
21. Shamasastry, *Kautilya's Arthashastra*, 175.
22. *Arthashastra*, Book III.2.45-47 in Kangle, *Kautilya Arthashastra*, Pt II, 200.
23. Kangle, *Kautilya Arthashastra*, Pt III, 153.
24. Kangle, *Kautilya Arthashastra*, Pt II, 200; some of these grounds for divorce, for example, desertion, impotence or threat to life by the husband or cruelty, are still valid in the law of divorce in contemporary India.
25. *Arthashastra*, Book III.3, Das, 'Position of Women', 545.
26. Das, 'Position of Women', 544; *Manusmriti*, IX, 80–81.
27. Shamasastry, *Kautilya's Arthashastra*, Book II.1, 47–48.
28. Shamasastry, *Kautilya's Arthashastra*, 47.
29. See Das, 'The Position of Women', 560.
30. Kangle, *Kautilya Arthashastra*, Pt II; *Arthashastra*, Book IV.15-25, 286–287.

31. *Arthashastra*, Book III.20.15-16.

32. Kangle, *Kautilya Arthashastra*, Pt II, 251–252; *Arthashastra*, Book 3.20.17.

33. Adultery is also prohibited in the *Shatapatha Brahmana* (11, 5.20), wherein it is mentioned that the divine raja Varuna seizes the woman who has adulterous intercourse with men other than her husband.

34. *Arthashastra*, Book IV.12.30.

35. *Arthashastra*, Book IV.12.35.

36. *Arthashastra*, Book IV.12.36-40.

37. Kangle, *Kautilya Arthashastra*, Pt II, 203.

38. Kangle, *Kautilya Arthashastra*, 202.

39. Boesche, 'Women in Kautilya's Arthashastra', 38.

40. For further comments and explanation, see Kangle, *Kautilya Arthashastra*, Pt II, 202.

41. *Arthashastra*, Book III.4.9-12; Kangle, *Kautilya Arthashastra*, 205.

42. *Arthashastra*, Book III.4.13; see Kangle, *Kautilya Arthashastra*, 206. A husband had to incur a fine of 12 *panas* in case he prevented her from the visit on such occasions.

43. *Arthashastra*, Book IV.8.17.

44. Kangle, *Kautilya Arthashastra*, Pt II, 290: *tadeva* refers apparently only to the punishment of death. Cs, however, includes *trilinga chedana* as well, which might mean cutting of the organ and the two breasts.

45. Bhattacharji, *Women and Society*, 52, 161; cf. Boesche, 'Women in Kautilya's Arthashastra', 38.

46. Laws of Manu (*Manusmriti*, 8.364, 190; 8.378, 192); Boesche, 'Women in Kautilya's Arthashastra', 38; It is difficult to believe that the same Manu is said to have said that a killing of a woman was equivalent to killing a *Sudra* and hence was not a big crime. Laws of Manu, (*Manusmriti*, 11.67, 257).

47. *Dharmasutras*, A2.20, 70.

48. See *Arthashastra*, Book III.13.11; III.20.16; IV.13.38-39, 291; IV.12.27-28.

49. *Arthashastra*, Book II.41, Kangle, *Kautilya Arthashastra*, Pt II, 188.

50. *Arthashastra*, Book III.5.9-10; Kangle, *Kautilya Arthashastra*, Pt II, 209.

51. Kangle, *Kautilya Arthashastra*, Pt II, Book III.6.8, no. 8, 212; *Manusmriti*, 9.118; *Yajurveda*, 2.114; allow 1/4th of a son's share to a daughter.

52. Kangle, *Kautilya Arthashastra*, Pt II, 204; *Arthashastra*, Book III.3.32.

53. *Arthashastra*, Book III.4.15; Kangle, *Kautilya Arthashastra*, Pt II, 206.

54. *Apastamba Dharamasutras*, A2.29.3; Boesche, 'Women in Kautilya's Arthashastra', 36.

55. Altekar, *The Position of Women*, 251.

56. The prostitutes, expert in lovemaking, have been used to spy on officials in power. Quoted in Shirin, 'Position of Women'.

57. Boesche, 'Women in Kautilya's Arthashastra', 40; *Arthashastra*, Book XI.1.34-35.

58. *Arthashastra*, Book XII.2.11-12; see also, *Arthashastra*, Book XII.2.14; cf. Boesche, 'Women in Kautilya's Arthashastra', 41.

59. Booth the dependent and independent prostitutes paid one-sixth of their income as tax to the state treasury. In times of financial crisis before the state, the independent prostitute paid half of her income as tax, while the dependent was to pay extra revenue to the state.

60. Shirin, 'The Position of Women', 123–134.

61. Shirin, 'The Position of Women', 125.

62. Kangle, *Kautilya Arthashastra*, Pt II, 147; *Arthashastra*, Book II.23.11-14.

63. Olugbade, 'Women in Plato's Republic', 516.

64. Bandyopadhyaya, *Development of Hindu Polity*, 47.

65. Olugbade, 'Women in Plato's Republic', 515.

66. Das, 'The Position of Women', 563.

Post-Kautilyan Political Science

6

Post-Kautilyan political theory may be relevant from two perspectives: first, it will tell us the nature of political science that evolved in the period following Kautilya, which may include the rule of Ashoka, the Guptas and of the Mughals to the British, and second, it will also help us understand the influences of Kautilyan political thought on the politics and administration of the later regimes. In other words, it will establish whether Kautilya's contributions to political science were specifically valid only during his times or his unique treatise on politics, economics, culture and society is timeless.

Let it be clarified at the outset that the comparative approach to the political theory of Kautilya is adopted only in relation to Ashoka without any reference either to his contemporary political thinkers such as Plato, Aristotle, Thucydides, Sun Tzu as well as Machiavelli with whom Kautilya is often compared or to the details of the polity and society under the Guptas or their successors so as to overcome the constraints of time and space. Appropriately, I have explored the issue of continuity and change or modification of the *Arthashastra* theory found in the post-Kautilyan political literature covering the age of King Ashoka.

The literature produced by the historians, the Indologists, the archaeologists and many others introduce the Mauryans to us from different sources such as *Puranas*, the Buddhist literature, the *Arthashastra* and the Greek sources in terms of their lives and times. But Ashoka's political and social philosophy can perhaps be best understood from the primary sources provided by his own orders and statements traced in his inscriptions written and found on the rock and pillar edicts spread over from Afghanistan to southern India, and from the West

to the East deciphered by James Prinsep, an Englishman, who categorized them into major rock edicts, minor rock edicts, pillar edicts and
miscellaneous edicts. 'We can understand his kingship', rightly avers
Nayanjot Lahiri, and 'his personality, his empire and his neighbours,
because he himself, fairly early in his kingly career, chose to speak'.[1]

The importance of his inscriptions as an evidence lies in the fact
that they explain the way Ashoka lived, the style that Ashoka used
for governance and the communication technology he employed for
disseminating his ideas and thoughts to his subjects and to those
surrounding him. Besides, I have also relied on the commentaries
thereon for purposes of understanding Ashoka's political philosophy.[2]
The objective is to not only locate the evolution of political science in
the post-Kautilyan period but also to situate the Kautilyan influence
on the later political thought and theory with special reference to the
organization, importance, nature and role of the political–social institutions in the administration and governance of society and polity and
to the politics and power configurations in those times. The discussion is mainly focused on examining the convergence and divergence
of Kautilya's perspectives on state, justice and law, bureaucracy and
society in a time following him. For example, it has been argued that
the principles of statecraft, enunciated in the epochal work of Kautilya,
have a perennial political value, and that the continuity is embedded
in the vocabulary and the concepts in the Indian tradition, and that
they have survived due to their own enduring logic.[3]

ASHOKA AND HIS POLITICAL PHILOSOPHY

Ashoka is the third Mauryan king, grandson of Chandragupta Maurya
and the son of Bindusara. Ashoka is a unique and distinguished historical figure insofar as he was not only a king ruling over a vast territory,
spread over most of India, covering its western borderlands, from
Afghanistan to Orissa (now Odisha) towards as deep south as Karnataka;
he was also a king who influenced the philosophical, religious and cultural thought in Asia in a more profound manner than any other king
of ancient times. His stamp of appeal as a model of rulership is visible
in various parts of the world like in Sri Lanka where King Devanampiya
Tissa established Buddhist faith after he received gifts and a message

from Ashoka inspiring him to take refuge in Buddhism.[4] It is not difficult to agree with what was stated by H. G. Wells in his seminal work, *The Outline of History*, about Ashoka. He said:

> The tens of thousands of names of Monarchs that crowd the columns of history, their majesties and graciousness, and serenities and royal highness and the like, the name of Ashoka shines, and shines almost alone, a star. From the Volga to Japan, his name is still honoured, China, Tibet, and even India, though it has left his doctrine, preserve the tradition of his greatness. More living men cherish his memory today than ever heard the names of Constantine or charmagne.[5]

It is pertinent to mention here that I have focused on the political thought of Ashoka without going into the controversy regarding his exact date of birth as well as about how he succeeded to the throne and his coronation.[6] His ideas on the nature of state and kingship, morality and goodness as an ingredient of his political theory and practice, consolidation and administration of the kingdom, the ecological aspects of governance, the idea of justice and his thinking on war form the mainstay of the present analysis. The questions addressed here in the discussion are whether both Kautilya and Ashoka can be placed on the same page on matters relating to issues of realism and idealism; on the issue of social and political ethic; on the role of force and violence in international relations; and on the problem of material and moral riches as the major foundation of the society. His theory of *dhamma* would form a major source of finding answers to these questions. I also seek to find out the affinity between the approaches of the *Arthashastra* and the edicts of Asoka about the state, society and the statecraft, and their efficacy in resolving the problems of our age of globalization and contemporary debates related to modern political science and modern civilization with the help of the conventional ideas represented by the two classical thinkers.

THEORY OF STATE AND GOVERNANCE IN ASHOKA'S EDICTS

Ashoka ascended the throne in about 273 BC[7] and fought a war of succession with his brothers, killing them all finally. Another important record about him is that he, who was called *Devanampriya*, conquered the state of Kalinga. The legend goes that lakhs of people lost their lives in this war against Kalinga, which prompted Ashoka to take recourse to Buddhist principles and renounce violence as a tool of social and political policy. He, no doubt, was convinced that the real peace and stability can be established through practising and establishing harmonious, just and righteous norms of social and political conduct. Professor Upinder Singh elaborates: *dhamma* includes what is good (*sadhu*), and the imperative to practice the good additionally endows it with the sense of duty. This imperative does not lie in an idea of goodness for the sake of itself but in an understanding of an individual's long-term self-interest through the operation of the law of *kamma/karma*.[8] Pointing out his tolerant and beneficial way of governance, H. G. Wells writes:

> Right Aspiration, Right Effort and Right Livelihood distinguished his career. He organised a great digging of wells in India, and the planting of trees for shade. He appointed officers for the supervision of charitable works. He founded hospitals and public gardens. He had gardens made for the growing of medicinal herbs. Had he had an Aristotle to inspire him, he would no doubt have endowed scientific research upon a great scale. He created a ministry for the care of the aborigines and subject races. He made provision for the education of women. He made, he was the first monarch to make, an attempt to educate his people into a common view of the ends and way of life.[9]

In order to lay and strengthen the moral foundations of his state, Ashoka invented, followed and pursued the policy of *dhamma*, which has social and political[10] underpinnings, combining the political philosophy of Ashoka and the principles of social organization. Digging further deep, it can be asserted that *dhamma* is the basis of state policy towards the people of his state and also in determining the relations with other states in the realm of international politics. One may conjecture here that Ashoka might have used his policy of *dhamma* to consolidate his power over the newly conquered territory of Kalinga and others as a part of meeting his political goals as well as to extend his support among the non-orthodox social groups, specially the commercial class. In this context, it may be pertinent to note the views of Romila Thapar that in his movement away from orthodox Brahmanism, though not opposing it, and his open support to Buddhism and certain other sects like the *Ajivikas*, Ashoka was seeking the potential support of non-orthodox elements, which may have eventually succeeded in weaning the people away from orthodoxy, and in the end making his own principles more acceptable to the populace.[11]

His edicts are also evidence enough to show that he invented policies that sought to weave together political sovereignty and reconciliation of heterodoxy—social and cultural, and often appearing as a discourse on governance and ethics.[12]

Thus, it is fascinating to note that the policy of *dhamma* owed its birth, as indicated by Anurag Anil[13], to the fragility of the empire conditioned by, 'the increasing vastness of the empire, potential assimilation of tribes and newer agricultural communities as by-product of its territorial expansion, the resultant political/social/economic strain on the Mauryan administration and military apparatuses, heterodox reactions to dominant and entrenched Brahminism in the guise of Buddhism and Jainism, the growing importance of "commercial" trade and, thus the emergence of the *Vaishyas* (the trading class)—challenging the established *varna*-based hierarchy'. In this competing and contending social environment, Ashoka thought it prudent to conceive and spread a theory of universal love and humanism rather than protecting one religious or social group and practices. This he did by attempting to circumvent the powerful *Brahminical* order for assimilating the new social classes in an egalitarian order for the sustenance of his empire.[14]

His government and politics were free from the biased considerations of caste, creed and ethnicity, negotiating and coalescing/aligning varied sectional interests through the policy of universal ethic. Thus, Ashoka partially deviated from the Kautilyan prescription that made it a part of state obligation to protect and sustain *dharma* and *Varnashrama* system, his recognition of high and low in the society notwithstanding. In another context, Ashoka tells Yasas (Ashoka's Minister) that it was the good conduct that constitutes the core of the human being, and not the caste, not at least in the matters of *dharma*. Ashoka says,

You, sir, are obsessed with matters of form and superiority and because of this attachment, you seek to dissuade me from bowing down at the feet of monks (some of whom were low caste).... You ... look at the caste and not at the inherent qualities of the monks. Haughty, deluded and obsessed with caste, you harm yourself and others ... for dharma is a question of qualities, and qualities do not reflect caste.[15]

One may argue, as does Bruce Rich, that the *dhamma* edicts of historical Ashoka reflect an egalitarian doctrine partially, if not wholly, against the caste system, in fact any hierarchical class system.[16]

According to Anurag Anil, 'multiplicity of issues and players converging on the scene of a nascent empire, and so a leader—for his and his state's survival—needed an alliance of sorts, which would mitigate all these differences, and look to.... "Pull the community (and-thus-the state) back together."' It is for this reason alone that Romila Thapar describes Ashoka as both a statesman and a social ethical thinker interested in changing the society through propagating the idea of social ethics and sustaining his empire in a particular historical period.[17] And so, we see the birth of the philosophy of *dhamma* (the *Prakrit* of the Sanskrit word *dharma*, meaning according to the context, the universal law, or righteousness or, by extension, the social and religious order) which was—definitely—a novel thought in the 'Indian political and social theory'.[18]

Viewed in this perspective, *dhamma* can easily be seen as a cementing force and a symbol of a new unity (insisting on the principles of Buddhism and also underlining the freedom of religion with equal respect for other religions).[19] However, some more questions await answers in relation to the policy of *dhamma*: whether *dhamma* was responsible for the weakening of the state and finally for its decline when it had to face several foreign invasions?[20] Does it reflect the sociopolitical ideas of Kautilya, forming the basis of government and administration, in any manner? Third, whether Ashoka's policy of *dhamma* was a religious policy tied with Buddhism.

The aforementioned questions are important to bring out the purpose and relevance of the policy of *dhamma* propagated and pursued by the great King Ashoka in the management and administration of national and international affairs. To begin with, it can be observed that Ashoka's policy of *dhamma* was not a religious policy tied with Buddhism, as is often understood. It was, in fact, an innovation or an invention of Ashoka himself who was inspired by the Buddhist principles or philosophy. D. D. Kausambi explains that '*Dhamma* is not Buddhism, but is some code of behaviour for all society which could be followed without damage to the various older group *dhammas*'.[21]

> Ashoka, after the slaughter at Dhauli, became fully convinced of the truth of Buddhist teachings and promoted a secular *Dhamma* or law of piety as a new ethic to guide his kingdom. But most authorities agree that Ashoka's law of piety, while inspired by Buddhism, is a practical, secular ethic quite distinct from Buddhist doctrine.[22]

Further, Edict VII underlines the desire of the beloved of the gods, King Piyadasi,

> that all religions should reside everywhere, for all of them desire self-control and purity of heart. But people have various desires and various passions and they may practice all of what they should or only a part of it. But one who receives great gifts, yet is lacking in self-control, purity of heart, gratitude and firm devotion, such person is mean.

Thus, it may not be wrong to say that Ashoka created an 'infrastructure of goodness' and pursuing and doing good, which, though he considered to be a difficult task, was his motto given expression in Edict V:

> One who does good first does something hard to do. I have done many good deeds, and, if my sons, grandsons and their descendants up to the end of the world act in like manner, they too will do much good. But whoever amongst them neglects this, they will do evil.

Dhamma can be identified as a policy or even strategy to weld together various strands forming the empire. Greeks define it as the law of piety. It was also an expression of his commitment to the welfare of his subjects whom he, time and again, describes as his children. It can be asserted that the philosophy of *dhamma* was, in fact, a theory of social ethics, tolerance and righteous government. Edict XI is a testament to this interpretation.[23] The essence of *dhamma* is clarified in the same edict as follows:

And it consists of this: proper behaviour towards servants and employees, respect for mother and father, generosity towards friends, companions, relations, Brahmins and ascetics, and not killing living beings. Therefore, a father, a son, a brother, a master, a friend, a companion or a neighbour should say, 'this is good, it should be done'. One benefits in this world and gains great merit in the next by giving the gift of *Dhamma*.

Dhamma is a concept used to define not only the relationship between the society and different sects based on the principle of righteousness in the thinking and behaviour of his people but also a policy influencing the ideas and ideal of kingship and governance. In other words, by *dhamma*, it meant a policy of having social, cultural, spiritual, political and economic ramifications, prescribing guidelines, and regulating the behaviour of the state and society in their mutual conduct. It was also a law of humanity, social order, enhancing spiritual capital and of prevention or denouncing of violence, including that against the animals. It exhibits his (Ashoka's) approach to shun coercive and aggressive conduct in managing domestic and international relations. *Dhamma* lays emphasis on a responsible and responsive individual conduct of which empathy forms a major characteristic. The 'essential doctrine' is featured by justness, reverence and deference for each other; our respect for

> that non-material order, to borrow from Vaclav Havel, which is not only above us but also In us and among us, and which is the only possible and reliable source of man's respect for himself, for others, for the order cf nature, for the order of humanity and thus for the secular authority as well.[24]

Dhamma, thus, can be taken to mean the theory and practice of sociomoral virtues of honesty, truthfulness, compassion, mercifulness, benevolence, non-violence, considerate behaviour towards all, non-extravagance, non-acquisitiveness, purity, generosity as well as non-injury to animals.[25] Ashoka refers to many sinful passions such as fierceness, cruelty, anger, pride, greed, envy and indulgence. It can be noted here that Kautilya also warns his king against indulgence in any of such vices because it will not only be ruinous of his image and the self but also weaken his kingdom. Thus, using *dhamma* in the sense of law and social order was by no means new to Mauryan India, and Ashoka, comments Romila Thapar, with the propagation of his *dhamma*, made an attempt to humanize it and show that in fact what mattered most was virtuous behaviour that transcends all barriers of sectarian belief. *Dhamma* was largely an ethical concept related to the individual in the context of his society, aiming to reform the narrow attitude of religious teaching, to protect the weak against the strong and to promote throughout the empire a consciousness of social behaviour so broad in its scope that no group could object to it.[26]

It appears that Ashoka is focusing on the value and utility of the spontaneity of a considerate behaviour of everyone without the compulsion of forced good behaviour[27] and seems to be contrarian to Kautilya in whose view it is the social institutions, through the use of force, restraint and punishment (*dandaniti*), that could ensure good human behaviour.

The importance and impact of *dhamma* are clearly brought out of Rock Edict IV, wherein it is recognized that the earlier time was characterized by lack of morality, lack of respect towards the *Brahmanas* and the *shramanas* and the relatives and the elders but now, thanks to the practice of *dhamma* on the part of the beloved of the gods, King Piyadasi, the sound of the drum has become the sound of *dhamma*, showing the people displays of heavenly chariots, elephants, balls of fire and other divine forms.[28]

DHAMMA IS NOT AN IMPOSING PHILOSOPHY

That propagation of *dhamma* was not in any way pitted against any other religion and neither was it given any preferential treatment by the state over other religions nor was it mandatory for any individual to renounce his religion to practice *dhamma* is clear from Rock Edict XII, wherein religious tolerance among all sects is clearly established. Perhaps, the policy of *dhamma* was emphatic about the possibility and necessity of coexistence of all sects/religions and harmonious relationship between a range of diverse societies and sects,[29] setting, at rest, the criticism by the other religious heads, that *dhamma* would dominate over other sects and impose his own ideas, or that it was meant to reduce the importance and influence of other sects among the populace. Edict XII explains:

> But beloved of the Gods, king *Piyadasi*, does not value gifts and honours as much as he values this that all religions must grow in their essentials constituting their ethical principles. Every sect will grow in its essentials through the practice of restraining oneself from praising one's own religion or condemning the religion of others without good cause, and if there is cause for criticism, it should be done in a mild way. But it is better to honour other religions for this reason.[30]

In the opinion of Ashoka, this act of respecting other religions benefits one's own religion as well as the other religions. The other way would harm both. Respect for the doctrines professed by others, listening to them and be connected to each other. Therefore, emphasis is on concord and coming together. Tolerance is the pathway of progress of all religious essentials because such behaviour implies that the views shall be placed in a manner that does not offend the other practitioner or believer, and the fruit of this is that one's own religion grows and *dhamma* is also illuminated.[31] Ashoka prescribes tolerance because it is evidence of the supremacy of man's thought and action if he shows magnanimity through such toleration. Thapar maintains that this approach also led to the progress and advancement of his *dhamma*, since the latter was based on the essentials of various sects. Thus, his intention was not to supplant the teaching of other religions with *dhamma*, but rather to insist on mutual toleration.[32]

One may observe here that Ashoka's philosophy seems to be emulating the philosophy of 'Sarva Dharma Sambhava'. The theory of tolerance was pushed ahead for various reasons—first, that the sectarian antagonisms and conflicts, if allowed to continue, were likely to harm the cause of *dhamma*; second, they would not allow the influence of *dhamma* to grow and spread as the subjects may treat *dhamma* as one other religious dogma; and third, tolerance and mutual religious concord would advance the cause of preventing religio-political sectarianism.[33] It may be added here that the policy of religious tolerance can be interpreted to mean establishing and reinforcing social and political stability and cultural unity within the precincts of the empire.

Furthermore, this policy establishes that Ashoka aimed at establishing and operating a secular polity rather than recognizing Buddhism as a state religion. Pillar Edict VII emphasizes that officers of *dhamma* were busy in many matters of public benefit. Ashoka says therein that

> both ascetics and householders, I have appointed some to concern themselves with the Buddhist Order, with Brahmins and *Ajivikas, with the* Jainas, and with various sects. There are many categories of officers with a variety of duties, but my officers of *Dhamma* are busy with the affairs of these and other sects.

Furthermore, Ashoka gave almost equal attention to all religions. He has been aptly depicted by Amartya Sen as the most 'articulate and ardent advocate of tolerance and mutual respect in India'.[34] Amartya Sen reiterates that Ashoka emphasized on not only the need for toleration but also appreciated the richness of heterodoxy for which he laid down what are perhaps the oldest rules for conducting debates and disputations, with the opponents being 'duly honoured in every way on all occasions'.[35] Ashoka seems to be deviating from the Kautilyan emphasis on discipline and order when he replaces it with tolerance and freedom.

Another important thing to emphasize is that Ashoka pleads for both inter- and intra-religious tolerance. For example, when it comes to dissidence or contra-opinions in the *sangha*, he acts as a disciplinarian and, in the words of Romila Thapar, since he is addressing a single sect, he naturally calls upon its members to be unified in their principles and in their policy '...If anything it would be more correct to say that he was far more concerned about the discipline of his own *Dhamma* than of any other sects. Peace between the various groups was of the utmost importance to his policy'.[36]

Dhamma, when seen as a policy and strategic methodology of governing internal affairs of the state, can be described as an all-inclusive concept, taking within its ambit a 'moral polity of active social concern, religious tolerance, ecological awareness, the observance of common ethical precepts, and renunciation of war'.[37] Ashoka links his glory and fame with the extent to which people follow and practice *dhamma*. It is mentioned in Edict X, beloved of the gods does not consider glory and fame to be of great account unless they are achieved through having my subjects respect *Dhamma* and practice *Dhamma,* both now and in the future. For this alone, the beloved of gods, Piyadasi desires glory and fame. And whatever efforts beloved of gods, king piyadasi, is making, all of that is only for the welfare of the people in the next world, and that they will have little evil. And being without merit is evil. This is difficult for either a humble person or a great person to do except with great effort and by giving up other interests. In fact, it may be even more difficult for a great person to do.

ASHOKA'S THEORY OF TOLERANCE IN THE CONTEXT OF INTERNATIONAL RELATIONS

Viewed differently, one may safely infer that the theory of tolerance propagated by Ashoka was meant not only for promoting the basis of social unity and integrity, desirable for ensuring a happy and prosperous state, despite the existence of several competing social and religious groups in his time, it was also meant to promote the philosophy of mutual peaceful coexistence at the international plane. *Dhamma* was a step in that direction. It explains how Ashoka used the policy of tolerance and mutual respect as a stratagem for conducting both the internal and external affairs of his kingdom in a peaceful manner. Ashoka says in the Pillar Edict I, thus:

> ...It is hard to obtain happiness in this world and the next without extreme love of *dhamma,* much vigilance, much obedience, much fear of sin, and extreme energy.... My subordinates too, whether high or low or of middle station, endorse it and practice it sufficiently to win over the wavering, and likewise do the frontier officials. For this is my principle: *to protect through dhamma, to administer affairs according to dhamma, to please the people with dhamma, to guard the empire with dhamma.* (Emphasis added)

He was aware that cruelty, harshness, anger, pride (he probably meant arrogance) and envy may be the causes of one's fall, and that should not be allowed to happen.[38]

V. L. Pandit seems to be pointing out the same peaceful approach to diplomatic and interstate relations when she writes: 'Emperor Ashoka was hailed as the most celebrated exponent of this peaceful approach, with the inscribed pillars he had erected all over India and the edicts he had carved on rock faces'.[39] That he got inscriptions of *dhamma* engraved for the happiness and welfare of the world is clear from the reading of Pillar Edict VI.

From the earlier text, it is clearly brought out that violence, a key feature of war, was a futile and unnecessary exercise as it only ended in the human sufferings and pain. So he appears to be prescribing non-violence as the solution for the problems of the people and of the empire, both internal and foreign. At the same time, Ashoka attracted different reactions to his theory of pacifism. Scholars like Raychaudhury[40] holds that his political ideology was responsible for the weakening and decline of the Mauryan Empire, while historians like Romila Thapar argue that the peaceful approach of Ashoka to the national and international conflicts, guided by humanist values and considerations, was based on realism and pragmatism. And, yet others, like Upinder Singh, propose that a real understanding of the theory of war and peace propounded by the great king, calls for its analysis within 'a larger web of ideas and should be understood as a strong and reasoned moral response to the problem of violence in the political sphere'.[41]

Ashoka's philosophy of war and violence finds its best expression in Rock Edict XIII, wherein he describes the horrors of war (reference to Kalinga War), though one comes across the same expressions against violence when he clearly comes out against harm/killing/injury to the living beings (human and animal). His aversion to war can be noted in Rock Edict IV, where it is inscribed that his practice of human values and righteous norms and rules of political conduct resulted in the replacement of sound of the war drum (*yuddha ghosa/bheri ghosa* with *dhamma ghosa*).

Thus, Ashoka not only rejected war as a desirable strategy or element of the statecraft, geographical expansion, but he seriously draws the attention of the empire and their heads to consider and focus themselves on the colossal loss of lives and material in the battlefield and the bickering, bitterness and pain thereafter not only among those directly affected but also those who are indirectly cursed by war and its consequences.[42] Explicating the political thoughts of

Ashoka on war, Upinder opines: 'It is seen as a reprehensible source of pervasive suffering, for which the king as initiator and possible beneficiary bears full responsibility and which must therefore be avoided as far as possible'.[43] Even then, it would not be out of place to mention that Ashoka did not rule out taking recourse to war in all situations like we see Ashoka having no objection to the killing of the forest tribes (*Atavikas*) if they refused to follow the policies and principles of *dhamma*; yet Emperor Ashoka made it explicit that, if the war could not be escaped, the conqueror should award only a mild punishment to the subdued.[44] At this point, Ashoka seems to be influenced by the ideas of Kautilya on the issue of war and peace to some extent, insofar as, though a believer in the theory of force and conquering the territories around, he also pleads for exercise of restraint and recommends compassion for the injured, fallen and the conquered as the conqueror should carry along all means and material for medical help (medicines, surgical instruments, the doctors and the women in charge of food and drinks, stationed in the rear).[45] For Kautilya, it is the duty of *vijigisu* to provide safety to the injured, enemy who surrenders and the fighters who have lost their weapons.[46] Even though a supporter of war, Kautilya was also aware of the large destructive consequences of war and, therefore, argued not to resort to indiscriminate firing as fire leads to huge devastation and destruction of 'innumerable creatures, grains, animals, money, forest produce, and goods. And a kingdom, with stores exhausted, even if obtained, leads only to loss'.

Unlike Kautilya, Ashoka does not believe in the efficacy of war alone for a king to become *chakravartin* for victory and fame can be situated in the moral or '*dhammic* sphere'. What follows from the edicts of Ashoka is that he sees the state as a 'fusion of politics, ethics and metaphysics'. So, for him, 'political' and 'moral' are inseparable elements of the state. Clearly, observes Upinder Singh, Ashoka's abjuration of war should not be understood merely as a pragmatic political strategy, but rather as a radical political stance rooted in ethical and metaphysical concerns.[47]

If one goes by variant interpretations of Ashokan epithet *Devanampriya*, it can be safely asserted that Ashoka might be underlining his desire to win over the hearts of other kings, his immediate neighbours by way of being beloved of the kings or beloved of his equals. Madhav M. Deshpande remarks:

> Ashoka does not use the term samrat to put him above other kings, but just uses the term raja/laja to refer to himself. If the term *deva* also refers to a king, then a possible understanding of *devanampriya* is that Ashoka would ideally like to rule his empire by endearing himself to the kings he may have subdued as well his neighbouring kings.[48]

DHAMMA VIJAYA

Proclamations made by King Ashoka in the Rock Edict XIII tell us that Ashoka considered *dhamma vijaya* (war won through *dhamma*, the righteous political behaviour and victory by practising *dhamma*) as the greatest conquest when compared to the conquest achieved through face-to-face war fought in the battlefield by use of the fiercest force/violence and every form of manoeuvrability. There was no place for military might in his foreign policy or if absolutely unavoidable, that, 'in whatever victories they may gain (they) should be satisfied with patience and mild punishment'.[49] Ashoka believed in winning over other countries through extending help, aid and assistance in the form of construction of wells, planting trees, both for the intent of shadow to the travellers and also medicinal herbs usable for the treatment of various diseases, construction of hospitals and roads instead of creating awe and fear in their minds, thus leading to the establishment of enduring relationship of peace and friendship with other nations. Perhaps, while he was certain that conditions of perennial conflict and war among nations might extend the territories of the empire and may also contribute to the rise of the heroic glory of the king, the war would hamper development and happiness of the subjects in the ultimate. So he propounded the theory of ethical war, and not a war through coercive subjugation. Even if war is undertaken, in future, as an unavoidable choice, victory must precede with utmost compassion.

In his edicts, Ashoka indicates the futility of war as it does not in any sense resolve the perennial security and happiness problems of the humanity; rather, it destroys civilization, culture and society; creates uncertainty in human life; sows permanent seeds of bitterness, revenge and hostility between countries at war; and gives rise to morbidity and callousness and inhuman values in man. 'The victory of power politics, Ashoka seems to be arguing, is no conquest of right. The success of politics and the victory in war are considered political wisdom, but in the scale of ethics victory thus scored is no real victory'.[50] The real victory for him is in establishing, accepting and universalizing the principles of morality than universalizing the political principles.

Even the *dutas* deployed by Ashoka to various countries mentioned by him in Rock Edict XII and to the Hellenistic lands were meant to serve the objectives of (some sort of) a 'Peace corps, consisting of men who would demonstrate their faith in many parts of the world by acts of service to other men, no matter what the land or language'.[51] The philosophy of non-violence and humanly behaviour with the tribal population and those living at the frontiers of the empire finds expression in Separate Edict II, wherein he assures all the people living in the border areas of happy living without fear of violence or injury on the condition of accepting, propagating and protecting *dhamma*. He reserves, however, the power to punish the disobedient. According to Bruce Rich, Ashoka proclaims that they (the tribals) understand that the king will forgive them as far as they can be forgiven, and that through him (i.e., following Ashoka) should follow *dhamma and gain this world and the next.*[52]

It is appropriate to quote a passage from Major Rock Edict (MRE) XIII to have a clearer understanding of *dhamma vijaya*. The inscription reads thus:

> The beloved of the Gods considers victory by *Dhamma* to be the foremost victory. And moreover the beloved of the Gods has gained this victory on all his frontiers to a distance of six hundred *yojans* (about 1500 miles), where reigns the Greek king named Antiochus, and beyond the realm of that Antiochus in the lands of four kings named Ptolemy, Antigonus, Magas and Alexander, and in the South over the Colas and Pandyas as far as Ceylon. Likewise in the imperial territories among the Greeks and the Kambojas, Nabhakas and Nabhapanktis, Bhojas and pitinikas, Andhras and Prindas, every where the people follow the beloved of the Gods' instructions in *Dhamma*. Even where the envoys of the beloved of the gods have not gone, people hear of his conduct according to *Dhamma*, his precepts and

his instructions in *Dhamma*, and they follow *dhamma* and will continue to follow it. What is obtained by this is victory everywhere, and everywhere victory is pleasant.

In my understanding of the concept of *dhamma vijaya*, Ashoka is arguing for, first, the adoption of humane strategy and tools to win the cooperation, confidence and support of the world; second, he was interested in increasing his moral and ethical authority to expand his political influence; third, he used aid to the other countries in the form of hospitals for both man and animals, construction of physical infrastructure like roads and construction of wells and developing other sources of water, including water reservoirs, as a strategic planning for running interstate relations. These measures together would contribute to the attainment of victory everywhere, and everywhere victory is pleasant. This pleasure has been obtained through victory of *dhamma*—yet it is but a slight pleasure, for the beloved of the gods only looks upon that as important in its results, which pertains to the next world.[53]

Dhamma vijaya of Ashoka has come in for severe criticism at the hands of several eminent scholars like Bhandarkar, Raychaudhury and Jayaswal. Bhandarkar terms his policy as 'politically disastrous, though spiritually glorious'. Similarly, Raychaudhury holds Ashoka responsible for failing of his Magadhan successor kings to effectively meet the forces of disruption since Ashoka had blunted the efficiency of the military forces. In the same vein, comments Jayaswal, that the accident of the presence on the throne, at a particular juncture of history, of a man who was designed by nature to fill the chair of an abbot, put back events not by centuries but by millenniums.[54] Many kings are said to have become indifferent, less vigilant, less connected in relation to army, resulting even in their dethroning at times.[55]

His policy of giving lavish grants in gifts and charity on his behalf and on behalf of his queens drained the treasury as well, leading, ultimately, to the weakening and decline of the Mauryan Empire. He is also held responsible for stopping the evolution of Indian political theory and thought because Ashoka took a deviant root to politics and foreign policy from the root adopted by his father as well as his grandfather.

However, many other authors reject this criticism as unfair and unfounded, if one can say so. This is so, in the eyes of Nilkanta Sastry and B. M. Barua, because the critics have reached their conclusions based on unreliable sources. For example, the reference to a Chinese Hou Hanshu's evidence who never visited India can hardly be taken as true. I have argued in the aforementioned pages that Ashoka's political model of pacifism guided by humanist and humane principles of governance and policy is still present, directly or indirectly, in the organization and working of national and international governments and agencies while designing their policies and approaches to resolving the complexities of the modern political systems and world politics. I may not be exaggerating to say that Ashoka could foresee the futility and fatality of hegemonic power structures and pursuits in international arena and presented a new model of cooperation, help and understanding between the people and the governments that would allow them to share the benefits of progress together and would permit every nation, especially the poorer ones, to grow. This is the call of the world even today.

It is not only his policy on war that alone can shape and direct the world to work collectively for the good and betterment of the whole world community but also his administrative reforms aiming at decentralization of power and authority through grant of autonomy to the officers in decision-making, within the general command and supervision of the emperor and the demands of *dhamma*, and decision implementation cannot be easily ignored.[56]

APPOINTMENT OF *DHAMMA-MAHAMATTAS*

Ashoka's unique initiative could also be noted in appointing a special state official known as *dhamma-mahamatta* to spread, support and persuade people into believing and practising the principles of *dhamma* and also ensure their welfare. The purpose of such an administrative arrangement was to expand the reach of *dhamma* to every household or the individual in the society. The *mahamattas* in charge of the women (*ithijhakha mahamattas*) and officers in charge of the outlying areas were also assigned the role and responsibility of achieving the growth of the essentials of all religions.

The institution of *dhamma-mahamatta* was conceived to serve the purpose of welfare of religious sects and orders. This institution also suggests that the policy of *dhamma*, instead of being any religious policy, was concerned with all aspects of life—political, social and economic. Had it been a part of any religion, the *dhamma-mahamatta* would not have been of much relevance, as in that case, it would have taken care of spreading itself through its devotees or followers. It is the reason why Romila Thapar argues that *dhamma* was above and apart from the various religious groups, and that the institution was an attempt made by Ashoka to provide some system of social welfare for the lower castes and the less fortunate members of the community.[57] Another objective of introducing this office was perhaps the desire of Ashoka to send a message across the empire that *dhamma-mahamattas* were meant to render or care for the welfare of the subjects and were vested with power to exercise control over every section of the society—high and low—without any discrimination and carry out the message of *dhamma* to all members. The *mahamattas* were also instrumental in establishing people's closeness to king or bringing people's issues to the knowledge of the king.

The institution of *dhamma-mahamattas* is first referred to in Rock Edict V of Ashoka and introduced in the 14th regnal year. They were very powerful and privileged groups of state officials enjoying the priority to direct royal access. These officers had their range of access not only in the towns but also the people in the frontier regions and among the neighbouring peoples.[58] To begin with, they were entrusted with the task of general social welfare and implementing *dhamma* in practice, but with the passage of time, there was quite an increase in their powers so much so that they could enter the homes of anyone in the society, including those of royal family. So it can be interpreted as a policy of social welfare of the subjects without any religious overtones. Some of the welfare activities mentioned in Rock Edict II include construction of hospitals, rest houses, plantation of shadowy trees, construction of roads, planting medicinal herbs, etc. Ashoka also focused upon the construction of means of communication for not only serving the interests of commerce and trade but also to take his ideas of *dhamma's* deeper roots on a wider scale. In brief, the functions and responsibilities of the *dhamma-mahamattas*, apart from spreading and enforcing *dhamma* among the people, for pursuing welfare, can be recalled as follows:

1. To be aware of the inspirations and problems of the subjects and be prompt in dispensing justice in an impartial manner
2. Relieving sufferings when found
3. Looking into the special needs of women, people living in the outlying areas, neighbouring population and of different religious communities
4. Achieving success through reasoning, not through commands
5. Construction of:
   a. Hospitals for men and animals and supply of medicines
   b. Roads, digging of wells and planting shadow trees
   c. Watering sheds and rest houses
   d. Prevention of cruelty against animals and curbing public laxities

It needs to be emphasized that Ashoka's philosophy of social welfare is reflected in his edict where he says that, 'all men are my children. As for my own children I desire that they may be provided with all the welfare and happiness of this world and of the next, so do I desire for all as well'. Furthermore, Ashoka seems to be following Kautilya who advised his king to follow the paternalistic path to win the hearts and support of the people of his empire. 'In the happiness of the subjects lies his happiness, in their welfare his welfare' is what was the basic principle of good governance in the famous work—*Arthashastra*. Ashoka ensures that his administration was not only welfare oriented but also empathetic and responsive to the needs of the subjects. For this to happen, he employed the techniques of exhortation and of firmness in punishing the non-compliance of his orders through issuing warning and surveillance, which is evident from the practice of carrying out inspection tours (Rock Edict III), and *dhamma yatras* undertaken by the king and the governors of the provincial administration and other officials. Additionally, the officials were responsible to convince the *avijitas* (unsubdued) territories/borderers about the benevolent person in the emperor. Such an act, one may infer, would not only complete the incomplete work of pacification but would also consolidate the empire after the military conquest of Kalinga.

It comes out from a separate Rock Edict II that Ashoka specifically instructed his officials to create confidence among the borderers that the king loves them like himself; that they should not fear him; that they should have confidence in him; that they may expect happiness and not misery from him; and that they should practise *dhamma*[59]; this edict further reassures them of getting fatherly treatment from him.

> Having done so, I may discharge my debt to them, by making known to you (officers) my will, my resolve and my firm promise. By these actions, my work will advance, and they will be reassured and will realise that the king is like a father, and that he feels for them as for himself, for they are like his own children to him.

And that by doing so, they could attain happiness in this world and the next. At the same time, he issued a warning to the borderers that the king will not pardon the unpardonable acts committed by them. It was like the one he issued in the case of the forest tribes as well.[60]

One sees the seeds of social-psychological theory of motivation in his exhortations to those involved in the task of administering and implementing good governance throughout the jurisdiction of the empire. On the other hand, his warning to the borderers implied his vow and commitment to upholding sovereignty and unity and integrity of the state. Upinder Singh explains:

> It is evident from the ideas expressed in the two separate rock edicts that Ashoka saw the essence of the problem of political consolidation and its solution primarily in psychological terms, but at the same time pragmatically put in place a surveillance machinery to ensure compliance.[61]

NATURE OF ASHOKA'S STATE AND ADMINISTRATION

The preceding discussion so far suggests that Ashoka's state and administration were characterized by *dhammic* nature of governance, laying emphasis on (a) following the principles of humanism, compassion, love, rule of piety and respect for all religions; (b) the policy of tolerance; (c) the policy of secular approach to the management of the society and the state; (d) the policy of welfare of the people of the empire and of the world and (e) the policy of peace instead of coercion and force in the conduct of national and the foreign affairs. This is why he believes in *dhamma vijaya*, that is, to extend his influence and moral authority all over the world that had consented to his theory of *dhamma*. According to Pillar Edict VII, thus speaks the beloved of the gods, King Piyadasi:

> whatever good deeds I have done, the world has consented to them and followed them. Thus obedience to mother and father, obedience to teachers, deference to those advanced in age and regard for *Brahamnas* and *shramnas*, the poor and the wretched, slaves and servants have increased and will increase.[62]

Furthermore, Ashoka appears to be arguing through the rock and pillar edicts that whatever the state does should be such that addresses the issues of governance relevant to the present generations and to the future needs too. The policies should be of perennial value to the living beings and serve the good of the humankind. According to Bruce Rich:

> we find in these ... an attempt to promote a continent-wide social ethic and system of governance grounded in the common, core social values of South Asia 2300 years ago.... Certainly there is a sense that Ashoka, in important ways, attempted to transform statecraft and governance from the Kautilyan rule of force to the primacy of morality.[63]

Unlike several political philosophers, including Hobbes and Kautilya, Ashoka did not subscribe to the view that man, by nature, is wicked, cruel and greedy. Rather, he believed in the goodness of man who can be persuaded and moved along the righteous path.[64] It is for his ethical and normative approach to administration and governance that sometimes he is described as a 'utopian idealist political theorist and statesman falling out of the lineage of the realists like Kautilya'. He may not be against accumulation and management of wealth as a system of politics and governance advocated by Kautilya, but he pleaded that this wealth must be distributed and gifted to the people under the politics of charity and welfare. According to Bruce Rich, 'rational analysis of the acquisition and management of wealth and power is useful in building the economy and the state but alone cannot inspire unity or long term loyalty'.[65]

Moreover, Ashoka took a long-term assessment of, in contrast to the short-term view adopted by Kautilya, material and power gains, a philosophy contained in the emphasis on the principles and transcendent values engraved in his inscriptions on the rock edicts although it should be remembered that Ashoka followed till the war of Kalinga the methods and means adopted by Kautilya to acquire power and expand the empire. Even after he took to *dhamma*, he did not rule out the use of force or violence completely. For instance, he prescribes repression and killing of the disobedient forest tribes or acceptance of torture as punishment. Patrick M. Hutchison in his 'Impressions of Ashoka in Ancient India' is of the opinion that although Ashoka professed and popularized *dhamma*, he did not move away from political realism. Ashoka's decision to promote *dhamma* was not necessarily a feeling of duty arising out of his own personal beliefs but merely the most effective solution at the problems that he faced.... Ashoka's adherence to the *dhamma* was extremely important, yet he was careful not to handcuff the dynasty:

> That my sons and great grandsons should not think of a fresh conquest by arms as worth achieving, that they should adopt the policy of forbearance and light punishment towards the vanquished even if they conquer a people by arms, and that they should regard the conquest through *Dhamma* as the true conquest.[66]

Still, it can be noted that, while retaining the form and structure of Kautilyan principles of administration and statecraft, Ashoka deviated from Kautilya at several places, particularly when we are told through the inscriptions that it is the 'political ethic' of compassion, non-violence and tolerance that form the core of the system of governance, kingly authority and power. And it is this new political ethic, which, according to some historians and commentator, led to the decline and disintegration of the Mauryan Empire, as it was far away from the practical ground realities of power politics and was naïve and too idealistic in nature and content. It was a case of misplaced idealism though good in intension and objectives. That is why some scholars compare Ashoka with B. C. Jimmy Carter or Gorbachev.[67]

Oftentimes, some studies hold Ashoka directly responsible for the decline of the empire as his policies derived from *dhamma* politics alienated the orthodox elements, the *Brahmanas*, for instance, of the society,[68] and this proved to be counter-revolutionary. While there may be an element of truth in this statement, it is difficult to digest unquestioningly as the nature of Ashoka's administration was that of a flexible, responsive and responsible mechanism.[69] The officials of the state were instructed by the king to devoting and committing themselves to the cause of welfare and equal treatment of all sects and individuals and to creating infrastructure—social and physical—for the benefit of the traders, travellers and other individuals. Yes, it could be the case that the attempts by the king to establish an egalitarian social system might have led to some unease and later retaliation by the earlier privileged sections of people. Similarly, his policy of non-violence might have made the king and his officers mild and meek to tackle the resistance and revolt from inside as well as from external forces against the state effectively, contributing to the decline finally.

Added to them may include static village economy, characterized by halted further growth, decline of productivity rate of state enterprises, diffusion of sovereignty and administration, inability of the economy to support and sustain the top-heavy bureaucracy, decentralization of state control responsible for a gradual but steady fall of the Mauryan Empire.[70] Though Ashoka tried to weaken, if not remove, the cultural, social, religious and economic divergences and differences through the introduction of *dhamma* as universal philosophy or law of coexistence, he seems to have been unsuccessful to install a real sense or consciousness of oneness from both the nationalist and sociocultural point of view in the minds of the subjects individually or the guilds. Arnold Toynbee argues that it was the Mauryan bureaucratic rule that probably could, and did, largely defeat the emperor's intentions.[71] However, the weight of these arguments seems to be losing sizably when seen in the light of the challenges and obstacles faced by the early empires like Egypt and Rome in ancient world history.

Administrative structure, it may be pointed out, was carved out as per the needs of a vast empire that was ruled by Ashoka. So the administration carried out its duties at three levels—the centre, the provinces and the district. At the central level, the king occupied the apex position who was assisted in the performance of his tasks by the ministers, that is, *mahamattas* and a council of ministers or officials known as *parishad*. The provinces were governed through the charge of governors comprising the princes of the royal blood, designated as *kumaras*.[72] There was another category of provinces that was governed by officers not belonging to the royal blood. Although no such categorization emerges out of Ashoka's inscriptions, one gets an example from the Junagadh inscription of Rudradaman, which introduces the reader to the province of Surashtra or Kathiawar under the charge of Vaishya Pushyagupta in the times of Chandragupta and under the charge of *Yavana* king—Tushaspa—during the reign of Ashoka.[73] Though no direct evidence is available from the Ashokan inscriptions about the nomenclature of the subdivisions of the province, the Siddapur copies of the minor rock edicts suggest that district heads were appointed by the person who was in charge of the province and not by the king himself.[74]

SOURCES OF AUTHORITY AND LEGITIMACY OF THE KING

The preceding discussion suggests that the basis of the authority and power of King Ashoka rested on his commitment to what Adams Smith terms as beneficence, prudence and justice.[75] The act of beneficence proves the magnanimity, charity, kindness and compassion as the qualities of the king, the paternalistic figure, concerned with distributing all accumulated wealth and establishes that power is meant for the good of the individual and the society. This further lends credence to the popular view of the king as a selfless ruler. Bruce Rich explains that:

> the spirit of giving emerges as a key element in the mythical accounts of Ashoka's efforts to reinvent the sources of state authority. The legitimacy of state power and wealth is at least partly grounded on the willingness of its possessors not just to distribute it but ritually and symbolically to periodically give it away.[76]

It further follows from the edicts and the policies introduced and executed by Ashoka that he was a powerful 'authoritarian moralist'. There are evidences, of course, that whatever social and political thoughts he gave birth to, he tried to ensure that they were properly carried forward by the officials of the state, and that people adhered to them. This might create an impression that the king was aggressive and forceful in imposing his philosophy on the people, but it is difficult to draw this conclusion from his messages in the inscriptions. What one gathers is that he preferred persuasion over fear or force, though not ruling out that authority lay with the king. That he left the tyrannical path of power after the Kalinga War is well taken.

Why did Ashoka not celebrate his victory, like many other kings of the time of his grandfather or his father: rather, he preferred remorse and held himself responsible for the unimaginable loss of people in deaths, capture and deportation. It is surprising that a person, who himself was a witness to several wars and who himself led the campaigns to suppress ruthlessly the revolts in some parts of the kingdom (Takshashila, Ujjain, for instance) during the reigns of his father, became so averse to fighting for extension of his power, domain of rule and consolidation of the treasury and gaining economic control over the territories bordering his empire.

It may be untrue to say that Ashoka was not interested in power politics or strengthening the economy or winning over the territories outside his domain. He wanted to achieve all these goals with reference to and through *dhamma*. One is reasonable to believe that King Ashoka wanted to present himself as the defender of peace for the cause of common progress of all the nations together, though sending a message that he would be considerate to all people and the kings, but would not compromise the strength of the treasury, so very important source of power and dominance verses others.

Second, peaceful approach to the kingly affairs and to the achievement of goals of the state to be pursued by his conviction that victory by *dhamma* was more enduring than victory through military force. Thus, he gave a new meaning and interpretation to the concept of power and the kingship. In him was reborn a virtuous king who believed in the extension of his influence, power and authority beyond the boundaries of his empire through the spread of humanly values of love, compassion, truth and non-violence. He saw the power of political ethic and morality as stronger than the power of sword; the power of mind and spirituality as more effective than the power of brutality expressed through the show of might and killings in the war fields. He exhorts everyone to follow these virtues and values. Hultzsch says (lines N–P of Brahmagiri edict):

> Obedience must be rendered to mother and father, likewise to elders; firmness (of compassion) must be shown towards animals; the truth must be spoken; these same moral virtues must be practised. In the same way, the pupil must show reverence to the master, and one must behave in a suitable manner towards relatives. This is an ancient rule, and this conduces to long life.[77]

Third, perhaps, Ashoka visualized that the authority of the king was better upheld if it was grounded on the ideology of winning the faith and love of the subjects as well as of the bordering kingdoms by acts of beneficence, prudence and justice, than through coercing them into obedience through physical subjugation and keeping them loyal through fear and awe. He was of the opinion that political stability and economic prosperity of the empire is better secured through the application of the first methodology; instead, it can be achieved by the employment of the second. Thus, he engraved a new concept of legitimacy of authority and the kingship in his territorial domain and beyond. His approach to legitimacy was linked to his commitment to transform the mental and attitudinal framework of the people and the monarch towards governance.

THE ASHOKAN PHILOSOPHY OF JUSTICE AND ITS ADMINISTRATION

It has been established in the discussion on the *Arthashastra* that only a just social and political order can guarantee a strong and stable rule. According to Kautilya, the prerequisite for such a rule was that everyone should enjoy the right to equality before law and the absence of discriminatory treatment, except by the authority of law. Kautilya argues that the state must give special attention to the weaker sections and the hapless and helpless such as the aged, the sick, the crippled, the old retired prostitutes and other women, on the one hand, and the king should make righteous use of *danda*, on the other hand. In other words, justice commands social justice, including within its ambit distributive justice, and criminal justice. Viewed in this perspective, I will examine Ashoka's idea of justice in the following pages.

Before discussing the idea of justice as envisioned by Ashoka and expressed through his edicts, it will be pertinent to first have a look at the dimensions of justice in the light of which it would be easier to understand Ashoka. Briefly stated, justice can be seen as:

1. Absence of conditions of injustice in the society.
2. Absence of partiality and presence of objectivity, neutrality and impartiality in the behaviours of the state.
3. Absence of the tendency of abuse of power by the wielders of power, from decision-makers to the implementers of the decisions and policies.
4. Equality and freedom—social, legal, economic and religious, both constitutional and real.
5. Absence of *Matsyanyaya* and freedom from exploitation, suppression and oppression of the weak by the powerful and resourceful.

It may be stated here that these materials of justice are not exhaustive; they are merely extended indicators of what constitutes justice or what can resist injustice. It can also be argued that justice ensures value and dignity to each member of a civilized society. It is a state of living without fear and threats.

How far do these principles and aims of justice find place in the political thoughts of Ashoka? Ashoka assigns an important place to the practice of impartiality in the operation of administrative machinery, which he thinks must behave without any favour or bias towards anyone. In the first separate rock edict at Toshali and Samapa, the two ancient provincial cities, the king tells his officers, including the magistrates, that they should strive to act impartially, avoiding jealousy, shortness of temper, harshness, rashness, obstinacy, idleness or slackness as he treats all men as his children, and tells them, 'you are in charge of many thousands of living beings' and that happiness of all the subjects was important to him'.

Ashoka warns his administration against abuse of power, which, if not checked, would lead to injustice. He says, 'Often a man suffers imprisonment or torture and then is released from prison, all without reason, and many other people suffer further'. The motive behind the Edict (XIII), which he wants to be read aloud at intervals, is to issue an order to the magistrates not to imprison or inflict torture on the people recklessly without establishing reasonable and sufficient grounds. Ashoka does not stop at that; rather, he takes steps to ensure his orders were implemented. Bruce Rich exerts that apart from exhortations, he proclaims specific measures of administrative review to prevent future abuses: 'I shall send on tour every five years,[78] an officer who is not severe or harsh, who having investigated this matter..., shall see that they carry out my instructions'.[79]

Further, we note in the Ashokan texts-edicts—that he emphasizes on the 'uniformity in judicial procedures and punishments', particularly to be followed by a class of rural officials known as *rajukas* since they enjoyed independent authority to work for the welfare and happiness of the rural population and dispensation of justice. Ashoka says in Pillar Edict IV, 'just as one entrusts his child to an experienced nurse, and is confident that the experienced nurse is able to care for the child satisfactorily, so my *rajukas* have been appointed for the welfare and happiness of the country people'.

The implication of the uniform judicial procedure and punishment is that there has to be equality in the eyes of law, and that it is an equal protection of laws. Stanley Tambiah seems to be in agreement with this view, terming Ashoka's proclamation of uniformity a 'startling contrast to the notion of graduated punishment and graduated legal privileges according to Varna status'.[80] Strangely, the Western Europe did not practise this principle till almost the end of the 18th century. This prescription of Ashoka was nothing less than a social, legal and political revolution of sorts. The judicial history saw the glimpses of change where the nature of crime, and not the caste or status, will determine the quantum of punishment uniformly. Elsewhere, it is stipulated that every citizen should be entitled to hold to his religion or faith without being hindered by the other practitioners of their respective religions. Moreover, as it follows, freedom from pain and enjoyment of happiness is the essence of justice for Ashoka.

It is also established, one may safely infer, that in matters of the administration of justice, Ashoka ordered and enforced a system of uniform criminal justice throughout his territorial jurisdiction. Bruce sees in this an element of due process of law, an extraordinarily progressive measure for its time.[81] Ashoka's penal code retains capital punishment as well as application of the technique of torture for investigation, thus following the principles of criminal justice administration prescribed in the *Arthashastra*.

Right of the relatives[82] of the convict to file an appeal for clemency within three days of the award of sentence to death to the convict was provided, as is evident from Pillar Edict IV.[83] The relations could also pray for the respite and reprieve for the convict. S. N. Mitra contends that Ashoka's expression 'for sparing of life' implies rather 'the barest sparing of life and reduction of punishment than release'. However, whether sparing was barest or full can be anybody's guess as nothing comes out clearly from the texts of Ashoka. It is further noted that

> Ashoka shows much concern for making arrangements to provide the prisoners with money to pay the ransom, to protect them against coercion and oppression and to see them released (*patividhanaye, apalibodhayo, mokhaye cha*), especially in the case of such prisoners as were minors or mere tools (*anubandha*),[84] or burdened with the maintenance of family (*pajava*), or entitled to consideration by reason of their good conduct (katabhkale) or aged (mahalake).[85]

There is a mention in Pillar Edict V of 25 releases of prisoners in 25 years of his consecration. He does not tell us though as to how many prisoners used to be released every year and on what occasions. This practice of premature release of prisoners still continues in India. Thus, one can claim that Ashoka's theory of justice was ahead of his times and had modernist elements of jurisprudence.

His idea of justice, it may be added, is reflected in personally hearing and addressing of complaints, efficient disposal of business, providing easy access to the king in matters of urgent importance at any place of his presence of the king from bed to the office to the field; his love and compassion for the poor and the aged, etc.

His concerns for justice were not confined to the human beings only. He equally was against the killing of the animals for the sake of feeding either the other animals or for the royal kitchens or others.[86] There are seeds of environmental justice and health implications in this instruction of Ashoka. This modernist philosophy is reflected in Pillar Edict V of Ashoka telling us his conscious commitment to the protection of environment and the enactment of laws there for.[87] Habitat protection was another measure, forming part of his forest policy. He prescribes that no 'forest should be put on fire either wantonly or for the destruction of life and that the chaff in the fields must not be set on fire along with the living things in it'.[88] Conservation of wildlife and forests was an integral part of the environment policy of Ashoka.

It is also pertinent to refer to the foundational feature of an effective justice delivery system. No one can imagine justice to all in the absence of independence of the judiciary. The modern constitutionalists, legalists and jurists and political and social activists are of the firm view that independence of the judiciary is a precondition of a just social, political and economic order. Strangely, though, the Ashokan state was a monarchy with legislative, administrative and financial powers belonging to the king, King Ashoka was emphatic in his view about keeping the judiciary free from bias and prejudice and ensure its independence.

Pillar Edict IV emphasizes about Ashoka's commitment and measures taken to enforce this important principle of justice:

> My *Rajukas* (rural officers) are appointed over many hundred thousands of people. In *judgement and punishment*, I have given them *independent authority* (emphasis added), so that the *Rajukas* may fulfil their functions calmly and fearlessly and may promote the welfare and happiness of the country people and benefit them.

Ashoka, however, was also aware that *rajukas* must know the limits under which they have to discharge their role.

> They must know the wishes of the king; they must obey the king and his envoys, they will learn what makes for happiness and unhappiness and they, the envoys, shall oversee the work of the *rajukas* in order to ensure that they will be able to give me (the king) satisfaction.

ASHOKAN STATECRAFT AND GOVERNANCE

Ashoka's theory of statecraft and governance seems to be rooted in his theory of social ethic, guided by the 'common, core social values of South Asia 2,300 years ago'. *Dhamma*, a social and political philosophy of Ashoka, travelled not only within the geographical domains of the empire but also across the world, 'something new and unprecedented in history'. He seems to be talking to the present and future generations of his people and beyond his precincts directly through his edicts. It appeals to say that he considered communication as an important aspect of statecraft, leadership and governance.

The many rock edicts, separate edicts and pillar edicts stand testimony to the fact that Ashoka was a great statesman and a political thinker with clarity of political vision about the state and statecraft, signifying his knowledge about politics and capacity to govern. 'The general principles of piety, duty and good conduct advocated by him in his edicts', explains Barua, 'fall all within the scope of the most advanced *rajdharma* or political thought of India, and had all the regulations of piety (*dhammaniyamani*) typified by Pillar Edict V, been recorded and preserved'.[89] Administrative reforms, changes and measures undertaken by Ashoka are enough to show his capacities and capabilities to devise and effect means and policies and adjusting them as the occasion demanded.

It is fascinating to note that Ashoka appears to be deviating from Kautilya insofar as he endeavoured to transform the statecraft and governance from the rule of coercion and force to the primacy of morality.[90] B. G. Gokhale in *Ashoka Maurya* remarks, 'Ashoka propounded an administrative philosophy which assumes that the basic nature of man is good'. Bruce Rich comments:

> In this view, Ashoka is one of the first avatars of a long lineage of utopians or idealists in politics, in distinct contrast to the realist school embodied by Kautilya.... He lays focus on the politics of *dana*, (gift giving and charity) instead of giving priority to acquisition and managing wealth.

However, this view does not place the entire truth because Ashoka was as much a realist as he was a moralist or idealist. We are reminded by Ashoka of the importance and relevance of prudence, justice and beneficence in the conduct of social and political affairs, both domestic and global. Even in the international arena, Ashoka seems to be present when we observe the efforts of the United Nations and its agencies not only to protect against violence against any member state but also to engage itself in the act of promoting peace, welfare, development, health, working for the cause of the poor by setting goals of poverty alleviation and environmental protection. The grant-in-aid provided by several developed rich countries such as Japan, the United States, France, etc., as well as by the UN to the poorer nations in their efforts to move forward in the field of education, health, social–physical infrastructure, etc., shows the presence of the Ashokan policy of gift, *dana* and charity.

Survival and welfare of humanity, based on deepening cultural values, form the core of the policies and politics of Ashoka. That is why, in his view, war is harmful for the good of society, people and the state in the long run. It is no remedy for the miseries of man; rather, war accentuates and perpetuates them. The Ashokan state is meant to be in the service of people, instead of people being adjusted to the political goals and crude power politics or observing universally the political principles since they are considered the foundations of the state of the pre-Ashokan times. The appointment of *dhamma-mahamatta* suggest that the Ashokan state believed in the theory of progress of man by way of promotion and adoption of morality as this is the only method that can put to an end the stumbling blocks to development and well-being such as hatred, jealousy, greed or pursuit of immoral politics. We can argue that the Ashokan state differs from the earlier Mauryan state (Kautilyan state) in the sense of purpose and means of the state and government.

The radical change that had been wrought by Ashoka in the spirit and form of the state was indicative of transvaluation of values. The sixth rock edict is a serious utterance of Ashoka. The affairs of the people were his affairs and their disposal was, in his thought, no easy task.[91]

His edicts speak less of the science of politics and more of the science of human relations and human progress both in this world and in the next. By creating a society by building on cooperation, integration and mutual service, underlines Ashoka in his text (edicts), the political leader can build four walls of a robust political state. The state exists for the sake of only the welfare of the people. He visualized a state, wherein the interest of the society and the state were shared ones and did not come in conflict with each other.

However, it may be reiterated that Ashoka, though renounced and critiqued war as a source of political domination and seeking power, he never disbanded his army. Even when he told his people and others at his frontier and beyond that he treated philosophy of *dhamma* as a better and efficacious arm to defend the empire, he did not rule out the use of violence in exceptional situations like people refusing to obey the rules and instructions of the state and challenged the sovereignty of the state even after all human and humane persuasive methods were applied and failed. Even so, it can be agreed that

> Ashoka was desirous of bringing the whole country under the sway of humanised culture with a view to deadening the universal law of politics and to developing the personality of man in the principle of humanism. This tendency of his was a signpost of a new culture of man.[92]

Winning through the heart philosophy of governance was equally a part of his foreign policy, as it has been stated elsewhere, he tells the other kings and people that they need not fear him as he is like their father and hence like the family (Second Separate Edict) and expected his officials to treat the people of the state as an experienced intelligent nurse treats her patients (with utmost care and love) [emphasis mine].

For Ashoka, the nature of the preceding political, technical power-driven state was indicative of a soulless state. Topa remarks:

To him, the political state was an embodiment of grossest instincts, finding outlet and expression in the field of politics. It sheds human blood without remorse for realising its ends; it creates and fosters hatred and disunity; it asserts, moreover, its own feigned superiority over political powers by infusing awe, dread and fear in the lives of the people. As an ugly and crude instrument of political forces, it debases and dehumanises the personality of man.

Ashoka could be described as a realist in the sense that he invented *dhamma* to manage properly an empire of the size and diversity he was the head of. He was certain that the challenge of uniting a multitude of population with different sects, ethnicity and multicultural characteristics could be better met through the persuasion of *dhamma*, which may become the source of commonality of purpose; *dhamma* was conceived as a means of creating a common political ideology founded on the secular reinterpretation of the shared transcendent values of the time.[93]

Ashoka's political realism is further inherent in his theory of war and peace as he warns against the disasters of war—both human and economic and ensuing miseries and pain—and insists on renunciation of violence and war. In the next moment, however, he seems to be not abdicating war totally in all circumstances and at all times. His statecraft and governance are wedded to the principles of enduring existence and well-being. He proclaims that his sons and grandsons, if they must conquer, be satisfied with the light punishments for the vanquished. It may be worth recalling that Kautilya also chooses peace over war, given a choice. Ashoka propounded, in the main, the moral, instead of technical materialist basis of power and envisioned a moral empire, even though, at times, it appears to be the case of 'authoritarian morality'.

KAUTILYAN LEGACY IN ASHOKA

The study of Kautilya and Ashoka together raises certain questions regarding the parallels between the political theory of the two—the Kautilyan legacy in matters of statecraft and governance in the political ideas of Ashoka and in issues of environmental law and justice in the governance framework of the time of Ashoka. It may be pointed out that both were for the conservation of forests and wildlife and both appeared to have a shared ideology on jail administration. Another area of convergence between the two was the area of approach to politics, in the sense that they both took the normative view of politics to quite an extent.

In the beginning, it seems that Ashoka followed or treaded a different path and evolved a political ideology of his own without being affected by the politics of his ancestors. I am saying so for two reasons: one, he completely ignores his ancestors—his father and the grandfather—from the text of his inscriptions, and, two, he deviated from the policy of expansionism and believed in the practice of consolidation of the empire. But as one moves further, one finds that Ashoka was initially found engaged in the expansion of the empire and fought a fierce bloody war of Kalinga. He renounced the path of war, it may be legitimate to argue, after he was not left with much to win or he realized that the survival and progress of the empire was of a greater significance than winning more and more territories; second, his conversion to Buddhism also moulded his approach to seeing the dark side of war and a false utility of domination by force in place of domination through peace, love, compassion and other transcendent human values and realization of futility of imperialist aspirations.

Ashoka did not abdicate the desire to dominate others, but the means he adopted were different—*dhamma*, not force. Coming back to the question of similarities between the Kautilyan and Ashokan approaches to statecraft and governance, it is worth paying attention to what R. K. Mookerji provides us, which is a list of 35 parallels between the two.[94] He tells us about the similarities between Kautilyan *Arthashastra* and the Ashokan inscriptions relating to ideas, and institutions and technical terms used in them. For example, both use the term, *mahamattas*, for high-ranking officers.[95] Likewise, Kautilya also mentions several such *mahamatyas*, *mahamattas* occupying high positions such as *nagrika* (the in-charge of the city administration (*Arthashastra*, Book IV.1), minister (*Arthashastra*, Book I.10,12, 13).

Similarly, both Ashoka and Kautilya accept the practice of torture, and both are against misuse of power. Again, both refer to the import of herbs and plants having medicinal value (refer to Ashoka's Rock Edict II and Kautilya's Book II.21). Both refer to the office of *yuktas* and *purushas* in Rock Edict III and Pillar Edict IV and VII, whereas Kautilya mentions the same officers in Book II.5. The term *aparanta* has been used in the edicts as well as in the *Arthashastra*. Ashoka's availability for the reporters and the officers at all times and at all places, including his harem, parks, inner apartments or ranches (Rock Edict VI), is an echo of the Kautilyan provision for the same duties of the king to perform public functions and attend to business of the state even when he is in *snanabhojajna* state. Further, both refer to the system of intelligence through *prativedikas* of Ashoka and *gudhapurushas* of Kautilya. There is a reference to the institution of *mantriparishad/parishad* in the government structure of both of them. The supremacy to the public interest, welfare and their happiness can be seen in both edicts and the *Arthashastra*.[96]

However, right to the people of all sects to settle down in any part of the kingdom (Rock Edict VII), which is in contrast to Kautilya who categorically states that *pashandas* and *chandalas* could live only near the burial places (*Arthashastra*, Book II.36). Rock Edicts IX, XI, XIII and Pillar Edict VII of Ashoka treat ceremony of *dhamma* as the best as it included regards, good behaviour and obedience for the teacher, the acquaintances, parents, father and mother; donations to *Brahmanas and sramanas*; regards for slaves and servants; and generosity towards friends and relatives. Kautilya too makes it a punishable offence if a slave is defrauded of his property and privileges; misemploying him like forcing him to carry corpses or sweep; not to pay wages to the *karamkaras* secured to him by law or ill-treatment of the *dasas* (slaves) and *bhritakas*.[97]

In sum, it follows that Ashoka followed the political thoughts of Kautilya in maintaining some political traditions and administrative organization and structure, rules of justice and governance, but he made a major deviation from the *Arthashastra* prescriptions in terms of inventing and applying the law of piety in dealing with domestic and interstate matters. He sought to increase his moral authority all over the world by transforming it into a humane system, on the one hand, and bringing the state–society relations to a level of trust in place of doubt and suspicion, on the other hand.

NOTES

1. Lahiri, *Ashoka in Ancient India*, 7.
2. The research also refers to the *Nitisara* by Kamandaka and *Nitisashtra* or *Shukraniti* of Shukracharya.
3. Gautam, 'The Nitisara'.
4. Lahiri, *Ashoka in Ancient India*, 5; she quotes the Ashokan message from *Dipavamsa* 12.5-6 sent to the Lankan king as: 'I have taken my refuse in the Buddha, the *Dhamma* and the *Sangha*; I have avowed myself a lay pupil of the doctrine of the *sakyaputta*. Imbue your mind also with the faith in this triad, in the highest religion of the Jina, take your refuge in the teacher' (p. 318); Oldenberg (1879), 167; other rulers like Wu of the Liang dynasty (pp. 502–549) erected *stupas* and forbade consumption of meat and alcohol.
5. Wells, *The Outline of History*.
6. It has been said that Ashoka was power hungry, and that he killed all his brothers (99) to acquire the throne; some others have it that his ascension to the throne was prophesied at quite an early age, by *Ajivika* and Buddha himself, for example.
7. Smith, *Asoka*, 73.
8. Singh, 'Governing the Self and the State', 135.
9. Wells, *The Outline of History*, 370–371.
10. From the political perspective, writes Upinder Singh, the major rock edicts can be understood as frontier markers, where the written commands of the king announced to the traveller that he was crossing over a luminal threshold into a new kind of space, a new kind of imperial domain; Singh, 'Governing the State and the Self', 133.
11. Thapar, *Ashoka and the Decline*, 143.
12. It is emphasized that his reading of political sovereignty, both the conquest of Jammudvipa and the welfare of his praja did not contradict his perspective on required policies. See Thapar, 'Ashoka', 31.
13. Anil, 'Negotiations and Coalitions', 6.
14. Cohen, 'Rulers and Priests', 210.
15. Strong, *The Legend of King Ashoka*, 235–236.
16. Rich, *To Uphold the World*, 103.
17. Thapar, 'Ashoka', 31–32.
18. Thapar, 'Ashoka', 31–32.
19. Thapar, 'Ashoka', 145.

20. Information about the foreign invasions and various revolts can be gathered from V. Smith's *History of India*, Chapter VIII.
21. Kausambi, 'Notes on the Kandahar Edict', 204.
22. Rich, *To Uphold the World*, 17.
23. Edict XI speaks, thus: There is no gift like the gift of *dhamma*, no acquaintance like the acquaintance with *dhamma*, no distribution like the distribution of *dhamma*, and no kingship like kingship through *dhamma*.
24. Vaclav Havel.
25. Rich, *Ashoka in our Time*; also see, Dhammika, *The Edicts of King Ashoka*, 2; II Pillar Edict, Bloch, *Les Inscriptions d' Asoka*, 162.
26 Thapar, 'Ashoka', 181.
27 Amartya Sen, Preface to the book, *To Uphold the World by Bruce Rich*.
28. Rock Edict IV, Girnar version, Bloch, *Les Inscriptions d' Asoka*, 98.
29. Ashoka, in Edict XII, disapproves the practice of glorifying or elevating one's own religion at the expense of someone else's. According to him, growth in essentials can be done in different ways. ...One should listen to and respect the doctrines professed by others.... An individual's religion grows through *Dhamma* and so all faiths are improved by tolerance and understanding.
30. Dhammika, *The Edicts of King Ashoka*, 8.
31. Dhammika, *The Edicts of King Ashoka*, 8.
32. Thapar, 'Ashoka', 165.
33. Thapar, 'Ashoka', 159.
34. Sen, *The Argumentative Indian*, 46–47.
35. Squarcini, 'Selling Tolerance', 480; also see, Sen, *The Argumentative Indian*, xxii–xxiii.
36. Ibid, pp. 159–160.
37. Strong, *The Legend of King Ashoka*, 4; cited by Squarcini, 'Selling Tolerance', 481.
38. Pillar Edict III, see Thapar, 'Ashoka', 263; the similarity of thought between Ashoka and Kautilya is clearly visible as later also held these vices to be the probable cause of the downfall of the king.
39. Pandit, 'India's Foreign Policy', 432–433.
40. Singh, 'Governing the State and the Self', 136.
41. Singh, 'Governing the State and the Self', 136.
42. It is difficult to deny that Ashoka's ideas on war and peace can be taken as inspiring components of the philosophy behind the establishment of the United Nations to pursue and ensure global peace and for resistance of violence across the world.
43. Singh, 'Governing the State and the Self', 142.
44. See Thapar, *Ashoka and the Decline of the Mauryas*, 167–169; Major Rock Edict (MRE) XIII.
45. Kangle, *Kautilya Arthashastra*, Pt II, 10.3.47; Rich, *To Uphold the World*.
46. Kangle, *Kautilya Arthashastra*, 13.4.52.

47. Kangle, *Kautilya Arthashastra*, 142.
48. Deshpande, 'Interpreting the Ashokan', 22.
49. Rich, *To Uphold the World*, 120.
50. Topa, 'Ashoka and His Dhamma Culture', 359.
51. Woodcock, *Greeks in India*, 56, Chapter 1, n. 32; Rich, *To Uphold the World*, 120–121.
52. Rich, *To Uphold the World*, 123.
53. See MRE XIII.
54. These scholars have been mentioned and quoted in B. M. Barua, *Ashoka and His Inscriptions*, 347–348. Also see the accounts given in the *Divyavadana* about the state of finances at the time Ashoka's rule.
55. For example, General Pushyamitra overthrew his king and the army did not act.
56. One can refer to the judicial administration under the *rajjukas*, wherein they enjoyed freedom and independence to decide the judgement and punishment, his ministers could meet together independently to discuss the matters of state; one does not find much interference with military organization and structure.
57. Ibid, 157.
58. Rock Edict V; Bloch, *Les Inscriptions d' Ashoka*, 101.
59. Separate Edict II states: 'if the unconquered people on my borders ask what is my will, they should be made to understand that this is my will with regard to them—the king desires that they should have no trouble on his account, should trust in him, and should have in their dealings with him only happiness and no sorrow.'
60. See Rock Edict XIII.
61. Singh, 'Governing the State and the Self', 141.
62. Thapar, *Ashoka and the Decline of the Mauryas*, 266.
63. Rich, *To Uphold the World*, 128.
64. See Gokhale, *Asoka Maurya*, 90–91.
65. Rich, *To Uphold the World*, 129.
66. http://www.inquiriesjournal.com/articles/55/impressions-of-ashoka-in-ancient-india (accessed on 13 January 2022).
67. Ibid, p. 133.
68. See Thapar, *Ashoka and the decline of the Mauryas*, 197–212; Mahajan, *Ancient India*, 275–280; Ambedkar, 'The Birth of a Counter-Revolution'.
69. This was ensured through the practice of *dhammayattas* undertaken by the king himself and also by the mandatory inspection tours of the governors of the provinces and *rajukas* and other officials of the state periodically, generally at an interval of five years.
70. See for details, Thapar, *Ashoka and the decline of the Mauryas*; Mahajan, *Ancient India*; Lannoy, *The Speaking Tree*, Chapter 1, n. 10; Wolpert, *New History*, 68 (Chapter 2, n. 55).

71. Toynbee, *Mankind and Mother Earth*, 229.
72. These provinces were those territories, which were of high political importance and required most loyal and trustworthy officer with proven administrative capabilities. These provinces have been mentioned as Takshashila, Suvarngiri and Kalinga with headquarters at Toshali and Ujjaini with headquarters at Ujjain.
73. EI. VIII.$# & 46-7; Roychaudhary, *Political History of Ancient India*, Chapter II, 49–50.
74. See Roychaudhary, *Political History of Ancient India*, 51–52.
75. Smith, *Theory of Moral Sentiments*, Vol. I, Chapter 3, n. 18; Vol. II, Chapter 3, n. 31.
76. Rich, *To Uphold the World*, 108.
77. Hultzsch, *Corpus Inscriptionum Indicarum*, 178.
78. In the case of Ujjain, it is said to be after every three years.
79. Rich, *To Uphold the World*, 123.
80. Tambiah, *World Conqueror and World Renouncer*, 58, Chapter I, n. 19.
81. Rich, *To Uphold the World*, 126.
82. Relations not only included kinsmen (*natikas*), near or remote, Pillar Edict IV, Separate Rock Edict I, but also the friends, associates, comrades and companions as well as neighbours; see Rock Edicts III, IV, IX and XIII.
83. Even in modern times in India, we note the existence of this right to those given a capital punishment as such a convict can appeal for clemency to the President of India.
84. The term includes the children as well as persons subservient to others command.
85. Barua, *Ashoka and His Inscriptions*, Chapter V, 200.
86. See Pillar Edict V.
87. Ashoka puts a ban on the slaughter of a number of animals and birds including tortoises, bats, ants, ducks, geese, swans, doves, porcupines, squirrels, deer, lizards, rhinoceroses and pigeons, in fact, all four-footed animals.
88. The landless poor population is demanding the chaff in field should not be burnt; the movement for sustainable agriculture is also a pointer toward the observance of this policy of Ashoka. See Rich, *To Uphold the World*, 127.
89. Rich, *To Uphold the World*, 221.
90. Rich, *To Uphold the World*, 128.
91. Topa, 'Ashoka and His Dhamma Culture', 362.
92. Topa, 'Ashoka and His Dhamma Culture', 361.
93. Topa, 'Ashoka and His Dhamma Culture', 129.
94. Mookerji, *Chandragupta Maurya and His Times*, 377–393.
95. Ashoka talks about *mahamattas* in charge of cities like Isila, Samapa (Kalinga Rock Edict [KRE II] or Kaushambi Major Pillar Edict [MPE]); associated with the princely viceroys (Toshali, KRE II or at Suvarnagiri, MRE I), or as in charge of thousands of lives; those appointed to inspect the work of the Judicial officials

as on other bodies or as head of the departments like that of *dhamma* and of women (*striadhyaksha-mahamtta* or *dhamma mahamttas*, Rock Edict XII) or were members of the *mantriparishad* to whom the king forwarded the matters for their deliberation (Rock Edict VI) and refers to the in charges of various religious sects (Rock Edict V, Pillar Edict VII).

96. *Nasti hi me toso ustanamhi atha samtiranaya va katavyamate hi me sarvalokahitam* (Rock Edict VI) is similar to what Kautilya prescribes as *Rajno hi vratamutthanam ... praja sukhe sukham rajnah prajanam cha hite hitam.*

97. For full details, see Mookerji, *Chandragupta Maurya and His Times*, Appendix III, 377–393.

CONCLUSION

Political science had been read and understood with the help of the Western lenses without focussing much on the alternative approaches to the study and interpretation of the subject coming from the East until the arrival of the *Arthashastra* on the intellectual plane, with the translation and publication of the text in 1915, followed by many other authentic translated works.

The book brings out that the Western political theory was unfair to the Indian political wisdom by ignoring the invaluable contributions of ancient Indian political thinkers such as Kautilya and Ashoka to developing a political theory having elements of universalism in terms of both thought and times. Kautilya, as a teacher and advisor of Chandragupta Maurya, explained the theoretical dimensions of the state as well as the pragmatic strategic aspects of politics, while Ashoka, as the king statesman, invented new and everlasting political ideas concerning the government and administration of his empire apart from developing a whole new approach to war and peace.

The *Arthashastra* refers to different forms of government, including the republican system. However, Kautilya supported bureaucratic monarchy with deep moral foundations. It may be noted here that India was not an exception in that regard. Even ancient European countries such as Greece and Italy had seen a shift from republic to monarchy. But India was a monarchy, grounded in morality, spirituality and public service and welfare. King was a *dharmapravartaka* and *dhritavrata*. Though king was theoretically the wielder of all powers—legislative, executive and judicial—in practice, it was almost impossible for him to overlook the customary law, the *Dharmashastra* traditions and the limitations of the *varnashrama* system in the exercise of state powers. The king was considered the servant of the people and was not above the law. Kautilya prescribed punishment to the king also, when he delivered unlawful or undue punishment to an accused. Kautilya not only dealt with the state as a political concept, but he also recommended, for the sake of its good health, that the head of the state and government should command freedom from vices such as anger (*krodha*), greed (*lobha*), arrogance (*madha*), on the one hand, and possess administrative skills, courage and valour of a leader and the capacity to inflict injury on the enemy apart from being owner of high human values, on the other hand. (Kautilya provides us with a list of leadership qualities[1] in the *Arthashastra*). It is observable that owning and exhibiting the qualities of a good leader by the executive head of the state was a significant factor of governance in ancient India in order to raise and maintain the trust of the people in the king (the head of the government) and in winning and sustaining political legitimacy.

In the political estimate of Kautilya and Ashoka, only that state could be strong and stable which is responsive, responsible and corruption free. The king must give priority to the interests and happiness of the subjects over his own when it comes to choice. He, thus, visualizes an ideal state that would provide people-centric administration and governance,[2] a theme at the core of the present theory of good governance. It is worth recalling that Kautilya, while being fully cognizant of the idea of the state and its institutions, deliberates and theorizes upon the matters of law and justice, public order and morality; the issues of international relations and politics; and the matters concerning good governance and gender justice.

It is undoubtedly true that Kautilya does not expressly identify any separate space in the *Arthashastra* for explaining the theory of the state's origin, but it can be discerned from different pages of his work that the state emerged out of the need to put an end to the prevailing environment of *Matsyanyaya/anarchy*, denoting the practice of the survival of the fittest in the like manner as Hobbs describes the state of nature, which compelled people to come together to surrender, by each one of them, their rights to a designated authority.

It should be pointed out, however, that there was no explicit social contract either between the people themselves or between the people and the king in the *Arthashastra*, yet it cannot be denied that there was an implicit agreement between the king and the subjects to the effect that the king will provide them protection against the powerful and the people will pay tax to the ruler in return. Even in the pre-Kautilyan times, it can also be gathered from various stories in the *Brahmanas*, *Jataka tales*, and the Mahabharata as well as from several other documents like the *Shanti Parva* that the state came into being after the God, being approached by the people, appointed (Manu, Indra, Virajas) a king for the safeguard of the human life and securing their material well-being. What can be suggested is that the traces of theory of origin of the state are found in various narratives of ancient Indian polity; in the Kautilyan narrative, one finds an implicit or latent theory of social contract, which later assumes another form to support the idea of the state in relation to the society and the individual, that is, the gradual evolution of the state with the evolution and development of the society, economy and government.

As for the nature of the Kautilyan state, it could be interpreted as a police state to begin with as maintenance of law and order and upholding the *dharmashastric* and customary laws, upholding of the *varnashrama*, protection of the property of the people and promulgation of rules and regulations and their enforcement were the primary objectives of the state. Then, one notices the elements of socialistic–capitalist state, based on a mixed economy model, insofar as we are told that the state would permit free agriculture, and trade, business and commerce within the empire and with other states, within the purview of certain regulations, of course; it itself owned many economic activities and enterprises, on the one hand, and would take measures to protect the interests of the consumer, on the other hand.

Moreover, the state followed policies for social welfare and justice to particularly assist the aged, the sick, the disabled, the helpless and the hapless sections of the society. It was the duty of the state to ensure that the labour was paid its due wages the violation of which was a punishable offence.

The debate regarding the centralized or decentralized character of the Mauryan state remains inconclusive as there is no unanimity among historians and other scholars devoting themselves to the study of the Kautilyan state in this regard. Some scholars such as R. S. Sharma, Romila Thapar and A. L. Basham opine that the Mauryan state, which Kautilya is apparently a part of, was a centralized bureaucratic state with concentration of all authority and power at the centre in the king, while some others, like Indologist J. C. Heesterman, argue that the Kautilyan (Mauryan) state was an apt example of a decentralized polity and government. His argument is that there existed many business and trade groups that enjoyed autonomy to take their own decisions, and even the local governments and officials were free to decide, on the spot, regarding the management of local affairs of the people. However, the truth lies somewhere in between the above two assertions. The Mauryan state, in fact, was a unique example of decentralization in centralization. It was a centralized polity with decentralized administration. Within the norm and aim of an effective government and efficient governance, the Mauryan state was divided into administrative units from the centre to provinces (under the charge of *pradeshtra/pradeshika*) to the districts known as *sthaniya* under the charge of an officer termed as *sthanika*, whereas the local administration was divided into rural and urban, the former was headed and administered by *gopa* and the latter by *nagrika*. The duties and responsibilities of each of them were well defined, and they enjoyed functional autonomy.

It is also not wrong to say that many elements of a centralized bureaucratic state of Kautilya have been, in some degree and form, present in the political regimes that succeeded the Mauryan state whether it was the Mughal or the British rule in India or the administrative system of independent India. Though one can find certain structural changes in the governmental organization and distribution of powers at different levels of the state to suit a federal democratic state that India is today, it cannot be denied that the centre has a domineering position vis-à-vis the states as states are in a predominant position vis-à-vis the local governments. Kautilya and the succeeding rulers practised a centralized system of government because they theoretically were convinced that a strong and powerful state was possible to be obtained only if the centre was in a strong position and the peripheral units served as subordinates to the central authority.

KAUTILYA ON THE ELEMENTS OF THE STATE OR HIS SAPTANGA THEORY

This research finds that Kautilya takes a wider and broader view of the state when he invents *saptanga* theory under which the state is defined as consisting of seven *angas/prakritis*, namely *swamy/swamin* (sovereign ruler), *amatya* (the minister), *janapada* (territory of the state and the people), *durga* (fortified city or capital), *kosa* (treasury of the state), *bala/army* and *ally*. It is worth noting that Kautilya does not only talk of the four elements identified by the Western political science, but he also goes further to include even those elements as part of the state definition that are necessary to protect the sovereignty of the state, that is, *kosa*, *bala/*army and the ally.

What separates the Kautilyan conception of the state from the Western conception is that he treats the state as an organism or an organist institution based on the integral ties of the seven *prakritis*, making it the defining feature of the state. In sum, the *saptanga* theory of Kautilya revolves around his theory of power, legitimacy and sovereignty. In doing so he appears to be quite close or ahead of his times as well as his contemporaries and others such as Plato, Aristotle, Machiavelli, Weber and Morganthau.

CONCEPT OF SOVEREIGNTY AND LEGITIMACY IN THE *ARTHASHASTRA*

Sovereignty and legitimacy have occupied the attention of the political philosophers almost in every age with the emergence of territorially settled population and the increasing focus on the concept of power. In fact, the whole concept of *Dandaniti* in the *Arthashastra* is based on the conception of power. The state and the citizen, it may be averred, are bound by mutual obligation to each other in which the basis of coercive power of the state is its obligation towards the citizens to provide them protection from internal and external threats to them as a society and as an individual, while the citizen is duty-bound to follow the edicts of the state. Thus, sovereignty and legitimacy are essential components of the government, and both are important from the point of view of providing efficacious and effective governance so as to enable people to peacefully enjoy peace and material progress.

It has been argued by some scholars that sovereignty resided in different centres instead of one place or person. But I intend to disagree with this proposition simply because Kautilya suggests nowhere, explicitly or implicitly, that while recognizing the existence of a number of social groups and guilds, there were many institutions enjoying parallel or coordinate powers to the state or that the state was one of the many associations, or 'an association of associations'.

KAUTILYA ON ADMINISTRATION OF LAW AND JUSTICE

It is amply clear from the earlier discussion that Kautilya developed a legal theory with modernist implications. He lists not only the matters that could be settled in court but also developed a comprehensive criminal and civil procedure code. The crimes and the punishment attached with them have been clearly prescribed, making it incumbent on the judiciary to follow a uniform sentencing policy (something missing from the modern jurisprudence, as, in many cases, the punishment is delivered as per understanding and discretion of the judge, since the quantum of punishment is provided within a range of 3–7 years for an instance instead of a predetermined or fixed penalty) since such a system was predictable and equitable, leaving hardly any space for the personal interpretation and/or discretion of the judge.

There were several courts beginning from the centre to the lower level. At the apex stood the king who was the fountainhead of justice (*kantakashodhana*) followed by the courts of the *dharmashthas* established each at the *janapadasandhi* (the frontier post), *samgrahana* (a place of 10 villages), *dronamukha* (unit of 400 villages) and the *sthaniya* (headquarter of 800 villages). This arrangement points out that Kautilya was conscious to the fact that justice delivery can be meaningful and effective if it is at the doorsteps of the people. In other words, he was convinced that justice should be easily accessible and less costly and reach the needy at the earliest. The second aspect worth noting is that Kautilya does not specify whether the courts were tied in a scheme of hierarchy or enjoyed the freedom of jurisdiction except saying that the king was the final arbiter of law. So a conclusion is drawn that every court could deliver its judgement without being challenged in the higher court as is the practice today (there is a long chain of appeals from district courts to high courts to the Supreme Court).

The judges could take the help of the *sabhasads* in matters relating to the cancellation of sale or purchase or gifts before deciding the amount of compensation to be paid to the complainant.[3] Moreover, the *dharmasthas* were to hear the cases involving *vyavaharikarthas*, that is, cases involving mutual transactions between the two parties/subjects (e.g., marriage, debts, sale, forcible seizure, criminal trespass, *kalaha* or scuffle involving monetary loss or any injury to the body). Kautilya does not leave anything to double interpretation and defines the conditions of valid and an invalid transaction, and accordingly, the cases could be decided.

The *dharmasthas* were free to start suo moto proceedings in only some special cases, while, in other cases, the matter had to be brought to the court by the aggrieved person (This practice is still in vogue in independent India). The *Arthashastra* also lays down the procedure to be followed by the court whenever it is approached by the complainant. It is surprising that the account of legal procedures to be followed, including the evidence, both witnesses and documentary evidence, the admissibility of the evidence, etc., can be compared to the present-day system of evidence and witnesses in the court. Perhaps there was no provision of the lawyers at that time as the judge himself used to put questions to the witness appearing before him. The witness of a kin or of the blood relation was not admissible in the court as he was suspected of having an interest in one or the other party in the dispute. Law of perjury was in vogue in the ancient period as evidenced in the *Arthashastra* and any person giving false evidence was liable to be punished. This arrangement is true till date in India.

Sometimes, the modern scholars have been very critical of the Mauryan rulers, especially the rule of Chandragupta Maurya and that of Bindusara on two counts: first, on account of developing a system of law, justice and governance that was based on the principles of discrimination and inequality, creating a big gap between the demand and supply of justice to everyone, irrespective of his place in the society, economy or the government; second, a related one, that Kautilya was biased and prejudiced in his approach to the matters of even gender rights and justice. But the critics forget that no political or legal theory can be seen in isolation of the time it was propounded in. This means that a dichotomous relationship between political thought of a time and the sociocultural and politico-economic context of the country is most likely a dishonest and a difficult exercise to undertake and sustain. It is the function of the society and politics of the future to read, understand, interpret and develop the political concepts and speculations of the past to adjust and mould them in accordance with the emergent new realities—social, cultural, legal, political and juridical.

Kautilya can be best appreciated for his thoughts on law and justice and his contribution to the legal theory only when one notices that he somehow entertained the basic principles of justice and agreed for a justice system that was governed by equal protection of laws, if not equality before law in the strict sense. He envisaged that true delivery of justice was impossible in the absence of proper codification of law. It can be safely averred that the principles of administration of law and justice evolved by Kautilya are much advanced in nature and with reference to his time.

The detailed discussion on judicial administration in Books III (deals with the civil law) and IV (discusses aspects of criminal law) suggests that he did not leave any aspect of law having a bearing on the dispensation of justice in his times, and that legal prescriptions have an everlasting value for both the practitioners of law and the legal philosophers in developing standards and norms of law and justice to suit the needs of the modern society, both Indian and global. It is remarkable that the organization and working of the

Indian judicial system in modern India are ingrained in her past so far as the form matters, though it has undergone change in scope, breadth and length, encompassing several new themes of the modern legal vocabulary.

It is true that justice theory of the *Arthashastra* is deficient in many ways as it does not treat all castes and *varnas* equal in matters of punishment for a crime committed against the higher *varna* people specifically against the *Brahmanas* and the ones against the *Vaishyas* and the *Sudras*. But it should be borne in mind that the king was duty-bound to uphold the *varnashrama* system and the traditions of the society. He was responsible not to allow opportunities to any member of his class to cross the boundaries of the respective profession, as it was likely to disturb the balance of society and introduce instability and conflict, throwing a challenge to the law and order.

It may sound to be hollow from the modern perspectives, but it is also a truism that there was neither a resistance to this discriminatory social system nor a demand for reforming the judicial system. The system changed with the change in the system of government as we observe now in a constitutionally guaranteed system of equality before law and equal protection of laws. It is worth noting, as Altekar does, that such a discriminatory justice system was not only the feature of the Indian administration of the Mauryas, but such iniquitous and unequal judicial practices were also common in all civilizations, Eastern and Western, and have not completely disappeared in modern times and form part of the judicial philosophy and administration even now.[4]

It is interesting to know that Kautilya lays stress on impartiality and independence of judiciary, a very recent modern perspective in the field of administration of justice. If any judge was found to be biased and prejudiced while delivering verdict, Kautilya prescribed punishment for him, for example, a judge was given *sahasdanda* of highest to middle to the lowest, depending on whether the judge was engaged in dereliction of duty or in threatening or browbeating or upbraiding a person coming to the court for filing a lawsuit or indulged in the act of abusing or defaming a party. They were further liable to pay double the fine imposed on an innocent person. This can be taken as an extraordinary measure to ensure judicial accountability in pronouncing correct punishment/judgement, something unheard of in modern judicial history, at least, of India.

KAUTILYA ON INTERSTATE RELATIONS, POWER DYNAMICS, AND WAR AND PEACE

The study points out that Kautilya not only contributed to the theory of state, law and justice, he has equally and competently addressed the problems of international politics within the framework of power, national self-interest and the idea of dominance in the global and/ or regional sphere by inventing a new theory of *mandala/rajmandala* and by prescribing the principles of *shadgunya* and the four *upayas* as strategic materials in the conduct of war, peace and diplomacy. It is concluded that Kautilya adopted an approach to the conduct of foreign affairs that can be termed neither as a completely rationalist, prudent nor realpolitik, based on the employment of cruel, crude and immoral means to serve the practical national self-interest at the cost of ignoring the moral concerns; it was not a theory to remain a silent spectator to the erosion of the power and influence of the king's state by taking a moralist stance of non-violence.

Rather, he can be seen as a neo-realist who pleads for initiating foreign policy measures based on a realist assessment of the power and resources of the enemy and of the self before launching a war. But realism is to be intervened by moralpolitik as well. The research on the close examination of his theory of international politics stresses that the students of this field are exposed to an alternative approach to the Western view of this field. The concepts developed and used by Kautilya to explain the techniques or methodologies, in which a king was interested in strongly defending his own boundaries as well as the one intending to expand his authority, influence and geographi-cal domain, are a pointer in that direction. The major assumption of the *mandala* theory is that the immediately neighbouring states are hostile and inimical to each other, while the countries with a common enemy tend to be friends to one another. The *vijigisu*, (the would-be conqueror) who is at the centre of the *mandala* or concentric circle has to work for overcoming the surrounding states in order to expand his suzerainty. It would be prudent to underline that Kautilya's assertions in this respect are only generally true, as, in some cases, it has been observed that a neighbouring state is not always an enemy. For instance, Norway, Sweden, Finland and other Scandinavian countries enjoy friendly relations with each other despite having contiguous territories, while France and Germany as neighbouring enemies and Switzerland as *udasina* country in that context may prove Kautilya right. In most other cases, Kautilya's idea of *mandalik* formation of states under different group leaders seems to be a reality. The argument finds its support from the examples of the kind of relationship existing between nations of South Asia and Southeast Asia, such as China, India, Pakistan, Nepal, Bhutan, Sri Lanka, Afghanistan, and Myanmar, extending up to West Asian and Middle Eastern regions and before that the formation of Western Bloc headed by the United States and the Communist Bloc led by the erstwhile Soviet Union can be cited as other such cases indicating global *mandala*. This theory further implies hegemonic power contests between nations, especially between neighbours, in order to establish, sustain and expand a state's zone of dominance and control of affairs of others.

The present research, having analysed six principles of foreign policy, subsumed under the concept of *shadgunya*, reveals to us the realist mind of Kautilya. The six policies refer to *sandhi*, (peace treaty), *vigraha* (hostility), *asana* (policy of keeping aloof or quiet), *yana* (marching on an expedition), *samsarya* (seeking shelter with another king or in the fort) and *dvaidhibhava* (following peace with one and war or hostility with the other simultaneously). This narrative of interstate relations teaches the ruler as to how to handle the issues of war and peace on a realist plane. The realism in Kautilya again comes out to the fore when we are told that apart from the six policies governing war and peace, the ruler must also employ the policy of four *upayas*—*sama*, *dana*, *danda* and *bheda*, which means the application of the principle of persuasion, gift or donations, use of force or coercion and sowing dissensions, respectively. The study establishes the efficacy, utility and relevance of both the six policies and four *upayas* as the guiding principles of modern foreign relations and international politics, particularly in times of war and hostility between two or more states. One can cite an example of China continuously trying to create a wedge between India and her neighbours such as Nepal, Myanmar and Maldives.

I have reflected in these pages that Kautilya not only indicates the ways and means to launch war and win but also the methods of consolidating the gains of victory and winning the hearts of the people subjugated by the *vijigisu*. Here comes in the idealist thought of the author of *Arthashastra* when he insists on the adoption of the policy of *yogakshema and lokasamgraha*.[5] Kautilya seems to be taking a mixed view of the political rational and the political moral while approaching the matters of international politics, making this classical text, as Deepshikha Shahi states, a document of 'Political realism between realpolitik and moralpolitik and that the philosophical base of Kautilya's Arthashastra definitely prioritised an alternative of exercise of power in international politics which was not limited to realpolitik, but consistently gripped moralpolitik'.[6]

STATUS OF WOMEN IN THE *ARTHASHASTRA*

The discussion on the status of women in the *Arthashastra* forms a significant part of investigation in the book and reveals to us his views relating to the rights and duties of women that is taken as the determinant of the status of women in those days and helps us make an opinion of the civilizational status of the country. It is notable that, in many cases, his views about the rights and duties of women were quite radical in nature when compared to modern age; for instance, the legalization and professionalization of the institution of prostitution and special rights enjoyed by them under the state. One is surprised to note that women had a right to remarry after the death of their husbands, a social taboo for a long time and still not so popular socially in modern India; they had a right to divorce and enjoyed inheritance of property rights, though within certain limitations. They also had the right to maintenance, among others.

POST-KAUTILYAN POLITICAL THEORY:
THE KING ASHOKA

It might have been noted during the preceding discussion that Kautilya's political philosophy, in many ways, was a precursor to modern political theory; rather, it provided a foundation for the understanding and analysing of a number of political concepts in theory and practice, but the Ashokan political thought and philosophy provide an immediate context of the impact and relevance of the *Arthashastra*, even though Ashoka did not refer to either Kautilya or to his ancestors, Chandragupta and Bindusara in any of his inscriptions.

The dialectic of relationship between Ashoka's ideas of state, power and ethics and the person and conduct of the king as coming out of his theory of *dhamma* and *dhamma vijaya* discerns his political thought and theory that is in many ways similar and dissimilar to the political theory propounded by Kautilya.

The study of Ashoka reaches the following conclusions drawn from the interpretation of major and minor rock edicts, separate rock edicts and the pillar edicts:

1. Ashoka did not worry much about the definition of the state, or how it originated. He perhaps took it as a given and inherited from the earlier Mauryas.
2. Ashoka was not an imperialist as was not the king of Kautilya, Chandragupta Maurya.
3. His empire was a moral and not a brute empire.
4. He believed more in the force of ethical and moral values and practices than in the military force.
5. His theory of dominance was based on the theory of *dhamma vijaya*, emphasizing upon the qualities of love, compassion, welfare and common good, trust and confidence. He exhorted his neighbours not to be fearful of him but have trust and faith in him.
6. When it comes to the qualities of the king (the chief executive or the head of the state of modern period), Ashoka underpins the good leadership traits like Kautilya does in the *Arthashastra*. Kautilya warns his ruler that he should be always away from the vices such as greed, arrogance, lust, anger, pride and foolhardiness, as, in his opinion, these are the six enemies and argues that any king not having control over the senses and not being free of the domination of the six enemies shall soon perish.

7. The Ashokan state was a secular ethical state from all angles of the term and that it is wrong to assign to him any approach favouring any one particular religion. All religions in his eyes were equal as all were similar in essential/characteristic fundamental values.

8. He propounded freedom of religion and faith and promoted harmonious relationship between different religious communities.

9. Ashoka understood the political exigencies associated with his concept of *dhamma*, which, in his view, could be an effective tool of establishing a sense of law and order, a kind of 'kingdom of righteousness'. In a way, it was a strategic intervention in the matters of good governance, responsive administration and peaceful interstate relations.

10. He followed a system of direct and open communication with his subjects and officers as evidenced from the account of *dhammayatras* undertaken by the king himself and the appointment of *dhamma mahamatras*. We come across the evidence in the inscriptions that Ashoka made it mandatory for a number of officers to visit the lower-level administrative units to see that the king's orders/edicts were put to practice.

11. Ashoka can be described as a realist, not a mere idealist or moralist, with firmness and strength of mind. But his realist approach to international affairs was punctuated, it can be assumed, with the qualities of spiritualism in which lay, observed Gelblum,[7] his innovation in the statecraft.

12. *Dhamma*, in the opinion of Cohen[8] was also used by Ashoka, a power-oriented king, as a tool to circumvent the powerful Brahminical order for assimilating the new social classes in an egalitarian order for the sustenance of his empire.

In sum, Ashoka can be praised for being a statesman and a social ethical theorist. As a statesman, he tried to evolve methods to sustain and consolidate and integrate his empire in a given historical context and as an agent of societal change by not only propagating social morals and ethics but also putting an end to the system of caste/*varna*, leaving an enduring lesion, in the words of Anurag Anil, for the modern political and social negotiators/policymakers too.

KAUTILYA AND ASHOKA

Though there has been a lack of unanimity among the scholars about the points of congruence and departure between Kautilya and Ashoka, pertaining to the uses and objectives of maximization of power and self-interests, it is reasonable to argue that Ashoka conformed in several ways to the political thought and ideology of realism propounded by Kautilya. The study shows that there is consonance between Ashoka's policy guided by political and social philosophy preached by Buddha and the political ideas pushed forward by Kautilya. The study notes that Kautilya was also against a march by the ruler to play an indiscriminate ruthless power game to establish his supremacy over others.

Expression of remorse in public by King Ashoka after the Kalinga War showed his strategic skills much as Kautilya argued to make skilful 'use of the science of Polity' to 'overreach other/s'. Even so he differed from Kautilya insofar as he preferred morality over force as a tool of international politics and achieving victory over others. In this context, his policy of *dhamma* and *dhamma vijaya* has been examined in detail to come to the conclusion that Ashoka renounced war as a strategy to conquer others, but not the idea of conquest. He became interested in establishing dominance over others through the *dhammik* means and by increasing his following worldwide at the international arena, which is termed as close to the Kautilyan fusion of realpolitik and moralpolitik by Shahi.[9] That in matters of exercise of power, Ashoka treated power of persuasion as a more effective method than the power through a mode of legislation is what comes out of deliberating the issue in the research work.

His theory of tolerance of and respect for others' interests—religious, social and material—arguably put, not only enhanced his legitimization skills among the member-actors in international politics and foreign policy but also established him as an undisputed leader of humanist moral political practices in that regard. Welfare of the world along with that of the national self was the central theme of his international relations theory governed by the principle of 'live and let live', a mantra of determining India's approach to world politics till date.

The research further points out that Ashoka, though a believer in Buddhist philosophy, never followed the policy of over-pacifism. He makes it clear in his inscriptions that he would forgive the wrong-doers only to the extent possible, and that he was still the owner of state authority through various rock edicts. He also did not rule out war when it became an absolute necessity. In that sense, his policy of war and peace could be seen as only a partial modification of the prescriptions of the *Arthashastra*. Ashoka can be further credited with entertaining the principles of giving gifts and charities apart from the politics of persuasion, just as Kautilya did, to advance the king's moral authority and worldwide acceptance of his leadership. This becomes evident when we are told through the inscriptions on the rock edicts and pillar edicts that the Ashokan state constructed social and physical infrastructure facilities—wells, water reservoirs and waterbodies; hospitals and herbal medicinal plants that could be used to cure the sick inside and outside boundaries of the empire; as well as developed roads and means of transport.

Ashoka was, like Kautilya, alive to the problems and challenges of environment protection and preservation along with the issues confronting the wildlife protection. Thus, several inscriptions to initiate work in that direction on behalf of Ashoka makes the will of the emperor clear. Viewed in this perspective, it cannot be denied that Ashoka, following the environmental concerns and canons of the *Arthashastra*, addressed himself to tackle the issues considered important for his times, but relevant for the modern times. What follows is that it is too late for the global community to recognize the human and material value of environment. It would have done better had it continued to follow the concerns and policies of ancient India of Kautilya and Ashoka and the problems like climate change would not have taken the shape they have assumed; moreover, the whole humanity could have been saved from the curse of destroying nature, and a fine balance between development and environment could have been possible to be maintained.

In the end, I would like to reiterate that the conception of *dhamma* was a unique invention of Ashoka, which not only defined the relationship between different sects based on the principle of righteousness in the thought and action of the people, but it also influenced the ideas and ideals of kingship and governance. *Dhamma* meant a policy of having social, cultural, spiritual, political and economic ramifications; prescribing guidelines regulating the behaviour of the state and society in their mutual conduct; and being a law of piety, humanity, social order, enhancing spiritual capital and of prevention or denouncing violence, including that against animals. Another important dimension relating to his political philosophy is the theory of *dhamma vijaya*, which implied his open declaration that *dhamma vijaya* was the greatest conquest indicating that there was little place for military might in his foreign policy, and whenever victories were gained, the victors should be satisfied with patience and mild punishment.

In sum, the focus of research was to trace the ancient Indian political thought from various treatises, *shastras*, *puranas*, commentaries and inscriptions on rock edicts; the nature of the state and the basis of its power and authority with respect to the domestic population and in relation to the states falling at the boundaries or beyond of the empire. In essence, it can be said that the roots of the Indian state were not in the crude pursuit of power within the empire or outside its territorial limits; there has been a moralist and ethical approach to governance even while striving to expand its influence and control over other states. Besides, the monograph also underlines not only the relevance of political theory of Kautilya in his times but also the influence he carried in the time to follow him both in the immediate context and in the modern Indian context.

Similarly, it can be reiterated that Ashoka evolved a different approach to politics and assigned higher importance to moral and human values and humane governance in the administration of the state and the affairs concerned with the conduct of interaction with other states near the state's boundary or beyond. Ashoka invented a new theory of *dhamma* to explain that it is the law of piety, humanness and respect for and tolerance of others' interests and thoughts, which establishes a conflict-free, mutually accommodative, cooperative and supportive society without facing a challenge of law and order or without fear of violence.

It may be underlined that the abdication of war by Ashoka as policy of victory or extension of territory and authority over others did not indicate anywhere that Ashoka was disinterested in expansion of authority or influence. His method was different. He wanted to achieve the goals of the state of the Mauryas through *dhamma vijaya*, a victory through righteous means, through winning the world by following world welfare and spread of love and compassion, instead of victory through force and violence.

NOTES

1. See Book VI.1.; cf. Shamasastry, *Kautilya's Arthashastra*, p. 287.
2. *Arthashastra*, Book I, Chapter 19, Section 34; cf. Kangle, *The Kautilya Arthashastra*, Pt. II, p. 47.
3. See *Arthashastra*, Book III.15.19 and Book III.16.5; Kangle, *The Kautilya Arthashastra*, Pt. III, p. 216.
4. See Altekar, *State and Government in Ancient India*, Chapter XVII, p. 385.
5. Happiness of the natives as well as subjects of other states.
6. Shahi, *Kautilya and Non-Western*, p. 129.
7. Gelblum, 'The Spirit of Ashoka', pp. 261–271.
8. Cohen, 'Rulers and Priests', pp.199–216.
9. Shahi, *Kautilya and Non-Western*, p. 133.

BIBLIOGRAPHY

TRANSLATIONS AND COMMENTARIES

Buhler, George. *Manusmriti (The Laws of Manu)*. Translated by George Buhler. Oxford: Clarendon Press, 1886.

Debroy, Bibek. *Mahabharata*. Translated by Bibek Debroy. New Delhi: Penguin Books, 2015.

Kangle, R. P. *The Kautilya Arthashastra*, Part II. Translated by R. P. Kangle. Delhi: Motilal Banarsidass Publishers, 1972.

Kangle, R. P. *The Kautilya Arthashastra*, Part II. Translated by R. P. Kangle. Reprint, Delhi: Motilal Banarsidass Publishers, 1992.

———. *The Kautilya Arthasastra*, Part I. Translated by R. P. Kangle. Reprint, Delhi: Motilal Banarsidass Publishers, 2000.

———. *The Kautilya Arthashastra*, Part III. Translated by R. P. Kangle. Reprint, Delhi: Motilal Banarsidass Publishers, 2000.

Muller, F. M. Vedic Hymns, Part II: Hymns to Agni (Mandalas I-V). In *The Sacred Books of the East 46*. Translated by Hermann Oldenberg. England: Oxford – Clarendon, 1897.

Olivelle, Patrick, ed. *Chandogya-upnishad, in Early Upnnishads: Annotated Text and Translation*. Translated by Patrick Olivelle. New York, NY: Oxford University Press, 1998.

Pandurangi, K. T. *Kshatravidya: science of politics or knowledge of Dharma Veda of the warrior class, Chandogya Upanishad*. Translated by K. T. Pandurangi. Bangalore: Vidyadisha Post-Graduate Sanskrit Research Center, 1909.

Rangarajan, L. N. *Kautilya: The Arthashastra*. Delhi: Penguin Books India, 1992.

Shamasastry, R. *Kautilya's Arthashastra*. Translated by R. Shamasastry. Mysore: Mysore Printing and Publishing House, 1915/1960.

Walshe, Maurice. *Digha Nikaya*. Translated by Maurice Walshe. Boston, MA: Wisdom Publications, 1986.

BOOKS

Aggarwal, V. S. *India as Known to Panini*. Varanasi: Prithvi Prakashan, 1963.

Altekar, A. S. *State and Government in Ancient India*. Delhi: Motilal Banarasidass, 1958.

—————. *The Position of Women in Hindu Civilization*. Delhi: Motilal Banarasidass, 1995/1959.

Ambedkar, B. R. 'The Birth of a Counter-Revolution'. In *Asoka 2300: Jagajjyoti, Asoka Commemoration Volume 1997 A.D./2541 B.E.*, edited by Hemendu Bikash Chowdhury. Calcutta: Bauddha Dharmankur Sabha, 1997.

Archer, Amitav. *The End of American World Order*. Cambridge: Polity Press, 2014.

Bajg, T. A. *Women of India*. New Delhi: Publications Division, Government of India (Originally from the University of Virginia), 1858.

Bajpai, Kanti, P., and Amitabh Matto, eds. *Securing India: Strategic Thought and Practice*. New Delhi: Manohar Publishers, 1996.

Bandyopadhyaya, N. C. *Development of Hindu Polity and Political Theories*, Part I, Part II. Calcutta: R Cambray & Co., 1927.

Bandyopadhyaya, Jayantanuja. *A General Theory of International Relations*. New Delhi: Allied Publishers, 1993.

Barua, B. M. *Ashoka and His Inscriptions*. Calcutta: New Age Publishers Limited, 1946.

Basham, A. L. *The Wonder That Was India*, 3rd rev. ed. London: Picador, 2004.

Bess, Michael. *Choices under Fire: Moral Dimensions of World War II*. New York, NY: Vintage, 2006.

Bhakri, S. K. *Indian Warfare: An Appraisal of Strategy and Tactics of War in Early Medieval Period*. New Delhi: Munshiram Manoharlal Publishers, 1981.

Bhattacharji, Sukumari. *Women and society in Ancient India*. Calcutta: Basumati Corporation, 1994.

Bisht, Medha. *Kautilya's Arthashastra: Philosophy of Strategy*. New Delhi: Routledge, 2019.

Bloomfield, Maurice. *Hymns of the Athrva-Veda*. Oxford: The Clarendon Press, 1897.

Boesche, Roger. *The First Great Political Realist: Kautilya and His Arthashastra*. Lanham, MD: Lexington Books, 2002.

—————. *Kautilya: The First Great Political Realist*. Noida: HarperCollins Publishers, 2002/2017.

Brekke, Torkel. 'Between Prudence and Heroism: Ethics of War in Hindu Tradition'. In *The Ethics of War in Asian Civilizations*, edited by Torkel Brekke. Abingdon: Oxon, 2006.

—————, ed. *The Ethics of war in Asian Civilizations*. Abingdon: Oxon, 2006.

Brown, D. M. *Indian Political Thought: From Manu to Gandhi*. Mumbai: Jaico Publishing House, 1964.

Burleigh, Michael. *Moral Combat: A History of World War II*. London: HarperPress, 2010.

Buzan, Barry. 'Rising Powers in the Emerging World Order: An Overview with a Reflection on the Consequences for India'. In *India's Approach to Asia Strategy, Geopolitics and Responsibility, Institute for Defence studies and Analysis (IDSA)*, edited by Teoksessa, Namrata Goswami, 21–31. New Delhi: Pentagon Press, 2016.

Chakravarty, Nilima. *Indian Philosophy: The Pathfinders and the System Builders* (700 BC to 100 AD). New Delhi: Allied Publishers, 1992.

Chakravarti, P. C. *The Art of War in Ancient India.* Delhi: Karan Publishers, 1987.

Chattopadhyaya, B. D. 'Autonomous Spaces and the Authority of the State'. In *Studying Early India: Archaeology, Texts and Historical Issues*, edited by B. D. Chattopadhyaya, 135–152. Delhi: Permanent Black, 2003.

Chattopadhyaya, Sudhakar. *Bimbisara to Asoka.* Calcutta: Roy and Chaudhury, 1977.

Chausalkar, Ashok S. *Authority and Forms of Political Protests in Indian Tradition.* Delhi: Kalpaz Publications, 2017.

———. *Revisiting the Political Thought of Ancient India Pre-Kautilyan Arthashastra Tradition.* New Delhi: SAGE Publications, 2018.

Childe, Gorden V. *Man Makes Himself.* London: Coronet Books, 1936/2003.

Chowdhury, Hemendu Bikash, ed. *Asoka 2300 Jagajjyoti: Asoka Commemoration Volume, A.D./2541B.E.* Calcutta: Bauddha Dharmankur Sabha, 1997.

Coetzee, Daniel. *Philosophers of War: The Evolution of History's Greatest Military Thinkers.* Santa Barbara, CA: Praeger, 2013.

Coomaraswamy, A. *The Spiritual Authority and Temporal Power in Hindu Theory of Government.* Delhi: Munshiram Manoharlal, 1978.

Cowell, E. B. *The Jataka, No. 132.* Cambridge: Cambridge University Press, 1895.

Das, Sudhir Ranjan. 'Position of Women in Kautilya's Arthashastra'. In *Proceedings of the Indian History Congress*, edited by Sudhir Ranjan Das, Vol. 3. Calcutta: Calcutta University Press, 1939. https://ir.nbu.ac.in/bitstream/123456789/2371/1/25903.pdf

Deshpande, Madhav M. 'Interpreting the Ashokan Epithet Devanampiya'. In *Ashoka in History and Historical Memory*, edited by Patrick Olivelle. Delhi: Motilal Banarsidass Publishers, 2009.

Dhammika, Ven S. *The Edicts of King Ashoka.* Kandy: The Wheel Publication No.386/387, 1993.

Dhar, Somnath. *Kautilya and the Arthashastra.* New Delhi: Marwah Publications, 1981.

Dikshitar, V. R. R. *Hindu Administrative Institutions.* Madras: The University of Madras, 1929.

———. *The Mauryan Polity.* Delhi: Motilal Banarsidass, 1993.

———. *War in Ancient India.* Reprint, New Delhi: Motilal Banarsidass, 1944.

Duraiswamy, Naresha. *The Arthashastra and the Welfare State* (Commentary, 2 January 2014). IndiaFacts. Available at IndiaFacts.org/the-arthashastra-and-the-welfare-state/ (accessed on 23 February 2020).

Elazar, Daniel. *Constitutionalising Globalisation: The Post-Modern Revival of Confederal Arrangements.* New York, NY: Rowman & Littlefield, 1998.

Engels, F. *The Origin of Family, Private Property and the State.* Chicago, IL: Charles H. Kerr & Company Co-Operative, 1884.

Fick, Richard. *Social Organizations in North-Eastern India in Buddha's Time,* 144–149. Calcutta: University of Calcutta Press.

Gautam, Pradeep Kumar. *One Hundred Years of Kautilya's Arthashastra* (IDSA Monograph Series No. 20). Delhi: Institute for Defence Studies and Analysis, 2013.

———. *Kautilya's Arthashastra Contemporary Issues and Comparison (IDSA Monograph Series No.47).* Delhi: Institute for Defence Studies and Analyses, 2015.

———. *The Nitisara by Kamandaka: Continuity and Change from Kautilya's Arthashastra (IDSA Monograph Series No. 63).* Delhi: Institute for Defence Studies and Analysis, 2018.

Ghosh, Partha. *The Politics of Personal Law in South Asia: Identity, Nationalism and the Uniform Civil Code.* India: Routledge, 2007/2021.

Ghoshal, U. N. *A History of Hindu Political Theories. From the Earliest Times to the End of the First Quarter of the Seventeenth Century A.D.* London: Oxford University Press, 1923.

———. *A History of Indian Political Ideas.* Oxford: Oxford University Press, 1959/1966.

———. *Beginnings of Indian Historiography.* Hounslow: Cosmo Publications, 2016.

Gokhale, B. G. *Asoka Maurya.* New York, NY: Twayne, 1966.

Griffith, R. T. H. *The Hymns of the Rigveda.* Translated by R. T. H. Griffith. Delhi: Motilal Banarsidass, 2014.

Halbfass, Wilhelm. *Tradition and Reflection: Explorations in Indian thought.* Albany, NY: State University of New York, 1991.

Hall, Edith. 'Citizens but Second Class: Women in Aristotle's Politics (384–322 B.C.E.)'. In *Patriarchal Moments: Reading Patriarchal Texts,* edited by Cesare Cuttica, and Gaby Mahlberg, 35–42. New York, NY: Bloomsbury, 2016.

Havel, Vaclev. *The Art of the Impossible: Politics as Morality in Practice.* New York: Knopf, 1997.

Heesterman, J. C. 'The Conundrum of King's Authority'. In *The Inner Conflict of Tradition: Essays in Indian Ritual, Kingship and Society,* edited by J. C. Heesterman. Chicago, IL: University of Chicago Press, 1985.

Hinslay, F. H. *Sovereignty,* 2nd ed. Cambridge: Cambridge University Press, 1986.

Hopkins, E. W. *India, Old and New.* New York, NY: Charles Scribner's Sons, 1901.

Hui, Victoria Tin-bor. *War and State Formation in Ancient China and Early Modern Europe.* Cambridge: Cambridge University Press, 2011/2005.

Hultzsch, E. *Corpus Inscriptionum Indicarum* (Vol. I: Inscriptions of Ashoka, Archaeological Survey of India), 178. Oxford: Clarendon Press, 1925

Jafferlot, Christophe, and Waheguru Pal Singh Sidhu. 'From Plurilateralisn to Multilateralism? G-20, IBSA, BRICS and BASIC'. In *Shaping the Emerging*

World. India and the Multilateral Order, edited by Teoksessa, Waheguru Pal Singh Sidhu, Pratap Bhanu Mehta, and Ja Bruce Jones, 319–339. New Delhi: Foundation Books, 2013.

Jayshankar, S. *The India Way: Strategies for an Uncertain World*. New Delhi: HarperCollins, 2020.

Jayaswal, K. P. *Hindu Polity, a Constitutional History of India in Hindu Times*. Bangalore: The Bangalore Printing and Publishing Co. Ltd., 1943.

Jha, K. N., and L. K. Jha, *Chanakya: The Pioneer Economist*. New Delhi: APH Publishing Corporation, 1997.

Jois, Rama. *Seeds of Modern Public Law in Ancient Indian Jurisprudence*. Lucknow: Eastern Book Co., 1990.

Jules, Bloch. *Les Inscriptions d' Ashoka*. Paris: Les Belles Lettres, 2007.

Juutinen, Marko. 'Emerging Dynamics of Conflict and Cooperation in a Post-hegemonic Age: A Kautilyan Perspective on BRICS'. Observer Research Foundation Occasional Papers No. 208, Observar Research Foundation, 2019. Available at https://www.orfonline.org/research/emerging-dynamics-of-conflict-and-cooperation-in-a-post-hegemonic-age-a-kautilyan-perspective-on-brics-54615/ (accessed on 13 January 2022).

Kamerling, Susane. 'China's Security Governance Conception for Asia: Perspectives from India'. In *China–India–Japan in the Indo-Pacific, Ideas, Interests and Infrastructure, Institute for Defence studies and Analysis*, edited by Teoksessa Jagannath, P. Panda, and Titli Basu, 47–63. Delhi: Pentagon Press, 2018.

Kane, P. V. *History of Dharmsastra*, Vol. I, III. Pune: Bhandarkar Oriental Research Institute, 2006.

Keith, A. B. *Classical Sanskrit Literature*. Oxford: Oxford University Press, 1923.

Keuning, Wytze. *Ashoka the Great*. New Delhi: Rupa Publications, 2015.

Khan, Shamshad A. 'Role of Forums and Institutional Mechanisms in the India–Japan Partnership of Prosperity'. In *Scaling India-Japan cooperation in Indo Pacific and Beyond 2025 Corridors, Connectivity and Contours*, edited by Teoksessa Jagannath, and P. Panda, 122–149. New Delhi: IDSA, KW Publishers, 2020.

Konow, Sten. *Kautilya Studies*. Delhi: Oriental Publishers & Distributors, 1975.

Kumar, Abhishek. 'The Arthashastra: Assessing the Contemporary Relevance of an Ancient Indian Treatise on Statecraft'. A Thesis Presented for The Requirement for the Degree of Master of Military Art and science, Fort Leavenworh, Kansas, 2016. Available at https://apps.dtic.mil/sti/pdfs/AD1020076.pdf (accessed on 13 January 2022).

Kumar, Niraj. *Asia in Post-Western Age*. Delhi: KW Publisher, 2014.

Lahiri, Nayanjot. *Ashoka in Ancient India* (Hedgehog and Fox). New Delhi: Orient BlackSwan Private Limited, 2015.

Lannoy, Richard. *The Speaking Tree*. Oxford: Oxford University Press, 1971.

Lath, Mukund. 'The Concept of Anrsamsya in the Mahabharata'. In *Mahabharata Re-visited*, edited by R. N. Dandekar, Papers presented at the International

Seminar on the Mahabharata by the Sahitya Academy at New Delhi, Sahitya Academy, 1990.

Law. N. N. *Aspects of Ancient Indian Polity*. Oxford: Oxford University Press, 1980.

Liebig, Michael. 'Kautilya's Arthashastra: A Classic Text of Statecraft and an Untapped Political Science Resource'. Working Paper no. 74, Heidelberg Papers in South Asian and Comparative Politics, South Asian Institute of Political Science, July 2014.

Lingat, Robert. *The Classical Law of India*. Translated by J. Duncanm Derrett (from the French with additions). New Delhi: Thomson Press (India) Limited, 1973.

Ludwig, Alfred. 'Der Rigveda'. In *Ancient Indian Political Thought and Institutions*, edited by Bhaskar Anand Saletore. London: Asia Publishing house, 1963.

Macdonell, Arthur Anthony. *A History of Sanskrit Literature*. London: Princeton University, 1917.

Macdonell, Arthur Anthony, and A. B. Keith. *Vedic Index I and II*. Reprint, Delhi: Motilal Banarsidass Publishers, 1995.

Mahajan, V. D. *Ancient India*, 275–280. New Delhi: S. Chand, 1974.

Majumadar, A. K. *Concise History of Ancient India*, Vol. I (Political History). Delhi: Munshiram Manoharlal, 1976/1992.

———. *Concise History of Ancient India*, Vol. II (Political Theory, Administration and Economic Life). Delhi: Munshiram Manoharlal, 1980.

———. *Concise History of Ancient India*, Vol. III (Hinduism: Society, Religion and Philosophy). Delhi: Munshiram Manoharlal, 1983.

Majumdar, R. C. *Corporate Life in Ancient India*. Calcutta: K. L. Mukhopadhyay and Co., 1969.

Mehta, J. L., 'The Discourse of Violence in the Mahabharata'. In *Philosophy and Religion: Essays in Interpretation*, edited by J. L. Mehta. New Delhi: ICPR and Munshiram Manoharlal, 1990.

Michael, Arndt. 'India's Foreign policy and Panchsheel-Multilateralism—The impact of Norm Sublimation, Norm Localization and Competing Regionalism on South Asian Regional Multilateralism'. Doctoral dissertation, University of Freiburg, 2008.

Michael, Arndt. *India's Foreign Policy and Regional Multilateralism*. Basingstoke: Palgrave Macmillan, 2013.

Misra, V. S. *Ancient Indian Dynasties*. Mumbai: Bharatiya Vidya Bhavan, 2007.

Mitra, S. K. *Politics in India*. London: Routledge, 2011.

Mitra, Subrata K., and Michael Liebig, *Kautilya's Arthashastra: The Classical Roots of Modern Politics in India*. New Delhi: Rupa Publications, 2017.

Mookerji, Radhakumud. *Ashoka*. Delhi: Motilal Banarsidass, 1928.

———. *Chandragupta Maurya and his Times*. Delhi: Motilal Banarsidass, 1999.

———. *Local Self Government in Ancient India*. New York: Palala Press, 2016.

Morgan, L. H. *Ancient Society*. Cambridge: Belknap Press of Harvard University Press, 1964.

Morgenthau, Hans J. *Politics among Nations: The Struggle for Power and Peace.* Cambridge: Cambridge University Press, 2013.

Mukherjee, Prabhati. *Hindu Women: Normative Models.* New Delhi: Orient Longman, 1978/1994.

Muller, Max, ed. *Sacred Books of the East,* Vol. 14. Oxford: Oxford University Press, 1885.

———. *A History of Ancient Sanskrit Literature.* London: Spottiswoode and Co., 1859.

Nagarajan, V. *Evolution of Social Polity of Ancient India: From Manu to Kautilya.* Nagpur: Dattsons, 1992.

Nehru, Jawahar Lal. *Discovery of India.* India: Indian Council of Cultural Relations, 1981.

Olivelle, Patrick. *Manu's Code of Law: A Critical Edition and Translation of the Maavdhramshastra.* New Delhi: Oxford University Press, 2005.

Oldenberg, Hermann. *The Dipvamsa: An Ancient Buddhist Historical Record.* London: Williams and Norgate, 1879.

Oldenberg, Hermann. *Buddha: His Life, His Doctrine, His Order.* Delhi: Motilal Banarsidass, 2006.

Pant, A. D. *Introduction to Beni Parsad, Theory of Government in Ancient India.* Allahabad: Central Book Depot, 1968.

Parmar, Ardhana. *Techniques of Statecraft: A Study of Kautilya's Arthashastra.* Delhi: Atma Ram & Sons, 1987.

Prasad, Beni. *Theory of Government in Ancient India.* Allahabad: Central Book Depot, 1968.

Prasad, R. U. S. *Rig-Vedic and Post-Rig-Vedic Polity: 1500 BCE-500 BCE.* Malaga: Vernon Press, 2015.

Radhakrishanan, S. *The Heart of Hindustan.* Madras: Natesan & Co., 1936.

Rao, M. V. Krishna. *Studies in Kautilya.* Delhi: Munshiram Manoharlal Publishers, 1979.

Rich, Bruce. *Ashoka in Our Time: The Question of Dharma for a Globalised World.* New Delhi: Penguin Books, 2007.

———. *To Uphold the World: A Call for a New Global Ethic from Ancient India.* Boston, MA: Beacon Press, 2010.

Rockhill, William. *The Life of Buddha.* London: Routledge, 2011.

Rosenau, James, and Ernst-Otto Czempiel. *Governance without Government: Order and Change in World Politics.* London: Cambridge University Press, 1992.

Roychaudhary, H. C. 'Kurus and Videhas'. In *Political History of Ancient India,* 49–50. New Delhi: Cosmo Publications, 2006.

Ruben, W. 'Inter-state Relations in Ancient India and Kautilya's Arthashastra'. In *Indian Year-Book of International Affairs,* edited by Charles Henry Alexandrowicz, Vol. IV, 139. Madras: University of Madras, 1955.

Saletore, A. B. *Ancient Indian Political Thought and Institutions,* New Delhi: Asia Publishing House, 1963.

Saran, Shyam. *How India Sees the World: From Kautilya to Modi.* Mumbai: Juggernaut, 2017.

Sarkar, Benoy. *The Positive Background of Hindu Sociology.* Reprint, Delhi: Motilal Banarsidass, 1937/1985.

Sastri, K. A. N. *Age of the Nandas and Mauryas.* Delhi: Motilal Banarasidass, 1988.

Scholte, Jan. 'Global Governance'. In *Building Global Democracy Civil Society and Accountable Global Governance,* edited by Jan Scholte, Cambridge: Cambridge University Press, 2011.

———, ed. *Building Global Democracy Civil Society and Accountable Global Governance.* Cambridge: Cambridge University Press, 2011.

Scott, David, ed. *Handbook of India's International Relations.* London: Routledge, 2011.

Senart, Émile. *Caste in India.* Translated by E. Denison Ross. London: Cambridge University Press, 1930.

Sircar, Dineshchandra, ed. *Select Inscriptions Bearing on Indian History and Civilization: From the sixth to the eighteenth century AD,* 2. New Delhi: Motilal Banarsidass, 1983.

Slakter, David. 'Sovereignty and Dharma: The Role of Justice in Classical Indian Political Thought.' PhD thesis, University of Liverpool, 2012. Available at academia.edu/2399450/Sovereignty_Dharma_The_Role_Of_Justice_In_Classical_Indian_Political_thought (accessed on 18 February 2020).

Sen, A. K. *Studies in Hindu Political Thought.* Calcutta: Oxford University Press, 1920.

———. *Hindu Political Thought.* Delhi: Gyan Publishing House, 2001.

Sen, Amartya. *The Argumentative Indian. Writings on Indian History, Culture and Identity.* New York, NY: Farrar, Straus and Giroux, 2005.

———. Preface. In *To Uphold the World* by Bruce Rich. New Delhi: Penguin Books, 2007.

Shahi, Deepshikha. *Kautilya and the Non-Western IR Theory.* Cham: Palgrave Macmillan, 2019.

Shamasastry, R. *Kautilya's Arthashastra,* Mysore: W. Mission Press, 1992.

Shankman, Steven, and Stephen Durrant. *The Siren and the Sage: Knowledge and Wisdom in Ancient Greece and China.* New York, NY: Bloomsbury, 2000.

Sharma, Arvind. *Modern Hindu Thought: Introduction.* London: Oxford University Press, 2005.

Sharma, J. P. *Republics in Ancient India (c 1500 B. C.—500 B. C.).* Leiden: E. J. Brill, 1968.

Sharma, R. S. *Aspects of Political Ideas and Institutions in Ancient India.* Delhi: Motilal Banarsidass, 1959/2005.

Shephard, Kuncha Ilaiah. *God as Political Philosopher: Buddha's Challenge to Brahminism.* New Delhi: SAGE Publications, 2019/2012/2010.

Sidhu, Waheguru Pal Singh. 'Of Oral Traditions and Ethnocentric Judgements'. In *Securing India: Strategic Thought and Practice,* edited by Kanti Bajpai and Amitabh Matto, 174–190. New Delhi: Manohar Publishers, 1996.

Sihag, Balbir Singh. *Kautilya: The True Founder of Economics.* Delhi: Vistara Publications, 2014.

Sihag, Balbir Singh. 'Kautilya on Administration of Justice during the Fourth Century BCE'. In *Kautilya: The True Founder of Economics*, edited by Balbir S. Sihag, 24. Delhi: Vistara Publications, 2014.

Singh, M. P. *Indian Political Thought: Themes and Thinkers*. New Delhi: Pearson, 2011.

Singh, Upinder, *Political Violence in Ancient India*. Harvard: Harvard University Press, 2017.

Sinha, B. P. *Readings in Kautilya's Arthashastra*. Delhi: Agam Prakashan, 1976.

Sinha, H. N. 'Sovereignty in Ancient Indian Polity.' PhD thesis, University of London, 1935.

Smith, Vincent Arthur. *Ashoka: The Buddhist Emperor of India*. Oxford: Clarendon Press, 1901.

Smith, Adam. *Theory of Moral Sentiments*, Vols I and II. London: A. Miller, 1759.

Spellman, John, W. *Political Theory of Ancient India*. Oxford: Clarendon Press, 1964.

Strong, J. S. *The Legend of King Ashoka. A Study and Translation of the Asokavadana*. Delhi: Motilal Banarsidass, 1989/2008.

Sukhija, Vijay. *Asian Maritime power in 21st Century: Strategic Transactions, China, India and South-East Asia*. Singapore: Pentagon Press, 2011.

Swaine, Michael D. *America's Challenge: Engaging a Rising China in the Twenty-first Century*. Washington DC: Carnegie Endowment for International Peace, 2011.

Swaine, Michael D., and Ashley Tellis. *Interpreting China's Grand Strategy: Past, Present and Future*. Santa Monica, CA: RAND.

Tambiah, Stanley J., *World Conqueror and World Renouncer*. Cambridge, Cambridge University Press, 1976/2010.

Thapar, Romila. *Ashoka and the Decline of the Mauryas*. Delhi: Oxford University Press, 1973/2005/2009.

Tharoor, Shashi. *Pax-Indica: The India and the World of 21st Century*. UK: Penguin, 2012.

Thomas, Cincy M. 'Concept of State and Nation in Indian Literature, Arthashastra and Islam'. Available at https://www.academia.edu/28022758/%20Concept_of_State_and_Nation_n_Indian_Literature_Arthashatra_and_Islam?auto=download&email_work_card=view-paper (accessed on 18 February 2020).

Topa, Ishwar. 'Ashoka and his Dhamma Culture' (in Appendix to Chapter IX). In *Ashoka and His Inscriptions*, edited by B. M. Barua. Delhi: New Age, 1946.

Toynbee, Arnold J. *Mankind and Mother Earth: A Narrative History of the World*. New York, NY: Oxford University Press, 1976.

Trautmann, Thomas, *Arthashastra: The Science of Wealth*. New Delhi: Penguin Books, 2012.

Verma, V. P. *Studies in Hindu Political Thought and Its Metaphysical Foundations*. Delhi: Motilal Banarsidass, 1974.

Vidyalankar. *Kautilya's Arthashastra* (Hindi trans.). Lahore: Motilal Banarasi Das, 1923.

Vivekanandan, Jayashree. *Interrogating International Relations: India's Strategic Practice and the Return of History*. Delhi: Routledge, 2011.

Vittal, Vinay. 'Kautilya's Arthashastra: A Timeless Grand Strategy'. A Thesis submitted to the Faculty of the School of Advanced Air and Space Studies, Maxwell Air Force Base, Alabama, for completion of Graduation Requirements, 2011.

Wells, H. G. *The Outline of History: Being a Plain History of Life and Mankind.* London: Macmillan, 1927.

Von Jhering, Rudolf. *The Evolution of the Aryan.* Translated by A. Drucker. London: S. Sonnenschein, 1897.

Wolpert, Stanley A. *New History of India*, Oxford: Oxford University Press, 2009.

Woodcock, George. *Greeks in India.* London: Faber and Faber Ltd, 1966.

Wheeler, Mortimer. *The Cambridge History of India* (Supplementary Vol., the Indus Civilization), 3. Cambridge: Cambridge University Press, 1960.

Zimmer, H. *Philosophies of India.* New York, NY: Meridian Books, 1957.

REPORT

RAND. *India's Future strategic Role and Power Potential.* Santa Monica, CA: RAND, 1992.

ARTICLES

Anil, Anurag. 'Negotiations and Coalitions under the Two "Greats" of Indian History: Ashoka and Akbar, An Analysis of "Dhamma" and "Sulh-I-Kul"', 6. History Discussion.net. Available at https://www.academia.edu/36041592/Ashoka_and_Akbar_docx (accessed on 13 January 2022).

Bergel, Jean Louis. 'Principal Features and Methods of Codification'. *Louisiana Law Review* 48 (May 1988). Available at https://core.ac.uk/download/pdf/235287967.pdf (accessed on 13 January 2022).

Budac, Cristiana. 'Mandala of Power'. *Procedia–Social and Behavioural Sciences* 183, no. 4 (2015): 129–134.

Bhagat, G. 'Kautilya Re-visited and Re-visioned'. *The Indian Journal of Political Science* 51, no. 2 (1990): 186–212.

Bhattacharjee, Miban. 'Position of Women in Kautilya's Arthashastra'. *International Journal of Humanities and Social Sciences* 6, no. 6 (January 2018): 108–114.

Boesche, Roger. 'Women in Kautilya's *Arthashastra*: Persons, Addictions and Weapons'. *South Asian Studies* 19, no. 1 (2003): 35–42.

Boesche, Roger. 'Han Feizi's Legalism Versus Kautilya's Arthashastra'. *Asian Philosophy, An International Journal of the Philosophical Traditions of the East* 15, no. 2 (2005): 157–172.

Chakravarti, Uma. 'Conceptualising Brahmanical Patriarchy in Early India: Gender, Caste, Class, and State'. *Economic and Political Weekly* 28, no. 14 (3 April 1993): 579–585.

Cohen, S. P. 'Rulers and Priests: A Study in Cultural Control'. *Comparative Studies in Society and History* 6, no. 2 (1964): 199–216.

Dumont, Louis. 'The Concept of Kingship in ancient India'. *Contributions to Indian Sociology* 6, (1962): 48–77.

Fussman, Gerard. 'Central and Provincial administration in ancient India: The Problem of the Mauryan Empire'. *Indian Historical Review* 14, no. 1–2 (1987–1988): 43–72.

Gautam, Pradeep Kumar. 'Understanding Kautilya's Four *Upayas*'. *The Journal of International Issues* 17, no. 1 (2013): 30–37.

Gelblum, T. 'The spirit of Ashoka'. *East and West* 8, no. 3 (1957) 261–271.

Heesterman, J. C. 'The King's Order'. *Contributions to Indian Sociology* 20, no. 1 (1986): 1–13.

Hillebrandt, Alfred. 'Altindische Politik. Jena: Fischer'. In *Kautilya's Relevance for India Today* by Michael Liebig, *India Quarterly* 69, no. 2 (1923): 99–116.

Jaiswal, Suvira. 'Female Images in the Arthashastra of Kautilya'. *Social Scientist* 29, no. 3/4 (March–April 2001): 51–59.

Kapur, Radhika, 'Status of Women in Ancient India'. Available at https://www.researchgate.net/publication/330220793_Status_of_Women_in_Ancient_India (accessed on 13 January 2022).

Karad, Satish. 'Perspectives of Kautilya's Foreign Policy: An Ideal of State Affairs'. *Modern Research Studies* 2, no. 2 (June 2015): 331.

Kaur, Kiranjit. 'Kautilya: Saptang Theory of State'. *Indian Journal of Political Science* 71, no. 1 (January–March 2010): 59–68.

Kausambi, D. D. 'Notes on the Kandahar Edict of Ashoka'. *Journal of the Economic and Social History of the Orient* 2, no. 2 (1959): 204–206.

Kielhorn, L. F. 'Epigraphia Indica'. *https://en.wikipedia.org/wiki/The_Indian_Antiquary*. *The Indian Antiquary* 9, no. 7 (1907): 113.

Kokanen, Jyrki. 'International Relations in Kautilya's Arthashastra'. A draft paper. September 2020.

Liebig, M. 'Kautilya's Relevance for India Today'. *India Quarterly* 69, no. 2 (2013): 99–116.

Ma, Li. 'A Comparison of the Legitimacy of Power between Confucianist and Legalist Philosophies'. *Asian Philosophy* 10, no. 1 (2000): 49–59, Available at https://doi.org/10.1080/09552360050001761 (accessed on 15 June 2020).

Marder, Lev. 'Adam Smith: So What If the Sovereign Hares in Ignorance'. *Journal of International Political Theory* (12 May 2017). https://doi.org/10.1177/1755088217705893

Mehta, J. L., 'The Discourse of Violence in the Mahabharata'. In *Philosophy and Religion: Essays in Interpretation*, edited by J. L. Mehta. New Delhi: ICPR and Munshiram Manoharlal, 1990.

Mishra, Malay. 'Kautilya's Arthashastra: Restoring Its Rightful Place in the Field of International Relations' *Journal of Defence Studies* 10, no. 2 (April–June 2016), 77–109.

Modelski, George. 'Kautilya: Foreign Policy and International System in the Ancient Hindu World'. *The American Political Science Review* 58, no. 3 (1964): 549–560.

More, Sachin. 'Arthashastra: Lesson for the Contemporary Security Environment with South Asia as a Case Study' (IDSA Monograph Series No. 31). Available at https://idsa.in/monograph/arthasastraforsouthasiasecurity_smore_240114 (accessed on 13 January 2022).

Mulgan, Richard, 'Aristotle and the Political Role of Women'. *History of Political Thought* 15, no. 2 (Summer, 1994): 179–202.

Nandal, Vikas, and Rajnish. 'Status of Women through Ages in India'. *International Research Journal of Social Sciences* 3, no. 1 (January 2014): 21–26.

Niaz, Ilhan. 'Kautilya's Arthashastra and Governance as an Element of State Power'. Available at https://www.academia.edu/2554826/KAUTILYA_S_ARTHASHASTRA_AND_GOVERNANCE_AS_AN_ELEMENT_OF_STATE_POWER (accessed on 2 May 2020).

Olugbade, Kola. 'Women in Plato's Republic'. *Indian Journal of Political Science* 50, no. 4 (October–December 1989): 129–136. https://doi.org/10.4000/etudesplatoniciennes.277

Pandit, V. L. 'India's Foreign Policy'. *Foreign Affairs* 34, no. 3 (1956): 433–434.

Prakash, Aseem. 'State and Statecraft in Kautilya's Arthashastra'. Paper presented at the Fall Semester Mini Conference, Indiana University, Bloomington, 11 and 13 December 11 1993. Available at http://dlc.dlib.indiana.edu/dlc/bitstream/handle/10535/5647/State%20and%20statecraft%20in%20kautilyas%20arthasastra.pdf (accessed on 13 January 2022).

Saad, Mohammad, and Liu Wenxiang. 'National Security in Kautilya's Arthashastra: A Content Analysis'. *Journal of Humanities and Education Development* 2, no. 2 (March–April 2020): 129–140.

Sarkar, Binoy Kumar. 'Hindu Theory of International Relations'. *The American Political Science Review,* 13, no. 3 (August 1919), 400–414.

Sarkar, Binoy Kumar. 'Hindu Political Philosophy'. *Political Science Quarterly* 33, no. 4 (December 1918), 482–500. https://doi.org/10.2307/2141603

Schottli, Jivanta. 'How India Sees the World Today: Kautilya to the 21st Century'. *Journal of Indian Ocean Region* 15, no. 1 (2018). doi.org/10.1080/19480881.2018.1550472

Set, Shounak. 'Ancient Wisdom for the Modern World: Revisiting Kautilya and his Arthashastra in the Third Millennium'. *Strategic Analysis* 39, no. 6 (2015). Available at https://doi.org/10.1080/09700161.2015.1090685 (accessed on 6 June 2018).

Shaffer, Ryan, 'The New Arthashastra: A Security Strategy for India'. *Intelligence and National Security* 33, no. 2 (2017). Available at https://doi.org/10.1080/02684527.2017.1380146 (accessed on 13 January 2022).

Shahi, Deepshikha, 'Arthashastra Beyond Realpolitik: The Eclectic Face of Kautilya', *Economic & Political Weekly* 49, no. 41 (11 October 2014): 68–74.

Shirin, Pratiti, 'The Position of Women in Kautilya's Arthashastra'. *Journal of the Asiatic Society of Bangladesh* 54, no. 1 (2009): 123–134.

Sihag, Balbir. 'Kautilya and Modern Economics: Introduction to Kautilya and His Arthashastra'. *Humanomics* 25, no. 1 (2009). Available at http://ignca.gov.in/invitations/About_the_lecture.pdf (accessed on 13 January 2022).

Singh, M. P. 'Two Contrasting Theories of Origin of State in Ancient India'. *Review of Politics* 26, no. 1–2 (January–June 2018): 7–11.

Singh, Ram Ranbir. 'Kautilya's Conception of State'. *The Indian Journal of Political Science* 65, no. 1 (January–March 2004), 41–54.

Singh, Upinder. 'Governing the Self and the State: Political Philosophy and Practice in the Edicts of Ashoka'. *South Asian Studies* 28, no. 2 (2012). 131–145.

Soloman, Hussein. 'Critical Reflection of Indian Foreign Policy: Between Kautilya and Ashoka'. *South African Journal International Affairs* 19, no.1 (2012): 65–78. Available at https://doi.org/10.1080/10220461.2012.670418 (accessed on 13 January 2022).

Squarcini, Federico. 'Selling Tolerance by the Pound: On Ideal Types "Fragility, Ashoka's Edicts and the Political Theology of Toleration in and beyond South Asia"'. *Philosophy and Social Criticism* 45, no. 4 (2019): 480.

Suresh, B. 'A Study on Ashoka's Inscriptions with Special Reference Karnataka'. *Journal of Emerging Technologies and Innovative Research (JETIR)* 5, no. 10 (October 2018): 234–240.

Thapar, Romila. 'Ashoka—A Retrospective'. *Economic & Political Weekly* 44, no. 45 (7 November 2009). Available at https://www.epw.in/journal/2009/45/perspectives/ashoka-retrospective.html#:~:text=Ashoka%20of%20the%20Maurya%20dynasty,entire%20span%20of%20Indian%20history (accessed on 13 January 2022).

Winternitz, M. 'Kautilya Arthashastra', 23. *Calcutta Review*, April 1924.

Uz Zaman, Rashed. 'Kautilya: The Indian Strategic Thinker and Indian Strategic Culture'. *Comparative Strategy* 25, (2006): 231–247. Available at https://doi.org/10.1080/01495930600956260 (accessed on 13 January 2022).

ABOUT THE AUTHOR

Rajvir Sharma taught at the University of Delhi for around 43 years. He was an advisor in social sciences at the Institute of Lifelong Learning, University of Delhi. He joined the Department of Journalism, Maharaja Agrasen Institute of Management Studies, New Delhi, as a professor and was a senior consultant at the Department of Public Administration, Indira Gandhi National Open University, New Delhi. He was awarded senior fellowship by the Indian Council of Social Science Research, New Delhi, twice to successfully complete two empirical research projects. Dr Sharma has been a visiting fellow at Loyola University Chicago, and a professor at Mizoram University and the University of Rajasthan. He has also been a fellow at the Indian Institute of Advanced Study, Shimla. Dr Sharma has contributed many research papers to peer-reviewed national and international journals and to edited reference books published in India and abroad.

INDEX

Adi Purana, 8
Aitareya Brahmana, 8
Amatya, 64–67
ancient Hindu politics
  nature, 4
ancient Indian political system
  political institutions, 27–31
ancient Indian science of politics
  Dharma and *Dharmashastra*, 21
anviksiki, 41
arsa marriage, 187
Arthashastra, 252
  argument, 38
  by Kautilya, xiii
  conception of law, 98–99
  concept of *dandaniti*, 87
  departure from past, 41
  females as slave, 202
  issues not covered, xix
  methodology and sources of study,
    xviii
  Naresha Duraiswamy's view, 36
  questions and arguments, 2
  rule of law, 100
  safety of king and kingdom, 58
  scheme of chapterization,
    xix–xxiii
  scope of study, xvi, xvii, xviii
  Shukrachary's conception, 4
  sources of law, 101

  sovereignty and legitimacy,
    256–57
  statement about king, 63
  status of women, 263
  treatment of prostitutes, 200–02
  Vedic and post-Vedic Legacy, 37
  welfare and social security of
    women, 202–03
Arthashastra and the Ashokan edicts,
  xv
articles
  *An Ancient Treatise and the Making
    of Modern India*, xiv
Ashoka
  authority and legitimacy sources,
    234–36
  dhamma vijaya, 224–27
  justice and its administration
    philosophy, 236–41
  Kautilya, 266–69
  Kautilyan legacy, 244–47
  nature of state and administration,
    230–34
  philosophy of war and violence,
    222
  Pillar Edict IV's views on
    commitment and measures, 240
  policy of *dhamma*, 213
  political philosophy, 211–12
  political realism, 244

post-Kautilyan political theory,
  263–65
survival and welfare of humanity,
  242
theory of state and governance,
  212–18
theory of statecraft and governance,
  241–44
theory of tolerance, 221–24
Ashvamedha, 26
  performance of sacrifice, 87
asura marriage, 187

bala/army, 72–74
Bhoja, 63
books
  janapada, 42
  The Evolution of the Aryans, 22
  The Outline of History, 212
Brahma marriage, 186
Brahmanas
  functions of king, 60

champion of Sudras, 196
civil code, 112
  division of inheritance, 114
  pledge/mortgage, 115
  recovery of debts, 115
  transactions/agreements, 112–14
codification of law, 111–12
criminal procedure
  act of murder, 118
  cases of adultery, 117
  misconduct with women, 117
  rape, 118
criminal procedure code, 116
  law of treason, 116
custom/tradition, 104

daiva marriage, 187
danda
  administration, 78
Danda, 8
  importance and relevance, 88

Danda and dandaniti, 41
Danda and Dandaniti
  ingredients of sovereignty and
    legitimacy, 19–20
Dandaniti, 20
  relation to sovereignty and
    legitimacy, 88
  theory, 21
Devanampriya, 212
dhamma
  concept, 217
  defined by Greeks, 216
  essence, 216
  importance and impact, 218
  symbol of new unity, 215
  Upindra Singh's view, 213
Dhamma, 265
  imposing philosophy, 218–21
  social and political philosophy of
    Ashoka, 241
dhamma-mahamattas, 227
  institution, 228
  objective of introducing, 228
  recalled, 229
dhamma vijaya
  Ashoka, 224–27
  concept, 226
Dhamma vijaya
  Ashoka, 226
  Bruce Rich's views, 225
dharma, 21
  defined, 22
  defined by Heinrich Zimmer, 22
  foundations of justice., 102
  Kangle's statement, 103
  meaning, 22
Dharmashastra, 101
Dharmashastra law, 102
Dharmashastras
  questions and arguments, 2
Dharma Sutras, 1
  A. K. Majumdar's views, 1
Digha Nikaya, 10
  Altekar points, 7

Discovery of India, 143
durga/fort, 69–70
Dvaidhibhava policy, 157

Five Power Defence Arrangements
  (FPDA), 167
foreign policy
  objective, 165

gandharva vivaha, 187
ganikas, 201, 204
government
  legitimacy, 51

H. G. Wells
  The Outline of History, 212
history
  post-Vedic period, 11
Hultzsch says
  obedience, 236

Indian Succession Act of 1925, 106
Indologists, 210
international relations
  Ashoka's theory of tolerance,
    221–24

janapada, 31, 67–69
judicial procedure, 132–34
  dimensions, 134
  forms of punishments, 134
justice, 123
  courts, 129
  features, 124–28
  Kautilya on administration, 257–61
  objectivity in delivery, 126–28
  organization and procedure,
    130–32
  principle of equity, 124–25
  to be fast, 125–26
  welfare, 128–29

Kapavya
  Mahabharata story, 24

Kautilya, 36
  administration of law and justice,
    257–61
  arguement on royal legislation, 109
  arguement on sanskriti, 39
  Ashoka, 266–69
  contract theory, 39
  cruelty against women, 196–97
  danda and *dandadhara*, 97
  forms of government, 45
  four sources of laws, 41
  ideas on *rajamandala*, 147
  interstate relations, power
    dynamics and war and peace,
    261–63
  legacy in Ashoka, 244–47
  legal philosophy, 110
  legal theory, 98
  mandala theory, 143
  Monarchical, 47
  nature of state, 254
  neo-realist, 169
  perspective of international
    relations, 167
  political ideas and philosophy, xviii
  political realism, 175
    pragmatism, 159
  pragmatism, 166
  protection of dignity and honour of
    women, 194–95
  realist/idealist, 168–78
  right to property and inheritance,
    199–200
  right to remarry, 188–90
  Saptanga theory, 256
  sexual crimes, 197–99
  theory of *shadgunya*, 153
  thoughts, xvi
  two assumptions, 39
Kautilyan scheme
  foreign policy, 165
  foreign relations, 150
Kautilyan state
  nature, 47–48

Khap Panchayats, 105
king, 57
 aggregate of people, 90
 definition of state, 57
 executive functions, 60
 functions, 60–77
 Kautilya's list of qualifications, 57
 quasi legislative authority, 108
 three powers, 165
kosa/treasury, 70–72
Kshatra Vidya, 40
Kshatriya power, 81
kumaras, 234

labour welfare, 49
land survey, 54
law
 balancing link, 111
 customary, 205
 defined, 98
 expression of sovereignty, 98
 Kautilya on administration, 257–61
 Kautilya's view, 98
law of marriage, 187
law of treason, 116
legitimacy, 86
 meaning, 90
 narrative regarding, 89
 political philosophy, 89
lekhakas, 107
Lokayat
 emergence of philosophy, 1

Maintenance and Welfare of Parents
 and Senior Citizens Act, 2007, 50
mandala
 concept, 145
Mandala, 144
Mandala doctrine, 143
mantrashakti, 144
Mantrashakti, xiv
Manusmriti, 8
Mauryan period, 16
Mauryan state, 255

mitra/ally, 74–77
 consideration, 74

N. C. Bandyopadhyaya
 opinion on state, 52

obedience
 Hultzsch says, defined by, 236
origin of state, 6
 evolutionary theory, 15–24
 Social contract theory, 9–13
 Theory of divine origin, 6–9

paishacha vivaha/marriage, 187
parishad, 234
peoples' welfare, 49
personal laws, 119
 divorce, 119
 maintenance, 120
 marriage, 119
 right of widow to re-marry, 120–22
 sexual morality, 122
political action
 four Upayas, methods, 160–68
political institutions, 42–43
political philosophy
 Ashoka, 211–12
political science, 252
post-Kautilyan political theory, 210
 king Ashoka, 263–65
prabhavashakti, 144
Prabhavashakti, xiv
prajapatya marriage, 187
Prakashyuddha, 149
pre-Kautilyan age
 Dharmashastra tradition, 40
Purohit, 81
Purush Sukta, 22

raja, 26
rajasasana
 R. P. Kangle's arguement, 103
Rajshastras, 4
Rajsuya, 26

rajukas, 238
rakshasa marriage, 187
religion, 102
right to divorce, 192, 193
right to maintenance, 193
right to remarry, 188–90
   man, 190–92
Rigveda, 12
royal edicts, 107–11
rule of law
   concept, 99
   importance in *Arthashastra*,
      99–101

sabha, *samiti* and *vidatha*, 28
Samaveda, 12
Samiti, 29
Saptanga theory
   conception of state in *Arthashastra*,
      54–56
   explained, 56
   Kautilya on elements of state, 256
   state, preceding discussion, 74
Satapatha Brahmana, 8
self rule
   Shukracharya's idea, 141
shadgunya
   concept, 153–60
Shadgunya theory, 142
Shukracharya
   idea of self rule, 141
social contract
   Indian theory and Western theory,
      comparison, 13–15
Social contract theory, 9–13
social shaming, 134
sovereignty, 25, 256
   ancient Indian political thought, 25
   Arthashastra, 256–57
   dimensions, 25
   ideas, 86
   mixed model, 75
   narrative regarding, 89
   pragmatic dimension, 87

spies, 62
state
   administrative functions, 84–85
   Aitareya Brahmana, 43
   Ashoka's edicts, 212–18
   basic functions, 78
   classification, 43
   draws power, 76
   financial powers, 80
   financial role, 79
   forms, 43–47
   functions relating to foreign affairs
      and national security, 86
   N. C. Bandyopadhyaya's opinion,
      52
   origin, 37–40
   Origin and theories, 6
   political functions, 81–84
   Swami, 56–59
   welfare schemes, 49
state and governance
   pre-Kautilyan ideas, 1
story
   Shanti Parva, 6

Tacitus., 30
Taittritya Brahmana, 8
Theory of divine origin, 6–9
The Outline of History, 212
Thirthankara, 8
Trayi and *Anvikshiki*, 4
Tribal Military Democracy, 16
Tusnimyuddha, 150
Tusnimyuddha/silent war, 162

Udasina, 161
unitary state
   centralized bureaucratic, 52–54
Ushansa, 4
utsah shakti, 144
Uttaradhyayana Sutra, 3

Vana Parva
   happy sketch, 11

varnashrama system, 102
Varnashrama system, 214
Vidatha, 30

welfare state, 48–52
Western scholars
    thoughts on *artha* and *dharma*, 2
women
    Arthashastra, welfare and social
        security, 202–03

cruelty against, 196–97
protection of dignity and honour,
    194–95
right to property and inheritance,
    199–00
sexual crimes, 197–99

yogakshema
    principle, xvi
Yudhishthira, 20